BUSINESS
@
THE SPEED
OF THOUGHT

Also by Bill Gates

The Road Ahead

BUSINESS @ THE SPEED OF THOUGHT

USING A DIGITAL NERVOUS SYSTEM

BILL GATES

WITH COLLINS HEMINGWAY

WARNER BOOKS

A Time Warner Company

Warner Books, Inc., 1271 Avenue of the Americas, New York, NY 10020
Visit our Web site at www.warnerbooks.com

A Time Warner Company

Printed in the United States of America

First Printing: March 1999

10 9 8 7 6 5 4 3 2 1

ISBN: 0-446-52568-5
LC: 99-60040

Text design by Stanley S. Drate / Folio Graphics Co. Inc.

Except as indicated, artwork is by Gary Carter, Mary Feil-Jacobs, Kevin Feldhausen, Michael Moore, and Steve Winard.

To my wife, Melinda,
and my daughter, Jennifer

ACKNOWLEDGMENTS

I first want to thank my collaborator, Collins Hemingway, for his help in synthesizing and developing the material in this book and for his overall management of this project.

I want to thank four CEOs who read a late draft of the manuscript and offered valuable thoughts on how to make it more meaningful for business leaders: Paul O'Neill, Alcoa; Ivan Seidenberg, Bell Atlantic; Tony Nicely, GEICO Insurance; and Ralph Larsen, Johnson & Johnson.

Details on the use of technology by business and public agencies came from worldwide travel and research by Collins and by Jane Glasser. Barbara Leavitt, Evelyn Vasen, and Ken Linarelli researched one or more chapters. The book gained from the careful editing of Erin O'Connor during manuscript development. Anne Schott served as combination research assistant and project coordinator.

I want to thank Bob Kruger and Tren Griffin, who offered thoughtful comments on many chapters as the book progressed. And Steve Ballmer, Bob Herbold, and Jeff Raikes for their thoughts about the book's organization and focus. David Vaskevitch, Rich Tong, Gary Voth, and Mike Murray helped shape important ideas. For their review comments thanks to Mich Mathews and John Pinette.

Thanks also to Larry Kirshbaum, chairman and CEO of Time Warner Trade Publishing, and Rick Horgan, VP and executive editor of Warner Books, for their incisive feedback. Thanks to Kelli Jerome, who has now managed the worldwide marketing of both of my books in a smooth and professional manner, and to Lee Anne Staller for her help in sales.

At Warner, thanks also to Harvey-Jane Kowal, VP and executive managing editor, and Bob Castillo, senior production editor, as well as Sona Vogel, copy editor, for their editorial assistance.

With all the search capabilities provided by technology, the researchers at the Microsoft Library remained an invaluable resource: Laura Bain, Kathy Brost, Jill Burger, Lynne Busby, Peggy Crowley, Erin Fields, April Hill, Susan Hoxie, Jock McDonald, Tammy Pearson, K.C. Rich, Deborah Robinson, Christine Shannon, Mary Taylor, Dawn Zeh, and Brenda Zurbi. For their general assistance, thanks to Christine Turner and Gordon Lingley.

This work gained enormously from the assistance of many people at Microsoft and others closely associated with our company. There are far too many people to mention here. I appreciate your help and support.

Finally, *Business @ the Speed of Thought* was possible only because of the commitment in time and energy of many of Microsoft's customers and partners. We were all amazed and encouraged by the willingness of customers to talk frankly about their successes and challenges, about their business and technical issues. These customers are listed in a special section at the end of the book.

CONTENTS

Introduction xiii

I

INFORMATION FLOW IS YOUR LIFEBLOOD

1 Manage with the Force of Facts 3

2 Can Your Digital Nervous System Do This? 22

3 Create a Paperless Office 39

II

COMMERCE: THE INTERNET CHANGES EVERYTHING

4 Ride the Inflection Rocket 63

5 The Middleman Must Add Value 72

6 Touch Your Customers 91

7 Adopt the Web Lifestyle 114

8 Change the Boundaries of Business 133

9 Get to Market First 141

III

MANAGE KNOWLEDGE TO IMPROVE STRATEGIC THOUGHT

10 Bad News Must Travel Fast 159

11 Convert Bad News to Good 184

12 Know Your Numbers 201

13 Shift People into Thinking Work 222

14 Raise Your Corporate IQ 236

15 Big Wins Require Big Risks 262

IV

BRING INSIGHT TO BUSINESS OPERATIONS

16 Develop Processes That Empower People 281

17 Information Technology Enables Reengineering 295

18 Treat IT as a Strategic Resource 317

V

SPECIAL ENTERPRISES

19 No Health Care System Is an Island 333

20 Take Government to the People 357

21 When Reflex Is a Matter of Life and Death 372

22 Create Connected Learning Communities 387

VI

EXPECT THE UNEXPECTED

23 Prepare for the Digital Future 407

Appendix: Build Digital Processes on Standards 417

Glossary 441

Customer Acknowledgments 453

Index 457

INTRODUCTION

Business is going to change more in the next ten years than it has in the last fifty.

As I was preparing my speech for our first CEO summit in the spring of 1997, I was pondering how the digital age will fundamentally alter business. I wanted to go beyond a speech on dazzling technology advances and address questions that business leaders wrestle with all the time. How can technology help you run your business better? How will technology transform business? How can technology help make you a winner five or ten years from now?

If the 1980s were about quality and the 1990s were about reengineering, then the 2000s will be about velocity. About how quickly the nature of business will change. About how quickly business itself will be transacted. About how information access will alter the lifestyle of consumers and their expectations of business. Quality improvements and business process improvements will occur far faster. When the increase in velocity of business is great enough, the very nature of business changes. A manufacturer or retailer that responds to changes in sales in hours instead of weeks is no longer at heart a product company, but a service company that has a product offering.

These changes will occur because of a disarmingly simple idea: the flow of digital information. We've been in the

Information Age for about thirty years, but because most of the information moving among businesses has remained in paper form, the process of buyers finding sellers remains unchanged. Most companies are using digital tools to monitor their basic operations: to run their production systems; to generate customer invoices; to handle their accounting; to do their tax work. But these uses just automate old processes.

Very few companies are using digital technology for new processes that radically improve how they function, that give them the full benefit of all their employees' capabilities, and that give them the speed of response they will need to compete in the emerging high-speed business world. Most companies don't realize that the tools to accomplish these changes are now available to everyone. Though at heart most business problems are information problems, almost no one is using information well.

Too many senior managers seem to take the absence of timely information as a given. People have lived for so long without information at their fingertips that they don't realize what they're missing. One of the goals in my speech to the CEOs was to raise their expectations. I wanted them to be appalled by how little they got in the way of actionable information from their current IT investments. I wanted CEOs to demand a flow of information that would give them quick, tangible knowledge about what was really happening with their customers.

Even companies that have made significant investments in information technology are not getting the results they could be. What's interesting is that the gap is not the result of a lack of technology spending. In fact, most companies have invested in the basic building blocks: PCs for productivity applications; networks and electronic mail (e-mail) for communications; basic business applications. The typical company has made 80 percent of the investment in the technology that can give it a healthy flow of information yet is typically getting only 20 percent of the benefits that are now possible. The gap between what companies are spending and what they're getting stems from the combination of not understanding what is possible and not seeing the potential when you use technology to move the right information quickly to everyone in the company.

CHANGING TECHNOLOGY AND EXPECTATIONS

The job that most companies are doing with information today would have been fine several years ago. Getting rich information was prohibitively expensive, and the tools for analyzing and disseminating it weren't available in the 1980s and even the early 1990s. But here on the edge of the twenty-first century, the tools and connectivity of the digital age now give us a way to easily obtain, share, and act on information in new and remarkable ways.

For the first time, all kinds of information—numbers, text, sound, video—can be put into a digital form that any computer can store, process, and forward. For the first time, standard hardware combined with a standard software platform has created economies of scale that make powerful computing solutions available inexpensively to companies of all sizes. And the "personal" in personal computer means that individual knowledge workers have a powerful tool for analyzing and using the information delivered by these solutions. The microprocessor revolution not only is giving PCs an exponential rise in power, but is on the verge of creating a whole new generation of personal digital companions—handhelds, Auto PCs, smart cards, and others on the way—that will make the use of digital information pervasive. A key to this pervasiveness is the improvement in Internet technologies that are giving us worldwide connectivity.

In the digital age, "connectivity" takes on a broader meaning than simply putting two or more people in touch. The Internet creates a new universal space for information sharing, collaboration, and commerce. It provides a new medium that takes the immediacy and spontaneity of technologies such as the TV and the phone and combines them with the depth and breadth inherent in paper communications. In addition, the ability to find information and match people with common interests is completely new.

These emerging hardware, software, and communications standards will reshape business and consumer behavior. Within a decade most people will regularly use PCs at work and at home, they'll use e-mail routinely, they'll be connected to the Internet, they'll carry digital devices containing their personal and business information. New consumer devices will emerge that handle almost every kind of data—text, numbers, voice, photos, videos—in digital form. I use the phrases "Web workstyle" and "Web lifestyle" to emphasize the impact of employees and consumers taking advantage of these digital connections. Today, we're usually linked to information only when we are at our desks, connected to the Internet by a physical wire. In the future, portable digital devices will keep us constantly in touch with other systems and other people. And everyday devices such as water and electrical meters, security systems, and automobiles will be connected as well, reporting on their usage and status. Each of these applications of digital information is approaching an inflection point—the moment at which change in consumer use becomes sudden and massive. Together they will radically transform our lifestyles and the world of business.

Already, the Web workstyle is changing business processes at Microsoft and other companies. Replacing paper processes with collaborative digital processes has cut weeks out of our budgeting and other operational processes. Groups of people are using electronic tools to act together almost as fast as a single person could act, but with the insights of the entire team. Highly motivated teams are getting the benefit of everyone's thinking. With faster access to information about our sales, our partner activities, and, most important, our customers, we are able to react faster to problems and opportunities. Other pioneering companies going digital are achieving similar breakthroughs.

We have infused our organization with a new level of electronic-based intelligence. I'm not talking about anything metaphysical or about some weird cyborg episode out of *Star Trek*. But it is something new and important. To function in the digital age, we have developed a new digital infrastructure. It's like the human nervous system. The biological nervous system triggers your reflexes so that you can react quickly to danger or need. It gives you the information you need as you ponder issues and make choices. You're alert to the most important things, and your nervous system blocks out the information that isn't important to you. Companies need to have that same kind of nervous system—the ability to run smoothly and efficiently, to respond quickly to emergencies and opportunities, to quickly get valuable information to the people in the company who need it, the ability to quickly make decisions and interact with customers.

As I was considering these issues and putting the final touches on my speech for the CEO summit, a new concept popped into my head: "the digital nervous system." A digital nervous system is the corporate, digital equivalent of the human nervous system, providing a well-integrated flow of information to the right part of the organization at the right time. A digital nervous system consists of the digital processes that enable a company to perceive and react to its environment, to sense competitor challenges and customer needs, and to organize timely responses. A digital nervous system requires a combination of hardware and software; it's distinguished from a mere network of computers by the accuracy, immediacy, and richness of the information it brings to knowledge workers and the *insight* and *collaboration* made possible by the information.

I made the digital nervous system the theme of my talk. My goal was to excite the CEOs about the potential of technology to drive the flow of information and help them run their businesses better. To let them see that if they did a good job on information flow, individual business solutions would come more easily. And because a digital nervous system benefits every department and individual in the company, I wanted to make them see that only they, the CEOs, could step up to the change in mind-set and culture necessary to reorient a company's behavior around digital information flow and the Web workstyle. Stepping up to such a decision meant that they had to become comfortable enough with digital technology to understand how it could fundamentally change their business processes.

Afterward a lot of the CEOs asked me for more information on the digital nervous system. As I've continued to flesh out my ideas and to speak on the topic, many other CEOs, business managers, and information technology professionals have approached me for details. Thousands of customers come to our campus every year to see our internal business solutions, and they've asked for more information about why and how we've built our digital nervous system and about how they could do the same. This book is my response to those requests.

I've written this book for CEOs, other organizational leaders, and managers at all levels. I describe how a digital nervous system can transform businesses and make public entities more responsive by energizing the three major elements of any business: customer/partner relationships, employees, and process. I've organized the book around the three corporate functions that embody these three elements: *commerce*, *knowledge management*, and *business operations*. I begin with commerce because the Web lifestyle is changing everything about commerce, and these changes will drive companies to restructure their knowledge management and business operations in order to keep up. Other sections cover the importance of information flow and special enterprises that offer general lessons to other organizations. Since the goal of a digital nervous system is to stimulate a concerted response by employees to develop and implement a business strategy, you will see repeatedly that a tight digital feedback loop enables a company to adapt quickly and constantly to change. This is a fundamental benefit to a company embracing the Web workstyle.

Business @ the Speed of Thought is not a technical book. It explains the business reasons for and practical uses of digital processes that solve real business problems. One CEO who read a late draft of the manuscript said the examples served as a template for helping him understand how to use a digital nervous system at his company. He was kind enough to say, "I was making one list of comments to give to you, and another list of things to take back to implement in my company." I hope other business readers discover the same "how to" value. For the more technically inclined, a companion Web site at www.Speed-of-Thought.com provides more background information on some of the examples, techniques for evaluating the capabilities of existing information systems, and an architectural approach and development methodologies for building a digital nervous system. The book site also has links to other Web sites I reference along the way.

To make digital information flow an intrinsic part of your company, here are twelve key steps:

For *knowledge work:*

1. Insist that communication flow through the organization over e-mail so that you can act on news with reflexlike speed.
2. Study sales data online to find patterns and share insights easily. Understand overall trends and personalize service for individual customers.
3. Use PCs for business analysis, and shift knowledge workers into high-level thinking work about products, services, and profitability.
4. Use digital tools to create cross-departmental virtual teams that can share knowledge and build on each other's ideas in real time, worldwide. Use digital systems to capture corporate history for use by anyone.
5. Convert every paper process to a digital process, eliminating administrative bottlenecks and freeing knowledge workers for more important tasks.

For *business operations:*

6. Use digital tools to eliminate single-task jobs or change them into value-added jobs that use the skills of a knowledge worker.
7. Create a digital feedback loop to improve the efficiency of physical processes and improve the quality of the products and services created. Every

employee should be able to easily track all the key metrics.

8. Use digital systems to route customer complaints immediately to the people who can improve a product or service.
9. Use digital communications to redefine the nature of your business and the boundaries around your business. Become larger and more substantial or smaller and more intimate as the customer situation warrants.

For *commerce:*

10. Trade information for time. Decrease cycle time by using digital transactions with all suppliers and partners, and transform every business process into just-in-time delivery.
11. Use digital delivery of sales and service to eliminate the middleman from customer transactions. If you're a middleman, use digital tools to add value to transactions.
12. Use digital tools to help customers solve problems for themselves, and reserve personal contact to respond to complex, high-value customer needs.

Each chapter will cover one or more points—good information flow enables you to do several of these things at once. A key element of a digital nervous system, in fact, is linking these different systems—knowledge management, business operations, and commerce—together.

Several examples, particularly in the area of business operations, focus on Microsoft. There are two reasons. First, customers want to know how Microsoft, a proponent of information technology, is using technology to run our business. Do we practice what we preach? Second, I can talk in depth about the rationale for applying digital systems to operational problems that my company actually faces. At the same time, I've gone to dozens of pioneering companies to find the best practices across all industries. I want to show the broad applicability of a digital nervous system. And, in some areas, other companies have gone beyond us in digital collaboration.

The successful companies of the next decade will be the ones that use digital tools to reinvent the way they work. These companies will make decisions quickly, act efficiently, and directly touch their customers in positive ways. I hope you'll come away excited by the possibilities of positive change in the next ten years. Going digital will put you on the leading edge of a shock wave of change that will shatter the old way of doing business. A digital nervous system will let you do business at the speed of thought—the key to success in the twenty-first century.

BUSINESS
@
THE SPEED
OF THOUGHT

I

INFORMATION FLOW IS YOUR LIFEBLOOD

1

MANAGE WITH THE FORCE OF FACTS

The big work behind business judgment is in finding and acknowledging the facts and circumstances concerning technology, the market, and the like in their continuously changing forms. The rapidity of modern technological change makes the search for facts a permanently necessary feature.

—Alfred P. Sloan Jr., *My Years with General Motors*

I have a simple but strong belief. The most meaningful way to differentiate your company from your competition, the best way to put distance between you and the crowd, is to do an outstanding job with information. *How you gather, manage, and use information will determine whether you win or lose.* There are more competitors. There is more information available about them and about the market, which is now global. The winners will be the ones who develop a world-class digital nervous system so that information can easily flow through their companies for maximum and constant learning.

I can anticipate your reaction. No, it's efficient processes! It's quality! It's creating brand recognition and going after market share! It's getting close to customers! Success, of course, depends on all of these things. Nobody can help you if your processes limp along, if you aren't vigilant about quality, if you don't work hard to establish your brand, if your customer service is poor. A bad strategy will fail no matter how good your information is. And lame execution will stymie a good strategy. If you do enough things poorly, you'll go out of business.

But no matter whatever else you have going for you today—smart employees, excellent products, customer goodwill, cash in the bank—you need a fast flow of good information to streamline processes, raise quality, and improve business execution. Most companies have good people working for them. Most companies want to do right by their customers. Good, actionable data exists somewhere within most organizations. Information flow is the lifeblood of your company because it enables you to get the most out of your people and learn from your customers. See if you have the information to answer these questions:

- What do customers think about your products? What problems do they want you to fix? What new features do they want you to add?
- What problems are your distributors and resellers running into as they sell your products or work with you?
- Where are your competitors winning business away from you, and why?
- Will changing customer demands force you to develop new capabilities?
- What new markets are emerging that you should enter?

A digital nervous system won't guarantee you the right answers to these questions. It will free you from tons of old paper processes so that you'll have the time to think about the questions. It will give you data to jump-start your thinking about them, putting the information out there so that you can see the trends coming at you. And a digital nervous system will make it possible for facts and ideas to quickly surface from down in your organization, from the people who have information about these questions—and, likely, many of the answers. Most important, it will allow you to do all these things fast.

ANSWERING THE HARD QUESTIONS

An old business joke says that if the railroads had understood they were in the transportation business instead of the steel-rail business, we'd all be flying on Union Pacific Airlines. Many businesses have broadened or altered their missions in even more fundamental ways. An unsuccessful maker of Japan's first electric rice cooker became Sony Corporation, a world leader in consumer and business electronics and in the music and movie industries. A company that began by opportunistically making welding machines, bowling alley sensors, and weight-reduction machines moved on to oscilloscopes and computers, becoming the Hewlett Packard we know today. These companies followed the market to phenomenal success, but most companies are not able to do this.

Even when you look at your existing business, it's not always clear where the next growth opportunity is. In the frenetic world of fast foods, McDonald's has the strongest brand name and market share and a good reputation for quality. But a market analyst recently suggested that McDonald's flip its business model. Referring to the company's occasional promotion of movie-inspired toys, the analyst said that McDonald's should use its low-margin burgers to sell a line of high-margin toys instead of the other way around. Such a change is unlikely but not unthinkable in today's fast-changing business world.

The important idea here is that a company not take its position in the market for granted. A company should constantly reevaluate. One company might make a great breakthrough into another business. Another company might find that it should stick to what it knows and does best. The critical thing is that a company's managers have the information to understand their competitive edge and what their next great market could be.

This book will help you use information technology to both ask and answer the hard questions about what your business should be and where it should go. Information technology gives you access to the data that leads to insights into your business. Information technology enables you to act quickly. It provides solutions to business problems that simply weren't available before. Information technology and business are becoming inextricably interwoven. I don't think anybody can talk meaningfully about one without talking about the other.

TAKING AN OBJECTIVE, FACTS-BASED APPROACH

The first step in answering any hard business question is to take an objective, facts-based approach. This principle, easier said than acted on, is illustrated in my favorite business book, *My Years with General Motors*, by Alfred P. Sloan Jr.[1] If you read only one book on business, read Sloan's

1. Sloan's book first came out in 1941. The current edition features an introduction by Peter F. Drucker (New York: Viking, 1991).

(but don't put this one down to do it). It's inspiring to see in Sloan's account of his career how positive, rational, information-focused leadership can lead to extraordinary success.

During Sloan's tenure from 1923 to 1956, General Motors became one of the first really complex business organizations in the United States. Sloan understood that a company could not develop a sweeping strategy or undertake the right ventures without building on facts and insights from the people in the organization. He developed his own understanding of the business from close personal collaboration with his technical and business staffs and by regular personal visits to the company's technical facilities. His greatest impact as a manager, however, came from the way he created working relationships with GM dealers across the country. He constantly gathered information from GM's dealers, and he cultivated close, productive relationships with them.

Sloan made a big deal out of fact-finding trips. He outfitted a private railroad car as an office and traveled all over the country, visiting dealers. He often saw between five and ten dealers a day. He wanted to know not just what GM was selling to dealers, but what was selling off the dealers' lots. These visits helped Sloan realize in the late 1920s that the car business was changing. Used cars would now provide basic transportation. Middle-income buyers, assisted by trade-ins and installment plans, would buy upscale new cars. Sloan recognized that this change meant that GM's fundamental relationship with dealers had to change, too, as the automobile business moved from a selling to a trading proposition. The manufacturer and the dealer had to develop more of a partnership. Sloan created a dealer council to meet regularly with GM's senior executives at corporate headquarters and a dealer relations board to handle dealer complaints, did economic studies to determine the best locations for new dealerships, and went so far as to institute a policy of "grubstaking capable men" who did not have ready capital to form dealerships.[2]

Accurate sales information continued to be hard to come by, though. GM's sales figures were inconsistent, out-of-date, and incomplete: "When a dealer's profit position was failing, we had no way of knowing whether this was due to a new car problem, a used-car problem, a service problem, a parts problem, or some other problem. Without such facts it was impossible to put any sound distribution policy into effect," Sloan wrote. He said he would be willing to pay "an enormous sum" and feel "fully justified in doing so" if every dealer "could know the facts about his business and could intelligently deal with the many details . . . in an intelligent manner." Sloan thought that helping dealers with these information issues "would be the best investment General Motors ever made."[3]

To address these needs, Sloan set up a standardized accounting system across the GM organization and all dealerships. The important word is *standardized.* Every dealer and every employee at every level in the company categorized numbers in precisely the same way. By the mid-1930s GM dealers, the auto divisions, and corporate headquarters could all do detailed financial analysis using the same numbers. A dealership, for instance, could gauge not only its own performance, but also its performance against group averages.

An infrastructure that provided accurate information led to a responsive organization that other carmakers didn't come close to matching for decades. This infrastructure,

2. Sloan, 288.
3. Sloan, 286–87.

Standardizing Worldwide Is Hard in Any Era

Microsoft's international business grew really fast once we got rolling overseas. We made a point of moving into international markets as early as possible, and our subsidiaries had a lot of entrepreneurial energy. Giving them the freedom to conduct their businesses according to what made sense in each country was good for customers and profitable for us. Our international business shot up from 41 percent of revenues in 1986 to 55 percent in 1989.

The independence of our subsidiaries extended to their financial reporting, which came to us in a number of different formats driven by a number of different business arrangements and taxation rules. Some subsidiaries accounted for products from our manufacturing corporation in Ireland based on their cost; others used a percentage of customer price as the cost. They'd reconcile the actual sales and profits in different ways. Some of our subsidiaries got a commission on direct sales to customers such as computer manufacturers selling PCs in their countries. Other subs facilitated direct sales from the parent company, and we reimbursed them on a cost-plus basis. The half a dozen different financial models gave us a lot of headaches.

Steve Ballmer, then executive vice president of sales and support, and I had to be pretty agile as we looked at the numbers. We'd be looking at a financial statement, and Mike Brown, then our chief financial officer, would say, "This is a Style 6 subsidiary, with cost-plus on this or that," meaning the financials were different from the other five models. We'd have to recompute the numbers for that sub in our heads as fast as we could so that we could compare them with other numbers.

"Not knowing any better," as Mike likes to say, he and our controller, Jon Anderson, decided to take advantage of the fact that everyone already used PC spreadsheets for other kinds of analysis. They designed a cost-basis profit and loss financial that didn't show any of the intercompany markups or commissions. Mike and Jon showed the new P&L around via e-mail and got quick buy-off on it. When we looked at our subsidiary financials after that, we had a much easier time seeing how we were actually doing, especially when we could pivot the data to see it from several different views. It's hard to overstate the benefit of being able to compare all of this data online. One critical aspect is being able to easily control exchange-rate assumptions in any view so you can see results either with or without the effects of exchange rates.

Later on, when we were ready to centralize our sales transactions in one corporate-wide system, we'd already done some of our homework. A lot of companies centralizing their sales systems lose time deciding how they want their financials organized. Because we had already figured that out, we were able to centralize our sales data far more quickly and inexpensively than many other companies.

what I call a company's nervous system, helped GM dominate automaking throughout Sloan's career. It wasn't yet digital, but it was extremely valuable. Knowing dealer inventory was something GM did better than anyone else, and GM got a huge competitive advantage from capitalizing on this information. And this use of information extended beyond GM's corporate walls. GM used manual information systems to develop the first "extranet"—a functioning network for GM, its suppliers, and its dealers.

Of course, you couldn't get nearly as much information flowing through your company then as you can now. It would have taken too many phone calls and too many people moving paper around and poring over paper records, trying to correlate data and spot patterns. It would have been immensely expensive. If you want to run a world-class company today, you have to track far more and do it far faster. To manage with the force of facts—one of Sloan's business fundamentals—requires information technology. What companies can afford to do, what it makes sense for them to do, what's competitive for them to do, has changed dramatically.

Now GM uses PC technology and Internet standards to communicate with its dealers and customers. Its solution, GM Access, uses a wide-area satellite intranet for interaction among headquarters, factories, and GM's 9,000 dealers. Dealers have online tools for financial management and operational planning, including total order management and sales analysis and forecasting. An interactive sales tool combines product features, specifications, pricing, and other information. Service technicians have instant access to the most current product and parts information through electronic service manuals and technical bulletins and online parts planning and inventory reports. E-mail links the dealers with GM headquarters, the factory, and one another. The private dealer solution is integrated with the public GM Web site, where consumers can get detailed vehicle information. Web technologies provide the foundation for a fundamental shift in the way consumers shop for vehicles, and they position GM for electronic commerce. Of course, other automakers have also improved their information systems. Toyota in particular has used information technology to develop world-class manufacturing.

DIFFERENTIATING YOUR COMPANY IN THE INFORMATION AGE

If information management and organizational responsiveness made such a fundamental difference in a traditional smokestack industry seventy years ago, how much more difference will they make propelled by technology? A modern automobile manufacturer may have a strong brand name and a reputation for quality today, but it is facing even greater competition around the world. All car manufacturers use the same steel, they have the same drilling machines, they have similar production processes, and they have roughly the same costs for transportation. Manufacturers will differentiate themselves from one another by the sum of how well they design their products, how intelligently they use customer feedback to improve their products and services, how quickly they can improve their production processes, how cleverly they market their products, and how efficiently they manage distribution and their inventories. All of these information-rich processes benefit from digital processes.

The value of a digital approach is especially apparent in information-centric businesses such as banks and insurance companies. In banking, data about the customer relationship and credit analysis are at the heart of the business, and banks have always been big users of information technology. In the age of the Internet and increasing deregulation of financial markets, though, how do two banks differentiate themselves from each other? It comes down to the intelligence of a bank's credit analysis and risk management and its responsiveness in its relationship with the customer. It's *brains* that gives one or the other bank the edge. I don't mean just the individual abilities of bank employees. I mean the overall ability of the bank to capitalize on the best thinking of all of its employees.

Today bank information systems have to do more than manage huge amounts of financial data. They have to put more intelligence about customers into the hands of business strategists and loan officers. They have to enable customers themselves to securely access information and pay bills online while the bank's knowledge workers collaborate on higher-value activities. Information systems are no longer only about back-end number-crunching. They're about enabling information to be put to work on behalf of the consumer. Crestar Bank of Richmond, Virginia, provides banking, mortgage application, and bill payment services over the Internet, and its tellers in remote locations such as supermarkets or malls can open accounts and initiate loans for customers—all by connecting the customer to the back-end systems by means of digital information flow.

I was speaking at a bank roundtable in Canada recently and got some questions about how banks should invest in the Internet. Today they have back-end database systems that store information, and they have applications for people doing customer service on the phone and for tellers and for branch banks. Now they're looking at adding new systems to present customers with data over the Internet. They said, "We don't want to pick up the additional cost and complexity of still another interface." I told them the solution was simple: They should build a great interface for customers to see data over the Internet, then use the same interface to view data internally. They'd have a small amount of additional data that the bank employees would get to see—customer data and background on recent interactions with the customers—but the interface would be the same. If they do the new system on a mainstream platform, they can replace all the different ways of viewing data. Over time, as it makes business sense, they can upgrade the back-end database to new technology, but meanwhile the Internet interface will simplify their lives, not make them more complex. The new interface "becomes" the bank, both inside and out.

PUTTING INFORMATION TO WORK

After the introduction of ENIAC, the first general-purpose computer, during World War II, computers quickly proved they were faster and more accurate than humans in many applications—managing the customer records of the largest institutions and automating almost any mechanical process that could be broken into discrete, repetitive steps. Computers were not functioning at a high level, though. They assisted people but not in an intelligent way. It takes brains to understand the physics and develop the underlying calculations for the arcs of artillery projectiles or ballistic missiles; it takes an idiot savant—a computer—to do the calculations in an instant.

Businesses need to do another kind of work, what Michael Dertouzos, director of MIT's laboratory for computer science and author of *What Will Be*,[4] calls "information

4. *What Will Be: How the New World of Information Will Change Our Lives* (San Francisco: HarperCollins, HarperEdge, 1997).

work." We usually think of information—a memo, a picture, or a financial report, say—as static. But Dertouzos convincingly argues that another form of information is active—a "verb" instead of a static noun. Information work is "the transformation of information by human brains or computer programs." Information work—designing a building, negotiating a contract, preparing tax returns—constitutes most of the real information we deal with and most of the work done in developed economies. "Information-as-verb activities dominate the terrain of information," Dertouzos says.[5] He estimates that information work contributes 50 to 60 percent of an industrialized country's GNP.

Dertouzos's insight into information-as-action is profound. When computers went from raw number-crunching to modeling business problems, they began to participate in information work. Even manufacturing firms have always expended much of their energy on information about the work rather than on the work itself: information about product design and development; about scheduling; about marketing, sales, and distribution; about invoicing and financing; about cooperative activities with vendors; about customer service.

When I sit down with developers to review product specifications, or with Microsoft's product divisions to review their three-year business plans, or with our sales groups to review their financial performance, we work through the difficult issues. We discuss feature trade-offs vs. time to market, marketing spend vs. revenue, head count vs. return, and so on. Through human intelligence and collaboration, we transform static sales, customer, and demographic data into the design of a product or a program. *Information work is thinking work.* When thinking and

5. Dertouzos, 230–31.

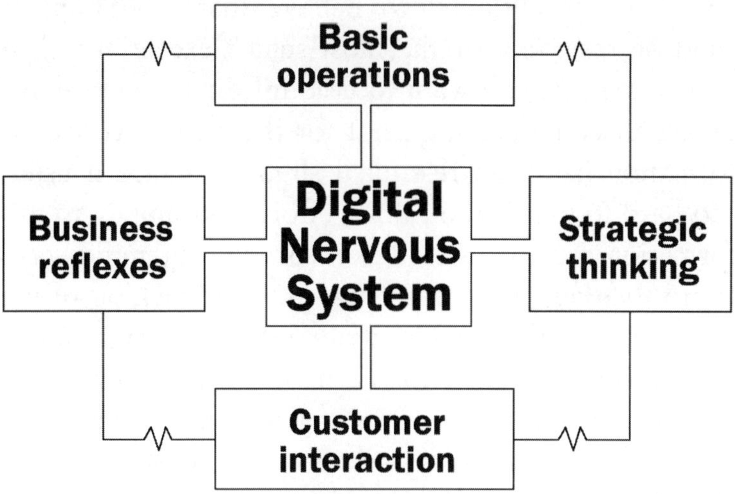

A digital nervous system comprises the digital processes that closely link every aspect of a company's thoughts and actions. Basic operations such as finance and production, plus feedback from customers, are electronically accessible to a company's knowledge workers, who use digital tools to quickly adapt and respond. The immediate availability of accurate information changes strategic thinking from a separate, stand-alone activity to an ongoing process integrated with regular business activities.

collaboration are significantly assisted by computer technology, you have a digital nervous system. It consists of the advanced digital processes that knowledge workers use to make better decisions. To think, act, react, and adapt. Dertouzos says that the future "Information Marketplace" will entail "a great deal of customized software and intricately dovetailed combinations of human and machine procedures"—an excellent description of a digital nervous system at work.[6]

GETTING THE NUMBERS EASILY

To do information work, people in the company have to have ready access to information. Until recently, though,

6. Dertouzos, 231.

we've been conditioned to believe that "the numbers" should be reserved for the most senior executives. A few executives might still want to hold information close in the interests of confidentiality, but for the most part access to information has been restricted simply because it used to be so hard to get. It took time, effort, and money to move information around. It's as if even now our mind-sets go back to the days when there was this big backlog of work that came from the need to write a custom program every time somebody wanted to see numbers in a new way. It was so expensive to pull data out of a mainframe, and it took so much labor to try to correlate the data, that you had to be at least a vice president to order up the work. Even then, the information was sometimes so inconsistent or out-of-date that you'd have VPs from different departments show up at high-level meetings with different data! The only way that Johnson & Johnson's CEO, Ralph Larsen, could get data about any of J&J's companies in the late 1980s, for instance, was to have the finance department prepare a special report. As we'll see in chapter 18, things at J&J are different now.

On today's computer networks you can retrieve and present data easily and inexpensively. You can dive into the data to the lowest level of detail and pivot it to see it in different dimensions. You can exchange information and ideas with other people. You can integrate the ideas and work of multiple people or teams to produce a well-thought-out and coordinated result. We need to break out of the mind-set that getting information and moving information around is difficult and expensive. It's just basic common sense to make all of your company's data—everything from the latest sales numbers to details of the 401(k) plan—just a few clicks away for everyone who can use it.

Executive Information Systems Evolve

One early effort to improve information flow, at least for executives, was the executive information system (EIS). Emerging in the late 1980s, EIS gave executives the ability to get sales information or other data without having to wait months for a special report. EIS was the right idea, but it was limited to senior ranks and wasn't connected up with the other company information systems. EIS tended to be just another proprietary system within a proprietary system. One large U.S. steel company discovered that the information provided by the new tool led senior executives to ask more questions of their subordinates, who didn't have the information to answer them!

With the benefit of PC-based platforms, tools for rapid application development, and improved graphical user interfaces, the executive information system has evolved into the "enterprise information system," also called a "performance measurement system." The new EIS systems are intended to provide information to a wider range of people in an organization.

As the vendors of EIS systems moved to a standard platform and tools, their roles evolved. The real value they offer is not in building the application, but in helping companies figure out what to do with it. Customers often arrive with their expectations so shaped by the idea that information is hard to get that they don't know what is reasonable to expect from their information systems. A leading EIS vendor, Comshare, of Ann Arbor, Michigan, starts out by asking a customer such basic questions as "What do you want from the sytem?" and "What are the outcomes you want to measure?" Comshare's sales analysis application comes with ninety specific questions about the kinds of data a company might want—performance, underperformance, regional performance, and so on.

Comshare, which offers a mix of systems using standard desktop applications or browsers as the front end, assists the customer with analyzing and shaping the right approach to the problem and will bring in consultants to help with business process reengineering if that seems to be needed. Only after analysis and any necessary reengineering of processes does Comshare deliver the technology.

A company's middle managers and line employees, not just its high-level executives, need to see business data. It's important for me as a CEO to understand how the company is doing across regions or product lines or customer segments, and I take pride in staying on top of those things. However, it's the middle managers in every company who need to understand where their profits and losses lie, what marketing programs are working or not, and what expenses are in line or out of whack. They're the people who need precise, actionable data because they're the ones who need to act. They need an immediate, constant flow and rich views of the right information. These employees shouldn't have to wait for upper management to bring information to them. Companies should spend less time protecting financial data from employees and more time teaching them to analyze and act on it.

Of course, every company is going to draw the line on information access somewhere. Every company keeps salaries confidential. In general, though, I believe in a very open policy on information availability. There's incredible value in letting everybody involved with a product, even the most junior team member, understand the history, the pricing, and how the sales break down around the world and by customer segment. The value of having everybody get the complete picture and trusting each person with it far outweighs the risk involved.

In many companies the middle managers can be overwhelmed by day-to-day problems and not have information they need to fix them. They may have reams of data in front of them—literally reams of paper reports—that are difficult to analyze or correlate with data in other reports. A sign of a good digital nervous system is that you have middle managers empowered by the flow of specific, actionable information. They should be seeing their sales numbers, expense breakdowns, vendor and contractor costs, and the status of major projects online, in a form that invites analysis as well as coordination with other people. The systems should notify them of unusual developments according to criteria they set—for example, if an expense item is out of line. This way they don't need to monitor normal expense activity. These capabilities are available at a few companies, but I'm continually surprised by how few companies use information technology to keep their line managers well informed and to avoid routine review.

I'm amazed by the tortuous path that critical information often takes through many Fortune 500 companies. I'm spoiled by being able to e-mail a view of the latest data to key managers and let them dig into it. At McDonald's, until recently, sales data had to be manually "touched" several times before it made its way to the people who needed it. Today, McDonald's is well on the way to installing a new information system that uses PCs and Web technologies to tally sales at all of its restaurants in real time. As soon as you order two Happy Meals, a McDonald's marketing manager will know. Rather than superficial or anecdotal data, the marketer will have hard, factual data for tracking trends.

As we'll see in the description of Microsoft's reaction to the Internet, still another sign of a good digital nervous system is the number of good ideas bubbling up from your line managers and knowledge workers. When they can analyze concrete data, people get specific ideas about how to do things better—and they get charged up about it, too.

People like knowing that something they're doing is working, and they like being able to demonstrate to management that it's working. They enjoy using technology that encourages them to evaluate different theories about what's going on in their markets. They get a kick out of running what-ifs. People really do appreciate information, and it's a big motivator.

A final sign of a good digital nervous system is how focused your face-to-face meetings are and whether specific actions come out of them. Pilots like to say that good landings are the result of good approaches. Good meetings are the result of good preparation. Meetings shouldn't be used primarily to present information. It's more efficient to use e-mail so that people can analyze data beforehand and come into a meeting prepared to make recommendations and engage in meaningful debate. Companies struggling with too many unproductive meetings and too much paper don't lack energy and brains. The data they need exists somewhere in the company in some form. They just can't readily put their hands on it. Digital tools would enable them to get the data immediately, from many sources, and to be able to analyze it from many perspectives.

GM's Alfred Sloan said that without facts it's impossible to put a sound policy into effect. I am optimistic enough to believe that if you have sound facts, you *can* put a sound policy into effect. Sloan did, many times over. At today's pace of business change, we need even more to manage with the force of facts.

What I'm describing here is a new level of information analysis that enables knowledge workers to turn passive data into active information—what Michael Dertouzos calls information-as-a-verb. A digital nervous system enables a company to do information work with far more efficiency, depth, and creativity.

Business Lessons

- ❑ Information flow is the primary differentiator for business in the digital age.
- ❑ Most work in every business is "information work," a term coined by Michael Dertouzos to describe human thought applied to data to solve a problem.
- ❑ Middle managers need as much business data as senior executives but often have less.
- ❑ Unproductive meetings, or meetings that largely involve status updates, are signs of poor information flow.

Diagnosing Your Digital Nervous System

- ❑ Do you have the information flow that enables you to answer the hard questions about what your customers and partners think about your products and services, what markets you are losing and why, and what your real competitive edge is?
- ❑ Do your information systems simply crunch numbers in the back room or help to directly solve customer problems?

2

CAN YOUR DIGITAL NERVOUS SYSTEM DO THIS?

A firm's IQ is determined by the degree to which its IT infrastructure connects, shares, and structures information. Isolated applications and data, no matter how impressive, can produce idiot savants but not a highly functional corporate behavior.

—Steve H. Haeckel and Richard L. Nolan,
"Managing by Wire: Using IT to Transform a Business"

Like a human being, a company has to have an internal communication mechanism, a "nervous system," to coordinate its actions. All businesses focus on a few basic elements: customers; products and services; revenues; costs; competitors; delivery; and employees. A company has to carry out and coordinate the business processes in each area, especially activities that cross department lines. Sales needs to quickly find out whether the company has the inventory or can get it quickly before promising delivery on a big order. Manufacturing needs to know what product is selling like gangbusters so that it can shift production priorities. Business managers throughout the company need to know about both and a whole lot more.

An organization's nervous system has parallels with our human nervous system. Every business, regardless of industry, has "autonomic" systems, the operational processes that just have to go on if the company is to survive. Every business has a core process at the heart of its corporate mission, whether it's the design and manufacture of products or the delivery of services. Every business has to manage its income and expenses. And every business has a variety of administrative processes such as payroll. No company will prosper for long if products don't go out the door or if the bills and the employees don't get paid.

The need for efficiency and reliability has driven the rush to automate many basic operations. With managers using whatever solutions were available, the result over time has been a proliferation of incompatible systems. Each independent system may operate smoothly on its own, but the data in each is isolated and hard to integrate with the data in the others. What has been missing are links between information that resemble the interconnected neurons in the brain. Extracting data from operational processes and using it in a meaningful way has been one of the more intractable problems of business. Although automation has been valuable, today's technology can make basic operations the cornerstone of a much broader, corporate-wide intelligence.

A company also needs to have good business reflexes, to be able to marshal its forces in a crisis or in response to any unplanned event. You might get a call from your best customer saying he's going with your biggest competitor, or that competitor might introduce a hot new product, or you might have a faulty product or an operations breakdown to deal with. Unplanned events calling for a tactical response can be positive, too. You might get an unexpected opportunity for a major partnering activity or an acquisition.

Finally, there's the conscious directing of your company's muscles, whether you're creating teams to develop new products, opening new offices, or redeploying people in the field to go after new customers. To be carried out well, these planned events need deliberation, strategic analysis, execution, and evaluation. You need to think about your company's fundamental business issues and develop a long-term business strategy to solve problems and take advantage of the opportunities your analysis unearths. Then you need to communicate a strategy and the plans behind it to everybody in the company and to partners and other relevant people outside the company.

More than anything, though, a company has to communicate with its customers and act on what it learns in that communication. This primary need involves all of a company's capabilities: operational efficiency and data gathering, reflexive reach and coordination, and strategic planning and execution. The need to communicate effectively with your customers will come up again and again in this book. I'll show how a digital nervous system helps successful companies bring all of their processes to bear on this most important mission of all organizations.

A digital nervous system serves two primary purposes in the development of business understanding. It extends the individual's analytical abilities the way machines extend physical capabilities, and it combines the abilities of individuals to create an institutional intelligence and a unified ability to act. To put it all together in the right context: A digital nervous system seeks to create corporate excellence out of individual excellence on behalf of the customer.

MAKING DATA AVAILABLE EVERY DAY

One way to think of a digital nervous system is as a way to give your internal staff the same kind of data for daily business use that you give a consultant for a special project. With their years of experience in the industry and their expertise in business analysis, consultants often come in with fresh ideas and new ways of looking at issues. After crunching through census-type demographic and sales data, consultants invariably surprise senior management with their profitability analyses, their comparisons to competitors, and their insight into better business processes.

From another perspective, though, it's just crazy that somebody outside your company receives more information than you use for yourself. Too often, important customer and sales information is pulled together on a one-time-only basis when consultants arrive. You should have that information available on an ongoing basis for your regular business staff.

If consultants get more insight from your systems than you do, it should be because of their unique abilities, not because you prepare information especially for the consultants that isn't otherwise available to your staff. If a consultant can find trends in your data that you can't, there's something wrong with your flow of information. Not all of your managers will have the expertise or breadth of knowledge that a consultant brings to your business, but your managers should have access to data of the same quality. They should be able to walk into work every day and see the freshest data and be able to analyze it in numerous instructive ways. As we'll see in the following example, good things happen when they can.

INFORMING STRATEGIC PLANNING

Since our direct sales force calls only on large corporations and partners, Jeff Raikes, our group vice president of sales and support, wrestles every year with the question of how to improve the effectiveness of our marketing to small and medium-size customers. We usually reach these customers through seminars, co-marketing activities with partners, and similar broad-reach programs. Jeff had been reviewing various approaches to reach our smaller customers. Should we do more marketing in the larger cities since more small and medium-size customers are concentrated there? Or should we expand our activities into the next half-dozen cities in each district according to population size? Given limited resources, what would be the best approach?

In Microsoft's culture of numbers you have to have good factual data to convince people of almost any business proposition, and no one had convincing evidence of the best way to proceed. Then somebody remembered an analysis Pat Hayes, operations manager for Microsoft's Central Region, had done. Pat had rationalized travel budgets among districts that had most of their customers in a major city, such as Chicago, and districts that had most of their customers dispersed across several states. His study had identified some small outlying cities with high concentrations of PC ownership. Would these cities be the best untapped source of new revenue?

Pat and a small team were charged with determining the best new marketing opportunities on a regionwide basis—eighteen U.S. states and Canada. What happened in the two months between November 1996 and January 1997 illustrates how the typical digital tools that many knowledge workers already have can integrate with back-end financial systems to help companies improve their sales.

How do you go about identifying the cities with the best sales potential among hundreds of cities of different sizes? What are the right metrics? How do you develop a marketing program that doesn't call for hiring dozens of people and spending tens of millions of dollars? You begin by putting the information you have to work.

Pat and a couple of other people began by culling data from MS Sales, our mission-critical revenue measurement and decision support system. This PC-based data warehouse has information from every reseller worldwide on the sales of every version of every product we sell. More than 4,000 employees use MS Sales regularly for decision support, supply chain management, sales force compensation, month-end general ledger close, fiscal budget planning, R&D planning, and market share analysis.

From the Internet, the team grabbed U.S. census data that showed the average number of employees per company per city. From an outside consulting firm, the team got information on the number of PCs per city. From field marketing managers around the region, the team manually gathered information on seminars and other marketing activities in each city. Finally the team included a list of the number of Microsoft partners in each city. This research, begun by two people using e-mail, intranet postings, and the phone to communicate, ultimately involved dozens of people around the country.

After merging and scrubbing all the data, Pat and the team began to analyze it in several different ways. Sometimes independently, sometimes in collaboration, and always with our electronic tools, they tried to spot a correlation between sales numbers and marketing activities across cities of varying sizes. MS Sales provided two sets of data that proved crucial: last year's sales data, which enabled them to calculate growth, and revenue by postal code. Having revenue numbers at the postal code level enabled very granular analysis by metropolitan area. With the census and PC data, they could create two other important metrics: revenue per PC and revenue per each company's employee.

By early January, when they had identified eighty cities

that were likely candidates for a new marketing campaign, Pat and the team met with Jeff Raikes. Jeff suggested that they develop a performance index and an activity index for each city. The indexes would provide the common measurement they had been looking for in order to understand the relationship among revenue, PC density, and marketing. The performance index would be the percentage of revenue divided by the percentage of PCs in the region; the activity index would be the percentage of all attendees at Microsoft events who were from the region divided by the percentage of PCs in the region. A number greater than 1 would mean that the city was outperforming other cities; a number below 1 would mean that the city was underperforming.

With a consistent set of metrics, the little group didn't have to have philosophical discussions about whether a city was in the Sun Belt or the Rust Belt or whether the economy in that area was generally good and therefore our sales should be up. Instead the discussion was straight math. They could relate each city's performance to every other city's and to the presence or absence of marketing activities. Most important, they had a way to extrapolate potential sales for those cities in which we were not doing any marketing at all. A number of small cities looked very promising.

I first heard about the project at the executive review in late January 1997, when Jeff presented the data. We were all intrigued and gave him the go-ahead to pursue a test-and-invest marketing strategy for some of these smaller cities. Before we spend big bucks, we want to find out on a small scale whether our idea will work. Jeff e-mailed Pat and told him to draw up a final set of recommendations for a pilot program and to plan to review it with Jeff within two weeks.

The day before that meeting, Pat and an associate were working on the final recommendations. Using his list of the number of Microsoft partners in each city, Pat had created a new index for partners to indicate the relative potential for co-marketing activities in each city. Not knowing where they'd end up, Pat and his associate decided to use the indexes to carve up the cities into different categories and come up with a recommendation for each category. At one end they'd have a city with high marketing activity that was overperforming. Their recommendation for such a city would be to lower activity and see whether performance dropped. If performance remained fine, the company could spend less for the same results. If marketing activity was high and performance was low, they'd check the partner index to see whether we had enough partners in that city to justify increasing marketing activity there. It was late when they got down to the last category, cities with an activity index of 0, meaning no marketing at all.

Overall, our average regional revenue for smaller companies was $2.90 per customer employee, but actual revenue per small-company employee varied tremendously. In a large city such as Dallas, where we have a district office and do marketing programs, our average was $8.43. In a smaller city like San Antonio, where we have no office but do marketing programs, our revenue was $3.44 per employee. In the eighty cities with no office and no marketing (the "zero activity" index), our average revenue was $0.89.

Suddenly they had their answer. New programs where we already did marketing would give us incremental results of some kind, but if new marketing programs brought even half of the eighty "zero activity" cities up to just our regional average of $2.90, we would double our revenue in those cities from $30 million to $60 million in a year!

Pat, who had never presented to Jeff before, had no

way of knowing that he'd never cover his plan in a formal way. Jeff has a habit of flipping through presentations quickly, to find the slides that describe action items. He can read faster than most people can talk, and skimming lets him get past the "status" aspect of a meeting and into the heart of the matter in a hurry. "We never got past slide one," Pat said. They dived right into the spreadsheets, answering Jeff's questions for two full hours. When Jeff saw the potential for the "zero activity" cities, he said, "Go do this."

Jeff made a final suggestion. Sift the eighty cities again with an eye to an 8-to-1 return on investment, the minimum ROI we think will justify a marketing program. Setting an 8-to-1 bar would enable them to weed out any cities where the percentage return might be high but the absolute dollar revenue would be too low. The 8:1 ratio represents our typical marketing spend as a percentage of net revenue. "Get this nailed, and then tell me what you need," Jeff said. In a follow-up e-mail he added, "Don't let head count and marketing budget get in the way. Just do it."

A week later Pat e-mailed Jeff with his final proposal to concentrate on forty-five cities (later pared to thirty-eight). Ultimately the marketing experiment was simple: two "Big Day" events in the year in each qualified city in which we hadn't been doing any marketing. Each Big Day would provide an overview of Microsoft strategy and our product line, and with our partners we'd present various sales offers. With a third party to handle logistics and with help from our partners for the Big Day events, the plan would entail just two new head counts and cost a total of just $1.5 million. The maximum ROI looked to be a staggering twenty to one: a $30 million revenue increase on a $1.5 million investment.

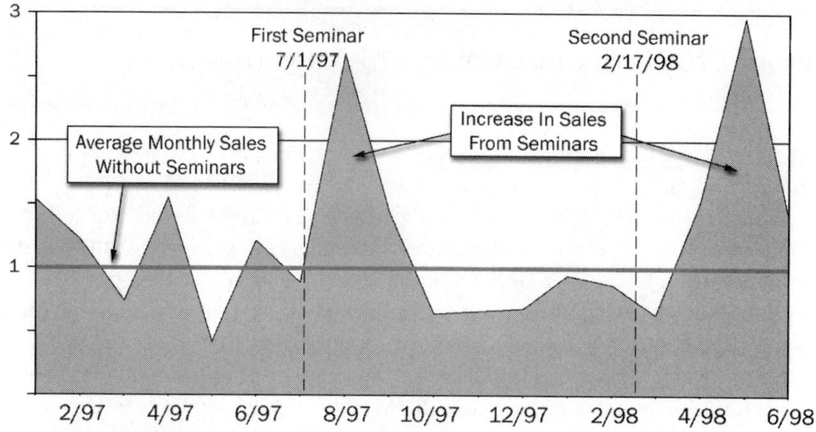

Microsoft's digital nervous system enables sales managers to pinpoint cities that are most likely to generate increased sales as the result of new marketing programs. Digital analysis led to a program that increased sales by 57 percent, more than 3.5 times the norm. Marketers can track the effectiveness of each marketing effort within days and, as these results from a Texas city show, test how often events should be repeated without diminishing returns. Digital data also shows what subject matter needs to be delivered next time.

As the Big Day events were carried out, we used MS Sales to constantly measure our progress in the thirty-eight cities against figures in similar markets to see if our new program was really making an impact. The results: After three quarters, we showed a 57 percent increase in revenue in those cities in which we did Big Day events vs. 16 percent growth in a control group of nineteen small cities that met the ROI requirement but sat out the test-and-invest period.

Our partners in the thirty-eight smaller cities, primarily value-added resellers and local retailers, were gratified by the Big Day program. Their sales increased an amount commensurate with ours, and the goodwill we achieved with them established a solid basis for future marketing cooperation.

We've continued to build on these early efforts at identifying new market opportunities. We've expanded the

From DISCO to Shirt Color, MS Sales Informs

MS Sales, our worldwide sales information system, has been responsible for a great deal of learning that has improved our marketing.

One of the most meaningful MS Sales reports is DISCO, for district comparisons. Using DISCO, our Northeast district manager discovered that the top districts overall in Fiscal Year 1996 were those that had done the best job of selling Microsoft Office to small business. She kicked off a direct-mail campaign to resellers in the small-business market that greatly increased district sales. By monitoring the results in MS Sales, she determined that the mailings needed to continue every six to eight weeks in order to keep driving increased revenue. The Northeast district finished FY '97 as the top growth district in this business sector, and the program has been emulated in other districts with similar results.

Microsoft India used MS Sales to track the effectiveness of programs designed to encourage customers to buy CD-ROM versions of our products rather than the floppy disk versions. The change would save customers a lot of disk switching to install products and reduce our cost of goods. India also used MS Sales to determine which special promotions to resellers actually increased sales for particular products.

In France Microsoft's large account team analyzed which accounts had enough software to qualify for our highest-volume discount program and went to those companies offering them great deals. In cases where customers had decentralized purchasing, we were able to tell them the locations of all of their PCs and help them better control their purchases.

In Argentina one of our salespeople was talking to a reseller who tried to impress him with somewhat inflated sales claims. Still on the phone with the reseller, our guy quickly checked MS Sales and found out exactly how much her company was selling, which was less than the reseller was claiming. When he casually mentioned the real sales numbers, she was surprised and asked how he had gotten the information so quickly.

He described MS Sales to her and went through all the data he could get from it. "That's not all," he said. "It also knows you're wearing a red polo shirt."

The phone went silent.

"How does it know?" she finally asked.

It was a lucky guess.

marketing program to other regions and to other countries. We recognized the value of the numbers we originally collected for onetime use, so we now have them in the sales system and keep them up-to-date. Anybody working on any sales analysis can view the data and do historical comparisons.

Also, while Pat Hayes's project was under way, another member of Jeff's group was working separately on an "opportunity map" for potential new business by different products. Jeff combined the work on products and Pat's work on the basis of revenue. Now we have a tool that allows anybody in the company to pivot through opportunities not just by revenue potential, but by product as well. Today, instead of scheduling a general Microsoft strategy tour in eight cities where overall revenue is low, we can determine whether one city needs a seminar on Office, another a seminar on Windows, and a third a seminar on Exchange.

MAKING AN INVESTMENT, NOT RELYING ON LUCK

MS Sales, our sales database, was a major part of our marketing solution for smaller cities. MS Sales was the result of our commitment to build a financial reporting system that would capture a wide variety of sales information and put it at our fingertips. MS Sales enables us to drill into data in every way imaginable—by region, country, customer size, product area, salesperson, even postal codes. Every business needs information systems that can quickly provide this granularity of detail. It should be just a click of a button away for your sales managers or for your people in the field.

It wasn't a matter of luck that we happened to have a crucial number like postal code revenue handy. We've made a real investment over a number of years in obtaining this kind of data and in getting our channel partners to feed sales data into our systems electronically. Because of our indirect sales model, integrating channel sales data digitally into our financial reporting is crucial. We didn't know beforehand all of the questions that would come up, but we had a pretty good idea of the kinds of data we'd need to answer a broad range of questions, at all levels of detail and from many perspectives.

A paper-based system could not do this work. Similarly, any system without easy spreadsheet access to allow different theories to be tested would not have worked. The need to combine census data and collaborate across the country required immense flexibility. Because much of the sales data now comes to us via the Internet in a format we can immediately use in MS Sales, the process is inexpensive, so our channel partners can afford it. By sharing the analysis from these tools appropriately with our partners, we also raised business discussions with them to a more strategic level.

Really difficult business problems always have many aspects. Often a major decision depends on an impromptu search for one or two key pieces of auxiliary information and a quick, ad hoc analysis of several possible scenarios. You need tools that easily combine and recombine data from many sources. You need Internet access for all kinds of research. Widely scattered people need to be able to collaborate and work the data in different ways. At one point Steve Ballmer, company president, was critiquing plans for Pat Hayes's project by e-mail from Europe. A back-end database was important to our solution, but more important was our decision to build our infrastructure around overall information flow. All of the important decisions were made in old-fashioned face-to-face meetings, but the program would not have been possible without the preparation enabled by our digital nervous system.

CHANGING THE ROLE OF DISTRICT MANAGERS

At Microsoft our information systems have also changed the role of our district sales managers. When MS Sales first came online, our Minneapolis general manager ran a variety of numbers for her district at a level of detail never possible before. She discovered that excellent sales among other customer segments were obscuring a poor showing among large customers in her district. In fact, the district was dead last among U.S. districts in that category. Finding that out was a shock but also a big motivator for the large-customer teams in the district. By the end of the year Minneapolis was the top-growing district for sales to large customers.

If you're a district manager at Microsoft today, you must be more than a good sales leader helping your team close the big deals, which has been the traditional district manager role. Now you can be a business thinker. You have numbers to help you run your business. Before, even if you were concerned about the retail store revenue in your area, you had no view whatsoever of those results. Now you can look at sales figures and evaluate where your business is strong, where your business is weak, and where your business has its greatest potential, product by product, relative to other districts. You can try out new programs and see their impact. You can talk to other managers about what they're doing to get strong results. Being a district sales manager in our organization is a much broader role than what it was five years ago because of the digital tools we've developed and their ease of use.

Customer Analysis Identifies Weaknesses

MS Sales also includes a central customer database, which we use to evaluate purchasing patterns of individual customers as well as groups of customers. Our Northern California district recently used MS Sales to analyze deployments for products such as Microsoft Exchange, Microsoft Office, and Windows. The team generated special reports with pivot tables to understand the number of licenses and the market penetration we were achieving among large customers in various customer segments.

Manipulating the spreadsheets to look at national, regional, and district data and to look at industries or specific accounts, Northern California realized that deployment of Microsoft Exchange, our messaging product, was weaker in certain types of accounts than in others. The district also found that in certain kinds of accounts IBM's Lotus Notes tended to be the main competitor, while elsewhere other products were the primary competitors.

This precise information helped the district put together programs to ensure that Microsoft met the market challenge by sending our systems engineers and consultants to the right accounts. The information also helped Microsoft engineers and consultants show up better prepared, having gotten more training on the chief competitor in an account so that they could answer tough questions about comparative strengths of our product vs. the competitor's.

DOING BUSINESS AT THE SPEED OF THOUGHT

A digital nervous system gives its users an understanding and an ability to learn what would not be possible otherwise. A good flow of information and good analytical tools gave us insight into new revenue opportunities among volumes of potentially impenetrable data. It maximized the capabilities of human brains and minimized human labor. The Central Region team had only two core members who pulled in many others, and everyone was doing the work on top of his or her regular duties. The same infrastructure gave us the right tools for executing, evaluating, and fine-tuning our marketing program.

To begin creating a digital nervous system, you should first develop an ideal picture of the information you need to run your business and to understand your markets and your competitors. Think hard about the facts that are actionable for your company. Develop a list of the questions to which the answers would change your actions. Then demand that your information systems provide those answers. If your current system won't, you need to develop one that will—one or more of your competitors will.

You know you have built an excellent digital nervous system when information flows through your organization as quickly and naturally as thought in a human being and when you can use technology to marshal and coordinate teams of people as quickly as you can focus an individual on an issue. It's business at the speed of thought.

Business Lessons

- ❑ Businesspeople need to shake loose of the notion that information is hard to get.
- ❑ Better information can expand the role of sales managers from being the closers of big deals to being business managers.
- ❑ Bringing together the right information with the right people will dramatically improve a company's ability to develop and act on strategic business opportunities.
- ❑ Integrating sales data with partners not only streamlines reporting processes, but also raises the business discussions to a more strategic level.

Diagnosing Your Digital Nervous System

- ❑ Is important data culled only for special onetime use, or can employees get access to it on a daily basis?
- ❑ Make a list of the most actionable questions about your business. Does your information system provide the data to answer them?
- ❑ Do your digital systems enable you to pinpoint sales areas that offer the most opportunities or that need the most attention?

3

CREATE A PAPERLESS OFFICE

It is sobering to reflect on the extent to which the structure of our business processes has been dictated by the limitations of the file folder.

—Michael Hammer and James Champy, *Reengineering Your Business*

Digital technology can transform your production processes and your business processes. It can also free workers from slow and inflexible paper processes. Replacing paper processes with digital processes liberates knowledge workers to do productive work. The all-digital workplace is usually called "the paperless office," a phrase that goes back to at least 1973. It's a great vision. No more stacks of paper in which you can't find what you need. No more pawing through piles of books and reports to find marketing information or a sales number. No more misrouted forms, lost invoices, redundant entries, missing checks, or delays caused by incomplete paperwork.

But the paperless office, like artificial intelligence, is

one of those "any day now" phenomena that somehow never seem to actually arrive. The first use of the phrase *paperless office* appeared in a headline a quarter of a century ago in a trade publication for phone companies. The Xerox Corporation (although it never called it a "paperless office") did more to promote the concept than anyone else. In 1974–75 the company was talking about "the office of the future" that would have computers and e-mail with information online. Between 1975 and 1987 several business publications promised that the paperless office wasn't far off and would radically change the workplace, but in 1988 I told a reporter, "This vision of a paperless office is still very, very far away. . . . Computers today are not yet fulfilling this vision."[1]

Today we have all the pieces in place to make the vision a reality. Graphical computing and better analytical tools make it easy to integrate data of various types. Highly capable, networked PCs are ubiquitous in the office environment. The Internet is connecting PCs around the world. Yet paper consumption has continued to double every four years, and 95 percent of all information in the United States remains on paper, compared with just 1 percent stored electronically. Paperwork is increasing faster than digital technology can eliminate it!

In 1996 I decided to look into the ways that Microsoft, a big advocate of replacing paper with electronic forms, was still using paper. To my surprise, we had printed 350,000 paper copies of sales reports that year. I asked for a copy of every paper form we used. The thick binder that landed on my desk contained hundreds and hundreds of forms. At corporate headquarters we had 114 forms in Pro-

1. James E. LaLonde, "Gates: Computers Still Too Hard to Use," *Seattle Times*, 1 June 1988.

curement alone. Our 401(k) retirement plan had 8 different paper forms—for entering and exiting the plan, for changing employee information, and for changing employee investments or contributions. Every time the government changed the rules, we'd have to update and reprint the forms and recycle thousands of old ones. Paper consumption was only a symptom of a bigger problem, though: administrative processes that were too complicated and time-intensive.

I looked at this binder of forms and wondered, "Why do we have all of these forms? Everybody here has a PC. We're connected up. Why aren't we using electronic forms and e-mail to streamline our processes and replace all this paper?"

Well, I exercised the privilege of my job and banned all unnecessary forms. In place of all that paper, systems grew up that were far more accurate and far easier to work with and that empowered our people to do more interesting work.

STARTING A JOURNEY WITH A SINGLE CLICK

Now, even before a new employee is hired, he or she embarks on an electronic journey. We receive 600 to 900 résumés from job applicants every day by postal mail, by e-mail, or via our Resume Builder on the Microsoft Web site.[2] Seventy percent of the résumés arrive electronically via e-mail or the Web, up from 6 percent two years ago and rising. Our software automatically acknowledges every electronic submission. Our recruiting database, from Res-

2. People mail their résumés to resume@microsoft.com. The link to Resume Builder is at www.microsoft.com/jobs.

trac of Lexington, Massachusetts, directly accepts information from résumés created at our Resume Builder Web site; e-mail submissions are parsed to deliver candidate information to Restrac. A paper résumé is scanned and converted into text that can go into the database. All résumés are electronically matched with open job positions within twenty-four to forty-eight hours of receipt.

Human Resources specialists search the Restrac database for promising candidates, consulting with hiring managers in person or over e-mail. They use scheduling software to set up job interviews. Every interviewer gets a copy of the résumé and any other background information in e-mail. After meeting with a prospect, each interviewer e-mails comments about the candidate to Human Resources, the hiring manager, and other interviewers, suggesting follow-up questions to later interviewers. This real-time sharing of interview information ensures that interviewers build on one another's work rather than duplicate it. One interviewer might suggest to the next that she probe for a better sense of how the person would work on a team, for example. For obvious hires, the e-mail alerts help us focus our time on explaining to the recruits why Microsoft is a good choice for them.

Let's say that an applicant named Sharon Holloway accepts our job offer. Sharon is a hypothetical new hire, but the description of her experience at Microsoft is typical of the experience of the 85 people we hire each week. While our intranet is a global solution for all 28,000-plus Microsoft employees worldwide, in this example we'll assume that Sharon is based at our main campus in Redmond, Washington.

Before Sharon arrives at Microsoft, an administrative assistant in her new group fills out the electronic New Hire Setup form on Microsoft's intranet to request a voice-mail account, an e-mail account, office furniture, and a computer with preinstalled software to be ready on Sharon's arrival. The same form ensures that Sharon gets added to the company phone list, receives a nameplate for her office door, and gets a mailbox in her building's mailroom. The single electronic form goes directly to the groups responsible for taking care of these items. Electronic logs ensure that everything is tracked.

After an orientation session with a Human Resources manager on the company's general approach to business and employee issues, Sharon and the other new employees are directed to the company's internal Web site for most of their administrative needs. Sharon goes online to review the employee handbook (it no longer exists in paper form), download any software she needs beyond the standard setup, and fill out her electronic W-4 form.

Next Sharon uses a procurement tool on our intranet called MS Market to order office supplies, books, a whiteboard, and business cards. MS Market automatically fills in her name, her e-mail alias, the name of her approving manager, and other standard information for the order. Sharon has to enter only the information unique to the purchase into a few designated fields. The vendors receive her order electronically and deliver the order to her office. An order above a certain amount of money requires additional levels of management approval before processing. Our electronic system routes the form to the right people for an electronic okay.

Sharon visits the Microsoft Archives, Library, and company newsletter sites to read up on Microsoft. By signing up for one or more of our library's news services, she sees the latest news about the company and the industry in electronic versions of publications such as *The Wall Street Journal*, *The New York Times*, *CNet*, and so on. The availability of these services online has increased the number of our subscribing employees from 250 to 8,000 for the *Journal* alone. The online library lists books, software, and videos that employees can check out online for delivery to their offices. Librarians also maintain Web pages containing news and research for each Microsoft product group.

New employees don't follow a standard route on our intranet site. We hire people who are intellectually curious, and they explore freely. After they get their basics set up, they'll dive into business or technical areas that relate to their jobs and interests. Our new employees use the site the way it's meant to be used: to learn and to get things done.

When Sharon's first paycheck "arrives," the payroll amount is deposited automatically into her checking account, and she can view her deposit confirmation and the details of her pay stub on a secure intranet page. As her banking needs change, Sharon can change her financial institutions online.

For travel, Sharon handles plane and hotel reservations online with a booking tool designed by Microsoft in partnership with American Express. AXI, available online twenty-four hours a day, seven days a week, gives Sharon direct access to corporate-negotiated airline fares and flight availability information, a low-fare search tool, airline seat maps, corporate-preferred hotels, and the ability to check a flight's status or request an upgrade. Microsoft's travel policies are embedded in the AXI software as business rules. Any nonstandard travel request triggers e-mail from AXI to a manager for review. Travel expenses are submitted digitally to her manager for electronic approval. We deposit the reimbursement into Sharon's checking account electronically within three business days of approval.

SUPPORTING CHANGING LIFESTYLES

Contrary to popular perception, Microsofties do have a life outside the company. Sharon gets married and after her honeymoon enters her vacation time online. When she and her husband move into a new house, Sharon submits her new address via an online form that automatically distributes the information to all of the organizations that need her address, such as Payroll, Benefits, and the vendors managing our retirement and employee stock option programs. She visits our intranet to get information about bus routes and ridesharing in her new neighborhood.

When Sharon and her husband have a baby, she goes online to learn about benefits such as parenting seminars, paid parental leave, and day care referrals. Sharon electronically submits the medical claims associated with the birth and goes online to change her benefits to accommodate the new baby. Microsoft has a "cafeteria"-style benefits program that pays a certain dollar amount of benefits to each employee. An employee can model different what-if scenarios to decide how the dollars should be allocated—with choices for medical, dental, and optical coverage, life and disability insurance, health club membership, and legal services—and see how an increase or a decrease in one benefit affects the entire package. She can set up a payroll deduction for any benefit combination that costs more than the company contribution.

An online tool is also the means for Sharon to manage her 401(k) retirement plan, her employee stock purchases, and her stock option grants. She can direct the total percentage of her salary to be withheld for retirement or stock purchases and can alter the percentage to be allocated to each retirement investment option. Fidelity Investments'

Giving Campaign Led to First Electronic Form

Our first electronic form at Microsoft was for our giving campaign to support United Way of America, a nonprofit organization committed to addressing health and human services needs. We wanted to make it painless for people to sign up to make charitable contributions.

Some users just want to quickly click on a button to give their "fair share." Other people want to drill down to see a list of eligible nonprofit agencies that they can give to through the campaign. Some employees want to designate their contributions to go to certain institutions or to certain fields such as education or cancer research. Others want to get information about volunteering in their communities or learning about philanthropic opportunities through United Way or other agencies.

Our Giving application makes it easy for both the person who wants to spend a few seconds and the person who might want to spend an hour browsing around at different charitable agencies before deciding what to do. And it offers simple choices such as giving through payroll deductions, in cash, or in stock donations.

Our efforts to support United Way taught us a lot about how to design a form that was easy to deliver over a network and easy to use. That learning has paid off in every other intranet application we've come up with since. And the Giving application raised 20 percent more money than the previous paper system!

Web site for the plan enables Sharon to view current account information and market indexes, to model loans, and to review her transaction history. The stock purchase tool enables Sharon to view the number and price of shares she's purchased, change her withholding amount during enrollment periods, or cancel participation. The stock option tool enables her to accept a grant with a secure electronic signature and view her options summary and exercise history. Salomon Smith Barney, the brokerage firm that handles Microsoft stock options, is creating a Web site that will enable Sharon to run scenarios to see how many shares she needs to exercise for such things as remodeling her house for her growing family. All employees can exercise their stock options online unless they live in countries that require paper forms.

As an employee and a shareholder, Sharon receives the company's annual report online—our income statement is shown according to the conventions and in the currencies of seven different countries, and my letter to shareholders is available in ten languages—and she can vote her proxy online. Microsoft was the first company to offer paperless proxy voting to employee shareholders, a step that has increased our employee participation from 15 percent to more than 60 percent.

USING ONE TOOL FOR MULTIPLE PLANNING NEEDS

One of Sharon's jobs as a marketer is product planning. Most of the management and financial information she needs is accessible from MS Reports, a single interface to many databases such as expense, customer, contract, and budget. MS Reports can also be used to access MS Sales, our sales reporting system; HeadTrax, our head count system; and a financial management system that includes general ledger, fixed asset, project accounting, and statutory information and management reports. MS Reports uses Excel pivot tables to show data from multiple views, enabling Sharon to focus on analysis instead of data structures. She can review revenue projections for her product from sales locations worldwide as the projections are updated. She can view historical information about previous marketing campaigns such as personnel, capital expenses, and marketing expenses.

With the relevant data from MS Reports to help her

plan, Sharon uses an online budgeting application to enter her projected head count and expenses for her new product, then is able to track her marketing budget throughout the project, answering questions such as "What is my spend rate?" "Where am I spending money?" and "How can I reallocate resources for new projects?"

Sharon may use an additional planning tool, OnTarget, to track expenses in more detail. OnTarget provides project accounting. A manager can get complete project expenses across multiple cost centers or across fiscal years.

REWARDING STAFF WHILE FOLLOWING POLICY

When Sharon is promoted to manager, one new duty is conducting performance reviews for each of her "reports" every six months. Each employee writes a self-evaluation, and Sharon adds her own performance evaluation to the original document. Sharon's evaluation of an employee incorporates peer review, and e-mail makes it easy to get feedback from people in other divisions or even around the world. Sharon and her manager review her appraisals of the work of her employees and her proposed ratings for them. Then Sharon meets each employee face-to-face to discuss performance and new objectives.

Microsoft managers used to spend more time on the paperwork for reviews than on the reviews themselves. Our review application simplifies the work of managers while ensuring that they follow company policies. The application calculates a default merit increase and bonus for each person based on Sharon's rating and on the employee's job level and current salary. Overriding the defaults is possible (for example, to "load up" the salary and bonus for a star performer), but managers have to adhere to the company's overall percentage guidelines. As Sharon enters the numbers for each employee, the tool automatically calculates the new group average. If she comes in too low or too high, she can go back and redo the numbers. After senior managers review the numbers electronically, compensation changes feed directly into the master employee data and stock option systems.

By translating a rating into compensation and by enabling the manager to visually compare such figures as ranking by performance and by salary, the review application helps managers to grade employees consistently according to both performance and policy. We estimate that the application also reduces managers' time spent on review administration by at least 50 percent.

SAVING AGGRAVATION AND $40 MILLION

Using our intranet to replace paper forms has produced striking results for us. As this book goes to press, we have reduced the number of paper forms from more than 1,000 to a company-wide total of 60 forms. Among those groups that started out with the most forms, Procurement has dropped from 114 to 1; Operations has reduced the number of its forms to only 6; and Human Resources is down to 39. Of the 60 remaining paper forms, 10 are required by law and 40 are required by outside parties because their systems are still based on paper. The last 10 paper forms are used so seldom that we haven't bothered to make them electronic, yet. Businesses have an incentive to persuade partners and governments to accept information electronically so that everybody can get to a fully digital approach with no paper.

Overall, the savings from our using the electronic

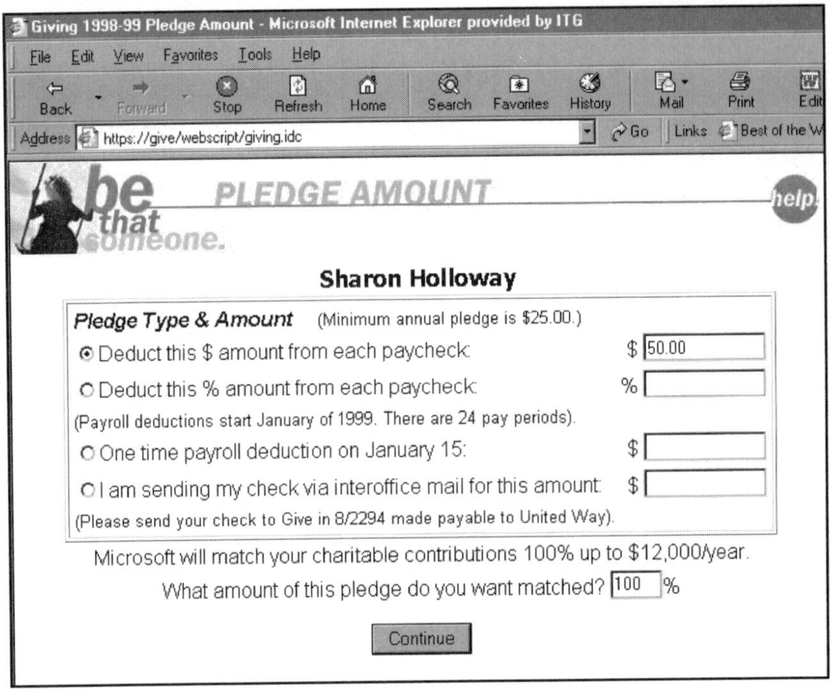

Intranet applications give employees control over changes to benefits, investment plans, or even community giving, putting responsibility directly into the hands of the people most motivated to act. Tools for self-service administration of benefits let employees model the results of changes before finalizing them. Data entered into the Microsoft Giving application, *top*, and the health benefits form go directly into Microsoft's payroll system, freeing human resources staff to work on strategic issues such as recruitment and training.

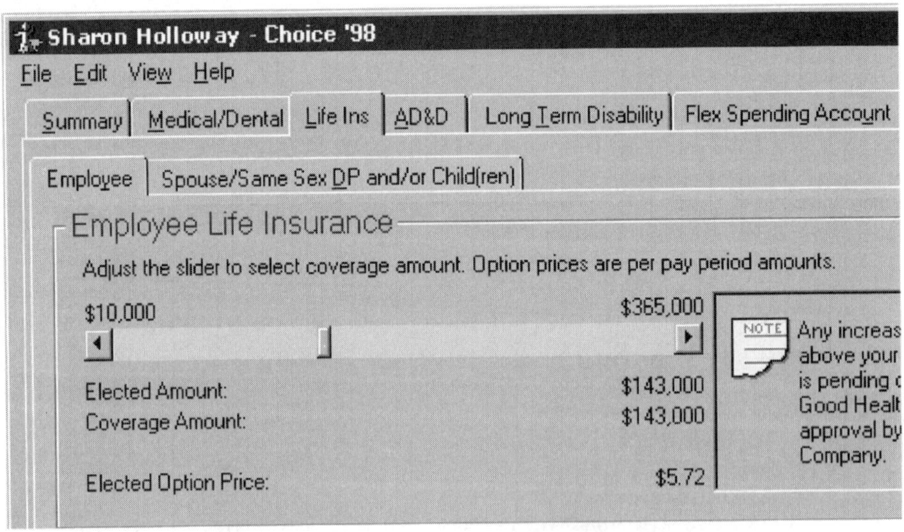

forms I've described in this chapter amounted to at least $40 million in our first twelve months of use in 1997–98. The biggest savings came from the reduction in processing costs. Accounting firms put the cost of paper orders—mostly the time of all the people handling the paper—at about $145 per transaction. Electronic processing at Microsoft, by comparison, runs less than $5 per transaction. In its first year MS Market alone handled 250,000 transactions involving more than $1.6 billion, saving our company at least $35 million in processing. Transaction volumes are increasing significantly. The $35 million figure includes $3 million saved through the reassignment of twenty-two procurement personnel worldwide. MS Market also directs employees to vendors with whom we've negotiated volume discounts, which saves us money on many purchases.

Using electronic forms for just the 401(k) plan, the employee stock purchase plan, and the stock options plan saved us another $1 million annually in labor. Attrition took care of some of the reduction in head count, but most of the staff moved on to more important tasks they weren't doing before because they'd had to spend so much time on rote administrative chores. One person who had been spending each day answering routine questions now manages the content for the Web page that provides the answers. Within a year, the number of employees using the online system to obtain account information and ask questions regarding Microsoft's 401(k) plan doubled from 24 percent to 51 percent. As a result, during the same period, assistance by service representatives decreased by half, from 35 percent to 17 percent.

Our new online travel system is expected to reduce overhead in our corporate travel group and to triple travel agent productivity from an average of eight to twenty-five completed itineraries (usually hotel, rental car, and airfare) per agent per day. Consistent employee use of preferred vendors will save us millions of dollars per year. The average time it takes an employee to make a domestic travel reservation is projected to go from seventeen minutes and six phone calls or e-mails to approximately five minutes.

All of the administrative applications and content I've talked about in this chapter run on a total of twelve servers, either dual-processor or quad-processor systems. Total cost for the hardware was about $300,000. Total development cost across two years was about $8 million. Ongoing support runs about $765,000 annually. Though far lower than comparable costs on other systems, our expenses were still higher than companies will see today because we pioneered a lot of solutions. There were no standards, for instance, for integrating third-party systems inexpensively; software products such as our commerce server provide this integration today. Companies will see lower costs going forward as the result of standards and of increased functionality in commercial software packages.

Even as we pioneered solutions, our central IT budget, which covers these and other major business applications, decreased 3 percent between 1996 and 1999, mostly from standardizing data and consolidating the number of information systems we have.

PUTTING RESPONSIBILITY INTO THE HANDS OF THOSE AFFECTED

Electronic tools give us benefits beyond reducing transaction costs. For example, by requiring proper sign-off before a request is processed, MS Market prevents inappropriate purchases that can easily slip through a paper-based system. Shipping information is typed instead of handwritten, so routing errors are almost nonexistent. Communication with our suppliers is documented, and we know the costs in advance so that there are no surprises. Our suppliers get paid faster, too, which motivates them to make swift deliveries. Business rules are implemented up front so that, for example, the system won't accept an order that has an incorrect budget code. This requirement eliminates hours and hours our finance group used to spend "scrubbing" records. Employee buying patterns can be tracked and used in vendor negotiations, too. The list of benefits goes on. We're always discovering new ones.

In our Human Resources, Procurement, and Employee Services groups and in the functions they touch throughout Microsoft, going digital has given us a mechanism for changing how we work. By enabling our employees to directly control such processes as entering address changes and making and changing retirement investments, we've put responsibility directly into the hands of the people most motivated to act. Self-service administration of benefits enables Human Resources staff to spend more of their energy on strategic personnel issues such as recruitment and training.

This fundamental process issue—how to get bureaucracy out of the way—is one that our Human Resources staff itself is driving. Human Resources had conducted a number of classic reengineering studies to understand what routine processes can be automated and what processes require their professional skills. Human Resources wants to do "thinking work, not manual work."

OPPOSING INFLEXIBILITY, NOT PAPER

With my insistence on eliminating paperwork, I must sound "antipaper." I am against paper forms, but even I still print out long electronic documents I want to read and annotate. Most people, when they're trying to organize a long document, like to spread out the pages on a table so that they can see them all at once—hard to do with a PC! Until we get a breakthrough in flat-screen technology—and furious research is going on at Xerox, the MIT Media Lab, Kent State, Microsoft, and other academic and corporate research sites in the United States and Japan—books and magazines still can't be beat for readability and portability.

High-quality displays are a necessity in the information-rich future. Microsoft showed, in late 1998, a technology code-named ClearType that allows color LCD screens to display text dramatically better than before. Combining this with improved hardware will be revolutionary. Some future screens will be flexible so that you can roll up or fold the display and take it with you, like a newspaper. Other screens will have the computer circuitry embedded in them, so that an entire PC could be as thin as the display part of a current laptop. One new technology enables a screen to retain its image after power is removed. Imagine true digital ink, where you can make a picture and hang the display on your wall.

Today PCs are better than paper for reading when you have shorter documents and lots of collaboration or when you're searching and pivoting through data. Easy searches and hypertext links are the major reasons electronic encyclopedias have overtaken print encyclopedias in popularity.

For forms, where you're filling in data that eventually has to be entered into a computer anyway, the time is ripe for abolishing paper. Otherwise you end up with groups whose job is to take paper forms and type the information into the computer system. Then you get people who measure their productivity by noting how great it is that their data entry error rate has gone down from 3 percent to 2 percent! If you start with electronic forms, you not only eliminate extra work, you also ensure consistency, easy measurement, and proper authorization.

When a paper form is confusing, you end up calling somebody or going somewhere to stand in line. On our intranet, every page contains summaries and details of plans, the ability to search, and links to related pages and to answers to frequently asked questions, or FAQs. A well-thought-out FAQ feature on a new intranet application can save us 200 or more e-mails from employees looking for basic information.

If you do find anything on an electronic form confusing, or if you think one of the fields should be filled in automatically for you, you can click the "e-mail to" line and type in a few words saying, "Hey, this should work better." Employee feedback has resulted in hundreds of improvements, small and large, to our intranet forms. And it doesn't take a year to get these changes made, which might be the case with paper forms. With a Web-based form, in most instances a change is made within anywhere from a few days to a few months.

Since you have no control over the paper that reaches you from outside your organization, your strategy should be to integrate it into your electronic systems. Companies such as Eastman Software and Platinum Software use imaging software to scan documents and integrate them into the digital flow. You can drill down through various levels of detail in cost summaries, all the way to an image of the original paper invoice, and you can index and search for original paper documents and include them in e-mail-based work-flow scenarios. While not as good as having data come in digitally, scanning enables you to go all digital internally while waiting for the rest of the world to catch up.

GETTING FEEDBACK THE OLD-FASHIONED WAY

Though most of the comments on our intranet applications come electronically, we occasionally also get face-to-face feedback from users. After a few months of use, our MS Market team had resolved most of the issues that employees had raised about use of the procurement tool. Only one senior executive stood between the MS Market team and 100 percent adoption, President Steve Ballmer, a guy who exudes exuberance.

The product manager for MS Market, Linda Criddle, resolved to meet with Steve personally to find out what would make him an MS Market user. She talked her way onto the calendar for Steve, whom she had never met. As she turned the corner to the hallway by his office, Linda says, she could see a couple of framed magazine articles in a glass case. One, from *Upside* magazine, showed Steve with a beatific smile and called him the Microsoft apostle; the other, from *Forbes*, showed Steve in a sterner pose and described him as the George S. Patton of software.

Linda, hearing Steve's voice through the thin conference room wall, quickly understood that he was meeting with the Office product group. His theme was that they needed to *listen* to customers more and needed to find out what customers *really* wanted, to learn *precisely* how they used our software *every day*. At each emphasized word, he'd bang on the wall. Few meetings with Steve are complete without sound effects.

Linda knew most of the executives in the meeting from a previous job, and when the attendees filed out of the meeting, she asked, "Did you tire him out or rile him up?"

One said, "I think we may have riled him up," which got everybody laughing.

Linda trailed Steve into his office, trying to introduce herself. Steve was distracted, with a bunch of things to do before he had to leave for the day. "So what can I do for you?" he asked.

"Actually, I'm hoping to give you the same kind of grief you just gave the Office guys," she said.

This got Steve's attention.

"I know you don't use MS Market," Linda said. "That doesn't help me. Tell me what you need to make it work." When Steve saw that she wasn't there to justify the tool's imperfections and that she intended to fix any problems, he stopped to concentrate on what frustrated him about the application.

"I don't want to get a ten-million-dollar order request and not know whether other managers have reviewed it before me," he said. MS Market needed to provide the ability to route orders through the management hierarchy. "And I want to see all of the supporting documentation that accompanies a purchase order, and I need to be able to approve orders offline."

Linda got the information she needed in less than ten minutes.

The routing feature was already under development, so Steve's first requirement for MS Market was implemented within two weeks. Access to supporting documentation was added three months later. The final feature, offline support, is in the queue for a future release.

This little tale illustrates several points about Microsoft's approach to digital information. Electronic applications have to solve the problems of our businesspeople, and we don't stop until they do. Everybody uses our electronic tools, starting with me. Steve could give Linda precise feedback because he'd made honest efforts to use the tool.

From Sales Analysis to Restaurant Bills

I use our Microsoft intranet for analyzing sales numbers. I do this before major business reviews and before a trip to one of our subsidiaries. I spend three or four weeks a year outside the United States on business. I go through the numbers thoroughly to uncover any issues I should take up with the business managers. It takes me only twenty minutes to understand how a country is doing compared to budget, to last year's results, and to other countries. I drill down on the areas significantly above or below my expectations so I am ready to discuss the numbers when I arrive.

I'll also review presentations by other Microsoft speakers while I'm preparing a talk for a major industry event. I use our multimedia streaming product to listen over the corporate network if I miss an important meeting we've taped. I don't sit in on quarterly earnings calls to financial analysis, for instance, but when I'm home at night reading, I might put on the audio and listen in. These tools keep me in close touch with what's going on in our company.

As the CEO, I'm supposed to be making decisions involving tens or hundreds of millions of dollars, but organizationally I am the only one who can approve the restaurant bill for Steve Ballmer, our president. I thought every company had this kind of explicit review for expense approval. I learned I was wrong when I demonstrated our intranet to a group of CEOs. Paul O'Neill of Alcoa, which is the world's leading producer of aluminum, came up to me after my talk and asked, "It's great that everything is digital and efficient, but why should you have to review expense reports? You've got better things to do with your time."

Paul got rid of explicit expense approvals at Alcoa ten years ago. Alcoa has clear rules about what are authorized expenses and what are not. The company audits expense reports from time to time on a sampling basis. "We trust our employees as a matter of employment," Paul said. "If we find that you're not trustworthy, you're gone. We don't have any problems."

Paul suggested that we could take the same approach, creating a new policy to simplify things and using our digital system to carry out the policy.

Paul's right. We're shifting from one-by-one approvals to a monthly e-mail summary combined with a special e-mail alert when there are unusual expenses. The e-mails will allow us to drill in on individual expense reports or a complete history if we choose to. Paul's comment is already saving me time.

KEEPING YOUR PRIORITIES STRAIGHT

While the move from paper to electronic forms is a vital step in the evolution of a modern organization's nervous system, you should use the change to improve important processes central to your business rather than just streamline what you have.

Once in place, a digital nervous system is easy to build on. A good network, a good e-mail system, and easy-to-build Web pages are everything you need for eliminating internal paper forms, too. You can add any number of intranet applications easily once this infrastructure is in place.

Our internal tools have two goals: to use software to handle routine tasks, eliminating wasted time and energy for our knowledge workers; and to free people to do more difficult work and handle exceptions. Our internal developers use the "soft-boiled egg" rule. A user must be able to get into and out of most administrative tools within three minutes. The metric ensures that we don't automate a process with a clumsy tool and cause more work overall.

Streamlining administrative and internal business processes is an important way to improve the overall efficiency of your employees. Giving knowledge workers good internal tools also sends them a subtle but important message. Companies talk about rewarding initiative and keeping workers focused on business. When employees see a company eliminate bottlenecks and time-draining routine administrative chores from their workdays, they know that the company values their time—and wants them to use it profitably. It's easy to measure when you make your factory workers more efficient. It's hard to measure when you make your knowledge workers more effective, but it's just common sense that knowledge workers who are not distracted or burdened by routine matters will do better work.

The benefit to customers is that your employees spend less time shuffling papers and more time on customer needs.

I know one thing for sure. You couldn't make Microsoft employees go back to the old way of doing things. The predictions that we'd have paperless offices were right—just premature by several decades.

Business Lessons

- ❑ Digital information enables process breakthroughs that are impossible with paper systems.
- ❑ Tally all your paper forms. Starting with forms-intensive areas such as procurement and human resources, develop programs to replace them with digital forms.
- ❑ A self-service approach can handle 90 percent of employee administrative needs.

Diagnosing Your Digital Nervous System

- ❑ Do you have electronic forms for your major internal business applications?
- ❑ Do you have people moving information around, or do your computers handle routine process flow while people handle exceptions and value-added issues?
- ❑ As you add applications, do you get more synergy or more complexity?

II

COMMERCE: THE INTERNET CHANGES EVERYTHING

4

RIDE THE INFLECTION ROCKET

The moment man first picked up a stone or a branch to use as a tool, he altered irrevocably the balance between him and his environment. . . . While the number of these tools remained small, their effect took a long time to spread and to cause change. But as they increased, so did their effects: the more the tools, the faster the rate of change.

—James Burke, *Connections*

Not too long ago I had a talk scheduled with the board of directors of a German financial institution. These were experienced businesspeople. The youngest person there was probably fifty-five, and many of them were in their sixties. They'd seen a lot of changes in banking, and beginning with mainframes, they'd lived through a lot of technology changes, too. The bank had not yet, though, embraced the new Internet technologies. On the day of my talk they'd heard a series of presentations from Microsoft employees about our strategy. When I walked into the briefing center, they were all sitting there with their arms folded across their chests, looking unhappy.

"Okay," I said. "What's the problem?"

One of them replied, "We think that banking is in the process of changing completely, and we're getting technical presentations from people here at Microsoft—more technical than we're used to." He took off his glasses and rubbed his eyes and said, "This is probably good, although it's making us tired." After a pause he continued. "It's good that you're just going to make all of your products better, but what is the overall plan? To view you as a long-term vendor, we need you to give us a vision of the future. What are your organizing principles for development?"

The senior Microsoft executive who concludes a customer briefing doesn't normally bring a prepared presentation. Instead the person answers questions and summarizes what we'll do to address any important issues that have come up. So as I stood in front of the German bankers I was thinking, Oh boy. We've spent eight hours talking to this bank and we haven't answered the customer's central concerns. Now I've got to do it off the top of my head. . . .

But by that time I'd given my talk on the digital nervous system a couple of dozen times, and I'd been working on this book for almost a year. I went to the whiteboard and began to go down the major changes that I thought were going to occur with technology in the near future.

"What I'm about to write down are ten inflection points that I think will fundamentally alter all industries," I told the bankers. My friend Andy Grove had written about different inflection points that changed various industries at different times. Here, I was using "inflection points" to mean ten significant shifts in customer behavior that were all related to digital technology and were all happening now. "I'm going to ask you whether you believe each of them will happen. Never mind for now how quickly, just tell me whether you believe they're ever going to occur. If you don't believe they will, then you shouldn't change what you're doing with technology. But if you believe they're going to happen, and it's only a matter of time, then you should start to prepare for that change today."

Do you believe that in the future people at work will use computers every day for most of their jobs? I asked. Today a lot of people use computers occasionally, but many knowledge workers may use their PCs only a few times a day. They may even go a couple of days without using PCs. Do you believe that today's paperwork will be replaced by more efficient digital administrative processes? They did. Their only concern was how to make the transition from a paper to a digital world.

Do you believe that one day most households will have computers? I asked. In the United States today about half the households have PCs. The percentage is a bit higher in some countries but much lower in most others. Do you, I asked, believe that one day computers will be as common in homes as telephones or TVs? They did.

Do you believe that one day most businesses and most households will have high-speed connections to the World Wide Web? I asked. They nodded agreement.

Do you believe e-mail will become as common a method of communication among people in business and homes as the telephone or paper mail is today? Currently not everybody uses e-mail even if they have a computer. Would that situation change? They agreed that it would.

Now, if most people have computers and use them every day, I asked, do you believe that most information will start arriving in digital form? Do you think your consumer bills will arrive electronically? Do you think you'll be booking your travel arrangements over the Internet? They agreed that these changes were on their way.

Do you think digital appliances will become common? I asked. Do you believe that digital devices for photography, video, TV, and phones will become ubiquitous? Do you expect that other new digital devices will proliferate around the home and be connected to the Web? It was only a matter of time, they agreed.

Do you foresee a time, I asked, when notebook computers become computer notebooks? I described what I meant, a computer notebook being a new device that enables you to take notes as you do today with a notepad and lets you carry with you all the personal and professional data you need. It's another aspect of having all information be digital. This will probably be the last inflection point to occur.

"The great thing about a computer notebook," I said, "is that no matter how much you stuff into it, it doesn't get bigger or heavier." They laughed. There was a thirty-second conversation in German before one of them said, "We thought you said something funny, and then we realized you said something profound."

"Am I wasting your time?" I asked. "Do you believe these changes are ever going to happen?" By now we were beginning to have a dialogue. They had a short conversation among themselves in German. The banker who had spoken before said, "We hired a management consultant, and we've been going through the same discussion at home, and yes, we believe it's going to happen. When it does, it's going to completely change the nature of banking."

"When is it going to happen?" I asked. "What do you think?"

They had a longer and more animated discussion in German. They came back and said, We didn't expect to make this decision here, but we have. First we were going to tell you twenty years, but then we decided that inside of ten years these inflection points will either have arrived or be very imminent. Banking will be a completely different thing.

To prepare for that change, I told them, you need to make digital information flow pervasive in your organization. I talked briefly about needing to take advantage of existing digital tools they already have for their knowledge workers; about digitally linking their knowledge systems with business operations systems and ultimately creating a new infrastructure around the PC and Internet technologies. If you do these things, I told them, you'll be prepared for the three fundamental business shifts that will occur as the result of all the digital inflection points:

1. Most transactions between business and consumers, business and business, and consumers and government will become self-service digital transactions. Intermediaries will evolve to add value or perish.
2. Customer service will become the primary value-added function in every business. Human involvement in service will shift from routine, low-value tasks to a high-value, personal consultancy on important issues—problems or desires—for the customer.
3. The pace of transactions and the need for more personalized attention to customers will drive companies to adopt digital processes internally if they have not yet adopted them for efficiency reasons. Companies will use a digital nervous system to regularly transform their internal business processes to adapt to an environment that constantly changes because of customer needs and competition.

Complex customer-service and business problems will require powerful computers on both sides of the relationship—customer and employee. The new relationships will be augmented by various electronic means such as voice, video, interactive use of the same computer screen, and so on. We'll see a world in which fairly simple personal companion devices proliferate side by side with incredibly powerful general-purpose PCs that support knowledge work at home or the office.

Life's going to be pretty exciting as these changes come about, I concluded, and within a decade it's likely that most of them will occur. This world will be radically different from the one we live in today. Microsoft's vision, I said, was to provide software that linked all these digital devices together and enabled people to create digital solutions based on the Web lifestyle. It was that simple.

The German bank board had a final question for me, which is the question on everyone's mind: What should they do personally to get ready for this new digital world? I left them with these thoughts: Practice hands-on usage. Senior executives should use e-mail and other electronic tools to get familiar with the new way of doing things. They should see what their competitors' Internet sites look like. They should become Internet users and consumers. Buy some books and arrange some travel over the Internet, I told them, and see what it's like.

As of late 1998 CEOs are beginning to explore this new medium. About 50 percent of the readership of *Chief Executive* magazine use the Internet an hour or two a week, but only 25 percent use it daily, and 11 percent have never used the Internet at all. Many, many consumers already use the Internet far more intensively. If you're going to lead the digital age, you need to become familiar enough with the Internet to be able to imagine what the Web lifestyle will mean for your industry—even if the change is going to take years. You should find ways to immerse yourself and your other executives in these new approaches and have retreats where you can determine the right strategy for applying them to your own business.

AVOIDING COMPLACENCY

For years and years enthusiasts have been saying that the Internet will happen "tomorrow." You're going to keep reading prognostications that the big change will happen in the next twelve months. This is just baloney. The social adaptations that have to occur take years, and the infrastructure has to be built out. But when the social and technical changes reach critical mass, the change will be quick and irreversible. The point will come where the Web lifestyle really will take off, and I believe that's sometime in the next five years. As I said in *The Road Ahead*, we always overestimate the change that will occur in the next two years and underestimate the change that will occur in the next ten. Don't let yourself be lulled into inaction.

One possible scenario is that you'll scramble to build some Internet sites, and then you won't see an appreciable portion of your customers or partners using them right away. This situation might mislead you into thinking, Oh, well, the Internet's not going to change our business after all, so let's not focus on it. Because it won't happen overnight, you might think nothing fundamental is going to change. Then, a few years later, all of a sudden the change will surprise you and you'll find it hard to catch up.

It's hard to think of a business category in which the Internet won't have an impact or in which there aren't already Internet start-ups. Lots of companies now wish they were the first Internet bookstore or travel agency or stockbroker, capturing the early customers, the word of mouth, and the name recognition.

Businesses that are out there early are not just getting ahead on the learning curve. They are also rushing to redefine business boundaries. Amazon.com, which established itself as an Internet book vendor, has begun to sell CDs. There's no reason for Amazon not to sell other merchandise as well. The initial impetus for your company to go onto the Web might be to obtain cost savings and attract new customers. Once you have customers interacting with you, you have an incredible ability to build on that relationship to offer a broader set of products. Portals like Yahoo! have created their own travel sites. An Internet business is not like a branch bank where you can train employees on only a small number of products. The virtual nature of the Internet enables whatever shopping your customers want to do. You'll see more Amazon-like cases in which a company that is strong in one online area expands its product offerings. The warning to every business is that even if no one in your industry jumps in early, big online players, trying to fill every commerce niche, will move into yours.

Learn about the Internet today. Find a microcosm of your customers who are already adopting the Web lifestyle. Use this group to develop models for how you might do business overall. Within a decade most of your other customers will have also made the shift, and you'll be prepared. The examples that follow in this section show companies that are taking this approach to prepare themselves for how the Internet is changing everything.

Business Lessons

- ❑ Most transactions will become self-service digital transactions, and intermediaries will evolve to add value or perish.
- ❑ Customer service will become the primary value-added function in every business.
- ❑ The pace of change and the need for more personalized attention to customers will drive companies to adopt digital processes internally.

Diagnosing Your Digital Nervous System

- ❑ Has your management team familiarized itself with the Internet and taken time to prepare a vision of how it will change your business in the next decade? Are you working with your IT team to implement that vision technically?

5

THE MIDDLEMAN MUST ADD VALUE

> Technology is reshaping this economy and transforming businesses and consumers. This is about more than e-commerce, or e-mail, or e-trades, or e-files. It is about the "e" in economic opportunity.
>
> —William Daley, U.S. Commerce Secretary

Here on the edge of the twenty-first century, a fundamental new rule of business is that the Internet changes everything. At the minimum, Internet technologies are altering the way every company, even a small one, deals with its employees, partners, and suppliers. Not every company needs to use the Internet to interact with its customers right now, but someday soon a corporate Web site where customers can do business with a company will be as essential as the telephone and a mailing address have been. Already the overwhelming majority of Fortune 500 companies have Web sites.

The Internet is driving down costs for transactions and distribution and reshaping the relationships of companies with their customers. The Internet produces more competition among vendors and more access to vendors by potential customers.

In pre-Internet days the only way consumers could get goods from most manufacturers was through tiers of distributors and resellers. Today consumers can transact business directly with manufacturers eager to offer Internet service. Nowadays any manufacturer can provide the Internet equivalent of a factory outlet.

Before the Internet, gathering all the information for financial products, travel options, and other consumer products required lots of time. A multitude of service companies made their money by collecting and organizing that kind of information for customers. Today, despite imperfect search tools, consumers themselves can go to the Internet to find much of the information they need. And any company can dispense valuable information cheaply by means of the Internet without branch offices.

The following chart shows typical savings in transaction costs when customers shop online.

In 1995, in *The Road Ahead,* I used the term *friction-free capitalism* to describe how the Internet was helping to create Adam Smith's ideal marketplace, in which buyers and sellers can easily find one another without taking much time or spending much money. Finding the other interested party is the first problem in most markets. The second is understanding the nature and quality of the goods and services being offered. The Internet makes it easy for a buyer to get background information about a product—how it's rated by consumer organizations or other independent reviews—and to compare prices easily. Buyers can also tell sellers more about their requirements, and sellers will be able to target their wares to the people most interested and to cross-sell related products.

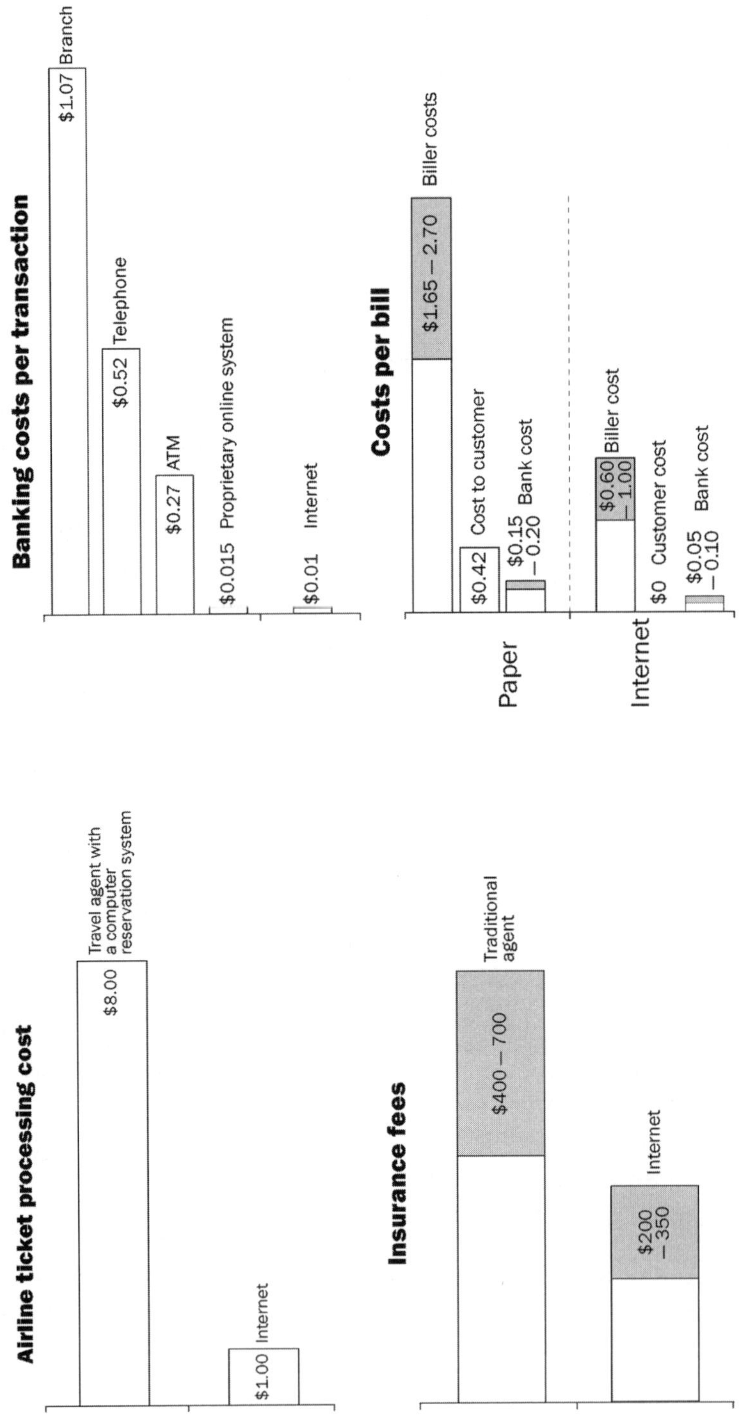

Source: The Emerging Digital Economy, U.S. Department of Commerce, 1998.

The Internet is a great tool for helping customers find the best deal they can. It is reasonably easy for consumers to jump from one retail Web site to another to find the best prices on some goods. At least two different services provide real-time pricing comparisons for consumers shopping for goods such as books and CDs. Some travel sites feature automated bargain finders that can track down low airfares. At least one company, priceline.com, reverses the buyer-seller relationship by having buyers bid the price they're willing to pay for a car or a plane ticket and shopping that price around to sellers. How broadly this approach will be used is yet unclear, but it is possible only through the reach of the Internet.

Over time, software will automate comparison shopping even more. "Haggling" over price will become effortlessly electronic. At least one online mall already checks other major sites for the prices of commonly purchased items and automatically reduces its prices to ensure that they're always slightly lower. It's an electronic form of "loss leader," though the merchant, without bricks and mortar, may still eke out a profit. Consumers will be able to join together electronically to get volume pricing in ways that have not been easy before. There will even be cases in which software representing the seller negotiates prices with software representing not one consumer but hundreds or thousands.

Existing major markets that have largely interchangeable products such as coal or steel are already well mediated. The Internet may not change the matching of buyers and sellers or price that much. The Web will provide more value in areas where matching buyers and sellers is more difficult, such as services, or where markets are small or dispersed. How does a consumer easily find a used product—car, computer, stereo—with certain capabilities and in a certain price range? People trying to buy or sell hard-to-find items of any kind, such as antiques, parts for older equipment, or specialty items, will benefit. The Gap, for instance, is finding that the most frequent customers of its online clothing store are people looking for sizes that are not normally stocked in physical stores. The Gap can meet the needs of these customers without adding to its stocking costs at its retail outlets. Virtual auctions provide a much wider array of goods than can be sold in an auction at a physical location and can draw people from all over the world, not just those in a particular locale. With its unique ability to bring people together, the Web will create markets that didn't exist before.

Some Web merchants will adopt flexible pricing. Flexible prices are already a fixture of the ordinary marketplace. Many electronics and appliance stores advertise price guarantees in which they promise to match the lowest price a consumer can find. This strategy lets them say that they won't be undersold, even while their marked prices stay higher. Some stores run so many sales that there are really two prices for most items—the regular price for the impulse shopper and the sale price for the patient shopper. Direct-mail marketers often publish different prices in different catalogs targeted at different market segments. When you call to order, the sales representative asks for your customer number or catalog number first so that he or she knows what to charge you.

The goal of these and similar pricing maneuvers is to capture the business of price-sensitive shoppers while harvesting higher margins from shoppers who aren't as diligent or as concerned about price. In effect, merchants are setting prices according to an individual's willingness to pay. This idea may sound radical, but it's as old as progressive taxation. College educations are priced this way, with a discount called *financial aid* that varies according to family income and assets.

The techniques used by direct marketers are crude compared with what the Internet will make possible. Sellers will identify repeat visitors to their online stores and give them personalized information and services. If a store's Web site comes to know what kinds of prices a customer has or hasn't been willing to pay in the past, it may reduce a price to spur that customer to buy.

Many Web sites ask users for registration information, including name, address, demographic data, and credit information. While this data enables businesses to offer better services and support for customers and do more targeted marketing, consumers should be able to approve in advance the use of any personal data and whether that data can be passed on to other entities. Today e-commerce runs on the honor system, with vendors asking users their permission for information use. We're working on technology that would let consumers predefine the type of data that their PCs would make available to other systems over a network. The software will put the control with the user, where it belongs, while also eliminating the need for the user to reenter the same data over and over.

Buying on the Web will increase the number of packages being delivered at the same time it reduces the number of letters, fliers, and bills. For low-cost items, the delivery charge may eliminate the savings of buying over the Web. Post offices and private delivery companies have a big opportunity to adapt their services to meet the changing demands in package delivery.

For the majority of products, which are available through many outlets, consumers will be the greatest beneficiaries. For unique products and services, sellers will find more potential customers and may command higher prices.

The more consumers adopt the Web lifestyle, the closer the economy will move toward Adam Smith's perfect market in all areas of commerce.

ADDING VALUE TO TRANSACTIONS

Now that customers can deal directly with manufacturers and service providers, there is little value added in simply transferring goods or information. Various commentators have predicted "the death of the middleman." Certainly the value of a "pass-through" middleman is quickly falling to zero. Travel agents who simply book plane fares will disappear. This kind of high-volume, low-value transaction is perfect for a self-service Internet travel reservation site. In the future travel agents will need to do more than book tickets; they will need to create a total travel adventure. A travel agent who provides highly personalized tours of, say, Italy or the California wine country will still be in great demand.

If you're a middleman, the Internet's promise of cheaper prices and faster service can "disintermediate" you, eliminate your role of assisting the transaction between the producer and the consumer. If the Internet is about to disintermediate you, one tack is to use the Internet to get back into the action. That's what Egghead.com (formerly Egghead), a major retail software chain, did after struggling for several years. Egghead closed all of its physical stores nationwide in 1998 and set up shop exclusively on the Internet. Eliminating brick-and-mortar expenses, though, is only a tactic, not a strategy. Egghead now offers a number of new online programs that take advantage of the Internet, such as electronic auctions for about fifty different categories of hardware and software and for reconditioned computers. It puts special liquidation prices on systems available on its Web site and sends out a weekly e-mail "Hot List" with exclusive offers available only to e-mail subscribers. The jury is still out on whether Egghead will thrive and meet the test of this chapter, which is that the middleman must add value, but the company certainly understands the principle.

Every retail store needs to take the Internet into account. The success of the Amazon.com bookstore, which exists only on the Internet, impelled Barnes & Noble to combine its successful physical bookstores with a strong presence in cyberspace and to team up with Bertelsmann, a leading international media company, in an online joint venture.

For service industries, the Internet requires you to be either a high-volume, low-cost provider or a high-touch, customer-service provider. For the high-volume, low-cost model you use Internet technology to create a self-service approach. You make a lot of information available to customers and you drive a lot of traffic and transactions through your Internet site offering the best price. Because only a few companies in any market will be the high-volume players, most companies will have to find ways to use the Internet not just to reduce costs, but also to deliver new services.

E * Trade Securities pioneered the low-cost, Internet self-service approach to financial services in 1992. The Forrester Group estimated that there were three million online brokerage customers in the United States at the end of 1997 and said that the number could top fourteen million within five years. By 1998 at least seventy brokerage firms provided self-service online stock trading, and the number was continuing to rise. Online trading accounted for more than 20 percent of all retail transactions. A few online brokerages, designed for experienced investors and offering no research, charge very little per trade. But most offer a range of research and services in an effort to set themselves apart, and they charge more per trade.

These new online financial services create an interesting challenge for the traditional brokerage houses accustomed to providing their services in person or over the phone. Most of the data that brokerage firms provide to their customers is now available for free on the Internet. These firms face a fundamental strategy decision: Do you use technology to play the same game that the e-traders play? And if you do that, how do you differentiate yourself from them? Or do you use technology to play to your traditional strengths—highly trained staff accustomed to managing long-term customer relationships? If you adopt the latter strategy, how can you use technology to be more efficient, and how can you turn the Internet's popularity to your advantage?

MAKING A FUNDAMENTAL DECISION

Merrill Lynch & Company, a longtime leader in traditional financial services, began an intense reevaluation of its approach to its business by asking just those questions in 1997. Merrill Lynch has managed its customer investments for more than a century by amassing vast amounts of financial data, analyzing it, and creating long-range financial plans. By 1997 the company had more than $1 trillion in client assets. But the growth of low-cost traders and then of Internet-based trading between 1992 and 1997 led senior managers to recognize that their current approach might not be sustained. As Howard Sorgen, senior vice president and chief technology officer of Merrill Lynch's private client business, put it: "Our customers were changing. The way people got information and made decisions was changing. We would have been foolish to think we didn't have to change, too."

At the heart of Merrill Lynch's concerns was the need to improve the efficiency of the company's most valuable asset, its financial consultants (FCs). Merrill Lynch's financial consultants were spending a great deal of their time tracking down data—stock quotes, research reports, customer account data, Merrill Lynch product information, interest rates, and other widely dispersed information—and less of their time acting as financial advisers. The company's mainframe-based information systems were expensive and hard to use. The customer database, product information, pricing, research reports—all of the different categories of data—were on different, incompatible systems. Financial consultants had several terminals on their desks, each one requiring fluency in a dozen different applications, all with different, esoteric keyboard commands.

Improving information access for its financial consultants was crucial to meeting Merrill Lynch's business goal: helping clients accrue wealth. Merrill Lynch's competitive advantage to date had been its collective knowledge of financial markets and the skills it brought to those markets on behalf of its customers. Merrill Lynch's future competitive advantage, its senior managers concluded, would be that same investment know-how augmented by technology.

Merrill Lynch decided to recast its information systems around the information flow its financial consultants needed. The new system had to be "FC-centric," providing rich content and great analytical tools on the desktop to help financial consultants develop, implement, and monitor financial plans for clients. This desktop environment would have to be robust and include audio and video capabilities so that financial consultants could see breaking news from around the world and video training materials and collaborate with each other. Merrill Lynch didn't want to hand-build everything, either. To save money and development time, the company wanted to use off-the-shelf products wherever it could.

When Merrill Lynch managers went before their board of directors, they asked for, in round numbers, a billion dollars' worth of technology to maintain the company's leadership position in financial services. One billion dollars is a pretty big bet on the future. The board's discussion, however, didn't center on the costs or on the return on investment. It was about survival and prosperity in the future. It was about continuing to differentiate Merrill Lynch from its traditional competitors and responding to the challenge from a new kind of competitor. The board agreed that the best way to compete was to give the company's knowledge workers great knowledge tools.

Management got the go-ahead for what became a five-year, $825 million project. The only admonition from the board was that the project had better not turn into an eight-year, $2 billion undertaking. It didn't. The Trusted Global Advisor (TGA) rollout was completed in October 1998, for approximately $850 million. With FC-centric requirements in mind, the company's IT team devoted a year to evaluation and designed a PC-based digital nervous system on which to build the company's future worldwide.

Merrill Lynch's system includes a new telecommunications infrastructure, upgraded PC hardware and software, and electronic market data feeds. Merrill Lynch spent a total of $250 million on software development. Much of the remaining expense—for the telecomm system and for electronic data feeds for stock quotes and news, for example—would have been required no matter what software Merrill Lynch used. Compared to maintaining the company's existing infrastructure and applications, the actual difference in cost netted out to about $250 million over four years. For slightly more than $60 million a year, approximately $3,500 per financial consultant, Merrill Lynch completely overhauled the information system for the 14,700 financial consultants in its 700 U.S. offices and for another 2,000 consultants internationally.

CTO Howard Sorgen showed me firsthand the Merrill Lynch solution, which represents a profound use of information technology to bring information to users quickly and intelligently.

Realizing that it would take years to rewrite legacy applications on old systems and integrate all of the company's core business systems, the IT team created a universal PC "shell," a common user interface for the TGA platform that ties together all of Merrill Lynch's systems—old, new, and future. This "superbrowser" shell enables Merrill Lynch staff to work with any number of local, client-server, legacy, and Web browser applications in a consistent, intuitive way.

Regardless of origin, related data is logically organized into pages of information. The pages are structured into sections, chapters, and books. Everybody understands the book metaphor, and a "loose-leaf binder" approach to the books provides flexibility in organizing the information. In the upper right-hand corner of the TGA screen is a customizable Information Center containing the real-time information that financial consultants need to monitor constantly. A financial consultant can monitor a dozen key stocks there, along with news alerts about key companies, broadcasts such as *CNN Live,* and important incoming e-mail. The folders in TGA are customizable, too. A financial consultant can click on a Stock Exchange folder and select a number of exchanges to watch: NASDAQ, New York, Tokyo, and so on. The financial consultant pastes new selections into the Stock Exchange folder, and real-time feeds for those exchanges start up.

The TGA platform enables fast measurement of a portfolio's performance against a client's financial goals. Tracking progress in a portfolio used to be very time-consuming. A financial consultant might see that the client's portfolio was behind goal but would need to manually run a lot of "what-if" scenarios to figure out what should change to get the client on track. Evaluating progress for 300 clients, many of whom might have several different accounts, was a challenge. TGA makes several views of the data available automatically. A financial consultant can tell with one glance whether a portfolio is performing to goal and can play with variables such as having the client increase savings, increase portfolio risk, downsize goals, and so on, to graphically see how various choices would affect the client's financial plan. Eventually clients will be able to run these what-if scenarios on their own PCs.

To take care of the administrative aspects of their jobs—filling out expense reports, calling clients, sending e-mail—financial consultants click on logically named tabs that automatically invoke the appropriate applications, such as a word processor, a spreadsheet, or a contact manager. A financial consultant doesn't need to know what these applications are called and doesn't need to worry about where the applications are running or how to summon them.

TGA has a user interface tuned for common scenarios. A financial consultant who has the News page up to see real-time news stories from the wire services can drag a company's stock symbol (say, MER for Merrill Lynch) from the live stock ticker in the Information Center over to the News page. The News page instantly displays stories related to that company. If a financial consultant has turned on a filter—say, for Asia—the News page brings up only the stories about that company involving Asia. A click on Stock History provides links to Microsoft Investor, which provides a history of the company's stock performance. If the market data vendor's stock feed dies, the TGA notices and puts a question mark in the stock quote field next to the last known number.

The system follows what a financial consultant does and notes special interests. Like a well-trained assistant, it carries out often repeated rounds of activity without being

How to Upgrade Ten Offices a Week

In a rollout that lasted a little more than a year, Merrill Lynch upgraded ten of its offices every week. Two weeks before conversion, a team would arrive to deliver mandatory training on the new system. The trainers would teach the staff basic functionality and use of the extensive online help system, which contains online cue cards and multimedia demonstrations. The Sunday before the system went live, the trainers would conduct a three-hour review session. After the system went live, they would stay for another week to make sure everybody was up to speed.

The Friday afternoon before the changeover, an installation team would arrive. Over the weekend this team would yank out the entire old infrastructure: the many terminals, older PCs, cabling, even inadequate electrical boxes. They'd install high-speed Internet links and Pentium Pro–based workstations for each employee and a pair of multiprocessor PC servers—one for stock quotes, other information feeds, and file and print services and the other for e-mail.

On Monday morning the office would go live. The assimilation rate was much higher than Merrill Lynch expected. The independent PC experience of many of the staff, the intuitiveness of the system, and the thoroughness of the training were the key reasons for this success.

asked. For example, a financial consultant can instruct the system to automatically bring up relevant news about a certain company, graph the stock's thirty-day and five-year performance, show similar graphs for the company's top three competitors, display the company's price-to-earnings ratio, bring up Merrill Lynch's research opinions of the company, and on and on. Every time the financial consultant clicks on that particular stock, all of this information will come up in about two seconds. In an effort to document and replicate best practices, Merrill Lynch is carefully monitoring how its most experienced consultants use the system. The plan is to create electronic models of their work habits and further enhance the TGA system for everybody.

In addition to seeing much of the same information as the financial consultants, Merrill Lynch's senior executives use a version of TGA that enables them to monitor company performance figures and other operational data. Branch office managers have a different custom set of "loose-leaf books," as do middle marketers, home office staff, insurance professionals, and support staff. Insurance professionals, for example, have access to underwriting tables and insurance regulations, while administrative staff can tap into travel information and reservation applications. Everybody feels that the system is tuned for him or her.

UNDERGOING A CONSULTANT PARADIGM SHIFT

The new technology has brought about a paradigm shift for financial consultants. Success now involves more than the slow accumulation of knowledge or knowing where to look for arcane information. A twenty-year company veteran says that in addition to cutting research from hours to minutes, the TGA system's ability to graphically chart a number of metrics (company performance, price-earnings ratios, and so on) allows an experienced financial consultant to zero in on the best-looking entry and get in on the ground floor of an emerging market.

Financial consultants have more time to build stronger relationships with clients. A financial consultant used to rely on notes and other documentation when talking with one of his or her 300 clients. When a client called, where was the information you needed? Did you have it? Your assistant? Now records of all client contacts are centralized in an electronic client contact file. Personal information—for example, the fact that the client has two children in college—gives the financial consultant opportunities to personalize a call and send the client pertinent information.

Merrill Lynch has spent a lot of time considering the impact of sharing a version of the system with its clients. There were long philosophical discussions within Merrill Lynch about how to use this technology to touch customers. The outcome was that Merrill Lynch decided that giving more information to customers would enrich the relationship between the financial consultant and customer, not diminish it. Merrill Lynch conducted extensive talks with customers and surveyed the competitive landscape. At this point customers were discovering the Internet and e-trades were growing. The company decided to move quickly.

Merrill Lynch created a version of TGA, called Merrill Lynch OnLine, for customers, giving them access to research, account information, basic bill payment, and other fundamentals. The company hoped to sign up 200,000 customers within the first year, an average of about 550 people a day. Instead, 700 to 800 people a day signed up, and Merrill Lynch hit its target in just seven months. One surprise was the demographic makeup of the clients attracted to the online service. Merrill Lynch had thought that younger, Internet-raised customers would bite first, but it was the older, wealthier clients who signed up.

The success of the pilot Merrill Lynch OnLine service encouraged the company to add more market data, more account information, and more bill-paying options for customers. Today customers can e-mail their financial consultants, get delayed stock quotes and daily mutual fund prices, view research reports, pay their bills, and do fund transfers. Merrill Lynch recently added the ability to enter trading orders.

Upon reflection, Merrill Lynch realized that the Internet was as much of an opportunity as a threat. The Internet provided more information to its customers, but information is not financial wisdom. A financial services firm should urge clients to use the Internet for information and communications so that its financial consultants can spend more time planning and interacting with them. Now a consultant can call a customer and say, "Did you see that research report on Merrill Lynch OnLine? . . . Have you read it? . . . Good. Now let's talk about how these issues impact your portfolio."

Informed clients ask better questions. Conversations are more in depth and to the point. Because they are more informed and have more control, clients are more confident in their decisions. A client with information is more likely to act on the advice of a financial consultant, whose strength is in providing financial insight into that information. With more dialogue between consultants and clients, clients will provide better feedback about what improvements or new services they want. The company won't be guessing about client needs. Eventually Merrill Lynch expects to provide total synchronicity between the financial consultant and the client—to have both of them looking at the same thing, on the same screen, at the same time. When that happens, Merrill Lynch people like to say, "the real magic" starts.

CHANGING THE COMPANY-CUSTOMER DYNAMIC

Merrill Lynch's investment in information technology is a statement of the value it places on its knowledge workers. While the system was being rolled out, the market experienced a strong bull period followed by a period of retrenchment caused by the Asian financial crisis, so it's difficult to directly measure the new system's financial impact. Merrill Lynch, however, can point to the more than $1 billion in additional assets that Merrill Lynch OnLine customers placed with the company. These funds might not have come Merrill Lynch's way without the new capabilities.

There's a hot debate raging between the online brokers and the full-service brokers that will repeat in other industries. The pure online companies believe low transaction costs are compelling. Full-service vendors believe that when customers want advice, they still need to work with an expert. For the consumer, the important issue is to know whether you're paying for transactions or advice and to be sure that you get what you pay for.

There's no doubt that the Internet is raising customer expectations. The seventy-plus online brokerages are discovering that the low-cost, self-service model creates intense competition to be one of the few that reach critical mass. Recognizing the need to offer differentiating value, even companies in the low-cost online market are experimenting with various combinations of service and price, trying to find the magic combination that customers are willing to pay for. Every company will need to adapt to get customers' attention in the crowded marketplace of the Information Age.

Business Lessons

- ❑ The Internet will help achieve "friction-free capitalism" by putting buyer and seller in direct contact and providing more information to both about each other.
- ❑ As the Internet drives down the cost of transactions, the middleman will disappear or evolve to add new value.
- ❑ Only a few businesses will succeed by having the lowest price, so most will need a strategy that includes customer service.
- ❑ If you take a service approach, arm your knowledge workers with digital information tools to connect with customers and manage those relationships.

Diagnosing Your Digital Nervous System

- ❑ Does your IT system enable your knowledge workers to spend most of their time analyzing information instead of collecting it?
- ❑ Are you using PC servers to integrate applications from multiple sources, particularly those from older, inflexible systems?
- ❑ Do you have a single infrastructure to support applications for your internal knowledge workers and your customers?

6

TOUCH YOUR CUSTOMERS

> What's my return on investment on e-commerce? Are you crazy? This is Columbus in the New World. What was his ROI?
>
> —Andrew Grove, Intel Chairman

As electronic commerce booms, it's not just middlemen who will find creative ways to use the Internet to strengthen their relationships with customers. The merchants who treat e-commerce as more than a digital cash register will do the best. Sales are the ultimate goal, of course, but the sale itself is only one part of the online customer experience. Some companies will use the Internet to interact with their customers in ways that haven't been possible before and make the sale part of a sequence of customer services for which the Internet has unique strengths.

It's important that customers come away from electronic interactions pleased enough to tell their friends.

Word of mouth is the most powerful means by which any product or company builds a reputation, and the Internet is a medium made for word of mouth. If a customer doesn't like a product or the way a vendor has treated him, he's likely to e-mail all of his friends or post a message on a heavily trafficked bulletin board. An Internet auto site called Autoweb.com queries customers about dealer service by e-mail and deletes dealers from its listings if they fail to improve their service as the result of complaints.

Today the primary competition for online stores is physical stores. Physical stores far outdo online stores in sales volumes. Online sales in 1998 were not much more than a rounding error in the world's overall business volume: only 0.5 percent of the total retail sales of the seven largest economies. But that percentage will grow radically in the next decade. As e-commerce takes hold, the main competition for Internet sites will no longer be physical stores but online stores.

Rapidly growing categories for online commerce include finance and insurance, travel, online auctions, and computer sales. Today's Internet customers are the technically savvy. Companies such as Cisco Systems, Dell Computer, and Microsoft are now doing billions of dollars each in annual transactions over the Internet. Tomorrow's customers will be the mainstream. Chrysler expects its 1.5 percent online sales volume to jump to 25 percent in four years. Even the most conservative estimates project an annual growth rate of about 45 percent for online sales. The highest projections are for more than $1.6 trillion in business by the year 2000. I think this number is too low.

In an online variant of the department store bridal registry, Eddie Bauer's online catalog enables a customer to post his name, his size, and a wish list of products he'd like so that his friends and family can buy him gifts he wants.

No more wrong sizes or ugly ties. Geffen Records promotes its own artists and artists from associated labels on its Web site, but it also sells music from other labels. The site cross-promotes T-shirts, other fan-type merchandise, and movies. To build a community, the site offers discussion groups for fans and twenty-four-hour response to e-mail queries.

Dell and Marriott International got into e-commerce early, convinced that "if you build it, they will come." Their objective was to use the flow of information made possible by the Internet to directly touch customers and create a level of customer service that would naturally drive more sales.

JUMPING ONTO THE INTERNET EARLY

Dell was one of the first major companies to move to e-commerce. A global computer supplier with more than $18 billion in revenue, Dell began selling its products online in mid-1996. Its online business quickly rose from $1 million a week to $1 million a day. Soon it jumped to $3 million a day, then $5 million. It's still rising. Computer buyers clearly like the friction-free purchasing environment of the Web. As of this printing, Dell has more than 1.5 million visits a week to its Web site, and 11 percent of its overall business is online. Dell intends to grow that portion to more than 50 percent, perhaps as early as 2000.

A lot of Dell's Web business is probably new since revenue on the Web is growing significantly faster than Dell's overall revenue, but the company doesn't spend a lot of time worrying about it. Instead the company just talks about "Web-enabled revenue," including the way the

Web supports other sales efforts. The Web streamlines transactions and reduces technical support calls, too.

Michael Dell, the company's founder, has a well-documented commitment to direct selling and computer-aided commerce. When he was twelve years old Michael netted $2,000 selling stamps by mail order. In high school Michael hustled newspaper subscriptions by using an Apple IIe to develop mailing lists targeting newlyweds or families who had just moved to town. He made enough money to buy himself a BMW. As a freshman at the University of Texas in 1983, Michael took excess inventory from local computer dealers at cost, upgraded the machines, and sold them over the phone for less than the dealers were charging. Within a year he had left school to build a computer company operating on the same direct sales principle.

When the Internet began to gain momentum, Michael was interested. He knew that the Internet could extend Dell's direct relationship with the customer from the customer's phone to the customer's desktop. Ultimately Dell figured out that to get into high gear the company needed to integrate the Internet into its overall business strategy. It established a business unit dedicated to online commerce and support.

Starting early, just as the Internet was reaching out beyond students and technologists and into the mass market, Dell broke into Internet commerce when many companies were talking about it but only a few were actually doing it. The company didn't know how customers wanted to use the Internet. The customers themselves weren't sure. Dell built an initial site that provided product information, enabled simple orders, and solicited feedback. Dell learned a lot from the customer suggestions that came in, mostly online.

Over time Dell has made hundreds of changes to its

Web site, including three major updates and many minor feature changes, such as turning menu options into radio buttons to make the options easier to select. Step by step Dell has added capabilities for customers such as the ability to track the status of any order and get service and support. Cumulatively these features have caused a major shift in Dell's business practices.

CHANGING THE ROLE OF THE SALES TEAM

Michael Dell characterizes the direct business today as "different combinations of face-to-face, ear-to-ear, and keyboard-to-keyboard. Each has its place. The Internet doesn't replace people. It makes them more efficient. By moving routine interactions to the Web and enabling customers to do some things for themselves, we've freed up our salespeople to do more meaningful things with customers."

Before, customers had a simple, convenient way to interact with the company: through the Dell salesperson who sold them the computer. And the Dell salesperson was trained to make the customer's problems go away. As it introduced its new technology, Dell had to ensure that two things happened: that the new solution would be at least as convenient as calling and that its own salespeople would change their way of doing business.

"We'd spent thirteen years building a culture based on high-quality customer service. A lot of it was based on our salespeople being on the phone to customers all the time. Now we wanted to insert another piece," Michael says. "The hardest part was not the technology but the behavior shift—for our own salespeople as well as the customers. Simplicity and convenience were paramount. We had to build an Internet system that was so convenient, customers

Dell Lowers Overhead for Service and Support

The Internet eliminates lots of costs, not just sales costs.

Each week about 50,000 customers use Dell's Web site to check their order status. If just 10 percent of these customers called instead of using Dell's online service, those 5,000 calls at $3 to $5 each would cost Dell between $15,000 and $25,000 a week.

Each week about 90,000 software files are downloaded from Dell's site. Answering the same number of requests for software by phone and sending each customer the software by mail would cost Dell $150,000 per week.

Each week more than 200,000 customers access Dell's trouble-shooting tips online. Each of these hits saves Dell a potential $15 technical support call. The savings over a year add up to several million dollars.

These self-service options improve Dell's efficiency, but the benefit also accrues to customers. Dell's online system saved one large company $2 million a year in help-desk costs.

got more value for their time than they did on the phone. That was the only way we could wean them off face-to-face or ear-to-ear contact. It was a high bar to clear."

Having more information online for customers didn't lessen the value of Dell's corporate sales team. With more reports and quoting tools online and available to customer and salesperson alike, the salesperson had fewer but meatier engagements with customers. Like Merrill Lynch, Dell found out that an educated customer is a better customer. Dell salespeople had already begun to play a consultant's role, helping the customer develop technology migration plans and leasing and asset-replacement programs and understanding the customer's business well enough to recommend ways that technology could help the bottom line more. Digital Web transactions reduced the time that sales representatives spent processing orders, checking order status, and fielding customer-service queries. Sales representatives now have more time for consulting, building the customer relationship, and selling. Representatives can still help out whenever they are needed. A customer can send a partially completed order form to a sales representative and get assistance before placing an order.

One of Dell's unique approaches to customer support was to create more than 5,000 specially designed Premier pages tailored to the needs of its major customers. About 65 percent of Dell's online business right now is from consumers and small businesses, and the Premier pages are one way Dell is growing its corporate business.

A large corporate customer, or a customer in a certain market segment such as government or higher education, logs on to a secure Dell page designed for that organization alone. The page shows purchasing options according to the organization's policies. It displays standard machine configurations and prices that have been negotiated in advance and shows order information, order history, and account contact information. Organizations can preapprove purchases up to any amount, so many orders can be processed immediately. Customers at U.S. government agencies see pricing for systems that have been approved through General Services Administration contracts. When an order ships, a customer can get an automatic e-mail notification and the order's airbill number.

A second secure page contains confidential information for senior purchasing managers or senior members of the organization's IT group. This page provides account information that used to reach customers only in monthly reports. One manufacturing company uses its page to track purchasing and spending to date by department, and an oil company uses its page to track the deployment of its widespread computer assets. This second page has reduced Dell's overhead for furnishing accounting information to customers by about 15 percent.

SHIFTING DEVELOPMENT PRIORITIES

The Internet approach changed the way that Dell develops applications. Dell used to build tools for its staff to use for phone support. Today every major tools development effort at Dell is evaluated first to see whether it should be built directly for customers on the Internet. If it's for customers, it gets first call on developer resources. Dell's last big internal development project for support tools came just as the Internet was reaching critical mass. The company used the tools internally for several months, made a few changes, and then "turned them over to customers."

The Internet also affected how Dell uses its back-end systems. The company's mainframe system supported the existing phone-ordering system, which had relatively few people inputting sales orders. This system could process hundreds of thousands of transactions a week, but it could *not* handle thousands of customers placing orders online. And the mainframe was usually taken down on the weekend for backup and maintenance. The Internet system needed to be available seven days a week, twenty-four hours a day.

Dell solved the problem by coupling the mainframe with a set of Dell's own PowerEdge servers equipped with dual Pentium Pro processors. These servers run PC Website management software and databases for order tracking and support. Using load-balancing technology, Dell feeds incoming Web requests through one of its many front-end servers. Content is mirrored on all of the servers so that the transaction load can be distributed. When traffic is particularly heavy, Dell can add a new server in about an hour. All the Internet team has to do is create a copy of the latest information on a new server, add this server to the network, and then notify the load-balancing system that there is a new server.

Dell had some kinks to work out in the procedures for uploading and downloading data. One day the software on the mainframe was changed, scrambling the pricing link to the Web servers. As a result, PC monitors were listed on the Web site at "zero" dollars. Approximately one hundred orders arrived in the short interval between the appearance of the zero price and Dell's correction of the problem. The company had to phone all of these customers to explain the error. The incident was a wake-up call about the kind of quality assurance required for Internet commerce, and Dell improved its software maintenance process to ensure that the mistake wouldn't happen again.

"In this instance, it was just embarrassing for us," says Scott Eckert, director of Dell Online, the organization established to build Dell's Internet business. "We were early in the game, and customers were understanding. But the lesson was clear. It alerted us that as our volume ramped up, the potential impact of any error was mind-boggling. A year from then, that kind of mistake would have been unacceptable for a high-visibility, high-volume Web site. While some people treat their Web site as a marketing brochure, or simply entertainment, our site does business. It requires even more care than you'd put into an internal accounting system. Any mistake will be instantly visible to the world."

Real-time flow of sales information through its Web site and order processing system is important to Dell's competitive situation. Instead of having eighty days of inventory, as indirect sellers have (although indirect sellers are trying to reduce that number), Dell keeps only eight days of inventory, and much of that is in parts such as chips and hard drives. Dell's manufacturing time is only four hours. Machines generally reach customers within three to five days of order.

Dell's business model is based on the evils of inventory. The more Dell can reduce its inventory, the more it frees up working capital to drive into other revenue-generating activities. Dell's reduced inventory translates to a savings of hundreds of millions of dollars in assets. At the same time, the requirement for great customer service means that you never want to be out of stock, either. Only information technology can provide the means to balance these needs. "Physical assets used to be a defining advantage," Michael says. "Now they're a liability. The closer you get to perfect information about demand, the closer you can get to zero inventory. It's a simple formula. More inventory means you have less information, and more information means you have less inventory. We're trading physical assets for information."

Going forward, Dell is taking the next steps in Web site development: customizing even more services on its Premier pages and making the entire ordering process for major customers totally paperless. Even with the ability of customers to order online, much of the approval process within a customer's organization has still been paper based. Dell will give companies an order application that integrates Dell's ordering database with the customer's purchasing system. Flexible reporting tools will give customers the ability to query Dell's information systems and generate their own status reports.

Dell is already offering Internet transaction capability in thirty-six countries and eighteen languages. The company plans to continue expanding its Internet services internationally so customers have a consistent Dell Internet experience everywhere.

EXPERIMENTING WITH A NEW SERVICE INITIATIVE

Marriott International, the world's largest hospitality company, also recognized that the Internet can do more than book sales. With greater than $10 billion in revenue, Marriott operates 1,500 hotels around the world under ten different brands. The company put together its first online reservation system in 1996. Although Marriott says it was rudimentary and experimental, the system did $1 million in business by the end of the year. This volume got the attention of Marriott executives. Like Dell's, Marriott's executives sensed a great but unclear potential for Internet business, and in early 1997 they created a special Internet team, Interactive Sales and Marketing, headed by Mike Pusateri.

From the start, Marriott's Internet execution benefited from strong internal corporate support and tight coordination between the business team and the technology team. Senior Vice President of Sales Rich Hanks was an important Internet champion. Hanks created Pusateri's department, hired Pusateri, got him in front of the right people, and helped him solidify his business case. Chief Information Officer Carl Wilson, new to Marriott at the time, not only worked with Pusateri on technical issues, but helped him win more executive sponsorship.

Marriott's marketing research consistently showed the high potential of the Internet for Marriott business. The 1997 American Internet User Survey by FIND/SVP showed that one of the most commonly researched topics on the World Wide Web was travel. According to the Forrester Group, the second largest online purchase category was travel. A Yankelovich study showed further that people shopping for travel services were looking for information about their destination above all.

And Marriott was in the destination business.

For Marriott, Mike Pusateri concluded, the Internet could create a communications loop that would provide a higher level of service, drawing in new customers. "Technology companies 'got' the Internet phenomenon several years ago, but most other industries are just waking up to it," says Pusateri. "The Internet is all about service—providing service to customers in a way that's faster, friendlier, and more personal than they or the company has ever experienced before. And service is Marriott's business. We don't even own the bricks and mortar in most of our properties."

HOW CAN WE HELP YOU?

Marriott was one of the first companies to build an interactive home page. Using a sophisticated search tool, you can find a Marriott hotel by any combination of location, on-site facility, in-room amenity, and recreational offering. You can quickly put together a list of hotels in Phoenix that have a business center, in-room data ports, and nearby access to a golf course. Or you can find all the Marriott hotels located within a ten-mile drive of your company's Dallas, Texas, branch office. You can click on a suggestion box icon to send feedback e-mail to the customer service departments of individual Marriott hotels.

Linked Web pages describe shops, restaurants, and other attractions close to a hotel. An integrated mapping system gives you access to more than sixteen million businesses and points of interest all over the world. You can get detailed driving instructions to any Marriott hotel from any location, or from any hotel to any nearby locations, complete with full-color road maps. If you want to go to a Chinese restaurant, or find the nearest copy shop, the mapping system gives you up to six options within a twenty-mile radius, along with directions to whichever you choose.

Once you've found the right hotel for your needs, you can easily check availability and rates and reserve a room. You can also book rooms through other popular online distribution services such as TravelWeb and Microsoft Expedia. Marriott's site has links to more than 1,000 other Web pages. Anywhere on the Web that you can book accommodations, Marriott has a presence.

CUSTOMIZING THE WEB SITE FOR EVERY VISITOR

Marriott personalizes its Web site services for each and every visitor. The site is not just a static list or links to static lists that users have to wade through. All of the information is kept in a database and is presented to the site visitor according to the visitor's search criteria. Because the back-end software is dynamically adapting the site as a session goes on, every visitor has a different experience on the Marriott site, one that speaks to his or her interests.

Marriott's Web site, which currently averages 15,000 hits a day, generated more than $2 million in Internet-related revenues a month in 1997. It's hard for Marriott to know what percentage of these revenues would have come its way anyway through traditional means, but Marriott does know that the Internet site is attracting more affluent customers who are opting to stay at its upscale properties. The average room rate of an online customer is higher than Marriott's overall customer average.

While other companies are just beginning to build interactive sites, Marriott is pushing forward with more sophisticated capabilities such as multimedia, which will give potential guests and travel planners a visual experience of a property. In place of static floor plans, customers will see panoramic views of the lobby and other facilities. Think of it as "reservations with a view."

Marriott has found, as others have found, that the more interactive a site is, the more business activity it gets from its visitors. A dynamic Web site creates more bookings and more business. Marriott plans to enrich its Web site and personalize it even further by adding a "customer profiling" feature. Say I want a relaxing weekend within a reasonable drive of Seattle. I'll be able to enter the names of two or three Marriott properties elsewhere that I really liked. Marriott will give me recommendations for similar hotels or resorts close to Seattle. The Web site might then let me read the comments from other guests who have stayed at one or more of those places.

"We've gone from monologue to dialogue in our Web site—from talking at our customers to talking with them," Mike Pusateri says. "Now we need to move from dialogue to forum. Building profiles of our customers will not only allow us to serve them better, providing suggestions for things and places we know they like, but it will allow us to put Marriott customers in touch with each other. It's sort of like a news group within your Web site, but the software is doing all the work for us."

Marriott believes that its value-added approach will differentiate it from other chains. The hotel is not interested in creating an "Internet flea market" where customers scrounge for the lowest price. Marriott is not always the cheapest option. The company would rather follow the Nordstrom model and give customers lots of nonprice criteria to shop by, intensifying its customers' loyalty with these new programs.

Instead of bypassing middlemen, Marriott is integrating them into its customer services. The company provides special places on its Web site for travel agents and meeting planners. The access enables agents and planners to serve their customers better. In the travel agent section of its Web site, Marriott tells agents how to tie into Marriott from most of the major travel reservation networks. Meeting planners can search for properties by location, amenities, number of available guest and meeting rooms, and meeting room dimensions and capacities. The site also suggests appropriate properties for various activities. Today the site provides detailed meeting room floor plans. In the future the presentation is likely to be in video.

Thousands of meeting planners visit Marriott's site, for the simple reason that they don't have to make a trip to view a hotel property. Everything they need to see, they can see on the Web. As for travel agents, Marriott succeeded in sending a message that this community is important to the hotel chain. Soon after going live, the Marriott site got good reviews in travel agent publications, and travel agent business at the site has been brisk ever since.

You might wonder how Marriott knew that it had enough meeting planners and travel agents visiting its site to make it worth the investment in special tools for them. Marriott used technology to find out. When it first launched its site, Marriott posted an online survey and got 7,000 responses in one month. A surprising number came from travel intermediaries. The company also found out that general respondents were split fifty-fifty between business and leisure travelers and that the two groups had radically different interests. Business travelers wanted to save time online. Leisure travelers wanted to spend time online. Marriott redesigned its site to be helpful to both groups. A red "reservation" button on the home page makes it easy for business travelers or other travelers in a hurry to quickly book a room. For leisure travelers, who wanted destination content without lengthy downloads, Marriott trimmed the number of pictures while adding maps and directions.

To keep in touch with its customers, Marriott is continuing its annual online surveys and analyzing its customer e-mail, now running about 1,000 e-mails a day.

"GETTING" THE INTERNET

To make the technology approachable and relevant to Marriott management, Mike Pusateri took an unusual step: He acquired twenty WebTVs and delivered them to the homes of Marriott's top executives. He wanted them to understand that the Web was becoming ubiquitous and that people were going to be embracing the Web in a big way. "As a company catering to guests' needs and desires, we needed to be speaking their language," recalls Pusateri. "I told them that within a very short time our guests would be demanding devices like this in our hotel rooms, so they could couch- and bed-surf from our properties. They listened."

Pusateri sat down with key executives and surfed with them through Web sites he knew they'd like. Within six months the Internet and the World Wide Web had become real to them. "Executives started looking me up in the cafeteria to tell me they had visited their favorite car site or had learned something about an illness," he said. "It was no longer a phenomenon 'out there.' It was something they could personally relate to."

Pusateri formed a Web Policy Board, an executive-level policy-making body with representatives from Information Technology, Sales, the hotel brands, franchisees, Legal, Human Resources, and Corporate Communications. Getting everyone, especially at the executive level, on board, organized, and thinking strategically about the Internet was the company's most important step. Later, Marriott also set up a Web Council, an informal working group of twenty-five to thirty people in charge of Web content in various areas. The working group meets monthly to improve coordination and share best practices.

Mike Pusateri and CIO Carl Wilson had established a connection from the beginning, and each made an effort to view the world from the other's perspective. When he first took the job, Pusateri, the business guy, had brought in a consultant weekly to educate him on technical issues. Wilson, the technology guy, recommended at the first policy board meeting that Marriott benchmark the business activities as well as the technical infrastructures of other leading companies on the Web.

At Marriott's request, its Web developer, fine.com, arranged for sessions at Boeing, which has probably the

How Good Is Your Web Site?

Many companies are hiring outside firms to build their Web sites, and many businesspeople may assume that they don't know enough about technology to judge whether they have a good site. Actually it's easy to judge the quality of your site: use it yourself. Is the experience easy? Is the information well organized? Can you quickly get answers to questions? Is it easy to gather goods into the electronic shopping cart—or is it hard to search for items, and do you have to jump back and forth? Every company that touches a consumer electronically has to build products that work intuitively. You need to be sure to rigorously test anything you put up on the Web for customers. You get only one chance to make a good first impression.

largest intranet in the United States, and Microsoft, which has one of the most active Internet sites. The Marriott team, including executives, technical staff, and the corporate communications people, got a "brain dump" on how Boeing and Microsoft use the Internet. They discussed technology, migration strategies, internal coordination, and coordination with outside groups such as Marriott's franchisees. Later, staff from fine.com put Marriott through a highly facilitated two-day executive discussion of the kinds of things each of Marriott's business units might do on the Internet.

In the future, hotels will integrate the Internet into more than just the process of learning about travel and accommodations. They will also make Internet access far more of a feature of the rooms themselves. Most major hotels now make modem connections reasonably simple from the room, and they usually have business centers where guests can get more computer-related facilities. In the future, hotels catering to business travelers will make high-speed connections a standard in every room, and leading hotels will offer docking stations and large, easy-to-read screens so that business travelers can plug in their portable devices and be as productive on the road as they are in their office.

PUTTING WEB SERVICE IN CONTEXT

Having founded a business on the principle of touching the customer directly, Michael Dell saw the Internet as a natural extension of that philosophy. Marriott found the Internet to be a great way to extend its relationship with customers. Both companies used the new capabilities offered by the Internet to add unique value.

The companies took similar steps to a successful deployment of Internet services. Internal coordination was first and foremost: corporate support for the Internet initiative, leadership from the business side, and the close cooperation of the technical departments. As a technology company, Dell needed less orchestration of its senior leadership, but like Marriott, it also formed a special Internet business unit. Marriott embraced the Internet with the help of high-level corporate sponsorship, a business evangelist, and a well-organized campaign to educate and involve its senior executives.

Both companies were smart enough to recognize that commerce should be a combination of interaction over the Internet and personal contact. It's not a matter of either-or. People think it's the cold screen vs. the warm face-to-face and assume that the person-to-person interaction will win. Because they don't see where the Internet belongs on the marketing-sales-service spectrum, they underestimate the Internet's capabilities. Smart companies will combine Internet services and personal contact in programs that give their customers the benefits of both kinds of interaction.

You want to move pure transactions to the Internet, use online communication for information sharing and routine communication, and reserve face-to-face interaction for the activities that add the most value. In addition to using the Internet simply to make reservations or place product orders, customers find the Internet the perfect medium for gathering information, assessing product value and price-performance, checking order status, diagnosing and solving simple problems, and other relatively straightforward tasks. More and more, in this scenario, sales personnel become consultants.

As Internet technology matures, customers won't have to distinguish between Web and phone support when they need help with difficult problems. As a customer browses a Web page, he'll be able to just click on a button to get either Web-based or phone-based support. For less critical business, he'll click on a button to send an e-mail. For a question that needs an immediate answer, he'll click on a button to talk to a customer service agent. To better understand the problem, the agent on the other end will be able to see the same Web page that the customer is looking at. At the same time, all of the customer's information will show up on the agent's screen.

There are two ways to make a voice connection. The first is to use the same Internet IP connection for both voice and data. With the IP connection, the agent can view the Web page the customer is looking at, and the same connection carries the voice exchange with the customer. Although it's the simplest way to achieve simultaneous voice and Web communications, the limited bandwidth that most consumers have today makes voice quality poor. As bandwidth and quality of service improve, this approach will be used on every Web site.

The second approach is for the software to check whether the customer's PC can establish a regular phone connection. When the customer clicks on the button to talk to an agent, the PC dials the phone number and connects with an agent over a regular voice line. The beauty of this method is that you can get high-quality voice today, but it is more complex to coordinate the voice connection with the Web connection.

Several companies are developing solutions based on one or the other or both of these technical approaches. One company, eFusion, has a "push-to-talk" button that companies can post on their Web sites. When a user clicks the button, he's connected directly to the company's call center, where both agent and caller can browse the same Web content simultaneously while speaking over a voice connection. This system works over the single telephone line installed in most residences. Users simply need a standard multimedia PC equipped with any Internet-compliant phone software, such as Microsoft NetMeeting. Dell is adding push-to-talk capability to its intranet for employees to get technical support and plans to add it to the external Web site as well. Simultaneous voice and Web communications will become common in many ordinary consumer transactions in the banking, mortgage, utility, and credit card fields as more and more people adopt the "Web lifestyle," a concept I describe in the next chapter.

As high bandwidth connections become common, neither businesses nor customers will think of Web support as distinct from other forms of support. Companies will need to be clever about their site design. Clicking a link to speak with someone won't be the first thing a customer does at most Web sites. Most companies will design sites so users are encouraged to look for answers for themselves and to click to speak to a service representative only when they really need to. The site might first guide a customer to a list of frequently asked questions or an automated help wizard that would guide them to a solution.

Over a low-speed connection, a photo of the customer service representative could come up to make the conversation seem more personal. Over a high-speed connection, the customer could also have a direct video link to the representative. This integration of Web and voice technology is going to be a huge change. Businesses already have the bandwidth today to do this internally, and it's only a matter of time before consumers have the capability, too.

As more companies move to e-commerce, how can anyone stay ahead? Companies that get there early, as Dell and Marriott did, benefit from the head start, from learning what works and what doesn't, and from name recognition. They benefit too from loyalty programs that tie customers to them. Dell uses electronic newsletters to stay in contact with customer segments, offering targeted news and promotions for subscribing customers. Marriott enables customers to redeem their Marriott Awards points via e-mail. Perhaps the most important competitive advantage from their early starts, though, is the constant feedback both companies have gotten about their sites and their programs. This feedback helps them continually improve their processes. Their goal is to keep their Web offerings several versions ahead of what a competitor will be capable of introducing. Michael Dell puts it well when he says that process innovation is now the fundamental source of competitive advantage.

For both companies, a highly interactive and customized Web site has been key to acquiring more customers at lower cost and retaining them through higher satisfaction. Interactive customization as exemplified by the Dell and Marriott Web sites will play a bigger and bigger role in online sales. Where physical stores invest substantial amounts of money in bricks and mortar for "location, location, location" and try to pitch their wares to the average shopper, online merchants can use digital information to customize their wares as they interact with each individual shopper. In Marriott's case, interactive customization draws more people to its hotel properties. In Dell's case, interactive customization helps to sell PCs. In both cases, the ability to touch their customers with individualized service is increasing their revenue.

Business Lessons

- ❑ A successful Web site requires the creation of a new customer experience that takes advantage of the unique capabilities of the Internet.
- ❑ Success on the Web requires high-level corporate understanding of the Internet's capabilities and support of early test-and-invest projects.
- ❑ The majority of your interactions with customers on the Internet will involve support rather than sales, and the word-of-mouth nature of the Internet means it's very costly if customers have a poor experience on your site.
- ❑ A good Web site can help turn salespeople into consultants.

Diagnosing Your Digital Nervous System

- ❑ Do your digital systems enable you to provide a personalized experience for customers who come to your Web site?
- ❑ Do your digital systems allow you to trade physical assets for information?
- ❑ Will your Web infrastructure enable you to easily incorporate video and phone support in the future?

7

ADOPT THE WEB LIFESTYLE

Throughout the territories of every civilized nation, wherever human language is known, or commerce has marts . . . the electric wires which web the world in a network of throbbing life utter their voices in all their varied tongues.

—A writer in 1878 describing the effects of the telegraph (from *The Victorian Internet*)

If you asked your friends why they use the phone to communicate with their friends or why they turn to the television for entertainment or breaking news, they'd look at you kind of funny. If you asked your friends whether they'd adopted "the electricity lifestyle," they'd think you were downright nuts. People in developed countries take their electrical devices for granted; we just use them. But people who are now in their fifties can remember when just a few families had TVs. Our grandparents can remember when much of rural America was without electricity. A few people alive today were born before the widespread use of electricity in cities. The telegraph first connected the far corners of the globe with fast communications a century ago. It's taken more than a hundred years for the "electricity lifestyle" to reshape civilization.

When streets and houses were first wired, the only use for electricity was for lighting. Electricity's potential to reshape everyone's lifestyle was unforeseen. Electric light was safer, cleaner, brighter, and more flexible than natural gas, kerosene, or candles. Once the infrastructure was in place, though, innovative new products were created that took advantage of electricity. Electric refrigerators, phonographs, and air conditioners were applications of the new technology to existing needs. The most revolutionary applications of electricity were the phone, the radio, and the television. All of these new devices reshaped our economies and our lifestyles. People hadn't dreamed of these devices before the infrastructure was available.

Because the Internet is a worldwide communications infrastructure that depends on electricity, you could say that its popular acceptance is an extension of the "electricity lifestyle." But the Internet is enabling a new way of life that I call "the Web lifestyle." The Web lifestyle, like the electricity lifestyle, will be characterized by rapid innovations in applications. Because the infrastructure for high-speed connectivity has reached critical mass, it is giving rise to new software and hardware that will reshape people's lives. Intelligent devices such as the PC are becoming more powerful and less expensive. Since they are programmable they can be used for many different applications. Within a decade most Americans and many other people around the world will be living the Web lifestyle. It will be a reflex for these people to turn to the Web to get news, to learn, to be entertained, and to communicate. It will be just as natural as picking up the phone to talk to somebody or ordering something from a catalog is today. The Web will be used to pay your bills, manage your finances, communicate with your doctor, and conduct any business. Just as naturally, you'll carry one or more small devices using a wireless connection to stay constantly in touch and conduct electronic business wherever you are.

For a lot of people the Web lifestyle is well on its way today. By 1998 more than sixty million Americans were using the Web regularly, up from twenty-two million the year before. By 1998 the average user accessed the Web eight to nine separate days a month, spending a total of about 3.5 hours a month online.

It's exciting to see that people living the Web lifestyle are using the Internet to learn and buy in new ways. When the *Sojourner* landed on Mars in the summer of 1997, NASA's Web site drew forty-seven million hits in four days from people seeking more detail than they could get from the traditional news media. Whatever you think of the Starr report on President Clinton, the Internet was the only feasible medium for disseminating the 445-page document quickly. Six to nine million people viewed it the first weekend after its release. Businesses are providing a wide variety of information and services, whether it's real-time stock quotes, sports scores, or city guides. You can buy almost anything on the Web, from Impressionist paintings to metal cartoon superhero school lunchboxes, which have become collectibles. The Web is an ideal vehicle for community building, too. There are sites for tracking missing children and helping people adopt pets and for every activity imaginable. Sites that involve citizens are getting excellent traffic flow. One Web site shows all the industrial polluters in the United States, offering maps and the ability to search by company name or locale. It drew 300,000 users in the first five hours it was up—almost all by word of mouth.

A cultural change as substantial as a move to the Web

lifestyle will be generational to some degree. It's the kids growing up with the new technology and taking it as a given who will show us the full potential. On most U.S. college campuses, the critical mass for a Web-ready culture already exists. Personal computer use, high-speed networking, and online communication are widespread. Universities are dispensing with paper forms and registering students for classes over the Web. Students can look at their grades and even turn in their homework over the Web. Teachers hold online discussion groups. Students e-mail friends and family as naturally as they call them. Students are the ultimate knowledge workers. Their "job" is to learn and explore and find unexpected relationships between things. The specifics of the academic courses don't matter as much as learning to think and analyze. Students are developing Internet skills that will help them learn throughout their lives. For business, there is an opportunity to learn from the way students use the Internet today to organize and manage their lives. Their approach is a guide to how the general population will use the Internet ten years from now.

The adoption of technology for the Web lifestyle is happening faster than the adoption of electricity, cars, TV, and radio, as illustrated in the chart that follows. Usage spreads through the workplace exposure to PCs and through friends and relatives. Many people who use PCs at the office install them at home for work and then use them for far more. A lot of people over fifty-five years old, who wouldn't usually integrate new technology in their lifestyle, are motivated to use the Internet as a way to stay in touch with their friends and families. A friend of mine recently received e-mail from two distantly related women in their seventies—they were "into the Internet" to research genealogy. Radical new uses of the Internet that none of us can accurately predict today will reshape the world as fundamentally in the twenty-first century as the unexpected uses of electricity did in the twentieth—and faster.

As consumers rapidly move online, one of the most fundamental shifts will be the degree to which consumers will manage their finances (including banking, mortgage, utilities, and credit cards) online. In 1998 only about one million of the fifteen billion total bills in the United States were paid electronically. Little online customer service was available. In fact, though consumers can pay some bills online, in almost every case they still receive them on paper. When consumers are able to pay online, the U.S. Commerce Department estimates, processing costs will drop more than $20 billion annually.

Within a couple of years electronic bill payment will be offered by most companies, and financial institutions

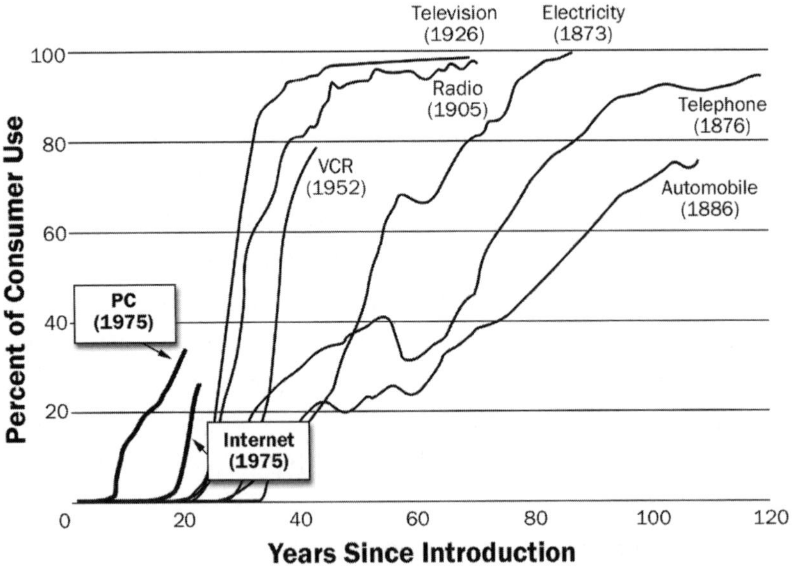

Source: W. Michael Fox and *Forbes* magazine

The PC and the Internet are both being adopted faster than the technologies that shaped the twentieth century. Just as people in developed countries today take for granted the lifestyles created by electricity and automobiles, they will soon take for granted the new lifestyle, the Web lifestyle, enabled by digital technology.

will maintain a single site where customers can go to pay their monthly bills. From your banking Web page, you'll click on the icon for your credit card company or department store or utility and go directly to that company's site for your account information. You'll have more information about your bills online than you have on paper today. You'll be able to drill into account and payment history. Rather than having to write a separate letter, you'll click on an e-mail button to ask a question about a bill. Merchants will use your online bill-review page to promote additional products and services.

Today you have to figure out on paper what bills you want to pay and how much you want to pay on each. In the future, software will enable you to calculate online the effect of various payments on your bank balance. You'll make your payment exactly when it's due. And bill payment systems will integrate with financial management software.

BRINGING ABOUT THE WEB LIFESTYLE

By late 1998 about half of all American households had PCs, and about half of those PCs were connected to the Web. The percentages are lower in most other countries. Reducing the cost of high-speed communications so people can remain constantly connected and making the software simpler to use are critical to making the Web lifestyle commonplace. I believe that by the year 2001 more than 60 percent of U.S. households will have PCs and that 85 percent of those homes will have Internet access. For other countries to reach these levels of use they will have to make large investments in communications infrastructure.

People underestimate the degree to which the hardware and software will improve. Take just one aspect: screen technology. I do my electronic mail on a twenty-inch LCD (liquid crystal display) monitor. It's not available at a reasonable price yet, but in two or three years it will be. In five years a forty-inch LCD with much higher resolution will be affordable. Screen quality will have a profound effect on how much people will read on the screen instead of on paper.

The cost of a personal computer is also coming down. Historically, innovation has focused on creating a more powerful PC at a given price point. Now innovation is reducing price as well. Capable PCs cost well under $1,000 today, and lower price points are expanding the market. Looking at a ten-year time frame, you're going to have PCs that cost the same as a typical TV set. In fact, the distinction between a TV set and a PC will be fuzzy because even set-top boxes that connect TVs to the cable system will have a processor more powerful than the one we have today in the most expensive PC.

Smaller personal companions will become prevalent. These will include the handheld PCs on the market today, new computer tablets, and wallet-size PCs that will carry identification and enable electronic transactions. The phone, radio, and TV will pick up new capabilities as they go digital. Some devices will be carried on your person. Some will be in different rooms in your house. Others will become standard in vehicles. Any of them will enable you to access such information as e-mail and voice mail, stock reports or other news, the latest weather, and the status of your airplane flight. These devices will connect through wires or through wireless technologies such as infrared and radio frequencies. Though the devices will function independently, they will synchronize data among themselves automatically.

CHANGING HOME AND TV EXPERIENCE

These devices will become part of the fabric of daily activities. When you leave the office for the day, your personal digital companion will download your e-mail, which might include a grocery list from your spouse. At the store, you can download a new recipe from a kiosk, which adds to your grocery list all the items you would need to use the recipe. Your digital companion is smart enough to update all the devices that need to know your home or work schedule but updates only the kitchen device with the recipe.

From a computer tablet in the kitchen or den, you check the house's status. The furnace icon may be blinking because the filter needs to be changed. A video of the front door area shows who stopped by while no one was home. Digital security cameras connected to a network are becoming cheaper and will be common to reduce theft. Some day care centers and schools are providing password-protected access to cameras to enable parents to check on their kids while they're at school.

While dinner is cooking, you go to a private Web site for your extended family and find out that everyone has been in the chat room discussing what activities to do at an upcoming family reunion. They used electronic polling to settle on any of half a dozen possible events, and they've asked you to go ahead and schedule as many of them as you can. A software agent, which knows you have already booked travel to the location, suggests several nearby activities, including rafting, which was on your family's list. The agent also alerts you to a new, lower airfare to your destination. You digitally book the rafting and the lower fares.

When you're ready to watch TV, you might scroll through the electronic programming guide on screen or use another software agent to see what's on. You've told the agent your viewing preferences and it's tracked your actual viewing patterns, so it recommends several shows among the many hundreds available on digital TV. You choose to see a rodeo. While watching, you use the interactive menu to enter a contest and to judge the bull-riding events. Viewer scores will count for half the final results. A commercial comes on advertising a minivan. Most viewers see an ad for pickup trucks, but demographic data that you voluntarily provided through your TV indicates that you're a better candidate for a family-hauling vehicle.

Using the interactive TV's menu, you also discover that there's a rodeo in the town where you're having the reunion. Your family wanted at least one more unusual outdoor activity, so you book the rodeo, too. The activity is automatically added to the reunion schedule, which you now e-mail to the rest of the family.

Development of intelligent, interactive TV will come as television moves from analog transmission, where video and audio are carried using signal strength, to digital transmission, where video and audio are carried as digital bits. Digital transmission is less subject to distortion, is easier to correct for errors, and provides for higher-quality video and sound. Better video and sound have been the main focus for broadcast networks with digital TV, in the form of high-definition television (HDTV). As of late 1998 forty-one U.S. stations had begun digital broadcasting for HDTV.

Digital TV can do a lot more than improve broadcast quality, though. Satellite and cable companies are already using digital TV to deliver more channels. Over time, the biggest impact of digital TV will be the ability to integrate other digital data, providing interactivity, smart agents, targeted advertising and sales offers, and access to the Web. Broadcasters will provide enhanced content such as links to relevant Web sites or entirely new Web content that complements the broadcast, or download music or software for a fee to a user's DVD. Many of the new features require a two-way link, which is easy for new cable TV systems. Older cable systems have to be upgraded. Satellite and over-the-air TV will use phone lines or wireless communication synchronized with their broadcast to achieve interactivity.

New technology will simplify the TV interface. Trying to record one or more programs at certain times and days remains frustratingly complex with analog systems. Recording a show on one channel while you watch a different show on another may require you to swap the cables among your TV, video, and set-top box! In the future, taping a show will be as simple as *telling* the TV the name of the show and the episode.

Using speech to interact with the TV, PC, or other personal companions will be common within ten years. The technology will combine speech recognition and natural language understanding, so that the computer can determine your intent. Speech synthesis will improve dramatically from the robot-sounding voices you hear today. Your TV and PC will include a camera so they can recognize gestures and facial expressions. They will be able to tell whether you're talking to the device or someone else (or another device) and determine your emotional reaction. If you appear confused, the TV or PC will offer interactive help on the current topic or issue. It will also adapt to your behavior, whether that has to do with the programming you like on your TV or the typical pattern of activities on your PC. Computers that "see, listen, and learn" will extend digital technology into many new areas where the keyboard or mouse interface makes interaction impractical.

The rollout of digital television will occur in three phases: the build-out of the infrastructure, which will take several more years; the integration of the new capabilities into broadcast, satellite, and cable systems; and, finally, innovation on the new infrastructure. A lot of exploration and a lot of customer feedback will be required before the best uses of the new infrastructure become clear.

Major networks such as NBC, MSNBC, CNN, and MTV and some local broadcasters are already experimenting with using interactive content to supplement their regular programming. During the Emmy Awards in September of 1998, consumers could access additional information on award categories and nominees, experience live on-scene video and audio, catch behind-the-scenes interviews, and participate in trivia quizzes, interactive fan balloting, and chat rooms.

Many technical issues need to be resolved to ensure a simple and totally digital television experience for viewers. There are too many incompatible encryption standards for different phases of digital transmissions: one for the airwaves, one for cable systems, and one for the link between the set-top boxes and the TV itself. And while PC vendors have agreed on the data formats for devices connected through a new standard called the *universal serial bus (USB)* that will connect many of the new digital devices, makers of consumer electronic devices have many different approaches.

Bandwidth, the information-carrying capacity of a digital communications system, remains the biggest obstacle to widespread adoption of the Web lifestyle in all countries. Bandwidth is also the biggest cost. In developed nations businesses can generally afford the bandwidth they need to work digitally because lots of telecommunications companies are wiring business districts with fiber-optic cable. But getting affordable wiring into homes, schools, and libraries, which is critical to achieving a fully connected society, will take much longer. Unquestionably we won't see the full benefits of a Web lifestyle until high-bandwidth systems are in place. Some governments, such as Singapore's, have committed to installing high-bandwidth systems as a matter of social policy. Governments in other countries, such as the United States, the United Kingdom, and Australia, can rely on competition between cable and phone companies to make sure that the infrastructure is built. Other countries are starting from scratch. The most important step for a country to achieve a high-bandwidth infrastructure is to encourage competition in telecommunications.

Because it's relatively inexpensive to add more cabling between major geographies around the world, bandwidth inside the Internet backbone continues to grow rapidly and will not be a limiting factor. The hard and expensive part is what's called the problem of the "last mile": getting increased bandwidth from the end of the "big pipe" of major transmission services to individual homes. Technology advances in the next ten years will help make this part less expensive. A technology called *DSL* (*digital subscriber line*), which uses digital signals instead of traditional analog signals over regular phone lines, is already giving us more bandwidth from twisted-pair copper telephone wire. Cable modems are becoming more popular.

Outside of a densely populated central business district, the laying of new fiber-optic cable is not cost-effective. Because the expense is primarily labor, there probably won't be any substantial reduction in price over time. For this reason, countries in both the developed and the developing world are awaiting satellite communications systems.

Five narrow-band satellite systems such as Iridium's are being constructed to provide voice communications. Another system, proposed by Alcatel, would provide regional broadband (high data rate) coverage. A third approach, by Teledesic, would provide broadband communications globally, an "Internet-in-the-Sky."

Operating only about 500 miles up, these low-Earth-orbit systems will provide the low latency that is essential for interactive applications on the Internet. Geostationary communications satellites 22,000 miles in space suffer half-second time delays every time data goes up and back. Because low-orbiting satellites are not stationary, though, a large constellation is required to ensure that at least one satellite is always in range of a receiver on the ground.

As with any pioneering concept, the people who are building, launching, and operating these satellite systems have a lot of work to do. They have to raise more capital, finish proving the technology, and establish the right distribution systems. But once in place, these systems will use small antennas to provide service to places such as offices, factories, oil platforms, ships, schools, and homes.

Because a satellite system that adequately covers all developed areas will also cover undeveloped areas, "extra" capacity will be available for developing countries. The benefits of the Information Age can be extended to areas of the world in which no one would build this capacity for its own sake, whether this locale is a suburb or small town in the industrial world or a remote region of an agricultural land. Nonprofit uses will likely be available at low cost.

Scientists all over the world are exploring new technologies. And old ones. Recently a British engineer developed a way to send high-speed voice and data signals on household electrical current, raising the possibility that Internet service could one day ride into homes and businesses over our existing infrastructure of electrical wires. Technologies such as DSL, cable modem, low-orbit satellites, and power-line transmission are exciting because they don't require us to dig up and replace the existing "last mile" of copper line that already connects most households in the developed world. Getting the Web infrastructure in place worldwide is a daunting task, but the advances on many fronts make it likely that the speed of improvement will surprise everyone in the next decade.

REMOVING WORK AND LIFE LIMITATIONS

The social implications of the Web lifestyle and workstyle are enormous. A lot of people fear that computers and the Internet will depersonalize experience, creating a world that's less warm and fuzzy. Some people were initially afraid that the telephone would reduce face-to-face contact, too. Just as two people might call each other when they would have talked face-to-face without the phone, two people sitting close to each other might e-mail each other when they would have met face-to-face without e-mail. Any medium can be misused. The evolution of personal and professional manners for the Web will continue. It's easy to speculate that the Web lifestyle, with everyone off in his or her own little world, will cause society to fly apart. I believe the opposite is actually true. Just as the phone and e-mail have increased contact between people living in different communities and between people on the go, the PC and the Internet give us another way to communicate. They don't take any away.

In reality, the ability to use the Internet to move or redefine boundaries in our communities is strengthening personal and cultural connections. The city of Amsterdam, the Netherlands, facilitates Internet discussions about issues such as city planning, safety, and drugs. Citizens can connect to the police via e-mail. An Egyptian site for children called the Little Horus Web site contains more than 300 pages of information and illustrations covering Egypt's 7,000 years of civilization. It also gives snapshots of Egypt today, including its economic, cultural, and social life. The Tour section includes tips on popular destinations for children. The Web lifestyle is about broadening horizons, not narrowing them.

With all this content available, screening becomes an issue, especially when children have access. The Internet reaches a global audience, yet definitions of objectionable content vary from country to country. At the same time, authors of illegal content are often hard to trace. In this environment, censorship is difficult. In light of the distinctive characteristics of the Internet, the most effective approach to content will combine the blocking of sites on a country-by-country basis with industry self-regulation and content-screening software. Content ratings and filtering technologies such as the Platform for Internet Content Selection (PICS) enable users to control the content they and their families can access.

Community building is going to be one of the biggest growth areas in the next few years on the Web. The Web dramatically increases the number of communities you can bond to. In the past you might have had time to be a part of your neighborhood community and one or two social organizations you took the trouble to join. In the Web lifestyle you are limited only by your interests. One of the most powerful socializing aspects of the Web is its ability to connect groups of like-minded people independent of geography or time zones. If you want to get together a group of avid bridge players or talk issues with people who share your political views or stay in touch with your ethnic group scattered all over the world, the Web makes it easy to do. If you want to keep up with the goings-on in your hometown, the Web can help. I've discovered that New Yorkers transplanted to the West Coast have an insatiable appetite for news from the Big Apple, and many of them satisfy that desire through the Web. A Web site such as Third Age, which offers an electronic community space for seniors, illustrates the power of electronic community building. The site provides advice on family, health, technology, warnings about scams targeting seniors, and discussion groups on topical issues.

The Web lets you join communities across the globe and provides the opportunity to strengthen connections in your own backyard. In Singapore population density and the government's focus on infrastructure have helped the city-state become perhaps the world leader in the deployment of fiber-optic cable and interactive applications built on top of it. Broadband cable is a required utility, like water, gas, electricity, and telephone service. Virtually all public housing has been connected with cable, and Singapore officials estimate that more than 50 percent of all homes have PCs.

Not all communities getting wired are urban centers. Parthenay, France, a town of 12,000 people, is one of four communities in three countries that have gone online as part of the European IMAGINE project, supported by the European Union and a partnership of cities and industry. Citizens are using the Web in their day-to-day lives for such things as ordering bulk groceries. French families still come down to the market every Saturday, but now they bring a small basket and buy only specialty items, making the excursion more of a social activity. An online Philosophers' Café encourages thoughtful discussion, and every

Wednesday cattle breeders have chat sessions to discuss issues of common concern. The goal of the three-year IMAGINE project is to pass on an integrated solution to another thirty European communities for deployment.

Various American towns are also hooking up. Coldwater, Michigan, in the American Midwest has all 4,000 households on a high-speed cable system that provides cable TV, Internet access, dial tone, and access to a community network. One family that had an interest in billiards built a Web site on the topic and sold $45,000 worth of billiard cues in the first sixty days. Lusk, Wyoming, a community of 1,500 where cows outnumber people a hundred to one, is wired with fiber-optic cable. The people use PC technology for everything from managing cattle herds and studying the prairie grass environment to operating a beeswax hand-cream business. A fifteen-year-old boy, a certified PC software engineer, acts as the town's technical consultant. The people of Lusk have embraced the Web lifestyle to keep their ranching lifestyle viable and to connect their kids so they don't have to leave in order to be part of the outside world.

How are we going to find the time to live a Web lifestyle and join more communities? The Web will make a lot of things more efficient than they used to be. You can quickly find out how much your used car is worth, plan a trip, or find out anything you need to know when you want to make a major purchase. These activities are easy on the Web today. And people will probably trade some of the time they now spend reading the paper or watching TV for the information or entertainment they'll find on the Web. A British study in 1998 showed that about 25 percent of the British adults who used the Internet watched less television than they did before.

MOVING PAST OLD LIMITS

Much of this book is about having all the information we want at our fingertips. Most people want to find the best price for a product or to be up-to-date on the important issues affecting their local or national communities. We have gotten by without this information because obtaining it has simply been too difficult. Without realizing it, we've been making do. The Web lifestyle isn't about changing human nature or the fundamentals of how people live. Instead the Web lifestyle gives more people a chance to pursue their interests in a better way.

For the consumer, the Web lifestyle will have a positive impact. With the Web as the world's biggest collection of shopping malls, consumers will have choices they didn't have before. They'll be able to find all the choices for goods they want and in many cases have them custom-made. They can have the final product delivered directly to their doors. The Web produces a true consumer-centric world. Because consumers are demanding faster service, stronger relationships, and personalization, the Web lifestyle will drive companies to develop a digital nervous system in order to keep pace with their markets.

The Web connects colleagues, friends, and families in new ways. Interest-based communities are forming with members from all over the world, and government has the potential to engage constituents more than ever before. By enabling people to shop, get news, meet each other, be entertained, and gossip in ways we're only now beginning to understand, the Internet is becoming the town square for the global village of tomorrow.

With a Web lifestyle, people can throw off many of the limitations that have been around for so long that we almost take them for granted. The Web lifestyle is not about adding complexity to already busy lives. As people embrace the Web lifestyle, they'll eventually take it for granted, just as they do the "electricity" lifestyle they live today.

Business Lessons

- ❑ As PCs continue to drop in price and more households are connected, the Web lifestyle will move most consumer transactions online.
- ❑ The Web lifestyle changes the way businesses relate to customers and governments relate to citizens. Ultimately the Web lifestyle puts the consumer-citizen in charge of the relationship.
- ❑ The PC-TV convergence will create a new user experience and a new programming and advertising medium.

Diagnosing Your Digital Nervous System

- ❑ Have you started interacting with your customers over the Internet?
- ❑ Have you considered what digital systems and tools you'll need when a majority of your customers prefer to conduct their business via the Web instead of via traditional methods?

8

CHANGE THE BOUNDARIES OF BUSINESS

Connectivity enables you to seize more independence while independence motivates you to get ever more connected.

—Stan Davis and Christopher Meyer,
BLUR: The Speed of Change in the Connected Economy

A flow of digital information changes the way people and organizations work and the way commerce is conducted across organizational boundaries. Internet technologies also will change the boundaries of organizations of all sizes. In changing the boundaries, the "Web workstyle" of using digital tools and processes enables both organizations and individuals to redefine their roles.

A corporation can use the Internet to work seamlessly with professionals such as lawyers and accountants who remain "outside" the corporate walls as consultants rather than as company employees. An important reengineering principle is that companies should focus on their core competencies and outsource everything else. The Internet allows a company to focus far more than in the past by changing which employees work within the walls and which work outside in an adjunct, consulting, or partnering role. Our core competencies at Microsoft are creating high-volume software products, working with other software companies, and providing customer service and support. We outsource a number of functions that don't fall into those categories, from help-desk technical support for our employees to the physical production of our software packages.

The Web workstyle makes it possible to deal better with unpredictable demand. Because you have an intense need for a skill, and then you don't, for some areas you want flexible staffing to deal with peaks and valleys. The Internet means that more companies can take a "studio" approach to running major parts of their businesses. Big Hollywood studios have full-time employees to handle finance, marketing and distribution, and other ongoing projects, but the creative side of the business, the full-time moviemaking staff, isn't very big at all. When a movie concept is agreed upon, a director assembles a large group of people to create the film. When they're done, they disband. Everyone, from the director to the actors to the cinematographer to the key grip, goes on to other projects.

Web technology makes it possible for many different kinds of projects to be structured as studio-type work. A project owner who wants to assemble a team can go online, describe the project, and find out who's available. People and organizations with the right skills can declare their interest, and the project owner can assemble a team quickly. People looking for work will find more opportunities for employment that meets their particular interests and requirements—if they have highly specialized skills, for example, or if they want to work only certain hours. The Web can mediate the gathering of resources for a project a lot more efficiently than the "my people will call your people" approach can.

Despite the emergence of new, flexible boundaries, big companies won't deconstruct themselves into per-project production companies. Companies need to excel in consistent in-house execution of their core competencies. Big firms will continue to load-balance that work as they always have—they'll just use technology to do it more efficiently. Every company will experiment to find its optimal size and organizational structure, though the dominant trend will be toward decreased overall size.

For Microsoft, outsourcing has been a way to temper the expansion of our workforce and reduce our management overhead, but it hasn't stopped the growth of our workforce. The Web workstyle, in which each contributor or company organizes itself optimally, enables us to extend our electronic web of partnerships and—I hope—keeps us from growing big in the wrong areas and becoming ineffective through too much overhead.

Medium-size and small companies can take advantage of the boundary-changing capabilities of the Web to act much bigger than they are without adding employees or offices. A small company with the right expertise can bid on and spearhead a movie production, a construction project, or an advertising campaign. By assembling other companies and professionals quickly, it can act as a virtual large company to see the project to its profitable end. Because the team can be disbanded at the end of a project, the company can manage labor resources without the administrative overhead of a large full-time staff. Smaller companies can use the Web to scale without permanent mass.

CHANGING THE WORKSTYLE FOR EMPLOYEES

Some employees in companies of any size are understandably nervous about the implications of the Web workstyle. They assume that if their company chooses to restructure itself around Web technologies, their jobs may disappear. Not so—unless "restructuring" is just a fancy term to mask layoffs. When a company downsizes, jobs are lost. When a company outsources, jobs move. The goal is not to eliminate work, but to move the responsibility to specialists outside. It's far more efficient for many companies, including Microsoft, to have an outside company handle installation and support for desktop machines, for example, because companies that specialize in such work can develop worldwide best practices and because we can solicit competitive bids for the job.

Employees who react to the prospect of outsourcing with fear are assuming that work belongs "in" the company and not "out." As companies redefine themselves, some people will be dislocated. Despite the understandable anxiety, employees should also look at boundary changes as opportunities to define their jobs the way they want them and to work for an organization of the size and personality they prefer. Or they can even use this sea change as a chance to start their own business. Not too long ago, one person who had been a freelance writer watched Microsoft outsource more and more writing assignments and recognized an opportunity. Today this person has a tidy business managing a dozen or so freelance writers, and Microsoft staff now spend their time specifying the work to be done instead of trying to manage the writing process for a bunch of different people. By and large the changes in organizational structure will empower good employees.

The Web workstyle is particularly well suited to lawyers, accountants, engineers, and doctors, who usually work independently or in small teams. One of the reasons professionals have traditionally organized themselves into firms is to deal with fluctuations in customer demand. Now, instead of clustering to make sure that the workload gets distributed, they'll also have the choice of being solo professionals and using the Internet to find customers. Laws or customs will hold back the rate of this change. Doctors and lawyers in most countries are limited in how they can solicit business. But even if they can't go directly to patients or clients, these solo practitioners can act as free agents to solicit work from established firms.

With the Web, becoming a free agent is no longer limited to athletes, artists, actors, and other big-name professional or creative types. It's now available to almost every kind of knowledge worker. Already the "free agent" labor pool, including self-employed workers, independent contractors, and workers at temporary agencies, totals about 25 million Americans. One benefit of self-employment is diversification—you're less likely to be out of work if you have several employers than if you have one.

Not everyone will choose the freelance approach. A lot of people want to work for bigger firms. They like the idea of belonging to one company, working on long-term projects, and having continuity in people and in the culture of a particular workplace. They invest in their career, and the company invests in them. A lot of the most interesting jobs, such as software design at my company, are core areas that won't be outsourced. Most companies, including Microsoft, work hard to make it attractive for good employees to stay long-term. A lot of developers and researchers joined Microsoft because they saw the chance to design software or develop technologies that will be used by millions of people. Like many artists, they want their work to reach the largest possible audience.

The Web Workstyle Eases Geographic Constraints

Before the Web, most workers were confined by geography. If you wanted to live in Greenwood, Arkansas, or Aiken, South Carolina, you couldn't easily work full-time or part-time for the best company in your field of expertise. If you wanted to work for a big firm, you were unlikely to live real close to the best fly-fishing country.

Web communication is changing the requirement that you have to live close to work. Within a few years telecommuting will not only become more common, but its essence will change. Today, most telecommuters do tasks that do not require a physical presence at the office—writing or analysis, for instance. E-mail and phone provide some interaction with colleagues or customers, but most of the remote work is solitary. In the future, videoconferencing, electronic collaboration on documents, and the integration of the phone and PC will create a telepresence at the office that is impossible today for home workers.

These technologies are already removing geography as a barrier to work. Several software companies in India are doing customer support for American companies. Taking advantage of the time zone differential, they work on problems while the United States is asleep and have solutions ready for customers first thing the next morning U.S. time. Not too long ago two Danish computer science students working at Microsoft's Redmond, Washington, campus became the first people in history to take and pass transatlantic oral exams over the Internet to complete their bachelor's degrees. By using a PC to eliminate the need to be physically present with their exam professor in Denmark, the students could stay in the United States longer and obtain more work-related training.

NetMeeting, the PC communication technology used by the students, has broad applicability for telecommuting. Pythia, a small software company in Indiana that makes software for legislative bodies, uses NetMeeting as part of its software development. Pythia has most of its customers and its software support engineers in the United States, but its chief developers live in Greece. The developers and U.S. employees use Internet telephony to discuss product requirements. Each side can take control of the PC screen to use it as a whiteboard on which to draw flow charts and even write code.

The Web will increasingly equalize opportunities for skilled people around the world. If you had to guess someone's income today and were limited to a single polite question, a good one would be "What country do you live in?" The reason is the huge disparity in average wages from country to country. In twenty years, if you want to guess someone's salary, the most telling question will be "What's your education?"

People who want to work for a big company will, and people who don't want to will have interesting alternatives. A Web workstyle also makes it easier for people who have good skill sets but who can't or choose not to work full-time. Because they can find more work over the Internet and do more work remotely, such people will have new opportunities, and society will benefit by better utilizing this huge pool of talent. Many knowledge workers will live where they want to live and structure their work the way they want it and still make major contributions to the businesses they work for or with. In the Web workstyle, employees can push the freedom the Web provides to its limits. When it comes to workstyle, the choice will be the worker's.

As a business manager, you need to take a hard look at your core competencies. Revisit the areas of your company that aren't directly involved in those competencies, and consider whether Web technologies can enable you to spin off those tasks. Let another company take over the management responsibilities for that work and use modern communications technology to work closely with the people—now partners instead of employees—doing the work. Also consider the employees who have strong expertise but decide they don't want to work full-time. Better communication tools may allow you to utilize their skills on an ongoing basis. The competition to hire the best people will increase in the years ahead. Companies that give extra flexibility to their employees will have the edge in this key area.

Business Lessons

- ❑ The Web redefines the boundaries between organizations and between people and organizations; it allows a company to structure itself to be more efficient.
- ❑ The Web workstyle makes it possible for employees to telecommute and to collaborate with employees and partners at other locations.
- ❑ The Web enables big companies to appear to be smaller and more flexible and smaller companies to become effectively much bigger than they are.

Diagnosing Your Digital Nervous System

- ❑ Do your digital systems allow you to work seamlessly with professionals such as lawyers and accountants who are "outside" the corporate walls?
- ❑ Do your digital systems help you focus on your core competencies and outsource everything else?
- ❑ Do your digital systems help you load-balance work more efficiently?

9

GET TO MARKET FIRST

You either move with speed or die. It's the converse of "speed kills."

—Richard McGinn, Chairman and CEO of Lucent Technologies

Customers want high-quality products at low prices, and they want them now. Every business, whether it's a producer of products and services or a supplier to that producer, has to deal with a shrinking time to market while keeping quality high and price low. Information technology has become a major contributor to the faster turnaround, the higher quality, and the low inflation that have characterized business in the last decade.

Few industries illustrate the twin pressures of collapsing time and improving quality better than the automobile industry. Japanese auto designs in the 1980s appeared fresher and their quality improvements more frequent than in American cars because Japanese automakers could take a car from concept to mass production in three years. American automakers typically took four to six years, and their costs were higher.

American companies responded by breaking down the organizational barriers that had cut off design, manufacturing, and sales divisions from one another and by improving communications with their external partners. Designers, engineers, suppliers, and manufacturing and assembly personnel began to work in tight teams that communicated electronically, cutting the time from product design to sales room floor by more than half. Other process improvements in the auto industry have been significantly augmented by technology, including the computer-aided design (CAD) of cars. The 3-D modeling capabilities of CAD applications enable engineers to design a vehicle without having to build a prototype by hand. The designers can see whether parts will fit together and can change part designs without building special tooling. The use of digital information flow to improve the efficiency in the supply system is covered in chapter 12, but it's worth noting that electronic links between car manufacturers and suppliers have already reduced the error rate in parts deliveries by 72 percent and saved up to eight hours per week per car in labor costs.

Consumers have benefited from better vehicles, produced more quickly. Ford's strides in production are representative of the entire auto industry. In 1990 the company took five-plus years to take a car from concept to customer, and it experienced 150 defects for every 100 cars, or 1.5 defects per car. By 1998 Ford had cut its cycle time by more than half, to less than twenty-four months. Its defect rate had gone down from 150 to 81 defects per 100 cars. Toyota Motor Sales, which had gotten a head start on the use of information systems, improved a comparable percentage in defects for the same period and remained the overall leader in quality, while the defect rate for the auto industry as a whole dropped to less than 1 percent.[1]

KEEPING PACE IN THE FACE OF RISING COMPLEXITY

In some industries the issue is not so much faster time to market as it is maintaining time to market in the face of astronomically rising complexity. Intel, for instance, has consistently had a ninety-day production cycle for its chips, which power most PCs. Intel expects to maintain this ninety-day production rate despite the increasing complexity of the microprocessor. The number of transistors in the chip has increased from 29,000 in the 8086 in 1978 to 7.5 million in the Pentium in 1998, and the microprocessor's *capability* has grown ten thousand–fold over the same twenty years. By 2011 Intel expects to deliver chips that have one billion transistors. This exponential improvement stems from Moore's law, which says that the power of microchips doubles every eighteen to twenty-four months. To put Moore's law in perspective, if products such as cars and cereal followed the same trend as the PC, a mid-size car would cost $27 and a box of cereal would cost a penny.

Intel uses a variety of management, production, and digital techniques to maintain efficiency while cramming more and more transistors onto a chip the size of a thumbnail. In the 1970s Intel's lab technicians wore smocks and used tweezers to move the silicon wafers from one process step to the next. Today Intel's technicians work in an environment a hundred times cleaner than the best medical operating theater. They wear the "bunny suits" you might

1. Sources for this section include *The Emerging Digital Economy*, U.S. Department of Commerce, April 1998, also at www.ecommerce.gov/danc3.htm, and the J. D. Power and Associates Initial Quality Studies 1987–1997.

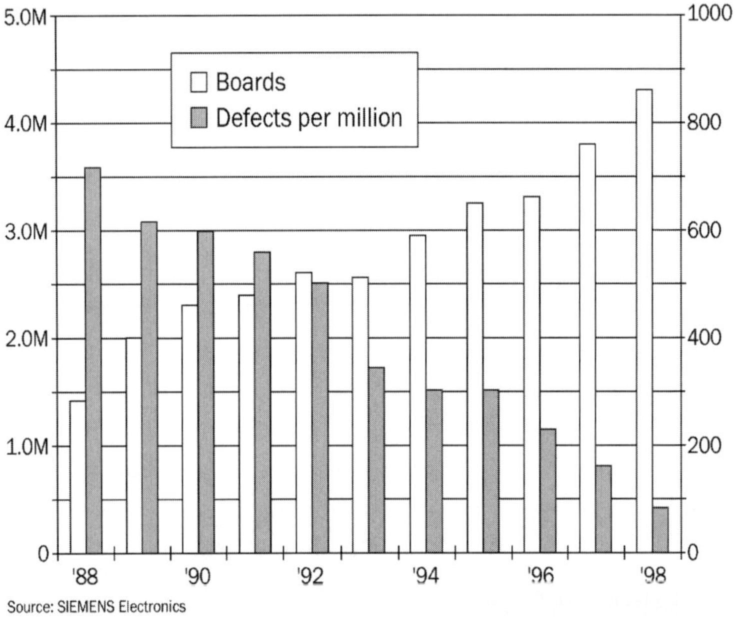

Siemens AG of Germany uses digital design tools and preproduction simulation tools to help reduce time to market and increase quality in the production of programmable logic controllers, or PLCs, the tiny devices that operate many industrial machines. Continuous feedback of production results into the design tools leads to constant improvement. In the decade between 1987–88 and 1997–98, Siemens cut its time to manufacture by a factor of more than 2.5 while reducing defects by a factor of 10. The use of digital tools to reduce time to market and increase quality will impact every industry.

have seen in Intel's TV ads. The real suits are white. They turn bright metallic colors only, Intel says, when put close to a marketing person. Now robots move large numbers of wafers between the processing steps.

Each generation of chips requires new high-volume factories that cost more than a billion dollars each. In 1998 Intel introduced an innovative "copy exactly" strategy to maintain a uniform level of efficiency and quality across its chip factories. To avoid the introduction of hundreds of varying trial-and-error processes as a new chip moves from development to different manufacturing plants, Intel involves the managers of the manufacturing facilities early on at the development plant, making sure that the production process is fine-tuned there for reliability and high volumes.

The perfected process is copied exactly to all of the plants, enabling Intel to bring new factories online quickly with high-volume best practices already in place.

To reduce the trial-and-error processes in its design work, Intel's Albert Yu, senior vice president of the microprocessor products group, also launched a program called Development 2000, or D2000, to ensure that every design engineer got the benefit of best practices from across the organization. By studying its design processes for the Pentium and Pentium Pro chips, Intel discovered that more than 60 percent of the problems that designers faced had already been solved by another team. It's very likely that any large-scale design or manufacturing company with manual processes in place would find a similar amount of overlapping or repeated work.

To ensure that designers began to build on previous work instead of starting over each time, Yu's organization created a database of best-known methods for addressing technical problems and used a browser interface to ensure access from its half dozen different design sites. Intel also developed software tools to help verify the correctness of a circuit design up front and to track manufacturing defects and identify problems in the manufacturing process. Together, the software tools involved in the D2000 program have helped Intel to almost double the speed at which it has ramped up new product production since 1994. Intel is well on its way to meeting the D2000 goal of achieving volume production from the first design of a chip, rather than having to go through several iterations of a design to perfect it.

Technology-driven shortening of time to market affects more than just manufacturing or high-tech industries. In book publishing, information tools have cut the cycle time from manuscript to publication in half, from eighteen months to nine months.

MAKING "FIRST" A CORPORATE MANTRA

Although banks have always been big users of information technology, as regulated businesses they have not had a reputation for innovation or for rapid time to market with new programs or services. Banco Bradesco, with twenty million customers the largest bank in Brazil, is a notable exception. Almost since its inception, this banking company has made "time to market" practically a mantra.

With nearly 2,200 branches, Banco Bradesco has $68.7 billion in assets and serves three million people per day. Banco Bradesco was the first private Brazilian company to use computers, in 1962, and it was the first bank to offer automated teller machines and home banking, in 1982. The history of inflation in Brazil forced banks there to keep account information up-to-date all the time. Even today banks in the United States and most other countries do not keep account information as current as Brazil banks do. Bradesco is sometimes called "the bank to beat in Brazil" because it uses technology to develop innovative solutions for customers faster than its competitors. Bradesco provides its customers not just traditional banking services, but any services related to finance—all in the name of keeping the loyalty of its customers.

To stay ahead of the competition, even six months is too long to bring a new idea to the market, so Bradesco focuses on short development cycles—weeks and months, no longer. The bank also wants to take a new product or service to its entire customer base at the same time, so it plans rollout logistics carefully.

For one small-business customer, Bradesco developed a cash-management software application to assist with payables and receivables. Now about 4,100 businesses are using the application. For another customer, Bradesco developed a salary card that enabled employees to be paid directly from Bradesco ATM machines without being required to have a bank account. The card is now in use at about 1,300 companies, quickly expanding to 2,000 companies and one million employees.

In each case, Bradesco was the first bank to offer such a service.

In 1996 Banco Bradesco became the first Brazilian financial institution—and only the fifth in the world—to use the Internet to offer banking services. In the summer of 1998 it became the first bank in the world to provide online banking for people with visual disabilities. A speech synthesizer reads aloud the content of the Web page to the user. By 1998, 350,000 of its 440,000 online customers were banking over the Internet instead of over the original proprietary dial-up service, and the number of Internet customers was growing at 12 percent per month. Online banking has caught on in Brazil faster than in any other country. Access to a full range of financial services is offered through the bank's Web site, BradescoNet.

In addition to the usual banking services, Bradesco also offers ten investment vehicles including mutual funds via the Internet, and it's joining many of its partners to develop Web stores accessible through BradescoNet or through a partner's own site. Each partner company—twenty and growing as of late 1998—provides a catalog of products, and the bank does everything else. Customers select the products they want to buy as they would at any online store. The difference is that payment is made through an immediate funds transfer from the customer's bank account to the partner's bank account. Because of this direct connection with the customer's bank account, the shopper doesn't have to provide a credit card number online. BradescoNet enables consumers to buy anything from chocolates to cell phones, pay their phone and utility bills, and even pay government taxes such as motor vehicle fees.

An example of Bradesco's desire to be first to market was its entry into Internet banking when most people saw the Internet as "an amusement park." While other banks were worried that the Internet would displace them, Bradesco plowed ahead. "We often hear complaints from companies, especially in the financial services industry, that technology empowers nonfinancial vendors to bypass them and offer direct services to their customers," says CIO Alcino Rodrigues de Assunção. "We don't buy that. At Banco Bradesco, we have taken a proactive stand. Technology threatens us if we sit back and let someone else use it. It helps us if we use it to move quickly to design services where the bank becomes the value-added intermediary to our customers."

By being the first major commercial Internet site in Brazil, BradescoNet has the opportunity to become a portal site—the primary way Brazilian consumers will access the Internet. What better way to keep customer loyalty?

Yet the bank recognizes that it needs to use its digital nervous system even better in the future. Today Bradesco collects a lot of information about customers independently through its separate services such as savings, credit cards, loans, insurance, and so on. The bank's goal is to collect information across all of these transaction types to create a complete profile of the bank customer. By targeting its customers demographically, the bank can offer more focused services or cross-sell the new services its technology enables it to develop so quickly. By identifying automobile insurance payments, for example, the bank could also offer automobile loans to customers who've financed their vehicle elsewhere. For customers with great payment records across a range of transactions, the bank might do special promotions whenever they have any new offerings such as low-interest mortgage loans.

This historical customer data is one of the bank's most valuable assets. Every financial transaction is already stored. It's up to the bank to devise the systems to best utilize that data as knowledge. The bank, which originally built its infrastructure around vertical applications, plans to take a horizontal view across departmental boundaries in order to better understand its customers as overall users of all bank services. It will take Bradesco several years to pull together all of this customer information, but then the bank will be able to rapidly devise and deliver still more customized services.

CONQUERING CYCLE TIME

Probably nowhere has the product cycle shrunk more than in the PC industry, and the changes caused by a shrinking time to market are an indication of how other industries will also be affected. In this situation a better flow of digital information does not simply make things better but, rather, is a requirement for success.

In just a few years the product cycle for Compaq Computer dropped from eighteen months to twelve months. By late 1998 it dropped to six to nine months for business products and to four months for consumer products. But with its older information systems, Compaq required forty-five days to roll up its worldwide sales information into a single set of numbers that it could use to complete its product planning. By the time it could communicate its manufacturing needs to suppliers, the company would be halfway through the four-month life cycle for important products. In an industry in which cycle time is king, the company had to have dynamic planning to remain competitive.

Compaq implemented an enterprise resource planning (ERP) system, using SAP software as the base. In manufacturing, a good ERP system tracks the way the enterprise is operating each day and gives business managers the ability to control the way the manufacturing system responds. ERP at Compaq enhances its ability to accurately schedule production, fully utilize capacity, reduce inventory, and meet shipping dates.

Compaq started the ERP projects several years ago when it had different financial and planning systems in geographies and factories around the world. Compaq now has all of its factories on SAP, including the factory that came with the acquisition of Tandem, and thirty-nine of Compaq's forty-six sales subsidiaries worldwide. In parallel, Compaq has implemented a planning system for production that consolidates supply, demand, and manufacturing capacity into one data warehouse sourced primarily from SAP.

This consolidation gives Compaq worldwide consistency of all data needed to plan sales and manufacturing. As Compaq has consolidated systems, it has shrunk its forty-five-day planning cycle to a weekly planning cycle. Generally a week's worth of sales information is necessary to get a real snapshot of the market for long-range sales planning. Compaq continues, though, to drive down its manufacturing cycle. It is now approaching daily "pull" capability to schedule materials from suppliers. Soon it will drop to a shift-oriented (eight-hour) pull schedule and ultimately to a four-hour pull schedule.

While shortening its regular planning cycle, Compaq is also implementing real-time systems to enable it to react to unplanned changes in demand. Using the same data sources, the company wants to take a separate snapshot three times a night, eight hours apart—at midnight, respectively, for the United States, Europe, and Asia—of information about its supply capability and committed order position. With real-time data instead of week-old or day-old data, Compaq wants to be able to see and react to, say, an unplanned order for 7,000 desktops, and work with suppliers to determine instantly whether the company can get all the critical parts and deliver on the order.

To develop this kind of corporate reflex, Compaq is moving its existing Electronic Data Interchange (EDI) systems to the Internet using Internet protocols and standards. Where the complexity of the EDI system limits response to a weekly interval, an Internet-based e-commerce solution offers the company the ability to develop an event-based, real-time response with partners. When an order comes in, the supplier can see the new demand on the extranet at the same time as the Compaq planner.

John White, who was CIO at Compaq for more than four years through 1998, likens Compaq's installation of its ERP system to changing out the wings and engines of a jet in flight. You have to keep the enterprise running even as you install the new systems. While Compaq was making the transition, the company's revenues grew from $7 billion to $35 billion and it absorbed Digital Equipment Corporation, which had just begun its own conversion to SAP with a slightly different approach.

White recommends that a manufacturing company put in the entire ERP package in one area, which could be by sales geography or sales subsidiary or by factory. Put in the complete portfolio once rather than disrupt an organization repeatedly to install purchasing, financing, manufacturing, and planning one by one.

A company can take one of two approaches to ERP.

One, buying all the software modules from one vendor, gives you the benefits of integration. The other approach is to buy each module from the vendor with the best product, the "best of breed" tack. In the current wave of adoptions, the ease of integration has led a lot of manufacturing companies to go with a single vendor for ERP. As more standards evolve to represent business information in a formal way, the use of different packages will become more feasible.

Another consideration is how much customization you do to the ERP system. Some packages let you customize in such a way that, as their new updates come along, your customized work will still function. In other cases you'll be constantly reworking your code to adapt to their new version. It's part of the revolution in component software, discussed in the appendix, to make it easier to separate and maintain your customized modules without having to spend a lot every time a new version of the ERP system comes out.

Both these areas—an easy exchange of data between packages and the preservation of customizations across versions—represent state-of-the-art work between applications vendors and Microsoft. Together we're pushing forward standards in each industry to ensure that companies can make the most of their large ERP and related investments.

INCREASING POWER AND DECREASING TIME

Greater computing power is a requirement to meet Compaq's goals of real-time execution. On the old minicomputer systems it took eight to ten hours to run a planning cycle. Using its own high-end PC systems, Compaq has gotten the time down to twenty-five minutes. But to obtain instant response to unexpected customer demands, Compaq requires memory-resident real-time databases. New 64-bit PC server software provides this capability, enabling Compaq to represent in memory the largest possible business problem it could calculate through any combination of 8,000 part numbers, 46 sales geographies, 6 major manufacturing facilities, and 12 distribution centers.

These new capabilities are good examples of how technology and business are intertwined and how technology enables new processes. Without powerful processors and digital information flow, it would simply not be possible for Compaq to shorten its business cycles. If it takes eight to ten hours to crank the numbers, and you can't update or access the database during that time, how can your information systems be as responsive as you need in an era of just-in-time delivery?

Publish-and-subscribe technology is another critical component for Compaq's future. It's the bridge between ERP and the planning systems. Publish-and-subscribe enables the company to extract data in a way that is reliable and near real time. As soon as changes are confirmed to the order or inventory position, the data system publishes the changes to a network server, which then pushes the information automatically to the PCs of the businesspeople who have signed up for notification. The technology gives Compaq the ability to replicate information to the people who need it while avoiding big loads on the central database.

Going further, publish-and-subscribe technology can generate events on the workstations of everybody involved in a business area, including suppliers on the extranet. The Compaq buyer and supplier won't have to constantly monitor the extranet site to keep an eye open for any changes.

If that order for 7,000 computers comes in, both buyer and supplier will get a real-time alert on their PCs.

SHRINKING TIME TO MARKET EVEN FURTHER

Digital processes make it possible for every business to dramatically shorten its time to market, although some amount of time and energy will always be required to deliver physical goods. MIT's Nicholas Negroponte describes the difference between physical products and information products in the digital age as the difference between moving atoms around (physical products such as cars and computers) and moving bits around (electronic products such as financial analyses and news broadcasts). Producers of bits can use the Internet to reduce their delivery times to practically zero. Producers of atoms still can't beam the physical objects through space, but they can use bit-speed—digital coordination of all kinds—to bring reaction time down dramatically. Almost all the time involved in producing an item is in the coordination of the work, not in the actual production. The British government did a study and found out that it required almost a year to take aluminum ore from the ground and deliver it as a can on the grocery shelf—almost all of that time spent waiting between steps in paper-based processes.

Good information systems can remove most of that waiting time. And makers of physical products will find that online service—another bit-oriented as opposed to atom-oriented effort—will become as much a part of the "product" and customer experience as the physical goods they deliver. The speed of delivery and the interaction with the customer made possible by the Internet effectively shifts products into services. Product companies today need to compare themselves not with the best of their competitors, but with the best of all service companies. Product companies need to ensure that their corporate cultures and their infrastructures support fast research, analysis, collaboration, and execution, and they need to treat their Web sites not as nifty add-ons, but as integral parts of product development and refinement.

Ultimately the most important "speed" issue for companies is cultural. It's changing the perceptions within a company about the rapidity with which everybody has to move. Everybody must realize that if you don't meet customer demand quickly enough, without sacrificing quality, a competitor will. Once the mind-set adapts to the need for action, digital technology enables fast reflexes.

Business Lessons

- ❑ Time to market is shrinking for every business, whether it sells physical or information products. Using digital information to be first to market can radically improve your competitive position.
- ❑ The most important "speed" issue is often not technical but cultural. It's convincing everyone that the company's survival depends on everyone moving as fast as possible.
- ❑ Moving to an enterprise resource planning package will help you instill the rigor and standardization you need in your financial data.

Diagnosing Your Digital Nervous System

- ❑ Do you use digital data flow to achieve faster turnaround, higher quality, and lower prices?
- ❑ Do you have electronic links among manufacturers, suppliers, sales, and other functions so that planning cycles are compressed?
- ❑ Do you have digital systems that enable you to react to production changes within the same eight-hour work shift?

III

MANAGE KNOWLEDGE TO IMPROVE STRATEGIC THOUGHT

10

BAD NEWS MUST TRAVEL FAST

The high-performance corporations are different. They worry about failure a lot. It makes them pay close attention to what is going on in their market.

—Guillermo G. Marmol, McKinsey & Company

I have a natural instinct for hunting down grim news. If it's out there, I want to know about it. The people who work for me have figured this out. Sometimes I get an e-mail that begins, "In keeping with the dictum that bad news should travel faster than good news, here's a gem."

A lot goes wrong in any organization, even a good one. A product flops. You're surprised by a customer's sudden defection to another vendor. A competitor comes out with a product that appeals to a broad new market. Losing market share is the kind of bad news that every organization can relate to.

Other bad news may have to do with what's going on internally. Maybe a product is going to be late, or it's not going to do what you expected it to do, or you haven't been able to hire enough of the right kinds of people to deliver on your plans.

An essential quality of a good manager is a determination to deal with any kind of bad news head on, to seek it out rather than deny it. An effective manager wants to hear about what's going wrong before he or she hears about what's going right. You can't react appropriately to disappointing news in any situation if it doesn't reach you soon enough.

You focus on bad news in order to get cracking on the solution. As soon as you're aware of a problem, everybody in your organization has to be galvanized into action. You can evaluate a company by how quickly it engages all of its available intellect to deal with a serious problem. An important measure of a company's digital nervous system is how quickly people in the company find out about bad news and respond to it. Digital technology speeds corporate reflexes in any emergency.

In the old days, an organization's response to bad news was necessarily slow. Business leaders often learned about problems only after they became serious, since the only quick way to pass information was to interrupt them with a phone call. Before handling a problem, people had to dig up information in paper files or go down the hall to find somebody who knew something about the situation. Once the information was in hand, however late and incomplete, people conferred over the phone or faxed data to each other. Every step in the process was very time-consuming. There was no way to gather scattered anecdotal information to get a complete picture.

Even with a combination of telephone and fax, it's hard to recognize a pattern of bad developments before it shows up in sales results. Even with mainframe computers storing customer data in a centralized location, extracting information in a timely way is so hard that the stored data is seldom of much help in a crisis. Though the dawn of the Information Age means we can send information fast, most companies don't gather the key information about customer issues in one place. By contrast, a well-designed digital nervous system operates as an early warning system.

CONQUERING THE WORLD AND GOING OUT OF BUSINESS

The Internet was not always the top priority in Microsoft's strategy. Its arrival changed our business and became the biggest unplanned event we've ever had to respond to. In fact, in 1995 various experts predicted that the Internet would put Microsoft out of business. This was bad news on a colossal scale. We used our digital nervous system to respond to that crisis.

On August 24, 1995, we introduced Windows 95, the most ambitious software product to reach out to the general consumer, with the biggest fanfare in computer history. The print news coverage was immense—hundreds of articles in the months leading up to the launch. We were described as invincible as we pulled away from our competitors on the desktop. *Windows* magazine said, "This year—for better or worse—Microsoft wins the war." A *Time* magazine editorial said that Microsoft was "the gravitational center of the computer universe."[1] The introduction of Windows 95 itself made major TV newscasts.

Within a couple of months, though, the press coverage cascaded in the other direction. The Internet had burst into

1. Mike Elgan, "The Day That Windows 95 Ships Is Sure to Be V-Day for Microsoft," *Windows* 6, no. 1 (January 1995): 61; Elizabeth Valk Long, "To Our Readers," *Time* 45, no. 23 (June 5, 1995): 44.

Suspend Disbelief, but Not Forever

Several years ago Microsoft was one of a handful of companies investing heavily in interactive television in the expectation that the market would develop quickly. We were working with Tele-Communications Inc. (TCI) and Southwestern Bell and in late 1995 had a pilot project in Tokyo with Nippon Telephone and Telegraph.

As we proceeded, there was a slow realization that the costs were higher and the customer benefits lower than we all had assumed they would be. Interactive television wasn't going to come together as soon as we expected or in the way we expected. But why did it take so long for all of us to figure this out?

The simple answer is that human nature made us reluctant to evaluate the bad news. The world was taking too long to move from analog to digital television, costs had not come down enough, and there weren't enough new applications to keep network providers enthusiastic about building out the infrastructure. Yet we didn't acknowledge these obstacles or didn't want to admit they were there.

You have to be able to make risky assumptions to undertake a new venture. To a certain extent, you have to suspend your disbelief and say, "Hey, we're going to go for this new business. Let's do our best." But every once in a while you also need to reassess the key assumptions to decide whether there will be a timely market for your new product or service. It's a thankless job. Would you want to be the one to call the meeting to say that the whole thing's too far off to be worth investing in?

In retrospect, there were serious doubts among the members of our interactive TV group about our progress and direction. Among other indicators, the number of people who transferred out of the group makes it clear that at least a few people knew we were off track.

Ultimately Craig Mundie, the division's senior vice president, called the "bad news" meeting. We decided to move some technology associated with the interactive TV project, such as cryptography and multimedia software, into products we could ship to the business market. Craig kept responsibility for small form factors and our Windows CE product. We retained a small core group to continue to work on our consumer TV efforts—basically, to dig in and wait for digital TV to arrive, which happened two years later.

To get into a new business, you have to believe—at least for a while. But you also have to be alert to bad news, and you have to be agile enough to adapt if the opportunity morphs into something new.

the public's awareness, and the perception was that Microsoft hadn't been invited to the new party. Now stories in the press said that we "didn't get it." The Internet signified our doom. Small, nimble competitors would put Microsoft out of business. Rick Sherlund, an analyst with Goldman Sachs & Company and a longtime Microsoft specialist, generated headlines when in mid-November he downgraded our stock because we didn't have "a compelling Internet strategy." Paul Saffo, a researcher at the Institute for the Future, a think tank in Menlo Park, California, summed up the views of many observers when he said, "The tide has turned against everything Microsoft has built."[2] By late fall the Internet phenomenon had eclipsed Windows 95 as the industry's story of the year.

On December 7, 1995, we held our first Internet Strategy Day, where for the first time we publicly previewed the array of technologies we were developing to integrate Internet support into our core products. Within a year of those announcements we had "Internet-enabled" our major products and delivered a number of new ones focused on the Internet. Now we lead in several major Internet areas and have a growing number of people using our browser. No one company will dominate the Internet, but Microsoft has come back to play an important role.

How, our customers and the press often ask me, did we turn the ship around so fast?

First of all, we were never as oblivious to the Internet as we might have seemed to outside observers. It wasn't as if somebody said "Internet" and we didn't know how to spell it. We had several Internet technologies on our list of things to do. Back in 1991 we'd hired J. Allard, a specialist

2. Dow Jones News Service report, November 16, 1995. Carried in a number of newspapers.

in internetworking, to ensure that we developed the right technologies for interoperability. Microsoft was a founding or early member of several Internet associations. By mid-1993 we'd built support for the basic Internet networking protocol into our Windows NT product, both server and desktop. By then we were also well under way with developing our approach to an online service, which became MSN.

We had an Internet site set up in a hallway of Building 2 to test our Internet connectivity. As a draw, so that we could test the compatibility of our Internet technologies with a range of outside systems, we made a minor upgrade to MS-DOS available on the site. J. Allard would drag everyone, from a new product manager to Paul Maritz, our group vice president of platforms, to Building 2 to show off the activity and fire up people about the Internet's potential. In a ten-week period customers downloaded twice as many copies of the MS-DOS upgrade from this site as from CompuServe, a level of activity that told us something big was brewing.

But let's also be clear. In 1993 we were not *focused* on the Internet. It was a fifth or sixth priority. Our new Microsoft Internet site consisted of three machines on an eight-foot folding table in J. Allard's hallway with handwritten instructions on how to connect to the Internet. The yellow network cable for the Internet tap, which J. had wheedled from our corporate IT group, ran out of his office over his wall to the machine in the hall. Four power strips bridged the outlet from another person's office to power all the equipment on the table. Duct tape held all these cords in place. It wasn't long before a fire marshal showed up, intent on shutting down Microsoft's site as a fire hazard. A week's reprieve enabled J. to transfer the machines to our corporate IT facility, where we began to transform our fledgling Internet support into a full-blown corporate program.

The Original Internet PC

The idea of an information empowerment tool is not a new one. It goes back to Dr. Vannevar Bush's "memex machine" described in 1945. Bush, director of the U.S. Office of Scientific Research and Development during World War II, predicted the development of a device in which you could store all your books, records, and communications and call up the data on a screen. This memex could hold hundreds of years of material, including longhand notes, annotations, and photographs. "Associative indexing" would create and maintain links between items to make "momentarily important" information easier to find and correlate from the maze of data.

Bush's memex, a big physical desk and microfilm storage operated by physical levers, now conjures up an image of the Wizard of Oz manipulating a clumsy contraption behind the curtain. But his analysis of the problem—that our way of handling information was inadequate—and his solution—a device that stored and organized all our information—were both fundamentally correct. He described, in the mechanistic terms of 1945 technology, the multimedia PC connected to the Web. He even predicted the equivalent of Internet search engines "establishing useful trails through the enormous mass of the common record."

Technological advances transmuted Bush's vision, making it seem old-fashioned even as it came true.

Original illustration by Alfred D. Crimi

Vannevar Bush's memex, though based on the microfiche technology of the 1940s, anticipated the idea of a PC connected to the Internet, able to hold vast amounts of data and using links to connect all information related to a topic.

At this time, we didn't have an overall Internet strategy for the company. We didn't see that the Internet, a network for academics and techies, would blossom into the global commercial network it is today. We were focused on broadband applications such as videoconferencing and video-on-demand. The Internet had such a limited capacity to carry digital information then that we saw it as a minor stop along the way. To our surprise, everything coalesced around the Internet protocols as it achieved broad critical mass.

The Internet's sudden growth in popularity changed all the rules, and its growth kept accelerating. People were willing to put up with the Internet's deficiencies because it made vast amounts of information available and enabled easy communication. Content providers raced to respond to the opportunity, creating a positive feedback loop and exponential growth. In 1993 alone Internet use doubled to more than twenty-five million people.

The impetus for Microsoft's response to the Internet didn't come from me or from our other senior executives. It came from a small number of dedicated employees who saw events unfolding. Through our electronic systems they were able to rally everybody to their cause. Their story exemplifies our policy, from Day One, that smart people anywhere in the company should have the power to drive an initiative. It's an obvious, commonsense policy for Information Age companies, where all the knowledge workers should be part of setting the strategy. We could not pull off such a policy without the technology we use. In many ways technology has shaped the policy. Do people all over my company feel free to send me e-mail because we believe in a flat organization? Or do we have a flat organization because people have always been able to send e-mail directly to me? For years everybody at Microsoft has had a

PC and e-mail access. It's a famous part of our corporate culture, and it's shaped the way we think and act.

MEETING PHYSICALLY AND ELECTRONICALLY

In true Microsoft fashion, J. Allard, Steven Sinofsky (my technical assistant then), and a few other people were the instigators of our response to the rising popularity of the Internet. In January 1994 J. wrote a memo in which he laid out the opportunities and dangers presented by the Internet. Coincidentally, within a week Steve went to Cornell University on a recruiting trip. While stuck there for two days in a snowstorm, he checked out how the university was using computers. A 1987 graduate who had worked for the IT group at Cornell as a student, Steve was amazed at the revolutionary changes Cornell had undergone since his visit the year before.

In his e-mail trip report Steve marveled at how "wired" the school was. About a third of the students had PCs, some school departments provided PCs, and kiosk PCs were available in public spaces. E-mail use by students was close to 100 percent. Many of Cornell's instructors were communicating with students online, and students were pestering their parents to get their own e-mail accounts. A wide variety of information, including much of the Cornell library catalog, was available online. A student could view her current course schedule, her previous grades, her outstanding accounts, financial aid information, and a directory of the school community online. Many faculty members were communicating with students online and used online chat services to collaborate with each other. There was a "huge movement" to make all sorts of information available to students via the Web. Steve even saw real-time videoconferencing over the Internet.

What struck Steve was how thoroughly this technology had become integrated into campus life "in practically no calendar time" and how students took it totally for granted. He said that for students "the online services are as ubiquitous and expected as regular phone service" and that "this pace of change in information access is faster than for any other technology I have seen in my lifetime, including the personal computer itself." Students were even complaining that they couldn't sign up for classes online.

J. and Steve made a number of recommendations about what Microsoft should do to participate in this revolution. Where Steve had focused on the users and cultural changes, J. drilled into the technical implications for a variety of Microsoft products. He noted that we were behind many of our competitors as far as the Internet was concerned but said that our "agility and creativity will allow us to catch up quickly" provided there was "efficient communication between the groups within Microsoft that these efforts impact." J. saw "a lot of potential synergy" among groups, although he also stressed "the potential for disaster" if we failed to coordinate our activities company-wide. He listed a wide range of Microsoft groups he thought needed to cooperate in an Internet effort.

Steve and J.'s memos quickly circulated by e-mail among a large number of people at Microsoft. They set off a firestorm of electronic deliberation. The number of issues to be considered was huge. How should our operating systems support the Internet? What did "Internet ready" or "Internet enabled" mean for Microsoft Word, Microsoft Excel, and the rest of our productivity suite? What did it mean for our e-mail products? What new products did we need? What Internet technologies should be packaged as new products, and what technologies should be incorporated into our existing products? Which technologies should we license? Should we focus initially on the ways businesses could use Internet technologies internally or on the ways consumers could use the technologies broadly?

Sometimes an idea got quick agreement. Sometimes the response was shrill mail saying you've got it all wrong. At different times people prodded me and other senior executives to move faster. We set up more taps to the Internet so that people could use it and learn about it firsthand. We told middle managers to go out and explore the Internet, to develop their own impressions and come to their own conclusions about what had merit on the Web and what didn't. We all had favorite sites we'd recommend to the others. Checking out competitor sites became something you did every morning. I still do. I have one PC in my office set up to rotate through a number of Web sites, including our competitors' sites, so that I can see how different companies are using the Web to promote their products and interact with customers.

These independent explorations led to dozens and dozens of great ideas. Quickly, over e-mail, people offered their opinions, fleshed out the issues, considered the options. The amount of e-mail was just fantastic. E-mail discussions led to many small group meetings—often loud, informal ones in the hallways—to hammer out recommendations. "Hallways and e-mail"—that's how it happened. As topics expanded, smaller groups would break off into their own e-mail chains to consider subsets. Before long, large numbers of people in different parts of our organization were participating. I was engaged in lengthy e-mail exchanges with dozens of people involving everything from our business strategy for online services to our technical approach to hyperlinking.

KEEPING FOCUSED, ACTING FAST

We kept our Internet development plan and action items on our network so that it was visible to everybody who cared. Managers at all levels would check the list regularly and follow up. When work in an area seemed to be lagging, people would rally around to focus on it.

To get a big company moving fast, especially on a many-headed opportunity like the Internet, you have to have hundreds of people participating and coming up with ideas. But you've also got to get them focused, or you'll never get any decisions made or get anything done. Our digital nervous system informed and propelled our decision making. E-mail generated the thinking and analysis, so teams moved quickly to develop strong points of view and recommendations. Once the e-mail chains got long enough and we had enough issues and recommendations to consider, we'd go off on retreats to produce the final decisions. Then we'd set priorities and ensure coordination among major groups. In 1994 we had three classic retreats several months apart. After the first one, on April 6, 1994, I e-mailed my staff to say, "We're going to make a big bet on the Internet."

I devoted my April 1994 Think Week to the Internet and multimedia topics. In a Think Week, which I do twice a year, I set aside all other issues to concentrate on the most difficult technical and business problems facing the company. We held our first major progress review in August 1994. Once again, it was the newer employees running the show. J., who at that time was a program manager with no direct reports, led the meeting with assistance from Steve Sinofsky and other people who had expertise in important areas. As J. put it, there were "no titles" in the presenter lineup, and they all felt it was like "the kids entering the boardroom" when the meeting began. One young guy went home before the meeting to change into Dockers and a button-down shirt to be more "appropriate," only to discover that his associates and a few of the senior staff were attending in T-shirts and Birkenstocks.

One of the biggest concerns at the time was whether we could convert our internal product and sales information from its database format into Internet-readable HTML format. Much of the massive amount of product information was appropriate for customers, and we thought it would be a great addition to our Web site as we were getting off the ground. One person at the meeting felt that the technical challenges of conversion would be too difficult. The next speaker—the fellow who'd put on the spiffy clothes—turned out to have already developed a converter. It had been a skunkworks project. His manager had told him the Internet would never be part of their group's business. By the time of this meeting, the small team had already converted thousands of files containing product information into HTML, and many of these files were already beginning to go online. I was pleased to see so much initiative.

By early 1995, months before we introduced Windows 95, every team at Microsoft had defined its Internet charter and begun development. In short order we were rolling out Internet add-ons, Internet integration, and new Internet products.

In a May 1995 e-mail memo called "The Internet Tidal Wave," I summarized our strategic directions and decisions and announced a corporate reorganization to map our Internet goals to every segment of the company. I made certain that the entire company understood the importance of our focus on the Internet: "Developments on the Internet over the next several years will set the course of our indus-

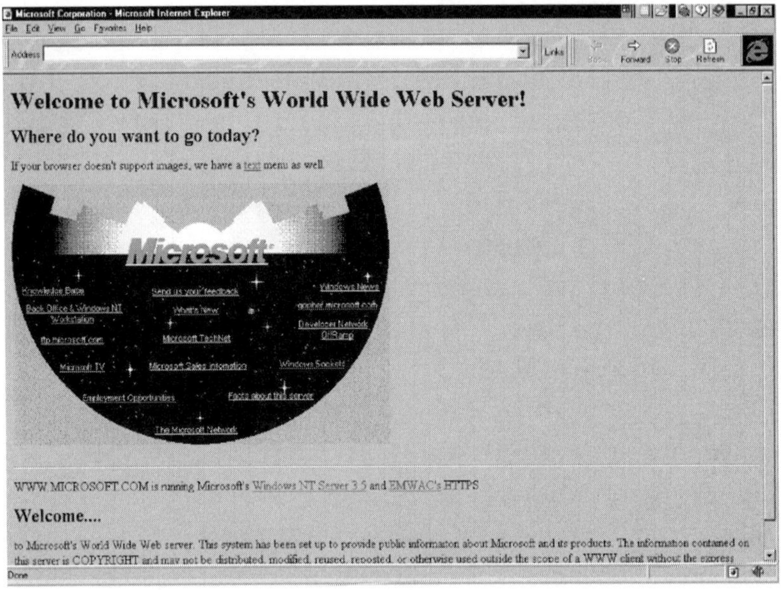

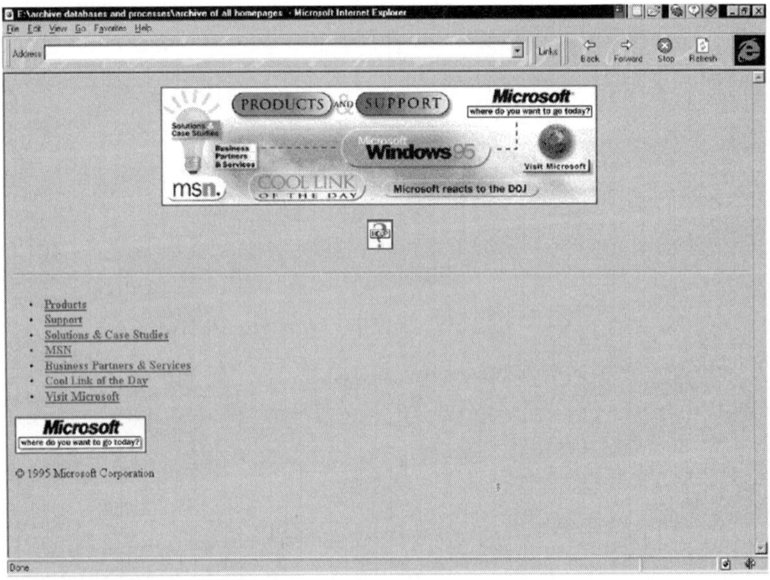

Electronic feedback from customers has led Microsoft to constantly upgrade and refine the design, organization, and content of the company's Web site, *www.microsoft.com*. The site has gone through more than one major revision a year, including these four. The original site, *top*, too closely resembled the "Death Star" and was quickly replaced. Another one, *bottom*, took the goal of a clean page design too far, requiring users to click on too many links to get information. More recent versions, *facing page*, display important news along the right side and a high-level site outline along the left, presenting an uncluttered look while making it easier for users to find what they need.

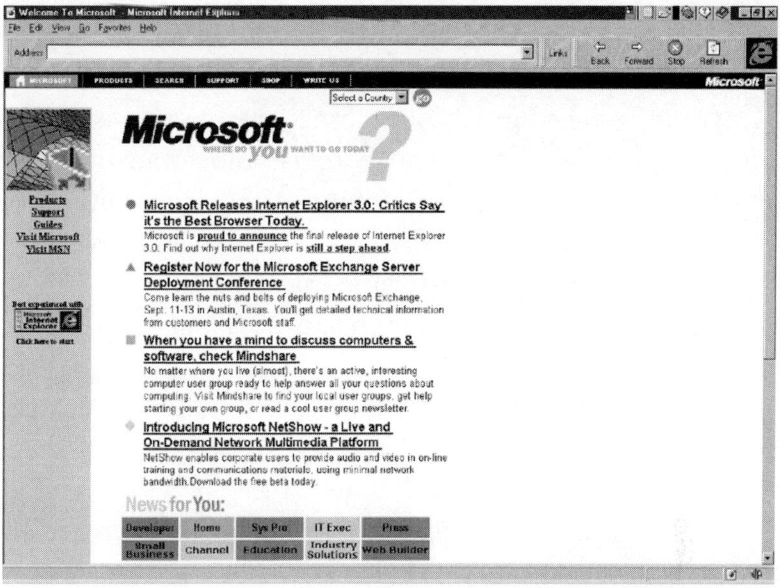
Welcome To Microsoft - Microsoft Internet Explorer
File Edit View Go Favorites Help
Address
Links
Back Forward Stop Refresh
MICROSOFT PRODUCTS SEARCH SUPPORT SHOP WRITE US
Microsoft
Select a Country
Microsoft
WHERE DO you WANT TO GO TODAY
?
Products
Support
Guides
Visit Microsoft
Visit MSN
Best experienced with
Microsoft Internet Explorer
Click here to start
Microsoft Releases Internet Explorer 3.0: Critics Say it's the Best Browser Today.
Microsoft is proud to announce the final release of Internet Explorer 3.0. Find out why Internet Explorer is still a step ahead.
Register Now for the Microsoft Exchange Server Deployment Conference
Come learn the nuts and bolts of deploying Microsoft Exchange, Sept. 11-13 in Austin, Texas. You'll get detailed technical information from customers and Microsoft staff.
When you have a mind to discuss computers & software, check Mindshare
No matter where you live (almost), there's an active, interesting computer user group ready to help answer all your questions about computing. Visit Mindshare to find your local user groups, get help starting your own group, or read a cool user group newsletter.
Introducing Microsoft NetShow - a Live and On-Demand Network Multimedia Platform
NetShow enables corporate users to provide audio and video in on-line training and communications materials, using minimal network bandwidth. Download the free beta today.
News for You:
Developer
Home
Sys Pro
IT Exec
Press
Small Business
Channel
Education
Industry Solutions
Web Builder

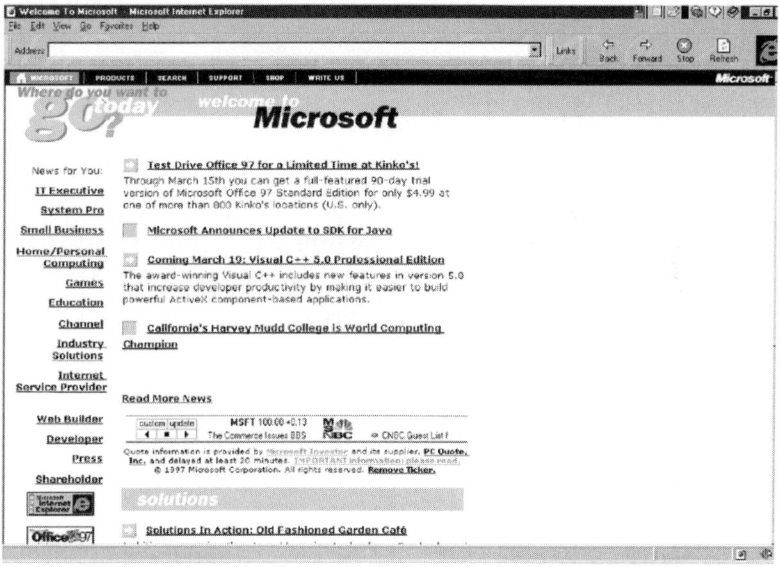
Welcome To Microsoft - Microsoft Internet Explorer
File Edit View Go Favorites Help
Address
Links
Back Forward Stop Refresh
MICROSOFT PRODUCTS SEARCH SUPPORT SHOP WRITE US
Microsoft
Where do you want to go today?
welcome to Microsoft
News for You:
IT Executive
System Pro
Small Business
Home/Personal Computing
Games
Education
Channel
Industry Solutions
Internet Service Provider
Web Builder
Developer
Press
Shareholder
Microsoft Internet Explorer
Office 97
Test Drive Office 97 for a Limited Time at Kinko's!
Through March 15th you can get a full-featured 90-day trial version of Microsoft Office 97 Standard Edition for only $4.99 at one of more than 800 Kinko's locations (U.S. only).
Microsoft Announces Update to SDK for Java
Coming March 19: Visual C++ 5.0 Professional Edition
The award-winning Visual C++ includes new features in version 5.0 that increase developer productivity by making it easier to build powerful ActiveX component-based applications.
California's Harvey Mudd College is World Computing Champion
Read More News
custom update
MSFT 100.00 +0.13
The Commerce Issues BBS
NBC
CNBC Guest List
Quote information is provided by Microsoft Investor and its supplier, PC Quote, Inc. and delayed at least 20 minutes. IMPORTANT information; please read.
© 1997 Microsoft Corporation. All rights reserved. Remove Ticker.
solutions
Solutions In Action: Old Fashioned Garden Café

try for a long time to come. . . . The Internet is the most important single development to come along since the IBM PC was introduced in 1981. . . . Since the Internet is changing so rapidly we will have to revise our strategies from time to time and have better inter-group communication than ever before. Our products will not be the only things changing. The way we distribute information and software as well as the way we communicate with and support customers will be changing."[3]

By the time we went public with our Internet strategy in December 1995, it was damn the torpedoes, full speed ahead. As I've said several times since, if we go out of business, it won't be because we're not focused on the Internet. It'll be because we're *too* focused on the Internet.

MAKING THE DIFFERENCE THROUGH E-MAIL

We reached most of the important decisions during this crisis in face-to-face talk. But our decisions were all informed, well ahead, by the exchanges taking place over e-mail. Electronic collaboration is not a substitute for face-to-face meetings. It's a way to ensure that more work gets done ahead of time so that meetings in person will be more productive. Meeting time is so precious that you want to be sure you're dealing with facts and good recommendations based on solid analysis, not just anecdotal evidence. You want to be sure that meetings produce actionable decisions, that you don't just sit around speculating and talking about philosophical stuff.

3. Bill Gates, internal Microsoft memo, "The Internet Tidal Wave," 26 May 1995. The memo was distributed electronically to all senior managers and included hypertext links to articles and research about the Internet and to more than two dozen of the best Web sites.

Our Corporate Presence on the Web Was Better, But . . .

During the mid-1990s we were not just building Internet-related products. Like other companies, we were also learning to use the Internet to promote our products and services. On the evening of November 2, 1995, I spent several hours browsing Microsoft's home page on the World Wide Web and then fired off an e-mail to thirteen senior executives whose groups had major amounts of content on the Web. The subject was "Microsoft Marketing on the Internet," and my main concerns were complex page designs, inconsistencies across different pages, and the overuse of big splashy graphics whose downloading slowed access to real information.

"Although I would say our corporate presence on the Internet is better, I still think it falls far short of what we need to do. It doesn't reflect our desire to show people we care about the Internet. . . . Our corporate site is still very weak. We have huge graphics with a collage of colors. It's as though someone thinks the measure of a good Web page is stepping back and looking at it after it downloads instead of its information utility. We need someone with the mentality of a front page editor who tries to put as much information onto a page as possible instead of creating a labyrinth of pages that you go to that just make you go further."

I pointed the senior executives to the *Boston Globe* site. "They use small pictures in order to make things move at a decent speed. They always try and grab you with some extra text—not just a button name—you want to go down into the next level, unlike our stuff."

Here are some of my specific reactions to a selection of Microsoft's pages:

"Look at how many clicks it takes to find your way to anything about Office that a) is a promotion you should think about, or b) encourages you to get the product because of what is in it. . . . The best material is actually confusingly in a place called 'news' 'top stories'—that is the first place I found that really had some meat in it. . . . Put a lot more on each page—some real meat about the products. Some real news. Some excitement about the offers. . . .

"There is nothing that grabs you on the consumer pages. You wouldn't know that we just shipped some amazing products. You wouldn't know we actually get good reviews on our products. . . . I couldn't even get the in-depth information I wanted."

In this case, the bad news came directly from the boss. And it sank in. By the time of our Internet Strategy Day a month later, the worst of these problems had been fixed.

To be sure, our competitors in this space also use electronic tools. In the high-tech industry, e-mail is considered old hat. We take it for granted, just as we do PCs. We take e-mail so much for granted that at the end of 1996 when I predicted in my syndicated newspaper column that e-mail would be used by a majority of companies by the end of 1997—a prediction that came true—two computer columnists gave me a hard time. "Bill Gates predicts the past" was basically what they said. Those of us in the PC industry had been using e-mail for fifteen to twenty years, but these writers didn't realize that even in 1996 less than half the companies in the world used e-mail. Having a critical mass of employees on e-mail today is not enough, though. Unless all knowledge workers use e-mail several times a day, companies will not get enough value from it to make it worthwhile. As a way of comparison, in a company where e-mail is integral to the culture, the average person will send five to ten messages a day and get twenty-five to fifty; heavy users will send or receive well over a hundred messages a day.

We in the PC industry sometimes forget that use of our own tools is one reason the whole industry has advanced so quickly. We can all move fast to see and respond to a customer problem or to what a competitor is doing. For a large company to be able to maneuver as well as or better than a smaller competitor is a testament to both the energy of the employees and the use of digital systems. Personal initiative and responsibility are enhanced in an environment that fosters discussion. E-mail, a key component of our digital nervous system, does just that. It helps turn middle managers from information filters into "doers." There's no doubt that e-mail flattens the hierarchical structure of an organization. It encourages people to speak up. It encourages managers to listen. That's why, when customers ask what's the first thing they can do to get more value out of their information systems and foster collaboration in their companies, I always answer, "E-mail."

PAYING ATTENTION TO BAD NEWS

Bad news can be really disheartening. When you get news of a product failure, there's a real temptation to think, Oh, that's as much as I want to know about that! I think I'll go home now. I think I'll work on something else. When you lose a customer, it can be tempting to tell each other, "That customer's not very sharp. They just made the wrong decision." Meetings in which colleagues try to explain away a product failure or a lost customer are the worst. But they are preferable to the meeting that isn't called, to the silence and inactivity when nobody tells you something negative is going on. If a competitor introduces a superior product, or if you lose a customer, resist the temptation to put it out of mind. Ignoring bad news is a formula for decline.

Only the Paranoid Survive is Intel chairman Andrew Grove's book about the need for a business to stay alert to change at what he calls "major inflection points" in the market. In the book Andy talks about how important it is for a company's middle managers, "often the first to realize that what worked before doesn't quite work anymore," to confront senior management with bad news. Otherwise, he says, "senior management in a company is sometimes late to realize that the world is changing on them—and the leader is often the last of all to know."

In one example of a major inflection point, Andy describes Intel's slow response to a crisis over early versions of its Pentium chip in late 1994. Certain chips contained a minor engineering flaw. Intel reacted to the problem on the basis of it being a relatively insignificant bug that would affect only a very small number of users. Customers, however, felt differently. Highly technical users cared about "minor" computational errors. The general consumers Intel was now courting were alarmed at the mere suggestion that something could be "wrong" with their PCs. Intel endured "unrelenting bombardment," as Andy described it—much the result of customers rallying together on the Internet—before offering a free replacement part to anyone who wanted it. Few customers took the company up on its offer, but the public anger subsided immediately.

An engineer himself, Andy confessed that he was one of the last to understand that his company now had to respond to a customer crisis as a consumer products company would—not in a month, as it had taken Intel this time, but in a matter of days. "It took a barrage of relentless criticism to make me realize that something had changed—and that we needed to adapt to the new environment. . . . The lesson is, we all need to expose ourselves to the winds of change. We need to expose ourselves to our customers, both the ones who are staying with us as well as those that we may lose by sticking to the past. We need to expose ourselves to lower-level employees, who, when encouraged, will tell us a lot that we need to know."[4]

Some experts say that companies struggle with the need for change because they haven't been designed for change. Hierarchy gets in the way. The corporate culture sees innovation as risky and suspect. "Worthy failure" (experimentation) is punished. A similar reaction can set in against bad news. Lower-level staff may hesitate to bring bad news forward, and many managers don't want to hear it. Corpo-

4. Andrew S. Grove, *Only the Paranoid Survive* (New York: Doubleday Dell, 1996): 21–23.

rate structure and culture can be a real roadblock, no question.

A change in corporate attitude, encouraging and listening to bad news, has to come from the top. The CEO and the other senior executives have to insist on getting bad news, and they have to create an appetite for bad news throughout their organizations. The bearer of bad tidings should be rewarded, not punished. Business leaders have to want to listen to alerts from salespeople, product developers, and customers. You can't just turn off the alarm and go back to sleep. Not if you want your company to survive.

Most of the excellent computer companies that Tom Peters and Robert Waterman cited back in 1982 in their fine book, *In Search of Excellence,*[5] have experienced serious setbacks since the book came out. IBM saw both its mainframe and its minicomputer businesses undermined by PCs in the 1980s and 1990s. Digital Equipment Corporation undercut IBM's mainframes with its smaller minicomputers, only to be undercut itself later by the still smaller PCs that Digital (and many other computer companies) had dismissed as toys. Wang didn't see the PC revolution coming either and lost the word-processing market to companies that provided software on the PC rather than on dedicated hardware systems.

These companies still talked to their customers. They still had smart, responsive people working for them. IBM's own skunkworks team had released the IBM PC in 1981, establishing a standard that made the PC a business tool. But IBM continued for two full decades to see PCs through the lens of its larger computer systems. This view distorted and slowed its response to a fundamental technology shift. After allowing Compaq to get out of the gate first with a

5. (New York: Warner Books, 1982)

32-bit PC system, IBM watched its share of the PC market drop from 55 percent to 15 percent within a couple of years. Its share now hovers below 10 percent. Digital, despite a reputation for high-quality products and services, struggled throughout the PC era until Compaq, a PC vendor, bought it in 1998. Wang went through bankruptcy before emerging again as a systems integrator.

Examples from the computer industry are only the most recent instances of an unwillingness to hear bad news. In 1920 Ford had 90 percent of the low-priced car market and was responsible for 54 percent of the total automotive manufacturing output in the country. Ford's position seemed to be invincible. Yet by May 1927 technical advances at General Motors and other automotive companies had forced Henry Ford to take the drastic step of shutting down his main plant for an entire year to retool for new designs. Today Ford is still a world leader in automobile production and quality, but it has never regained its pre-1927 position in the industry. Somebody at Ford saw the changes coming in the 1920s. An engineer who came up with a new design was fired for his temerity. The senior leadership wouldn't listen.

In commercial aviation, Douglas Aircraft, with its DC series, had a major lead over Boeing immediately after World War II. Douglas was so focused on filling all of its orders for the propeller-powered DC-7 that it failed to move quickly enough to jet engines. Boeing built the jet-powered 707 on speculation, without a single customer order in hand, and never looked back. Douglas is now part of Boeing.

An unwillingness to hear bad news and take action isn't just a business phenomenon, either. History is full of far more serious examples. Many books have been written about why the United States was not prepared for the attack on Pearl Harbor that hurled the country into World War II. According to historian Gordon Prange, the American military could not overcome its "psychological unpreparedness." Communication of the bad news of potential war was flawed, too. Cable after cable warned U.S. admirals and generals in the Pacific of the imminent likelihood of war. Yet cryptic cables made for confusing orders to the forces in Hawaii. In the last twenty-four hours lower-level officers with tantalizing clues to the time and place of the attack scurried around, hand-carrying paper folders up through the chain of command. No one could bring together all of the pieces of information until it was too late.[6]

It doesn't do any good to be receptive to bad news if you can't get bad news up through your organization and then do something about it in a hurry. Today's digital technology can ensure that you get the news and that you can put your organization into action fast.

ACTING ON BAD NEWS

How fast a company can respond in an emergency is a measure of its corporate reflexes. People in the organization will feel lousy and threatened by bad news, but that's okay as long as they feel it as a group. As an act of leadership, I created a sense of crisis about the Internet in 1994 and 1995. Not to leave people paralyzed or unhappy, but to excite them to action. The leader needs to create an environment in which people can analyze the situation and develop a good response.

6. Gordon Prange, *At Dawn We Slept* (New York: McGraw Hill, 1981). Prange mentions "psychological unpreparedness" on page 641. See chapters 54 through 59, pages 439–492, for the long string of communications breakdowns and "fundamental disbelief" that occurred on the U.S. side the weekend of December 6–7, 1941.

I like good news as much as the next person, but it also puts me in a skeptical frame of mind. I wonder what bad news I'm not hearing. When somebody sends me an e-mail about an account we've won, I always think, There are a lot of accounts nobody has sent mail about. Does that mean we've lost all of those? This reaction may seem unwarranted, but I've found there's a psychological impulse in people to send good news when there's bad news brewing. It's as if they want to lessen the shock. A good e-mail system ensures that bad news can travel fast, but your people have to be willing to send you the news. You have to be consistently receptive to bad news, and then you have to act on it. Sometimes I think my most important job as a CEO is to listen for bad news. If you don't act on it, your people will eventually stop bringing bad news to your attention. And that's the beginning of the end.

In three years every product my company makes will be obsolete. The only question is whether we'll make them obsolete or somebody else will. In the next ten years, if Microsoft remains a leader, we'll have had to weather at least three major crises. That's why we've always got to do better. Ask anybody who's ever worked at Microsoft and they'll tell you that if there's one cultural quality we have, it's that we always see ourselves as an underdog. I see us as an underdog today, just as I've seen us as an underdog every day for the last twenty years. If we don't maintain that perspective, some competitor will eat our lunch. I insist that we stay on top of the news, as well as pursue longer-term developments on the research front, and that we use "bad news" to drive us to put innovative new features into our products. One day somebody will catch us napping. One day an eager upstart will put Microsoft out of business. I just hope it's fifty years from now, not two or five.

Business Lessons

- ❑ A company's ability to respond to unplanned events, good or bad, is a prime indicator of its ability to compete.
- ❑ Strategically a major function of the CEO is to look for bad news and encourage the organization to respond to it. Employees must be encouraged to share bad news as much as good news.
- ❑ The flatter the corporate hierarchy, the more likely it is that employees will communicate bad news and act upon it.
- ❑ Personal initiative and responsibility thrive in an environment that fosters discussion.
- ❑ Reward worthy failure—experimentation.

Diagnosing Your Digital Nervous System

- ❑ Do your digital systems enable you to learn about bad news anywhere in the company and communicate it quickly?
- ❑ Do your digital systems enable you to assemble the necessary data and get teams working on solutions quickly?
- ❑ Can you put together virtual teams from separate departments and geographies?

11

CONVERT BAD NEWS TO GOOD

Outstanding service firms differentiate themselves on the basis of quality dimensions that are important to their customers and that explicitly or implicitly guarantee results.

—James Heskett, W. Earl Sasser, and Christopher W. L. Hart, *Service Breakthroughs*

Once you embrace unpleasant news not as a negative but as evidence of a need for change, you aren't defeated by it. You're learning from it. It's all in how you approach failures. And believe me, we know a lot about failures at Microsoft. Back in the 1980s our Multiplan spreadsheet product couldn't make any headway against Lotus 1-2-3. We spent the last half of the 1980s working on a database called Omega before we finally abandoned the project in 1990. We based our long-term operating system strategy on jointly building OS/2 with IBM, but that project came to an end in 1992 after we'd sunk hundreds of millions of dollars and countless hours of developer time into it. In the early 1990s we had to can our

Newton-like personal digital assistant because the technology wasn't good enough. In 1993 we had a project we thought would revolutionize office machines such as copiers and faxes called "Microsoft at Work," but it never worked. In the mid-1990s our TV-style Internet shows on MSN were a flop.

The weight of all of our failures could make me too depressed to come in to work. Instead I am excited about the challenges and by how we can use today's bad news to help solve tomorrow's problems.

What we learned in our Multiplan spreadsheet effort helped us develop Microsoft Excel, the most advanced graphical spreadsheet when it came to market in 1985, and it still leads the competition. A lot of what we learned from the Omega database project paid off several years later when we shipped Microsoft Access, which became the most popular desktop database. That modern, built-from-scratch, world-class operating system initially intended to be OS/2 version 3.0 became Windows NT instead. Our early experiences with small devices and office form factors helped us understand the technical requirements for a growing market we now serve with our Windows CE operating system. And our Internet media investments taught us that our customers thought our role on the Internet should be as a provider of practical, software-intensive products such as Microsoft Expedia (travel), Investor (finance), and Sidewalk (leisure).

Learning from mistakes and constantly improving products is a key in all successful companies. Listening to customers is a big part of that effort. You have to study what customers say about their problems with your products and stay tuned in to what they want, extrapolating from leading-edge buyers to predict future requirements.

In software, customers always want more. If you improve software reliability, customers say great, but what about scalability? If you improve scalability, they want more integration. Our customers are always upping the ante, as they should.

Listening to the customers means hearing their complaints about current product shortcomings. But getting bad news from customers passed all the way to the product design groups is surprisingly hard to do. Most companies have an inefficient chain of people and paper between customers and the people who can make major improvements. When the customer data finally reaches the product design group, it often isn't easy for the team to digest its significance and prioritize it accordingly. All of the delays taken together mean that improvements don't happen as fast as they should.

I recommend the following approach to integrating customer complaints and wish lists into product and service development.

1. Focus on your most unhappy customers.
2. Use technology to gather rich information on their unhappy experiences with your product and to find out what they want you to put into the product.
3. Use technology to drive the news to the right people in a hurry.

If you do these three things, you'll turn those draining, bad news experiences into an exhilarating process of improving your product or service. Unhappy customers are always a concern. They're also your greatest opportunity. Adopting a learning posture rather than a negative defensive posture can make customer complaints your best source of significant quality improvements. Adopting the right technology will give you the power to capture and convert complaints into better products and services fast.

GIVING CUSTOMER GUARANTEES SOME TEETH

Hotels and airlines usually offer a "satisfaction guarantee." If you're unhappy with the company's service, you receive a discount or an upgrade that's good the next time. The satisfaction guarantee is actually a sales tool designed to get you to come back.

A radically different approach comes from Promus Hotels, based in Memphis, Tennessee. Promus (pronounced "promise"), which generated $5 billion in revenue in 1997, has a family of hotels. The best known are the Hampton Inns, Embassy Suites, and Doubletree Inns. Promus was the first hotel chain to guarantee no charge for your current visit if you have any complaint about your stay. And *any* Promus employee can make good on that guarantee—a front desk clerk, a maid, a maintenance engineer—anybody.

For obvious reasons, customers love the Promus guarantee. Debbi Fields, president and chief executive officer of Mrs. Fields, the chain of cookie and baked goods stores, stayed at a Hampton Inn one time and mentioned at checkout that there hadn't been any soap or towels in her room when she'd arrived. The desk person ripped up her bill and told her the stay was free. She was so impressed that she made Hampton Inn her company's corporate hotel and ultimately ended up on the Hampton/Promus board.

A guarantee of this kind is not just a feel-good device for the customer, although making the customer feel good certainly makes sense. The larger business reason for offering such a guarantee is to create an environment in which customer complaints drive service improvements. The rationale is laid out in the book *Service Breakthroughs: Changing the Rules of the Game* that a guarantee encourages "the entire organization to focus on customers' definitions of good service, not on executives' assumptions about what good service is." Reliable data about the firm's service delivery system helps identify failure points, and the guarantee "invariably injects a sense of urgency into all of these activities. The end result, of course, is unshakable customer loyalty."[1]

A no-questions-asked guarantee from a service company such as Promus makes complaints mean something. Customers like the guarantee going in—even if they're a little skeptical about how hard it will be to get you to deliver on it—and when you do deliver on it, you have a very gratified customer.

Equally important, the guarantee creates a financial incentive to fix the underlying problem right away. Because it costs the hotel money immediately, the problem doesn't get overlooked. It doesn't get filed away. Tying complaints to immediate payouts "lowers the water and exposes the rocks" relating to service quality.

Because every employee is empowered to act on the guarantee, everybody is on the hook for quality. The everyday hotel workers, who make or break quality and who can administer the guarantee, have more pride in their own jobs and pride in the hotel. Peer pressure comes into play within the different groups to hold up their end. And if you're going to give all hotel employees the power to make a customer's stay free—a lot of power for service personnel—then you'd better train them all to do a good job.

When Promus first proposed this policy, some franchisees said, "You're nuts. Deadbeats will just take advantage of us. They'll kill us." So Promus inaugurated the policy with a mix of company-owned and franchised hotels. It

1. James L. Heskett, W. Earl Sasser, and Christopher W. L. Hart, *Service Breakthroughs: Changing the Rules of the Game* (New York: Free Press, 1990): 94–95.

turned out that refunds were much lower than anticipated, averaging 0.3 percent of revenues. Promus also discovered that "intent to return" was 50 percent higher for customers who invoked the guarantee than for other customers.

Franchisees quickly got with the program.

USING TECHNOLOGY TO BACK UP GUARANTEES

How can you put your money where your mouth is like this and not go broke? Technology. Promus uses information technology to track unhappy customer experiences and convert them into continuous service improvements—and to prevent too many exercises of its guarantee.

Complaints are tracked centrally on the chain's corporate database, so Promus management can see where the complaints are coming from. Promus can quickly identify any hotels experiencing the same repeated complaint (say, unfriendly desk clerks or dirty rooms), so the company can work with hotel managers to fix the weak point. The same technology gives Promus a way to track any customers who might be tempted to take advantage of the chain's generosity. The company can quickly identify anybody who goes from hotel to hotel, claiming poor service and getting free rooms. When such a pattern develops, Promus immediately sends a nice letter to the customer lamenting the fact that the hotel chain can't meet his quality standards and inviting him to stay in a competitor's facility.

The central customer database also enables Promus to track the paths of the chain's favorite customers, the regular guests. If you're a businessperson who stays at four or five Promus properties on a regular basis and you suddenly stop going to any of them, you'll receive a special promotion to entice you back.

Booking Gets Smarter with Every Transaction

Promus franchisees now have access to corporate revenue data that helps them determine how to price and sell their rooms. Using chainwide booking data and a hotel metric called "revenue per available room" (RevPAR), Promus's System 21 predicts the best rate that franchisees can get for any room, any night.

Monitoring current availability and the number of days left before the reservation date, System 21 compares these figures with historic usage. If reservations are slow, the system will make more low-priced rooms available; if bookings are brisk, it will keep more rooms at the standard price. The software can compare the opportunity cost between a two-night booking today against the likelihood of a four-night booking beginning tomorrow. It can alert the clerk that bookings will be slow tonight and recommend that a frequent guest be upgraded to a better suite. The system advises the reservation clerk on all kinds of booking decisions.

In a business where front desk staff are often put on the spot by "rate shoppers" insisting that they can get a better price across the street, System 21 relieves staff and customers of the need to haggle over room rates. Promus staff can quote the lowest possible rate without sacrificing profitability. Customers are assured that they're getting the best rate for their date and situation.

Every booking and every transaction goes into the central database, so that Promus and franchisee staff increase their aggregate wisdom and make smarter decisions. "It gives our franchisees a more educated basis from which to make moment-to-moment booking decisions rather than just shooting from the hip or guessing," says Promus CIO Tim Harvey. "We want each franchisee to get the benefit of the entire chain's learning."

The customer database of about thirty million records, which is updated every night, helps Promus personalize a stay. Everybody—the hotel, the travel agent, and central reservations—can see the individual customer's preferences. When you arrive at a Promus hotel, the receptionist knows that you prefer a nonsmoking room or a double instead of a king-size bed or that your allergies require you to have special pillows.

Promus designed and is implementing an end-to-end infrastructure for information flow. This infrastructure has enabled the hotel chain to use its information not just to handle reservations or support guarantees, but to extend the use to operational and revenue management systems that enable hotel employees and managers to make better decisions and improve hotel operations. Because of the comprehensive way in which they assist franchisees in their day-to-day business operations, Promus calls the management systems "a hotel manager in a box." Training costs for a front desk person—a position with 100 percent annual turnover—have gone from $11,000 per employee to $3,000. Instead of spending two weeks in formal classroom training in Memphis, new front desk employees now spend only two to three hours in training at their hotel properties, moving Promus closer to its goal of "Day One Performance."

Employees in every hotel have a single way to do all of their many tasks, from conference room scheduling to accounting to check-in; the checkout process has been reduced from twenty screens to three. Individual hotel managers now have access to operational and revenue management information that helps them track data that used to be available only to the corporate executives in Memphis. A franchisee who owns ten Embassy Suites, for example, can log on to a PC every morning and see how every one of his hotels did the night before, how they stand against plan, and which came in under plan. If the numbers for one of the hotels don't look good, the franchisee can fire off an e-mail to his hotel managers to get everybody involved in devising plans for boosting occupancies or revenues. The operational folks at Promus can see the same information and get in on the collaboration, too, offering assistance to properties that are lagging.

As business needs change, the PC architecture will enable new applications to be developed at modest incremental cost, further integrating the information and activities in Promus's corporate offices and franchises.

CAPTURING AND CONVERTING BAD NEWS TO GOOD

Most retail product companies take a different approach to guarantees than service companies with their "perishable inventory" of only so many rooms or seats for a given date. Microsoft offers the common thirty-day, money-back product guarantee to our customers. Like Promus, though, we have recognized the importance of using technology to capture and convert customer feedback into improvements as fast as possible.

We began collecting data about customer problems from support engineers in 1985 and began the steps to create a regular feedback loop in 1991. First we used a phone system and then developed different tools for gathering data from sources such as e-mail, Internet newsgroups, and the Web. Then we began to consolidate the data. We're now in our third generation of computer-based customer feedback tools. The team specifically charged with using our customer feedback tools to convert bad news to good is the Product Improvement (PI) team in Microsoft Technical Services.

Product Improvement is the voice of the customer. The people in this group sift through a lot of bad news and some good news all day long. They focus exclusively on what our customers are telling us that we might not want to hear—but should. They analyze customer feedback and lobby on behalf of the customers for fixes and new product features to improve the customers' experience with our software. Although they sit in the customer support group, they're not in the customer support business. They're in the product improvement business.

The Product Improvement team has a tool for incident management and analysis that makes sense of seven to eight million pieces of raw customer data per year. Six million pieces of data come from support incidents, mostly by phone but also from the Web. One million come in from Premier, our more sophisticated support service for enterprise customers. The rest of the customer data comes from a variety of other sources. Support engineers enter problems reported via phone into the database as they handle calls. Online problem reports go directly into the database. E-mails, already electronic, are easily converted into a structured format for entry.

From this database the data is extracted in statistically valid random samplings for each product and scrubbed for accuracy and categorization. Because each problem report is weighed for both frequency and the labor involved in resolving the problem each time it surfaces, the most difficult issues bubble to the top—either by topic and product, such as the number of network problems experienced by users of Windows; or by topic and groups of products, such as whether file management is a concern across all of Microsoft Office.

Not all of the customer feedback is negative. We also get lots of "wishes." Some customer wishes we can't do anything about, as with the guy who asked for a date with actress Sandra Bullock. Other wishes we could help with but choose not to, like the ones by people who ask for a tour of my house. Then there are those that just baffle us, like the one from a fellow who wished he could get Microsoft Flight Simulator to fly him on the computer to the island of Fiji. We finally discovered that the numbers he was entering into the program came from a map on his shower curtain and bore no relationship to earthly coordinates.

We pay much more attention to customer wishes involving new product features, which pour in from customers and from our sales representatives and technical account managers—over the Web, by e-mail, by fax, and by mail, at a rate of more than 10,000 per month.

By analyzing the aggregate data, the PI team develops prioritized lists of problems and recommends to each development team a variety of solutions, including new product features. This structured feedback gets to our development teams early enough in the development cycle for appropriate corrections or new features to be included in the next release. For example, we shipped Internet Explorer 4.0 in September 1997. Two months later we shipped a minor upgrade primarily to deliver features that made Internet Explorer easier to use for people with disabilities. But that upgrade also contained, among other fixes, the solutions for six of the top ten customer complaints from that brief interval between the two releases.

We acted so quickly because every morning the PI team ran a report to analyze the most severe and time-consuming problems for customers and presented its findings to the Internet Explorer team, which would assign developers to solve the biggest problems. As a result of the fixes, our support call volume dropped by 20 percent after the upgrade shipped.

On a larger scale and over a long time frame, this kind of monitoring and response goes on for all of our major products. The process is constant and iterative.

We also use our corporate intranet to disseminate information to all interested parties, integrating Web pages with e-mail. For our major products, any employee can go to our Web site to see the current status of the data on customer complaints and requests. When a product is released, PI posts reports on immediate customer reaction. More detailed reports are posted monthly, organized by major product groups. These monthly reports include a problem's symptoms, a short-term solution, recommendations for a longer-term fix, and any response from the product group. Microsoft subscribers get e-mail with links to new monthly reports as they are done. Other employees will see the most current reports when they browse the intranet site. The most frequent visitors are the program managers, developers, and testers for various products. Writers of online articles regularly review the site to ensure that they develop content focused on the most important issues to customers, and another team uses the site to evaluate what new software tools customers may need. The status of customer issues is included in the major quarterly product reviews that go to senior management.

HELPING USERS STEP SAFELY THROUGH PROBLEMS

In recent years Microsoft and other software vendors have been moving from a base of technically sophisticated customers to consumers who care less about technical wizardry than about basic ease of use. As software becomes increasingly prevalent in business, more and more employees who aren't necessarily savvy about technical issues are using computers. And many companies that would never consider themselves to be in the software business at all are getting involved by virtue of publishing Web pages and communicating electronically with customers. For less sophisticated customers, it's not good enough that we're merely prompt in helping to fix bugs or providing smart

Error Message "Help"

We could eliminate a lot of customer help calls at Microsoft by fixing such simple things as error messages. It's pretty shocking how confusing or cryptic they are. Here's one of my favorites, which perhaps one user in a thousand might understand: "The DHCP client could not obtain an IP address. If you want to see DHCP messages in the future, choose 'yes'; otherwise choose 'no.' "

I love that "otherwise choose 'no.' " The message assumes that everybody understands the meaning of DHCP—a method for allocating computer addresses on a network—but that nobody understands the difference between yes and no. I didn't know what this message meant the first time I saw it, so like other users, I chose "no"—I never wanted to see this particular message again. I showed this error message in a recent slide presentation while making the point that we need to push for simplicity in our software, and a few people thought I'd run into a technical problem in the middle of the speech! We have fixed this message in our latest version of Windows.

Have you ever seen the error message that says the system can't associate a file with the right application? That one is really frustrating. If the system doesn't know what files go with what programs, how likely is it that you will? And how many different error messages have you gotten when you've tried unsuccessfully to connect to a Web page? Could anybody, on the basis of one of those error messages, figure out the real reason for the failure?

The problem is not just that the messages are confusing. It's that the system as a whole is not smart enough to help the user through a problem. Instead of simply alerting the user to some inscrutable error, the software needs to fix the problem automatically or walk the user through the necessary steps to fix it. We now have software wizards, for instance, that help users through printing problems or give users shortcuts to certain procedures, and we plan to provide more wizards in the future.

tools to solve problems. They want us to keep things simple in the first place. A goal for companies in many industries now is to use the customer feedback loop to build more intelligence into every aspect of their products so that there's less and less occasion for "bad news" to begin with.

As they move into electronic commerce, a lot of businesses will have to start using electronic tools to furnish the kind of customer support we're working toward at Microsoft. They'll need to recognize that customers at least for the near future will hesitate when they consider purchasing any electronic product or service. How hard will it be to install? Will it work the way I expect it to? If I have problems, how will I get help? Also, users associate one experience with another. If they have trouble setting up their basic online service, they'll be reluctant to set up online banking. If they have problems conducting e-commerce at one site, they'll assume that the problems are a function of e-commerce technology in general, not of a poor Web site.

CREATING A CUSTOMER FEEDBACK LOOP

Using a guarantee to focus corporate attention on customers and using information technology to ensure quick response to customer problems is a strategy that works for Promus Hotels, and it will work equally well for any other service company. Using information technology to instantly drive customer complaints into product development groups, as we've done at Microsoft, is a strategy that will work for any product company. Whether you sell insurance or real estate or you make trucks or breakfast cereal, the principle of using digital systems to tie customers back to your core business is central to future success.

You can collect information from customers even if you don't have a digital system, but you can't analyze it quickly. You can't make nondigital information integral to the development process for a service or a product. Nondigital systems won't enable you to route information directly to product developers. Digital systems give companies the ability to do all these things and transform into adaptive learning organisms. Customer service changes from an add-on activity to an integral part of product development.

The process has to begin with a corporate decision to put the customer at the center of the solution. Once you do that, digital information enables you to create a tight loop that runs between customer needs and your company's reactions. Promus can focus its staff on the problems that customers most care about. At Microsoft we can put our software engineers to work on the problems that are giving customers the most grief rather than on problems the engineers think are the most technically "interesting."

ALWAYS GOING BACK TO THE CUSTOMER

If you accept customer feedback electronically, you need to be prepared to answer quickly. When a customer mails a letter to a company, he or she doesn't expect a reply for a week. But when a customer e-mails a query to your company, he or she knows that the e-mail arrives in a matter of minutes, if not seconds. Business protocol is to respond to e-mail within a few hours or overnight. A few days is "slow." If you take weeks to reply, consumers will take their business to a more responsive company. Because e-mail is so much easier to send than paper mail, you're likely to get many more responses, too. So when you ask

About Those Longer Phone Calls

Electronic feedback loops will change the nature of your existing customer support patterns. As we've rolled out our online support systems at Microsoft, we've discovered that our Web site is handling most of the easy questions from customers. Phone support now handles the most difficult calls. We're getting fewer and fewer calls per product unit sold, but each call is averaging more time.

At first you might be dismayed by such a trend, because longer calls usually mean that your support problems must be getting worse. But in this situation longer calls are a good sign. Your Internet site is handling the novice and intermediate questions, and more difficult problems go to your support staff, which has the training and experience to solve them.

Dell Computer has experienced the same phenomenon as it's provided more and more support online. I believe the trend to longer but fewer calls will show up for many companies that offer online support, regardless of product. As a result, you may need more experienced support personnel on the phone than in the past, but they'll also be helping customers in more profound ways.

for electronic feedback, make sure you have the staff and the internal systems in place to handle it promptly.

Listen to your customers and take their bad news as an opportunity to turn your failures into the concrete improvements they want. Companies that invest early in digital nervous systems to capture, analyze, and capitalize on customer input will differentiate themselves from competition. You should examine customer complaints more often than company financials. And your digital systems should help you convert bad news to improved products and services.

Business Lessons

- ❑ Embrace bad news to learn where you need the most improvement.
- ❑ Your most unhappy customers are your greatest source of learning.
- ❑ Implement policy and business structures that tie complaints directly to a fast solution.

Diagnosing Your Digital Nervous System

- ❑ Can you capture and analyze customer feedback electronically to find out how customers want you to improve your product or service?
- ❑ Do your digital systems enable you to quickly deliver customer feedback to the employees who can fix the problem?
- ❑ Can you respond to electronic customer feedback promptly?
- ❑ Can you drive simple customer queries to your Web site and reserve your phone support for difficult customer questions?

12

KNOW YOUR NUMBERS

To achieve nirvana, you must have perfect information about every customer order (new and old) and every asset in your business (both permanent physical assets and various inventory components). And guess what? The only way to secure, maintain, and harvest this information is through the aggressive use of information technology.

—J. William Gurley,
"Above the Crowd"

If you take your car into a Jiffy Lube station for an oil change and ask for 10W-40, a good oil for hot-weather driving, the service technician will first check his PC terminal before doing anything to your car, to make certain that the manufacturer recommends 10W-40 and not another grade of oil for that make and model.

In fact, the technician can tell you all of the manufacturer's recommendations for service intervals and for the vehicle parts that Jiffy Lube might service: oil, filters, headlights, windshield wipers, transmission fluid, grease—even the number of grease fittings. All from a PC-based point-of-sale system in the service bay.

Cars get in and out fast. A typical Jiffy Lube outlet

services forty-five cars a day and is able to do so more quickly and efficiently with the new system. Technicians don't have to look things up in print manuals anymore, and the system helps managers calculate the number of employees needed to handle traffic patterns for the time of the day and the day of the week. It cuts back on overtime. Most important, it reduces lines. In this business, when customers see a line, they drive away. The old paper system was a productivity bottleneck.

Three months after your visit you'll get a service reminder for your next oil change, one of the 300,000 reminders that Jiffy Lube sends out a week. Having a historical record of customer service to enable timely customer contact is a prerequisite for doing business in many service industries today. Jiffy Lube's system monitors the number of miles driven between visits and, after a couple of visits, learns about the customer's driving habits. Knowing the timing and nature of each customer interaction means that a company can take advantage of cross-selling opportunities.

Jiffy Lube was the world's number one franchiser of fast-lube centers—but unprofitable—when the Pennzoil Company bought it in 1991. In 1997 Jiffy Lube earned $25 million, the highest earnings in its history and an increase of 14 percent over 1996 earnings, on gross revenues of $765 million. Jiffy Lube serviced 21 million cars, an increase of 1.2 million over 1996.

Driving this new success is a daily flow of information from each store to headquarters and back. Customer-service information from each of the 600 company-owned and 1,000 franchisee-owned outlets is uploaded to Jiffy Lube headquarters in Houston each night. With the merger of Quaker State's Q Lube stores, the total number of outlets will increase to more than 2,100 locations. The data goes into multiple servers, including the company's 120-gigabyte customer database, which was recently cut over from a mainframe to a PC server. Headquarters does immediate analysis on a number of operational measures—number of cars handled, costs, revenues, and actual vs. projected profits—and on sales trends. Beginning as early as five A.M., up-to-date performance data is available to all Jiffy Lube managers nationwide, who can log on to the database to get performance figures. Each manager uses the information on a daily basis to see current revenue status, average ticket price, the time required to do each job, and overall throughput for the day.

Corporate management can see historic comparisons of figures for all Jiffy Lube centers. Franchisees with multiple stores can see consolidated activity in all of their holdings. Jiffy Lube's regional managers, who typically supervise ten outlets each, use the operational data to help their outlet managers build their businesses and be more profitable and efficient. The system is quite flexible. If a regional manager develops a special report—say, to detect fraud or abnormalities—it can be sent electronically to different outlets for local analysis.

The Jiffy Lube manager usually isn't an expert in market research, so headquarters employees do marketing and trend analysis. The information they use includes statistics, maps, and profiles of Jiffy Lube customers. The data shows sales by different neighborhoods, including neighborhoods in which the Jiffy Lube outlet isn't as effective as it might be; or which neighborhoods are statistically ripe for a promotion.

If customers are bypassing a neighborhood Jiffy Lube center for another one farther away, the system gives Jiffy Lube an opportunity to investigate. The pattern might be a result of natural traffic flow, or it might signal specific problems at the closer store.

Jiffy Lube is beginning to use its information system to help with promotions. A manager who looks at the weather forecast on a Tuesday afternoon and decides to run a wiper-blade special in a certain market can have the system updated with the promotional details and pricing for the local stores first thing Wednesday. In the future, follow-up information will help the manager determine whether the promotion was profitable enough to try someplace else or whether a special on transmission services was more successful.

Its extensive demographic data analysis and mapping software also helps Jiffy Lube scout and develop potential outlet locations. The software plots existing Jiffy Lube locations, competitor locations, and potential new sites according to the demographics of sites that have already been successful. The company can overlay a map with market data to see where sizable numbers of prospective customers don't have a nearby Jiffy Lube service center. That kind of analysis strengthens the company's relationship with its franchisees, since Jiffy Lube can provide the franchisee with data on land costs, proximity to other stations, and other variables that he would not ordinarily have.

Today information about the individual customer is stored in a database at each local Jiffy Lube store. Depending on size, each service center has a database of 8,000 to 50,000 customers. Jiffy Lube has an initiative to consolidate its eighteen million vehicle records and eighty-five million service records into a national database that is connected to each store. A customer will soon be able to drive into any Jiffy Lube service center in the United States and the outlet will know that vehicle's service history. When any service is done, the data will be updated in a single place and available to outlets all over the country.

The ability to perform this kind of customer service

has changed the way Jiffy Lube does business. It doesn't sit back and wait for customers to come in. It learns as much as possible about its customers and markets and adapts accordingly. Jiffy Lube finds out the kinds of promotions that customers respond to and then ties promotions to customer demographics. The result is more targeted promotions. It might send a certain kind of promotion to customers with a certain income within two miles of a particular outlet, for example.

The company also compiles data on the preferences of individual customers so that it can send service reminders and other promotions via e-mail to customers who prefer electronic rather than paper reminders. Handling the reminders via e-mail will make it possible for Jiffy Lube to personalize promotions and cut costs while improving convenience for customers.

Jiffy Lube is also considering putting up a Web site where a customer, whether an individual or a fleet manager, will be able to get an online Jiffy Lube vehicle service history and manufacturer's recommendations. The Web site would provide details about any current promotion and encourage a visit to the nearest Jiffy Lube store. Jiffy Lube has the infrastructure in place to do all of these things because it built its flow of information around customer data.

KNOWING YOUR NUMBERS FOR SHAPING YOUR BUSINESS

"Know your numbers" is a fundamental precept of business. You need to gather your business's data at every step of the way and in every interaction with your customers. With your partners, too. Then you need to understand what the data means. I'm not saying that you should be single-mindedly driven by bottom-line concerns. I'm saying that you should objectively understand every aspect of your business that you can. If you're considering trading off short-term profits for long-term gains, for instance, you need to know as precisely as possible the cost of that trade-off. Companies can use the data they collect to improve the efficiency of their core businesses, strengthen their relationships with both customers and partners, extend their businesses in new ways, and develop better service and new products.

The Jiffy Lube example illustrates the two dimensions of using customer data. The first is aggregating data for statistics that track trends and patterns on which to base analysis, planning, and decisions. The second is collecting detailed information on the individual customer so that you can provide personalized service. Most of the examples in the rest of this chapter illustrate both ways of using customer data—often from the same set of data. By creating a flow of digital information from start to finish, businesses are able to create tight loops among knowledge management, commerce, and business operations.

To use either kind of data effectively, you need to capture it digitally at the outset and analyze it in digital form at every juncture of your business processes. "Every juncture" includes not just what happens within your corporate walls, but also what happens with both your customers and your suppliers. Knowing your numbers can help you transform all of your business relationships and give you a significant competitive advantage.

COLLECTING YOUR DATA

To ensure accuracy, get your data into digital form at the point of origin. Initial digital data entry reduces reentry labor and virtually eliminates errors. When a new customer pulls into a Jiffy Lube today, the technician takes down the customer information on a paper form on a clipboard and then enters it again into the bay terminal. In the future, Jiffy Lube will use a handheld PC that will eliminate the data reentry step. Reentry takes only a minute, but it increases the chance of an error, and meanwhile the customer is waiting.

At Microsoft we realized immediate, dramatic improvements as soon as we switched from taking customer orders by fax to taking orders digitally. Our application for digital ordering, named MOET (for Microsoft Order Entry Tool), quickly evolved into an advanced Web site for electronic commerce worldwide. MOET makes it easy for our distributors to enter their orders digitally by either creating orders online or uploading them in batch files. Because MOET has all of the part numbers and validates all orders, order entry errors have dropped from 75 percent to zero and the distributor's order is priced automatically. Distributors can find delivery dates, other products, and services at the MOET Web site, too. Today the MOET site, which handled $3.4 billion in revenues in 1998, runs neck and neck with Cisco Systems' order site as the highest revenue-processing Web site in the world.

Once MOET has captured and verified an order, it's electronically routed to the appropriate Microsoft regional manufacturing system for fulfillment. Our manufacturing plants use the MOET information to automatically generate product build schedules, saving time that used to go into manually creating manufacturing schedules. There's no way we could have achieved this related benefit if we hadn't had the data in digital form.

Making data digital from the start can trigger a whole range of positive events. The Coca-Cola Company, whose information systems are described in more detail in chapter 14, is collecting data directly from smart vending machines via cellular phone or infrared signals. These machines, already in use in Japan and Australia, transmit such information as the number of cans dispensed, coin status, and any leakage problems. A PC restocking program at the local bottler office analyzes the data and produces a delivery slip that tells drivers which products and locations need to get stocked the next day. Need-based delivery in Australia has reduced the number of out-of-stock machines on any given day from 20 percent to less than 1 percent, which improves Coke's sales. Drivers are happy, too. They get paid by the case, and their productivity has risen 50 percent. This efficiency in managing its stocking and routes has Coca-Cola on track to double its Middle and Far East business in three to five years without adding more bottlers.

Taking advantage of digital data at its source can even create new business opportunities for a mature market such as soft-drink sales. Panels on new Coke vending machines use interactive technology to display commercials, weather reports, even subway maps. A pilot program in Texas lets customers use a credit or debit card to pay for Coke drinks while fueling at a gas station. Since most people who pay at the pump don't go into the building, the digital sales system at the pump creates a whole segment of new customers for Coke.

SPEEDING AND EXPANDING THE SALES PROCESS

Siemens Information and Communication Networks, part of the global technology giant Siemens AG, is a leader in telecommunications systems used inside a company, known as a private branch exchange, or PBX. Each customer selects from an array of options for PBX equipment to create an internal phone system customized to its needs. Siemens has created a fully digital sales process system that quickly provides quotes, captures and adjusts order information going in, ensures parts compatibility, and drives order information all the way through to the company's manufacturing process.

In the early 1990s Seimens's complex product configurations required a salesperson to assemble a lot of intricate detail before presenting a quote. Every quote involved Engineering, which had to ensure that the parts in an order would be compatible. Any change order was complex, wasting sales time and often leading to a start-over in manufacturing that would delay customer delivery.

To resolve these problems, Siemens put together a team of some 200 people representing sales, systems engineering, customer support, manufacturing, logistics, finance, and IT to develop a new set of tools to make the sales process go faster and easier. The team came up with a set of PC-based applications called CRAFT, or customer requirements and fulfillment tools. CRAFT enables salespeople to develop and present a variety of quotes to customers, without the need for detailed calculations or engineering analysis up front. Engineers who used to work on order configurations can now spend their time developing new products. With CRAFT a salesperson can compile an order in under an hour instead of in several hours, with greater accuracy. Less time with the tool means salespeople have more time to spend with customers. CRAFT provides a set of selection criteria that graphically display what components go together, reconciling any parts incompatibilities as the salesperson creates the order so that a final order can be logged, configured, and booked in real time.

Used by 400 to 500 sales representatives nationwide,

CRAFT passes orders directly to the manufacturing system. This direct path reduces sales order errors and in turn decreases the number of change orders, saving significant costs. Previously, change orders would come in throughout the production process, sometimes until the product was almost out the door. Discounts are no longer attached to a specific option; rather, they are integrated into the total order and are automatically adjusted as parts are added to or dropped from the order. Manufacturing employees are better able to plan for long-lead items and receive much more consistent data sooner. Prompt data has reduced the time to produce a small system from five or six days to less than three days. Emergency requests can be met in less than twenty-four hours. CRAFT has contributed to a significant increase in sales without the addition of sales representatives.

CUSTOMERS DRIVING BUSINESS

Digital data gives you higher-level business benefits, too. Capturing and analyzing digital data in real time can create an information cycle between a business, its partners, and its customers that can reshape a company's entire behavior. Retailer Marks & Spencer, a British institution with 300 stores in the United Kingdom and another 400 around the world, cycles customer information to respond immediately to consumer preferences and to achieve the kind of personalized service that's impossible to get at a typical supermarket chain. Marks & Spencer is tying itself closely to customer buying patterns so that those patterns will drive its business processes in real time.

Marks & Spencer sells a unique mix of dry goods, mostly clothing, housewares, and gourmet foods throughout most of the English-speaking world. It operates Brooks Brothers in the United States. Total revenues in 1998 were £8.2 billion. Marks & Spencer's 15 percent profit is almost five times the median American retailer margin of 3.2 percent reported by *Forbes* magazine in 1998. (In its first quarter of 1999, the Asian crisis and a major build-out program reduced Marks & Spencer's profits somewhat.) The company attributes a large part of its success to its ability to use information to make its supply system highly responsive to customer needs.

Only a few years ago the company's information situation was run-of-the-mill. Like most retailers, Marks & Spencer's buyers ordered and allocated goods to stores according to their best judgments of what customers might like. The information system provided only a basic analysis of historical data to help. It was impossible to predict sales accurately enough to avoid either selling out of stock or having to discount or discard leftover inventory. Both outcomes hurt profitability.

Its 1980s-era point-of-sale system could tell Marks & Spencer on a daily basis that the chain had sold, say, 3,000 navy blue suits, 10,000 French baguettes, and 300,000 roast beef sandwiches, but it couldn't tell the store who bought those sandwiches and suits, what else those customers bought, or how the customers paid for them. The system couldn't alert the company to whether customers were buying substitute items if the goods they originally wanted were sold out, or whether the purchases of regular customers were consistent with their typical buying patterns. The system couldn't help the store detect changing buying patterns as sales were happening during store hours.

And when Marks & Spencer competitors were getting more aggressive on pricing and beginning to stay open later—some even twenty-four hours a day—its old batch-processing system wouldn't allow Marks & Spencer to change prices in real time or extend store hours much beyond nine P.M. As the chain opened stores in different time zones through the 1990s, it began to run out of dead time in which to crunch company-wide sales data. Finally, as its system vendor's customer base dwindled, Marks & Spencer bore more and more of the cost of development. When Marks & Spencer had to buy secondhand gear to get enough equipment, the company started looking for a better way.

Determined not to be stuck with a single system supplier again, Marks & Spencer is outfitting its 300 U.K. stores with PC technology that allows competitive bidding on all aspects of its hardware and software solutions. Each store now has a central quad-processor PC server and forty to fifty top-of-the-line Pentium II PCs acting as point-of-sale devices. Each of these PC tills runs a complete pricing database, so customers can buy any item at any location in the store—socks in the food department if they want. Because the workstations process sales faster than the old devices, Marks & Spencer needs fewer per store. The PCs are having no trouble keeping up with the millions of pounds a day in revenue that the largest stores take in—15,000 transactions a minute across all stores. If anything else in the system fails, the tills keep running.

Marks & Spencer piloted the new system in the peak Christmas season of 1996 and will finish rolling it out worldwide in 1999.

KNOWING CUSTOMERS THROUGH THE SANDWICHES THEY BUY

With its new digital infrastructure in place, Marks & Spencer is beginning to capture an incredible array of data on customer buying patterns. Data from each store is sent electronically to the main data center in London. Fully implemented, the dynamic flow of information will enable Marks & Spencer merchandisers to analyze purchases as they occur instead of waiting overnight. Marks & Spencer will be able to adjust stock throughout the day across the whole chain. Before, the company would stock its stores with gourmet sandwiches according to sales from the day before and would have to make the sandwiches at night. The retailer's 400 food suppliers worldwide will be able to make less product initially and then complete the orders in response to regular sales reports from Marks & Spencer during the day. A store won't need to run out or end up with excess inventory, and customers get fresher consumables. The system will even get automatic feeds from local weather services and be able to make appropriate food stocking suggestions—soup, maybe, if the forecast is for stormy weather, or meat for barbecue if the day will be sunny.

A similar application of information technology enables Marks & Spencer to work closely with its more than 300 clothing manufacturers. When Marks & Spencer launches a dress in two colors—say, red and blue—it quickly knows which one is selling better in which markets. Suppliers work on a just-in-time basis: they make smaller quantities initially and then tune production to actual sales.

Other industries have used just-in-time techniques for manufacturing components and mechanical parts. Marks & Spencer is the first to apply just-in-time inventory techniques to perishable foods and well-tailored finished clothes.

Marks & Spencer's growing database of specific customer data includes not only what item an individual customer bought on a particular day, but what else the buyer purchased in other departments and the time of day of the purchases. Marks & Spencer can aggregate this information to create highly targeted marketing initiatives. Knowing that British customers frequently buy strawberries and whipping cream together and coffee and cookies together, the company can promote and cross-sell the related items in store displays. Or Marks & Spencer can use the data on the individual level to make customer service a proactive invitation to do more shopping. Knowing that you're a lover of fine wines and seafood, the local store can send you a postcard or one day an e-mail inviting you to a special wine-tasting event and send you a packet of complimentary seafood recipes. Knowing your preference for a certain designer's clothes, the store can let you know when the new styles from that designer arrive.

PROVIDING AN OBJECTIVE STARTING POINT

The business side of any company starts and ends with hard-core analysis of its numbers. Whatever else you do, if you don't understand what's happening in your business factually and you're making business decisions based on anecdotal data or gut instinct alone, you'll eventually pay a big price. Microsoft is a product company, and I care deeply about product development. But anyone who has participated in a budget review with the executive committee at Microsoft knows that we insist on having accurate numbers and insightful analysis of those numbers. Numbers give you the factual basis for the directions in which you take your products. Numbers tell you in objective terms what customers like and don't like. Numbers help you identify your highest priorities so that you can take fast tactical or strategic action.

There's no substitute for understanding your numbers

at a working level. Sometimes my friend Steve Ballmer, Microsoft's president, surprises the members of a product group by knowing their pricing schemes and sales numbers—and the competitors'—better than the people presenting a plan to him. He has a way of striding into a room and immediately asking the one question the team doesn't have an answer to. He's done his homework, and he's thought hard about the issues that come out of the numbers. He sets a high priority on fact-based decisions.

The line managers at a company need to be doing the numerical analysis. Other groups can help, but the people who deal with customers and with competitive problems need to be engaged in looking at their business in every way possible every day. The analysis should always support action, not just more analysis. Analysis should lead you step by step to a decision and to action. You have to think, act, evaluate, adapt.

Starting with digital numbers doesn't merely eliminate redundancy of effort and errors. It also sets in motion optimal ways to process the data afterward. Being digital from the outset drives efficiency in manufacturing, shipping, billing, and other operational processes. Getting the data digitally is also the only way to ensure that you get information quickly enough to respond to customer needs before your competitor does.

This need for good, timely information to drive employees to quick action is one reason that "paper numbers" bother me as much as paper forms do. A printed sales figure or a printed number on customer trends is static. You don't have the ability to get in and see detail or to e-mail the number and its context off to somebody to talk about it. You can't analyze what's behind the number. With a paper number that looks out of whack, you have to get hold of somebody and say, "I'm looking at this report, and this number surprises me." A lot of the time, the anomaly is easily explained: Some customer has put in a big order or has backed one out. There's nothing actionable involved, but you still want to know quickly why the month's results look skewed. If you spot a trend in a paper report, it's hard to send the paper around and get people to work together to dig into it. Over time you stop paying close attention because it's so hard to investigate.

When figures are in electronic form, knowledge workers can study them, annotate them, look at them in any amount of detail or in any view they want, and pass them around for collaboration. A number on a piece of paper is a dead end. A number in digital form is the start of meaningful thought and action.

EXTENDING YOUR BUSINESS

Going digital changes your business. Without a modern information system, an oil-change company would have no chance of expanding its services, using well-timed specials to entice customers, or offering special promotions to targeted customers. Coke's ventures with smart vending machines are a good example of "starting digital" and also of creating a new business model. Coke vending machines are evolving into self-managed stores, able to advertise their own wares, offer their own promotions, and order their own supplies or merchandise. None of that would be possible without a digital starting point. Smart machines communicating from remote locations will become more and more common.

SPINNING A WEB OF PARTNERSHIPS

Digital technology also enables a company to create a web of partnerships that serves its customers better. You can create a virtual company in which commerce, knowledge management, and operational systems integrate everyone. Your partners are better integrated with you, benefit more from your success, and are naturally driven to respond to the same precisely tracked patterns of customer behavior that you are. When your information systems are designed to promote a flow of information to and from your customers, the business processes of the entire supply system will naturally align in efficient directions. Just-in-time delivery can be a reality for any industry.

Digital information flow makes it possible for a company to create a boundaryless organization, but it takes a new corporate mind-set and culture to turn suppliers from "them" into "us." In the traditional business model, suppliers have often been merely tolerated for what they provided but were not treated as an integral part of the overall business process needed to serve customers. The old phrase *supply chain* implies links in a linear relationship, looking back from the retailer to distribution to transportation to manufacturing. Today's approach is that of a "value network," a web of partnerships enabled by digital information flow. Everyone who touches the product must add value, and communications go both forward as well as back.[1] Companies in the value network aren't restricted to their places in line by heavy chains of process but can interact and do business with multiple vendors as they need to.

Wal-Mart began the change in how major buyers viewed their suppliers, giving Procter & Gamble access to its sales data so that P&G could do what it does best—manage inventory and distribution—and Wal-Mart could do what it does best—sell lots of products. This degree of

1. The phrase "value network" has been used to describe a number of different ideas. The particular sense of a computer network of partners is developed in Don Tapscott's *Paradigm Shift: The New Promise of Information Technology* (New York: McGraw-Hill, 1993).

openness is the only way to get the full benefit of freely flowing numbers. Wal-Mart, according to *Forbes,* reduced its expenses by $2 billion in 1997 through better inventory management. Much of this savings came from its continuing drive to use information to work better with its supplier partners. Marks & Spencer has demonstrated that information sharing not only reduces costs, but can also reduce reaction time to just a few hours anywhere in the world.

General Electric's CEO, Jack Welch, was one of the first people to talk about "boundarylessness," the idea that solutions to business problems should encompass everyone in the critical path, whether inside or outside the formal borders of the corporation. Not surprisingly, GE, the largest diversified industrial company in the United States, has begun to create for its twelve operating units what will probably become the largest extranet in the world. An extranet is a private Internet site that enables several companies to securely share information and conduct business. GE expects to do more than $5 billion, or 14 percent, of its projected $35 billion in capital procurements over the extranet by 2001, compared with less than 1 percent in electronic purchases today. Fully deployed, the extranet could involve as many as 40,000 trading partners. In addition to being a system for straight transactions, GE's extranet will include software that enables real-time collaboration. GE employees and partners will be able to view and edit the same electronic documents and to discuss them at the same time over the Internet.

In a value network, companies can free up capital that would otherwise be tied up in inventory and dramatically reduce inventory management costs, as Wal-Mart has done. GE expects to save between $500 million and $750 million with its extranet through reduced errors, contract leverage, and other efficiencies. Companies can improve quality, too.

About 70 percent of the value of Ford's products comes from components provided by independent parts manufacturers, and Ford's digital network enables the company to quickly work with these suppliers to address quality issues with parts. Companies in a value network can respond faster and more accurately to the market.

DOING MORE DIGITAL INFORMATION WORK

If the benefits of knowing your numbers and creating a value network are so compelling, why don't more companies do it? Why don't more companies develop their aggregate numbers digitally to track trends? Why don't they track customer history?

The main reason is that too few businesses start with digital input. Grocery stores were among the first to go digital at the point of origin. The original use of scanners was to speed up checkout, but the more important business value became inventory management and trend analysis. Starting with digital data requires diligence, though. If six-packs of soft drinks are on special for $1.99, a checker might key in "two" for a six-pack, even if one is a Dr Pepper and the other a Pepsi. The customer's price total will be correct, but the inventory numbers for both beverage brands will be off.

Connecting digital data among vendors using mainframe-based computers and private networks has also been too expensive. Even though the benefits of data exchange are obvious, less than 5 percent of all U.S. businesses use the old EDI standard. Sometimes only one side of the transaction is electronic: "EDI to fax" is a common approach. And most of that 5 percent are using EDI just for purchase orders and invoicing. They aren't exchanging sales and logistics data to optimize inventory and transportation management. Cost and technical complexity have been holding people back, but the PC and the Internet give us an infrastructure that makes exchanging all kinds of digital information very inexpensive. The more homogeneous the software platform, the less complex the connectivity issues and the better able you are to form a value network.

Not enough people are using digital data in the office. Existing paper systems lead people to assume that data is hard to get and customize. Because their data isn't digital, they have to work with stacks of paper they can't navigate or analyze. They can't find patterns in their data. They can't turn their paper information into action. Because so few companies are using digital tools internally or with partners today, those firms that act quickly to create a digital nervous system have the opportunity to jump ahead of their competitors.

To make the transition to an empowered virtual enterprise, a CEO needs to look first at all of the paper on desks of knowledge workers and ask, How could digital systems get rid of these stacks of paper? As part of this examination, think of your business processes as extending far beyond your walls to encompass the entire web of your partnerships and your customers. You need to develop business processes supported by a swift, reliable flow of information that will enable the customer to drive your responses and the responses of all of your vendors as if you were one entity. If you find your efforts to link up with your partners and your customers to be more focused on costs and just keeping things running, and less on building solutions that add business value, evaluate your technical underpinnings. You need to step back and come up with a new approach.

Business Lessons

- ❑ Knowing your numbers is more than balancing your books each month. It's being able to use data for marketing and sales as well as for financial purposes.
- ❑ A number on a piece of paper is a dead end; a number in digital form is the start of meaningful thought and action.
- ❑ Quick, accurate numbers make it possible for customer actions to drive an immediate response by you and your partners.

Diagnosing Your Digital Nervous System

- ❑ Do your digital systems capture your business's data at the point of origin and in every interaction with your customers and partners?
- ❑ Can you integrate your partners' numbers with yours?
- ❑ Do you have a complete customer database that you take full advantage of?

13

SHIFT PEOPLE INTO THINKING WORK

> We view this pile of data as an asset to be learned from. The bigger the pile, the better—if you have the tools to analyze it, synthesize it, and make yourself more creative.
>
> Britt Mayo, Director of Information Technology, Pennzoil

The inevitable consequence of better computer systems is a smarter use of people's time. With intelligent software continuously scanning through its sales data, tracking trends, and noticing what's selling and what's not, Marks & Spencer can use its 500 to 600 buyers far more effectively. Instead of plowing through fat paper reports from the previous day to try to determine whether sales are going well, the buyers can spend their time more effectively to capitalize on what up-to-the-minute data is telling them. If sales are proceeding as desired, no human intervention is needed, but the new system monitors sales data and flags items whose sales fall above or below preset bounds. Exception reports are created automatically, and buyers handle only exceptions.

"With these smart systems in place, we're able to shift people from repetitive, nonthinking work to more productive activities," says Keith Bogg, Marks & Spencer's divisional director for IT and logistics. "They use their intelligence to deal only with the exceptions, letting the computers make decisions about everything else. We can redeploy those people to do new product selection, market analysis, and other value-added activities instead of babysitting daily stock. Buyers are spending their time much more effectively, adding a lot more value than they were before."

Desktop tools can make sophisticated analysis easy. Investment firms use electronic spreadsheets in the areas of risk management and portfolio analysis for such things as managing the real-time exposure of a given option to changes in its underlying price or analyzing the spread of a portfolio across different industry sectors.

Morgan Stanley Dean Witter uses spreadsheets in its Equity Division to examine complex data structures and provide multiple views to its sales and trading staff as well as to its clients. In Tokyo, for example, some clients wish to see individual trades and executions for a given day, while others wish to see only the average executed price across different accounts. Complementing this functionality are proprietary risk models that can often offer more detailed insight into a client's risk and performance.

Pivot tables, which quickly flip data from one view to another, have enabled the firm to adapt to the use of a common currency, the Euro, by several European countries. A typical international portfolio, divided across national currencies, no longer applied. Pivot tables could create sector-based views of the same information, providing clients with a more relevant representation of the data.

Using software to handle routine data chores gives you

the opportunity to provide the human touch where it really matters. There's a pretty dramatic difference between getting a note that was clearly written by a person vs. a computer-generated form letter, or receiving a phone call about some new product or special event from a person vs. a computer. It's of incredible value to have a person working with a customer who is unhappy about something really important or who has special needs. In a hotel, for instance, smart software can dramatically shorten the check-in and checkout time and solicit routine feedback, freeing up staff time. How much more would people enjoy their hotel stay if there were half a dozen additional people acting as concierges instead of as clerks?

Electronic commerce, though, brings new challenges. In a physical store a salesperson can use clues such as the customer's questions, dress style, and body language to better assess interests. However, on a Web store no one sees the customer, and the goal is to let the customer do as much shopping as possible for himself or herself. Web store owners have an interesting piece of detective work. Based on customer browsing behavior and purchase history, how do you construct a model of who the shopper is? It requires sophisticated data analysis capability.

EXTENDING THE REACH OF HUMAN ANALYSIS

Digital analytical tools such as the ones Marks & Spencer uses, which enable people to focus only on exceptions rather than on the routine, are also changing the nature of work. The tools are so powerful that some Marks & Spencer employees were initially afraid they'd be replaced by computers. There's a natural resistance to giving up any decision-making function and letting a machine do it.

When a database gets big enough and complex enough, though, the computer can do the initial searching and sorting far better than a human being. We're simply incapable of recognizing patterns in large amounts of data. And the available data—in databases, file systems, messaging systems, and Web sites—is growing exponentially. The only way we can get the full value of all of this data is to use computer tools to get at it and sift it for actionable information.

Using software algorithms to find useful patterns in large amounts of data is called *data mining*. The first major step in data mining was online analytical processing (OLAP), which makes many kinds of querying much more efficient. Data originally collected for accounting and bookkeeping purposes was recognized as a potential mine of information for modeling, prediction, and decision support. Companies began creating corporate data stores, or *data warehouses*, to satisfy these new demands for business analysis. Data subsets focused on one aspect or department of a business are often called *data marts*.

HarperCollins, the publishing company, uses a PC-based OLAP system to track book sales in real time so that it can print just enough books to meet distributor demand. That way HarperCollins won't be caught with large stocks of unsold copies in the channel, which publishers have to take back as returns. After only a year in operation the new system has helped HarperCollins reduce returns of unsold copies on its most popular titles from over 30 percent to about 10 percent. Each percentage point represents millions of dollars in savings.

Its OLAP system enables HarperCollins to ask questions such as, What was the profitability of this title this week with this distributor? But OLAP needs a human being to direct the querying, and neither traditional data-

Digital Tools Slice and Dice

In most business organizations, people need to see information in a variety of ways. Senior executives often want to see a consolidated view of sales, then a view by region, then by country. Sales managers want to see numbers by team and individual sales or by customer accounts. Product managers want to see numbers by sales channel or to drill down to see what SKUs (Stock-Keeping Units) are selling well or poorly. Different people need to see month and year-to-date sales, actual sales vs. budget, year-over-year changes in sales, and sales in U.S. dollars or other currencies. Typically, a company's finance department produces a very large number of separate reports to meet these various business needs.

Often, all of these reports can be produced digitally using an electronic spreadsheet. Outline controls enable businesspeople to begin at a summary level and click on any item in order to drill into successive levels of detail. Another capability known as pivot tables enables people to see the same data in multiple ways. If you're viewing sales by salesperson and you want to shift to a view by customer, you change the view by dragging the customer label to the proper row position. When these capabilities are combined with templates that build the underlying data into standard formats, the results are powerful, flexible digital reports that each person can personalize to meet specific needs. Such reports can also be e-mailed around for further analysis and discussion.

Pivot tables are particularly powerful when combined with a company's data warehouse. Each database in the warehouse usually has limited reporting capabilities, restricting creation to more technical personnel. Typically, people aren't sure when they will need additional detail, so they do massive database queries that might take twenty to thirty minutes to run. Pivot tables linked to a database extend data warehouse access to all business users, and a spreadsheet interface enables users to do summary-level queries and refine them step by step to obtain more detail. With little data involved with each refresh of the data, response is very fast. This interface can extend to a dynamic data source such as real-time stock-market feeds.

For the businessperson, digital tools mean faster and deeper analysis. For accountants, digital tools mean less time spent producing reports and more time assisting with business analysis and exploring exceptions. For the people managing business data, digital tools mean much faster and higher-quality information, with monthly closings taking a couple of days instead of weeks. With the same headcount, finance departments can then take on assignments involving new data, such as long-term planning and analysis of head count usage or fixed assets.

What digital tools do that paper reports cannot is give everyone the ability to ask the next question. Because you never know what that question is going to be, you need tools that help you explore the answers on your own.

bases nor OLAP can find answers in the data for less-well-defined but important business questions such as, Which of my customers is likely to prefer product A over product B? What distinguishes my satisfied customers from my unsatisfied customers? Which customers in my database are "similar" to other customers in my database? The results of nonspecific queries such as these would swamp the user of an OLAP system and wouldn't be meaningful. Sophisticated forms of data mining will use software to navigate an information-rich environment, helping users answer business questions without requiring them to be experts in statistics, data analysis, or databases.

Among the challenges that data mining can help with are these: Predicting the likelihood of customers buying a specific item based on their age, gender, demographics, and other affinities. Identifying customers with similar browsing behaviors. Identifying specific customer preferences in order to provide improved individual service. Identifying the date and times involved in sequences of frequently visited Web pages or frequent episodes of phone-calling patterns. Finding all groups of items that are bought together with high frequency. This final technique is usually valuable for merchants to uncover buying patterns, but a correlation between two billing codes for the same procedure enabled an Australian health care provider to uncover more than $10 million in double-billing fraud.

Data mining is also a valuable tool for forecasting sales and sharing that analysis with partners and customers. Data mining is being used in manufacturing, banking, telecommunications, planetary geology/remote sensing, and in running interactive Web stores. By recognizing patterns of consumer activity on a Web site, for instance, Microsoft Site Server Commerce 3.0 can predict shopper interests and can customize the online shopping experience for each visitor. Web stores can tailor ads, promotions, and cross-selling offers for every visitor. Data mining techniques can also ensure that an online store doesn't send a mass e-mailing to its customers with offers they're unlikely to be interested in, avoiding a cost that is often ignored: the price of annoying customers with irrelevant information.

Some less typical but interesting applications of data mining include analysis of foster children records to help design better social services, and the scouting of NBA basketball players. Data mining gave the Utah Jazz basketball team a complete profile on every tendency of the Chicago Bulls' Michael Jordan, including an isolation play in which he takes two or three dribbles before pulling up for a jumper. Analysis is only as good as your ability to execute, though. Even knowing Jordan's profile, Utah couldn't stop him from using that dribble move to hit the winning shot in the game that gave Chicago the 1998 NBA championship.

The most common business use of data mining is for database marketing, in which companies analyze data to discover customer preferences and then make targeted offers to specific sets of consumers. For example, American Airlines uses information about the twenty-six million members of its frequent flier program—such as the rental car companies, hotels, and restaurants they use—to develop targeted marketing efforts that have saved more than $100 million in costs.

Cost savings come from the ability to create more precise models of customers and reduce the amount of mailings. A direct marketing campaign for something like credit cards, for instance, would normally generate a return of about 2 percent. Mellon Bank USA in 1997 had a target of acquiring 200,000 new accounts, a number that would require mailing offers to 10 million prospects. Instead the bank used data mining techniques to produce 3,000 models of the most likely prospects. A subset of the models was refined to create a smaller number that, testing showed, would generate a response rate of 12 percent. This rate enabled the bank to mail only about 2 million offers to acquire the desired 200,000 customers instead of mailing to the original population of 10 million. In addition to reducing cost, the average profitability of an acquired customer was three times higher than usual because data mining had targeted the customers whose needs best matched Mellon Bank's services.

This example illustrates two important aspects of data mining. The first is the sheer scale of it: The amount of data involved and the number of models explored are far beyond traditional statistical analysis. The second is that even highly trained specialists can benefit from data mining, as seen in the Mellon Bank example by the ability of an outside team to get six times the results in one-fourth the time of customary methods used by an in-house dedicated statistical analysis department. A major goal is making the tools so easy to use that the business end user, not a specialist, can apply them.

Data mining will become a requirement for online interaction. Lars Nyberg, chairman and CEO of NCR, described to me the standard menu his bank ATM prompts him with: Does he want instructions in English or Spanish, which account does he want to access, what kind of transaction does he want, and when he's done, does he want to do another transaction? At the end, the ATM displays an ad with a phone number to call if he wants a mortgage from that bank. Most ATM users have worked through a menu like this.

Yet Lars withdraws the same amount of money from the same account almost every time he uses the ATM. He already has a mortgage from this bank and pays them a lot of money every month for it. When he puts in his bank card, why doesn't the machine ask him in the language he usually uses, "Lars, would you like your normal withdrawal from your primary account?" And why doesn't it promote a service he doesn't already use, one that fits his customer profile? Such specialized service would be better for him and better for the bank. The information needed to create these more relevant questions is in a computer somewhere. NCR actually makes the ATM for Lars's bank and is developing a major practice in data mining. Lars is keen on solving these kinds of problems for his customers.

Data mining is part of customer relationship management (CRM), in which information technology helps companies manage customer relationships on a one-to-one basis instead of on the mass-marketing model. Data mining is actionable for reaching the individual customer when there is a channel for customized delivery, whether it's an ATM or a Web site or direct marketing via e-mail promotions and offers. With the patterns revealed by data mining, you can present your products to a customer in a way that's most likely to increase your value to him and his value to you.

This personalization has profound implications for advertising in all media, including television and magazines. As digital TV becomes prevalent and electronic books become the preferred way to read magazines and newspapers, virtually all advertising will move away from mass advertising to personalized advertising. The ads that appear onscreen will differ according to the demographic profiles of the viewer.

Instead of having to buy every household in the United States with mass media to advertise a car or other item, companies will be able to buy the demographic that's most efficient to reach their potential customers. If, for instance, somebody's already bought a certain type of car and you think the time frame is right for him or her to be in the market for a new one, you could target that customer narrowly. A big car company may still buy other demographics to keep its brand awareness high but would focus its advertising on the best demographics.

We're already seeing personalization a tiny bit on the Web. If a user types in a location in a search engine—"San Francisco," for example—or indicates that he or she wants to buy a book related to travel or certain other topics, an ad about that location or topic comes up along with the other information. A context-sensitive ad, which you can associate with a customer's preference or something that the person is trying to do, is worth dramatically more than a generic hit-or-miss ad.

The ability to personalize ads means that different neighborhoods or even different households in the same area could be seeing different ads. Big companies can become more efficient with their advertising, and small companies can begin to consider TV and magazine ads for the first time; today many advertising vehicles are too expensive for any but true mass-market products. Even the corner grocer would have the potential to afford TV ads for people living near the store.

Targeted ads should make consumers happy. They're more likely to see ads that are relevant to them. Some people may be concerned about advertisers having too much information about them, but as I say in chapter 5, software will make it possible for consumers to reveal only the information they want to reveal. Giving advertisers access to viewing patterns is not unreasonable, as just one example. Most subscribers to a specialty publication—whether the topic is sports, science, gardening, homemaking, or autos—peruse the ads as carefully as the articles. If you watch TV in the same way, primarily for one or two interests, you probably wouldn't object to seeing ads focusing on those interests.

Soap operas—that staple of daytime TV in the United States—are so named because the advertisers were traditionally the big soap companies going after the audience of largely female viewers. So the idea of targeted TV marketing is not new. The dimensions of it are radically different, though, with data mining as a way of gleaning information and digital TV and electronic books as a way of narrowly targeting the audience in a more personal way. The combination will bring very much a revolution in how you think of advertising and marketing. Personalization greatly increases the value of understanding whom you want to target with your products and services.

GETTING THE MOST OUT OF DATA MINES FOR EVERYONE

Today most data mining systems are quite expensive, ranging from $25,000 to $150,000 for a small or medium-size business to millions of dollars for a high-end customer such as Wal-Mart. One insurance company spent more than $10 million for a data mining solution five years ago. The CEO said he knew he could obtain the same solution for a good deal less money with today's technology but the results had been worth the $10 million investment. That remark gives an indication of the value of data mining, but these high prices reflect the old world order of software complexity, in which only the largest organizations, using a lot of staff or hiring specialized vendors, could make good use of data.

With the growth of competition in our information-based economy, customer data has become an increasingly important asset. Every company, and every knowledge worker at a company, has an imperative to get the most out of the company's data assets. These new users can't afford big database budgets or specialized database experts. Fortunately, as data mining capabilities become available on the high-volume PC platform, you'll see prices drop dramatically and the use of data mining explode in companies and departments of all sizes. Soon every business user will be able to do the high-end analysis that used to be reserved for the companies that could shell out big bucks. Data mining will become pervasive, a standard capability of every business's information system infrastructure.

The greatest value of data mining will be to help companies determine the right products to build and the right way to price them. Companies will be able to evaluate a variety of packaging options and price points to see which ones are most appealing to customers and profitable to themselves. Such capabilities are of special interest to companies that sell information products. Unlike a car or chair, products such as insurance, financial services, and books have far more cost tied up in development than in production and have a value determined more by the customer than by the physical cost of goods. The secret to success with information products is understanding the profile and buying habits of your most likely customer.

Insurance companies, for instance, have products that are very profitable with some customers and less profitable—or unprofitable—with others. The difference is related to loss experience with policyholder claims. Data mining can provide an insurance company with the customer profiles and geographies where its loss experience is very low or very high. The company can determine whether to do heavy marketing and attractive pricing to people in an age group or geography with good loss experience and whether to raise prices or do less marketing in groups with bad loss experience. When you have that kind of variability, it's worth a lot to do data mining to help develop your product strategy. Banks have similar opportunities to use data mining to target new customers. People are now more willing to switch banks, and there are many new financial services companies. Banks will have to do a lot more marketing to acquire customers, and this marketing will pay off only if they figure out which customers are most valuable.

But you always have to ask what's actionable. If your customer profiles are quite similar or your customer base is small, data mining is not nearly as actionable. A grocer selling specialty items to a small neighborhood clientele probably doesn't need to do data mining. A national grocery chain does.

The powerful capabilities of data mining will help companies determine how to acquire new customers, whom to market to, how to tailor and price their products, and how to attract individual customers. Human creativity and skill are needed to use this information to come up with the new packaging and pricing approaches, to see the seed of new products in the patterns the computer returns, and to figure out intriguing new offers. The better tools they have, the more creative they can be. Management needs to invest in advanced tools that enhance people's jobs. You should budget 3 to 4 percent of the salary of your knowledge workers to make sure they have the best tools, which free people to direct their mental energies toward finding creative responses to the patterns and trends identified by the computer. Using information to develop innovative new products and services and to collaborate more closely with partners and customers will always remain a uniquely human endeavor. As software extracts more and more ore from the mine of information, people will always have work turning it into gold.

Business Lessons

- ❏ Analytical software enables you to shift human resources from rote data collection to value-added customer service and support where the human touch makes a profound difference.
- ❏ Apply software analysis first to those aspects of your business where you are most able to act on the results.
- ❏ Consider how the move from mass advertising to targeted advertising will change your marketing approach.

Diagnosing Your Digital Nervous System

- ❏ Can you do sophisticated analysis of customer buying patterns and use the results for either trend analysis or individualized service?
- ❏ Can you determine which customer groups are the most profitable and the most unprofitable for you—by income, age group, geography, or other demographics?
- ❏ Do your digital systems enable people to shift from dealing with the routine to dealing with the exceptions?
- ❏ Do your employees have easy, digital access to numbers? Can they go from summaries to detailed data? Can they see numbers in different dimensions and pivot across those dimensions?

14

RAISE YOUR CORPORATE IQ

An organization's ability to learn, and translate that learning into action rapidly, is the ultimate competitive advantage.

—Jack Welch, Chairman, General Electric

A few years ago we discovered we were missing some blueprints for the existing buildings on our Redmond campus. We needed the blueprints as background for our next stage of construction. Our longtime head of real estate and facilities had just retired, so we had to call him up at home to see if he knew where the plans were. He directed us to an electrician who fortunately still worked with one of our outside vendors. Sure enough, the electrician had the blueprints. In fact, that electrician was the only person in the world who had all of the plans for all of our buildings.

Traditional societies often rely on one or two people to remember the group's history and traditions, but modern organizations need a better way to record and pass on their folklore. Yet at Microsoft we were relying pretty much on oral tradition, too. Here we were, the largest developer of office space in the Seattle area, embarking on a period of construction in which we would put up between half a million and a million square feet of new office space a year, and our entire "knowledge base" of crucial information was being carried around in the heads of just a few people and in a few stacks of blueprints we didn't even have on file.

Alarmed by this incident, the Microsoft real estate and facilities group decided we needed a digital repository to preserve and augment all the knowledge we'd accumulated over two decades of construction. We put all of our blueprints, diagrams, and other construction information into computer-aided design (CAD) files, and created a CAD standard for our vendors to implement going forward. We moved existing electronic documents from vendors' systems into our in-house system. Then we created an extranet site for our vendors to access for as long as they are part of a project. Everyone has access to records of problems and solutions from earlier phases of construction. Because we've regained control of the information, we can bid out projects more broadly to get better pricing and flexibility.

Our business and financial planners use the extranet site to prepare for an office expansion or the opening of a new subsidiary. Microsoft personnel can get educated on issues and costs related to major real estate projects, and international groups can use our main campus real estate expertise as they plan for business development. Floor plans are also posted on our intranet so space planners in separate buildings on our main campus can view the same floor plans as they discuss major moves. Regular employees use the floor plan page to see where their new offices will be after a move. In fact, except for a brief flurry of visitors to the food page while we were changing cafeteria vendors, the floor plan page has been the most commonly visited spot on our intranet.

DEFINING KNOWLEDGE MANAGEMENT

Our electronic real estate library and a similar one on trademarks and patent law are examples of corporate knowledge management. As a general concept—to gather and organize information, disseminate the information to the people who need it, and constantly refine the information through analysis and collaboration—knowledge management is useful. But like reengineering before it, knowledge management has become infused with almost any meaning somebody wants to associate with it. News articles on the topic, analysis, and even reviews of the "category" appear regularly. Consulting practices and Web sites are devoted to knowledge management, and a "knowledge management" magazine started up in mid-1998. If reporters talk to a database company, they find that knowledge management is the newest thing in databases. If reporters talk to a groupware company, they find that knowledge management means the next generation of groupware.

So let's be clear on a couple of things first. Knowledge management as I use it here is not a software product or a software category. Knowledge management doesn't even start with technology. It starts with business objectives and processes and a recognition of the need to share information. Knowledge management is nothing more than managing information flow, getting the right information to the people who need it so that they can act on it quickly. It goes back to Michael Dertouzos's idea that information is a verb, not a static noun. And knowledge management is a means, not an end.

The end is to increase institutional intelligence, or corporate IQ. In today's dynamic markets a company needs a high corporate IQ to succeed. By corporate IQ I don't mean simply having a lot of smart people at your company—although it helps to start with smart people. Corporate IQ is a measure of how easily your company can share information broadly and of how well people within your organization can build on each other's ideas. Corporate IQ involves sharing both history and current knowledge. Contributions to corporate IQ come from individual learning and from cross-pollination of different people's ideas.

The workers in a company with a high corporate IQ collaborate effectively so that all of the key people on a project are well informed and energized. The ultimate goal is to have a team develop the best ideas from throughout an organization and then act with the same unity of purpose and focus that a single, well-motivated person would bring to bear on a situation. Digital information flow can bring about this group cohesiveness.

A company's high-level executives need to believe in knowledge sharing, or even a major effort in sharing will fail. Leaders must further show that they themselves are not locked in an ivory tower, isolated from everyone else, but are willing to engage with employees. Jacques (Jac) Nasser, automotive operations president at Ford, sends e-mail every Friday afternoon to 89,000 Ford employees worldwide, sharing the week's news—the good and the bad—with everybody. No one screens the e-mail. He talks straight to the employees. He also reads the hundreds of responses he gets each month and assigns a member of his team to reply to any that need follow-up.

I don't send out weekly reports, but I do e-mail employees worldwide on major topics. Like Jac Nasser, I read all the e-mail that employees send me, and I pass items on to people for action. I find unsolicited mail an incredibly good way to stay aware of the attitudes and issues affecting the many people who work at Microsoft. We also use Windows Media Player, which continuously streams audio and video across the corporate network or the Internet, in order to broadcast press and industry events to employees. Because the client machine does not have to download all the content before playing it, streaming media reduces the wait time and storage requirements on the user's PC.

Having established an atmosphere that encourages collaboration and knowledge sharing, business leaders need to set up specific knowledge-sharing projects across the organization and make knowledge sharing an integral part of the work itself—not an add-on frill that can safely be ignored. Then leaders need to ensure that the people who share knowledge are rewarded. The old saying "Knowledge is power" sometimes makes people hoard knowledge. They believe that knowledge hoarding makes them indispensable. Power comes not from knowledge kept, but from knowledge shared. A company's values and reward system should reflect that idea.

Knowledge management can help any business in four major areas: planning, customer service, training, and project collaboration. If you haven't done any explicit work on knowledge management in your company yet, consider picking one or two areas in which to launch knowledge management projects. You can use the success of your projects in those areas to encourage knowledge management projects in your other business areas. Within a few years all leading companies will have achieved levels of digitally charged knowledge sharing that are on par with the ones I describe in this chapter.

SUPPORTING CROSS-BORDER BRAND PLANNING

No company has a better-known brand than the Coca-Cola Company, which makes four of the world's five top-selling soft drinks. About two-thirds of Coca-Cola's sales and nearly 80 percent of its profits come from international markets. Coke uses technology to create a flow of information that supports its most important business planning function and worldwide brand management. And not just for its carbonated drinks. Coke has more than 160 brands of beverages that include juices, teas, coffee, sports drinks, and milk-based drinks across almost every country in the world.

Coke was one of the first companies to establish worldwide communication, with its own custom e-mail system, in the 1980s. In 1997 CIO Bill Herald conducted the company's first-ever information technology strategy review to make sure its technology was aligned with the company's business strategy. In the course of the review the company realized that despite its earlier investments, it too often treated information technology as an expense to control rather than as an enabler of better business. As a result of this realization, the thinking at Coke moved from "how much can we save" to "how much can we grow share globally so that we don't have to reinvent the wheel." From this review came initiatives to standardize the worldwide desktop environment, applications, the network operating system, the database system, and the Coca-Cola system's entire technology architecture.

The worldwide system for information flow has consolidated the company's business processes for research, brand planning, and global marketing. Marketing has usurped finance as the biggest user of information technology at Coca-Cola. Where cost analysis was once the primary motive for information gathering, now it's consumer and market analysis.

If Coke wants to understand why people in the Bronx drink half as much Coke as consumers on Staten Island, or compare Coke consumption in France to Coke consumption in Belgium, marketers use its analytical tool, Information For Marketing, or Inform, to examine the data: ethnic composition, penetration of sugar-sweetened or carbonated soft drinks in the market, brand relevance, and other demographics. The Inform tool integrates data from the company's own sales and marketing sources with data from research sources such as Nielsen, focus groups, and UN-supplied country per capita incomes. Inform shows what's going on by country or multiple countries and by brand information—volume share, preference imagery, why consumers consume and purchase certain brands.

Sales data is available on Inform by market, outlet, time period, or location. Inform incorporates more than 1,000 research studies on how to determine company or brand preference levels in a particular country. Inform can tell you what types of people in a specific township in South Africa are daily drinkers of Sprite and what their total daily consumption was last March.

All of this information makes it possible for Coke to develop better marketing plans across many countries and to develop very targeted new products. Coca-Cola Japan, for instance, produces more than twenty-five new soft drink, tea, and coffee products a year. It needs good information tools to plan these products and evaluate their success.

While brand planning has gone on at Coke for decades, the different Coke companies used to collect their research data in different ways. Some data was quantitative, some was qualitative, some was a mix of both. The different kinds of data resulted in huge variations in brand plans in the 200 countries Coke sells in. Now the brand plans grow out of Inform data. A new planning system contains 150 questions to be answered in all brand plans and organizes the information according to repeating processes. What is the per capita income? Percentage of disposable income spent on beverages? Market penetration of carbonated soft drinks? Inform ensures that each planner considers these questions by taking the planner to the related data. This instant data access enables the user to develop a brand plan quickly. A planner seldom has to ask for manual research. The planner learns from previous research and the accumulated corporate wisdom.

A planner in Zimbabwe who wants to figure out the best way to launch Sprite in his country might discover that a Coke marketer in Thailand launched the same product six months ago. The Zimbabwean marketer can review the results of the earlier launch and even e-mail the Thai planner to discuss the fine points. When planning is completed, the business plan and its supporting material are stored together in one place. Inform ensures that every planner covers the same comprehensive steps in building a brand plan, but a corollary goal is for each planner to add his or her unique thinking to what has gone before. Coke wants to continually improve the quality of thinking throughout its system.

Information sharing also supports the company's global ad campaigns—about 250 ads a year, 50 for the Coke brand alone. The company's global brand process uses a standard methodology to test ads by market. Using Inform, a marketing brand manager can search the global pool of tested ads to find ads appropriate for the attributes of a particular target population group or country. The marketer can usually even determine whether to customize the ending to make the ad locally relevant.

Because information tools such as Inform spread learning in the organization, new Coke employees or recent transfers come up to speed faster. People aren't dependent on knowing people in the research group or in a certain city. The same information and planning templates are available worldwide. The company can transfer a brand manager from France to Argentina and expect the initial quality of work to be much higher than it might have been in the past.

"We use our consumer information system to enable business disciplines and manage the routines across borders," says Tom Long, vice president and director of strategic marketing at Coke. "We use our information to help us gain best practices from what we do over and over—brand planning, business planning, advertising testing, and consumer image analysis. Technology enables us to take new people, point them to where the information is, and have them deliver a robust business plan."

Inform was initially developed in 1995–96, and Coke employees started using it widely in 1997. Users of Inform increased from 400 headquarters-based marketers to more than 2,500 general managers, researchers, brand managers, and midlevel marketing staff worldwide by mid-1998.

The information system has resulted not in leaner staffs, but in smarter staffs who focus on anticipating the market rather than reacting to it. In fact, because of Inform, Coke puts a higher premium on human thought. Information enables good employees to shine. Information creates accountability. Information eliminates excuses. "The brand planning tool comes with no brains included—you get great information that you add value to," Tom Long says. "This has raised our expectations of how knowledge should be used. We move from description to explanation. It's the explanatory whys of consumer behavior that marketers now have to uncover to repeatedly deliver results. Inform gets us to that focus. We take information to new levels of insight."

SPEEDING CUSTOMER RESPONSE

When customers need answers to important product questions, a company often has to scramble behind the scenes to get them the answers. Both Yamanouchi Pharmaceuticals, at $3.9 billion the third largest pharmaceutical company in Japan, and Microsoft have made Web-based information systems a key component in improving the quality and timeliness of answers to customers' tough technical questions.

Product support personnel at Yamanouchi can immediately answer about half the questions that come in from doctors or pharmacists. To find the answers to more difficult questions, they use Yamanouchi's Web-based PRoduct INformation CEnter Supporting System, or PRINCESS. Using optical storage for some documents and a real-time search engine, PRINCESS enables support personnel to do sophisticated electronic searches on products and keywords. They transfer urgent questions they can't answer to product experts. Less urgent queries are e-mailed to experts, who have a goal to respond within one to seven days. Results are relayed to the customer and entered into PRINCESS for future use. To ensure follow-up, every question is tracked electronically.

In 1998 Yamanouchi made this product information system available to its sales representatives over its internal Web site, improving their access to information and their ability to support customers and reducing the load on the call center. The obvious next step would be to make the knowledge base directly available to doctors and pharmacists, but for now such publishing could be construed under Japanese law as illegal pharmaceutical "advertising." The Japanese government is working on guidelines that will make posting the knowledge base possible.

Information gleaned by the call center has enabled Yamanouchi to provide more information on the administration of some medicines to doctors and pharmacists up front and has prompted Yamanouchi to arrange for an extra trial for one medication. Long-term, Yamanouchi has high expectations for collaboration in general among all of its offices in Japan, Europe, and the United States. The company believes it may be possible one day to implement a system that would automatically notify the right people according to the circumstances and automatically set up tasks and deadlines according to the information reported.

Like Yamanouchi, Microsoft uses a Web-based tool to ensure timely responses to complex questions coming into our product groups from our sales representatives, support engineers, and technical account managers worldwide. Such questions can hold up a customer's purchase decision or halt a deployment, so Rich Tong, vice president of applications product management, has for several years driven his teams to a crisp objective: 90 percent of all questions from the field must be answered within forty-eight hours. Product managers at Microsoft live frantic lives giving presentations to customers, doing research, tracking and supporting sales, talking with the press, creating marketing materials, and working with program managers to define future product releases. Even with high-level management pressure and the ability to divide questions up among team members, getting product managers to reply within forty-eight hours has been a challenge.

Now a field sales representative can go to the InfoDesk

Web site, pick a product or an issue from a drop-down list, and submit the question. The question, along with the representative's contact information, is logged into a database. Representatives can also submit questions even when they are at a customer site or traveling. A representative immediately receives return e-mail with a log number and the name of the team that will handle the question.

When a question arrives, the database triggers the messaging system to e-mail the appropriate product manager. If the product manager hasn't answered within forty-eight hours, both he and his manager receive regular e-mail reminders until someone replies. Any manager can query InfoDesk to view open questions—even to track questions that may have been forwarded one or more times. When another team member is asked to contribute to a reply, he receives e-mail and a link to the Web site for additional information. InfoDesk provides query management statistics as well. If a team complains about receiving too many questions, for instance, Rich or any of the management staff can quickly see whether the numbers show that they really do get more questions per person.

In addition to receiving a response, each sales representative receives an online questionnaire about the timeliness, quality, and sales effectiveness of the answer. Answers must satisfy the sales force. You can't get away with a fast but lousy answer. Most of the comments that come back are positive. When they aren't, managers have the information they need to ensure that a product manager does better next time.

InfoDesk is more than just a place for salespeople to submit questions. A section answering the frequently asked questions (FAQs) cuts down on the number of repeat questions; links to other internal resources and information provide a rich knowledge store for our sales force. InfoDesk now has about 20,000 questions and answers in a database going back three years. This trove of information not only has helped us with particular questions, but also had helped us track trends. Analysis of questions allows us to improve our Web site, perhaps creating a new category or generating new pages for issues such as the Year 2000. It's particularly valuable for us in tracking field activity during product beta tests. Questions from the field have led us to make product changes or improve documentation, and they've helped us resolve licensing and pricing questions before a product became broadly available.

TAKING THE PAIN OUT OF TRAINING

Training is the most basic and sometimes most overlooked form of knowledge sharing that needs to go on in a company. Sometimes it seems impossible for busy people to find the time for classes, though. Finding out what courses are available can be difficult. Registering for a course is time-consuming. The training often requires you to leave your office for long stretches of time, and class hours never take an unexpected business problem into account.

A well-designed online training management tool can eliminate these obstacles to employee training. An online catalog of courses and an online registration system take the pain out of class registration. People can view course descriptions and the dates and times the courses are offered; find out whether a class is full and how long the waiting list is; and ask to be notified by e-mail when particular classes they're interested in will be offered. When people register online, they can add a class to their electronic schedules with the click of a button. When the course is over, each participant can be sent an electronic survey to evaluate the course's effectiveness. Freed of managing most of the logistics, trainers and administrators can concentrate on class content. We use such a system at Microsoft, and colleges and universities are adopting similar systems to handle basic course registration.

Even more significant, online systems allow an employee to take training courses at his desk at his own pace and when his schedule permits. Multimedia streaming technology is a great tool for self-paced training. Streaming technology enables the use of audio and video information over corporate networks or the Internet. The presentations can use PowerPoint slides to complement the video and audio. The streaming media format is most appropriate for courses that have long shelf lives and a broad audience in the company. Another good training technology is online chat, which makes the live session interactive and can be recorded for employees who view the session later. The ability to electronically annotate multimedia presentations with comments by later viewers creates living content.

Training companies themselves are using streaming media to conduct classes over the Internet. USWeb, a company that specializes in training people to use technology in business, has developed SiteCast to broadcast interactive seminars. Attendees can view the sessions and participate through chat technologies, and they can replay the sessions when they want to.

Online training has been really popular at Microsoft. In 1998 online participation increased five times faster than classroom participation, and total online participation was more than double our physical class attendance. This increase indicates to us that people want to improve their knowledge and job skills but simply haven't had time-efficient ways to get training before. Streaming media makes it possible for our product experts and executives at headquarters to present information and training to any employee, anywhere in the world.

MANAGING PRODUCT DEVELOPMENT

Digital information flow can really help in the collaboration required to improve products. Through years of internal and external benchmarking, Nabisco has created leading-edge development processes that have produced some of the most popular snack food brands in the world and made the company number one or number two in nearly every category in which it competes. Its 1997 revenues were $8.7 billion.

Historically, roughly a third of Nabisco's new products become blockbuster successes, a third do okay, and another third underperform. These results are better than the industry average; only 20 percent of new products introduced to grocery store shelves each year succeed. But with competition increasing, and with forty to sixty new product projects going on at any one time—each team involving about eight core people and another thirty stakeholders—Nabisco realized that it needed to use information technology to get a competitive advantage in its product development process.

Lots of ideas for new food products are spurred by market research, by what the competition is doing, and by developments in food science. The hard part is determining what to do with ideas after they pop up. It was the winnowing and refining process that Nabisco wanted to improve.

Nabisco didn't need a new product development process. Nabisco needed information technology that would enable it to follow its existing rules of when and how to proceed with development and dramatically improve its success rate. The technology needed to provide well-defined checkpoints, improve communication among team members, and enable people to make decisions with all the facts available. To meet these requirements, Nabisco created Journey, an electronic product development system. Using e-mail on the desktop and e-mail and database technology on the server, Journey organizes the project information that used to be in the file cabinets or scattered around on team members' hard disks and in people's heads. A rigorous set of security features grants or denies authorization to peek into a project.

Say that Nabisco is investigating the feasibility of coming out with a new ginger-lemon cookie. The core people on the ginger-lemon team represent Product Development, Manufacturing, Marketing, Sales, and Finance. Another twenty people are attached to the project as stakeholders—managers, field people, finance people, teams working on related ideas, and so on. Any time a project member wants to communicate with the other core team members or with the larger group of stakeholders, he does it through Journey.

When the product manager clicks on the ginger-lemon project, he can review all the information related to the project by clicking on the appropriate electronic tab. He can see financial analyses and market research. He can see status updates with a chronological, up-to-the-minute listing of all milestones, past, present, and future. He can see current activities—the cookie is entering its first round of focus group testing today; financials will be completed this Friday; R&D is testing a more lemony filling. An electronic discussion forum might include debate about current hot topics such as "advertising strategy," "how much lemon?" and "fat content." All other supporting documents for the project are stored as well. In addition, it would be easy to add another tab to invoke full-featured project collaboration software to access Gantt charts or other visual displays of what tasks depend on other ones, or detailed analyses of the duration of the project and resource assignments.

Recently, during the development of one product, the manufacturing team reported a problem: The product developed an undesirable texture during baking tests. Rather than conduct a traditional, limited dialogue among themselves ("Try adjusting the oven temperature"), Manufacturing entered the problem into the Journey forum for discussion. Journey immediately notified the entire project team by e-mail designated "urgent." R&D got involved and offered a solution—add a new ingredient to modify the texture. Another team member reminded everybody that the addition of a new ingredient would involve a packaging revision. Packaging got involved and made the change. In the end the problem was solved in a few days, vs. the weeks or months it might have taken the old sequential process to play out.

ESTABLISHING FIRM GO/NO-GO GUIDELINES

Beyond serving as a repository for project documents and information on project activities, Journey incorporates the business rules that guide Nabisco's new product development efforts—how the company defines financial success, what kinds of jobs and volumes the company's bakeries are set up to handle, what scores a product has to achieve in consumer tests, what manufacturing costs should be. Journey evaluates whether new equipment has to be purchased and whether that equipment can be reused for other products. The application has the intelligence to monitor a project's compliance with the rules, move the project along from stage to stage, notify everyone of the next step, and ensure that someone immediately reviews the product if it doesn't make the grade at some critical juncture. If the ginger-lemon cookie falls short of the minimal consumer test score, for example, Journey notifies key project members and stakeholders by e-mail so that an immediate review takes place. When the new review is posted on the system, Journey notifies the people who need to read it so that they can determine whether the project should proceed to the next stage.

Before Journey, an enthusiastic team might find a way to brush past poor consumer test scores or manage not to hear warnings from the bakery that the product would be too complicated to produce. Today Journey provides firm, quantitative, go/no-go hurdles that every team must negotiate before proceeding to the next step. Exceptions are possible. Nabisco might decide to green-light a project that will be low-volume overall but strong in certain regions, for instance.

Once a project is done, Journey serves as a central archive, keeping all project documentation in corporate memory. If somebody starts thinking about another lemon cookie idea down the road and wants to tap into the corporate brain to find out about earlier efforts, he or she can find all the documentation, organized by topic.

In the first year and a half after the system rolled out, Nabisco's trial budgets are down by a third. Nabisco has been able to eliminate marginal projects before they got to the trial phase and concentrate on trials for a smaller number of products with better prospects. Eileen Murphy, Nabisco's senior director for new product development, says, "Any good new products program should be a Darwinian competition in which projects compete for scarce internal resources. Some projects live and evolve, and some die, pushed aside by stronger projects. Journey has changed the rules of the competition from one based partially on facts and partially on the persuasiveness of the team leader, to one based primarily on facts—the same kinds of facts for every project."

GAZING INTO AN UNEXPECTED CRYSTAL BALL

A serendipitous benefit of Journey is that Nabisco now has the information it needs to create a "full portfolio view" of new development projects. Senior managers can quickly and easily see what they have in the pipeline and determine whether the company has the right product mix for the near and the long terms. Putting together or updating a rolling eighteen-month aggregate plan used to be an enormous task that required someone to check with all project teams, track down numbers, and knit information together manually. Journey does this automatically by generating a Web-based report that lays out project milestones along a timeline. In addition to this high-level view, managers can get project-specific information by drilling down on a project.

Using Journey, Nabisco has been able to identify gaps in product lines two to three years out, in time for the company to speed up projects or come up with new ideas to fill the void and keep the product portfolio balanced. Its ability to provide an extended view of Nabisco's product plans was an unexpected but tremendous discovery. "Product gaps directly impact our revenues," Eileen Murphy explains. "With Journey, we can take action early to ensure that we are well positioned to capitalize on potential changes in consumer tastes."

Now when Nabisco asks the three key questions of any new product idea—Does the consumer want it? Can we make it? Can we make it at a profit?—Journey helps Nabisco ensure that the answers are "yes" before it proceeds.

INVESTING IN YOUR GREATEST ASSET

In addition to realizing the management and financial benefits of Journey, Nabisco has seen the morale of its employees rise. An employee in any company can spend a lot of time just trying to find out what's going on and seeing that other people get notified, too. Spinning your wheels is one of the biggest frustrations of employment. Using an application like Journey, team members can find out what's going on with a few keystrokes. They can find out what the problems are and make suggestions that won't get lost. They can see how all the pieces of a project fit together. Everyone, not just the project leader, can see the big picture. These benefits are hard to measure, but they go a long way in motivating employees.

To recruit and retain smart people, you need to make it easy for them to collaborate with other smart people. That makes for a stimulating, energized workplace. A collaborative culture, reinforced by information flow, makes it possible for smart people all over a company to be in touch with each other. When you get a critical mass of high-IQ people working in concert, the energy level shoots way up. Cross-stimulation brings on new ideas—and less experienced employees are pulled along to a higher level. The company as a whole works smarter.

Knowledge management won't work, though, unless it's a goal that informs every team's business planning and processes and unless employees are rewarded for sharing information. At the end of each consulting engagement, we require a Microsoft consultant to post technology solutions to a central Web location, called InSite, for the benefit of other technical employees, and we evangelize the use of InSite to reduce preparation time and risk in consulting engagements. In performance reviews product managers are graded on the speed and quality of their teams' responses to field queries, and salespeople are graded on how well they maintain up-to-date information in our customer tracking system. At Coke, knowledge management is one consideration for job performance, and senior managers who evaluate marketing plans also review the collaborative resources such as Inform that went into the project. Nabisco does "360-degree" performance reviews, in which employees are critiqued by everyone around them. If someone is not sharing information or not building on the information of others, that fact will show up in job reviews.

Exercise your ingenuity to reward people for making an information investment in the company. Texas Instruments awards the "Not Invented Here But I Did It Anyway" prize to encourage information sharing. Some companies use inducements such as a night on the town, department store gift certificates, or handheld computers to encourage salespeople to take the time to fill in good data for customer-tracking systems. We gave away InSite polo shirts to the first several hundred contributing authors to help prime the site with quality technical content, and we gave financial awards for the top ten contributions—as judged by employees, who can rate the usefulness of submissions with an electronic voting button on the Web site. Nabisco has a Success Sharing program, which rewards information sharing every month, and an annual chairman's award for team accomplishments. Winners get recognition and money. Wide recognition and even a modest monetary award can go a long way toward creating a spirit of knowledge sharing at any company.

Perhaps the biggest incentive for our sales staff to keep our customer database up-to-date is the knowledge that senior managers, up to and including me, regularly review the customer information provided by the sales force, and budget reviews are based on the information. Salespeople know that their information is being used. They see maintaining the database not as busywork, but as a way to help advance our business and their sales.

Think of knowledge management as an investment in intellectual capital that will ultimately lead to a higher corporate IQ—an enhanced ability of your company to get the best collective thought and action. The idea of intellectual capital is more than a management concept. Intellectual capital is the intrinsic value of the intellectual property of your company and the knowledge your people have. Properly managing this capital raises your corporate IQ and could have a major impact on your company's valuation. More and more, financial analysts are looking beyond a company's physical assets and current market presence to how it manages its intellectual property and its intellectual resources. Financial analysts are betting that companies with well-managed intellectual capital will be market leaders for years to come, regardless of where they are today, and are valuing companies accordingly.

APPLYING TECHNOLOGY TO KNOWLEDGE NEEDS

Any sophisticated application of knowledge management will involve a number of building blocks. The systems for knowledge management in this chapter's examples use different combinations of numerical analysis technology (databases), product or marketing information documents (files), and formal routing and task checkoff software (e-mail and work-flow applications), and most include ad hoc search capabilities (Web technology). Back when the projects cited here were started, the world of databases was separate from the world of e-mail, which was separate from the world of the Web. Each of these projects built on the technology most central to its needs and did a good job of integrating the other technologies.

In the future you won't have to think about which building block to start with. Software technology is bringing together the richness of database, document, and work-flow applications to make solutions much easier to build than before. For today, be sure that any solution you build or buy supports PC and Internet standards so that the solution can easily "plug and play" with other technologies as your needs evolve. You want to be sure, for instance, that numerical data and non-numerical data can be accessed together. Too often objective data such as monthly sales numbers is in a rigid format, and you can't simultaneously get to both the numbers and the subjective data such as focus group transcripts or project postmortems. If you can't integrate all of the information, separate communication channels develop, and extra energy goes into tracking down the different kinds of data.

The worldwide information sharing that Coke practices, or the coherent flow of product development work within Nabisco, simply could not occur without digital information flow. Coke wanted to make a fundamental cultural and business shift, from a company that had a global vision but was locally run to one that has global vision and is globally run. The use of e-mail and other collaborative digital tools integrates people into the organization faster and has made all of the company's knowledge workers

I Say Computer, Computer Says Potato

Any knowledge management solution should include the capability for users to easily search for information—whether for specific numerical data, all of the documents and files related to a specific project or topic, or a wide assortment of information off the World Wide Web.

Internet searches usually return too many or too few results. First you get thousands of responses. Then you make the search a bit more precise and get almost none. If you want to learn about the fastest computer chip available, you might end up with information about potato chips delivered in fast trucks.

Microsoft and other system vendors are working on technology that will catalog material across a variety of storage mechanisms—Web, file, database, and e-mail—so that a single search will offer a much higher likelihood that you'll find what you're looking for quickly. Microsoft is also supporting the industry standard called XML (eXtended Markup Language), an updated version of the Internet standard HTML (HyperText Markup Language).

Where HTML tells the PC how to lay out content on a Web page for display or printing, XML does this and also describes the nature of the content. XML provides a way of indexing data for retrieval and for other kinds of manipulation. For example, it can tag "Bill Gates" as a customer name and "One Microsoft Way" as a business address. Other applications can act on the metadata or metatags (data that describes other data)—for example, copying the customer information into the proper fields of a record that needs to be updated in another application.

XML solves the twin problems of searching for information across different storage mechanisms and integrating applications over distributed systems. The flexibility of XML creates a risk that people will generate incompatibilities by describing data differently. Is "Bill Gates" formally a "name" or a "customer"? This danger of incompatible definitions is why we're working with leading solution providers in such industries as retail, finance, and health care to get industry-wide agreement on tag definitions.

When computer software can understand natural language better, we'll have another way to improve searching. Experimental software that understands natural-language queries, parsing regular sentences into meaningful patterns, can already return two-thirds fewer responses than today's search engines, with a greatly increased likelihood of a match.

Continued advances mean that in the future we'll speak or type regular questions into the computer, and the computer, understanding the context, will return the most likely match across all the different storage mechanisms. If you search the Web for the speed of chips, the result will be about computers, not potatoes.

aware that they have a global audience. "Globally run" does not mean that a manager in Atlanta makes all the decisions for the manager in Nairobi, Kenya. It means that the manager in Nairobi has the same access to information as the manager at headquarters and that the same analytical and communication tools make him part of one worldwide integrated unit. Feudal mind-sets are giving way to a consciousness of global context. The brand management process really took off when the digital tools came out of the executive suite and into the hands of the worldwide marketing teams. Technology has empowered local business teams at Coke, but not in ways that create incompatibilities and inconsistencies within the company. And digital information has enabled Coke to shift from quarterly planning and reporting to continuous planning.

Knowledge management is a fancy term for a simple idea. You're managing data, documents, and people's efforts. Your aim should be to enhance the way people work together, share ideas, sometimes wrangle, and build on one another's ideas—and then act in concert for a common purpose. The CEO's role in raising a company's corporate IQ is to establish an atmosphere that promotes knowledge sharing and collaboration, to prioritize the areas in which knowledge sharing is most valuable, to provide the digital tools that make knowledge sharing possible, and to reward people for contributing to a full flow of information.

Business Lessons

- ❑ Foster knowledge sharing through policies, rewards, and specific projects that establish a knowledge-sharing culture.
- ❑ Teams should be able to act with the same unity of purpose and focus as a well-motivated individual.
- ❑ Every new project should directly build on the learning from any similar project undertaken anywhere else in the world.
- ❑ Training should be available at the employee's desk as well as in the classroom. All training resources should be online, including systems to provide feedback on the training.

Diagnosing Your Digital Nervous System

- ❑ Do you have a digital repository where you preserve and augment your organization's accumulated knowledge?
- ❑ Do your digital systems allow numerical and non-numerical data to be accessed together?
- ❑ Can employees, partners, and suppliers get access to appropriate corporate knowledge with a few simple commands?
- ❑ Do your information systems ensure that the proper reviews happen as products move through development?

15

BIG WINS REQUIRE BIG RISKS

If you want to look at it that you're betting the company, I hope we keep doing it. And I'm pretty damn sure we will.

—T. Wilson, Boeing CEO, 1972–88

To be a market leader, you have to have what business writer and consultant Jim Collins calls "big hairy audacious goals." You can't look at just the past or current state of the market. You have to also look at where it's likely to go, and where it might go under certain circumstances, and then navigate your company based on your best predictions. To win big, sometimes you have to take big risks.

Big bets mean big failures as well as successes. I recounted some of Microsoft's failures in chapter 11 and how the lessons learned helped us change our products and strategy. Today, with the benefit of hindsight, it's easy to believe that Microsoft's current success was preordained.

Yet at the time we made our big bets—including the founding of the company as the first microcomputer software firm—most people scoffed. Many industry leaders hesitated to move to new technologies for fear of undercutting the success of their existing technologies. They learned a hard lesson. If you decline to take risks early, you'll decline in the market later. If you bet big, though, only a few of these risks have to succeed to provide for your future.

Microsoft's current audacious goals include making the PC scale in performance beyond all existing systems, developing computers that "see, listen, and learn," and creating software to power the new personal companion devices. These initiatives are Microsoft's response to digital convergence, in which all devices will use digital technology and need to work with one another. Whether these initiatives succeed, one fact is clear: We have to take these risks in order to have a long-term future.

Risk taking is natural in an emerging industry. The computer industry is about as far into its development as cars were in the 1910s and planes were in the 1930s. Those industries underwent radical and often chaotic technical and business change before they matured, and the same phenomenon is happening in the computer industry. The phrase *mature industry* implies less risk taking, but in well-developed industries, where vendors approach parity in most areas, taking a risk that information technology can change the rules is the best way to create product and market breakthroughs. A primary competitive differentiator will be the way companies employ the Web workstyle.

BETTING THE COMPANY EVERY TWENTY YEARS

One of the largest manufacturing concerns in the world, Boeing has a corporate tradition of betting the company on breakthrough aviation products every couple of decades. In the 1930s Boeing gambled on a new bomber that became the B-17 of World War II fame. In the 1950s Boeing gambled to build the first all-jet commercial passenger plane in the United States, the 707, and in 1968 Boeing built the first jumbo jet, the 747, without enough customer orders to guarantee it could break even. If any of these projects had failed, Boeing probably would have gone out of business.

By the 1990s Boeing's bet-the-business challenge was its next-generation passenger plane, the 777. Boeing's first aircraft to be designed entirely by digital means, the 777 was also the first Boeing plane to totally use fly-by-wire technology, in which computers drive the control systems, eliminating the heavy cables used by mechanical systems. And it was the first Boeing plane built with major international suppliers, necessitating digital collaboration—so much digital collaboration that Boeing needed a new fiber-optic cable across the Pacific to Japan to handle the electronic traffic. This large-scale knowledge problem required enough pioneering to make it a major risk—with an equally great potential for reward.

Key project objectives were to reduce error, rework, and change by 50 percent. The 777 team succeeded. The digital mock-up identified more than 10,000 points of interference, where parts did not fit together properly, so that designers could fix the problems before production began. Without a digital design, these interferences would not have been found until the plane was being manufactured. Toward the end of the 747 project, Boeing was spending $5 million a day on engineering, mostly in changes. The company did not experience those costs with the 777. When the 777 was built, laser alignment tools found that one wing was perfectly aligned, another was out of alignment by only two-thousandths of an inch, and over the

Automated Design Instead of Automated Waste

Two events convinced Boeing that it needed to go digital. Both occurred when Phil Condit, now Boeing's CEO, was managing the company's 757 project in the mid-1980s. The first was a capital request for a multimillion-dollar machine, an automated shim maker. Shims are thin pieces of metal that are wedged between parts to ensure a tight fit. The million-dollar shim maker could turn out lots of them, fast. He rejected the request for what he called "automated waste." Wouldn't it make more sense, he wondered, if Boeing could design planes so they fitted together without shims?

The second occurred at about the same time. Boeing was already using digital design on small projects. In one, a numeric controller was bending titanium hydraulic tubes into specified shapes based on a digital design. The first ones made had to be redone because they didn't fit the mock-up. A few days later, however, someone brought Condit a correction to the mock-up. When the mock-up was redone, the computer-designed tubes fit perfectly. They had been made correctly to begin with. It was the mock-up that was wrong. When digitally designed parts served to check the accuracy of physical mock-ups instead of the other way around, Boeing knew a new approach was required.

209-foot length of the aircraft the fuselage was off by only three- to eight-thousandths of an inch. This virtual perfection of alignment translates into increased aerodynamic performance, better fuel efficiency, and less rework during the assembly process.

Digital information flow changed the way Boeing collaborated with Japanese suppliers who built fuselage sections and other components. Without digital tools, Boeing would have had to create all the designs in Seattle and send hard copy to Japan. Boeing would not have learned of problems until the parts were built and delivered. Instead Boeing did the conceptual design and sent these drawings electronically to Japan, where local engineers could then do the detailed design. The Japanese designers could quickly check with their manufacturing people about the difficulty of building the part and bring any problems to Boeing's notice early. Electronic collaboration redefined the roles of partners and streamlined the process for everyone involved.

But though the use of digital processes in the design of the 777 worked well, the design phase represents only 20 percent of the actual work that goes into the production of a complex modern aircraft. Boeing's use of digital information was only just beginning. Boeing's next step was to tackle the remaining 80 percent—the production processes that went back to the days of the B-17. This production system comprised at least 1,000 custom-made, intertwined computer systems—some from as early as 1959—built in "every computer language ever known," according to company officials. The system's inefficiencies allowed the wrong parts to be manufactured or the right parts *not* to be manufactured.

When demand for Boeing's most popular aircraft, the 737, soared in 1997–98, the production system created a bottleneck. Compounding this problem, Boeing was in a fierce price war with rival Airbus in the commercial sector, and it was reengineering its primary production processes while trying to keep down production costs. Aviation customers make purely economic decisions. They know the maintenance and fuel costs of their existing fleet, and aircraft manufacturers have to bring in a plane that will lower their costs. If you do, you'll replace old aircraft. If you don't, nobody will buy.

Boeing's challenge—to design better and better aircraft while paring its production costs—could be met only with new processes and new ways of using information technology, the adoption of the Web workstyle from start to finish.

The design of a new airplane or spacecraft is a huge integration task. Each vehicle is structurally complex to begin with. Then propulsion systems, air-conditioning, electrical systems, hydraulic systems, avionics, and other systems are added. The biggest debate is territorial: what systems get to go through the many restricted spaces. Digital tools enable Boeing engineers to see something as "simple" as whether the electrical and hydraulic designers both ran lines through the same hole, to something as complex as the overall design of the new international space station, which will not be physically brought together until it is assembled in space. Digital tools make it possible to solve multidimensional, multivariable problems, such as determining the structural impact of extreme heat and cold, by bringing together a variety of experts who understand their own piece but not necessarily others. The work to be done remains complex. It's not as though you can push a button and get great aircraft design. Digital tools enable engineers to see conflicts and begin the discussions by asking the right questions.

A new digital process will also drive Boeing's entire production chain, from obtaining raw materials, engineering the parts, defining the airplane, and machining the parts to controlling configuration and assembly. The new system, which 25,000 employees are already using, provides a single source of product data in place of thirteen independent systems. The goal is for all 100,000 manufacturing employees to use it.

What makes Boeing's efforts unique is the degree to which it plans to integrate digital data from end to end, including integration with its partners, and the sheer scale of the intellectual and manufacturing processes that it is digitizing. The company already operates the largest Web-based parts-ordering system in the world and is using digi-

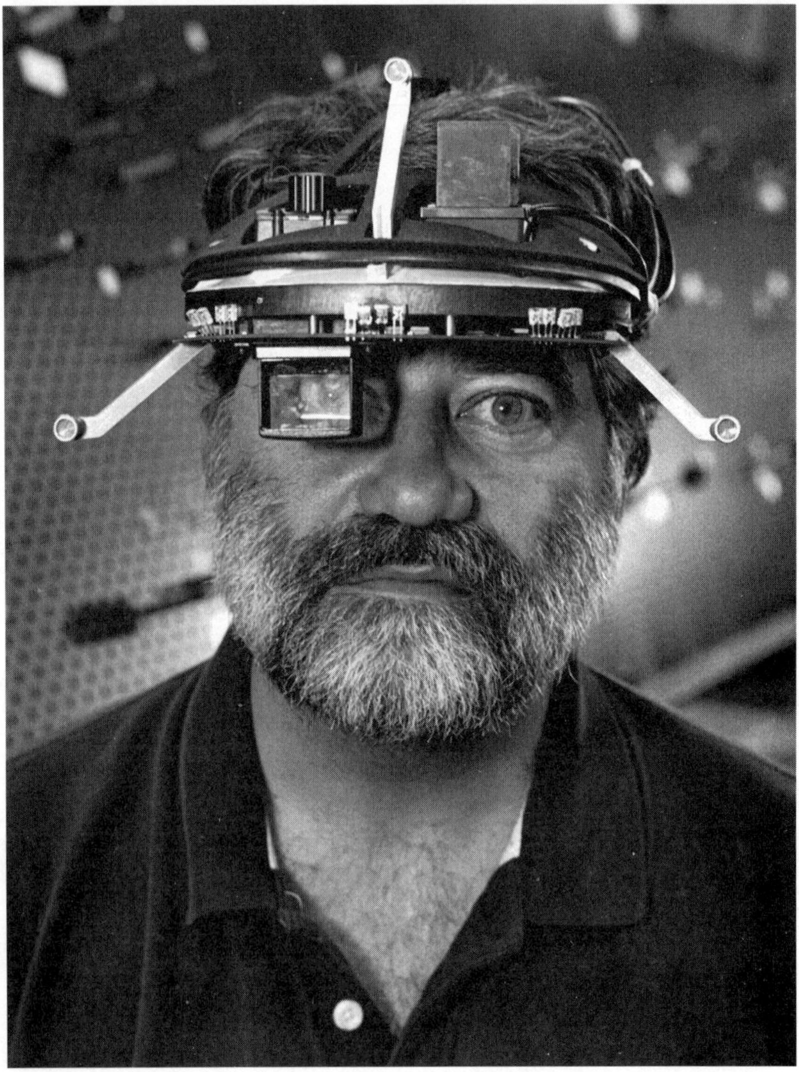

Photo by Norman Mauskoff

Use of digital information at Boeing extends not only to the design and manufacture of aircraft, but to the installation of aircraft systems as well. In one plant, virtual reality goggles show workers how hydraulic and electrical cables are supposed to be routed through the aircraft body. Boeing is betting that end-to-end digital systems will ultimately cut 30 to 40 percent out of the cost of building aircraft, savings that are necessary for success in the fiercely competitive commercial aircraft market.

tal tools to bring together virtual teams such as its collaboration with Lockheed Martin on the new F-22 fighter. All told, Boeing believes its efforts will cut 30 to 40 percent of its production costs.

Networked PCs are central to Boeing's plan for information flow throughout the company. When the 777 was designed with the computer-aided design application known as CATIA, eight mainframes in the Puget Sound area and several more in Japan, Canada, and other locations in the United States supported 10,000 specialized workstations used by designers and manufacturing engineers to define and manufacture the airplane. Technology being implemented in the near future will allow access to the data from anywhere via a PC. Even customers will be able to access some data, getting a custom CD of all the parts and systems for the planes they purchased.

CEO Phil Condit offers a bit of tough advice to other manufacturers facing the question of how and when to go digital: If you're going to go digital, you have to go digital all the way. If you try to maintain the old paper system and a new digital one, you'll have a lot of nonproductive effort and cost, people won't really be committed, and everyone will simply default to using the old system. Part of the go-ahead is an act of faith, and part of it is trust in the people who've designed the new system, but "you have to make the tough decision and take away everyone's crutches."

ACCELERATING THE SEARCH FOR CANCER CURES

While digital information can put new life into existing industries, it's also helping create new industries. A good example is the high-risk field of genetic research, where companies have to expend huge resources for years without any guarantee of success. In a pure knowledge field such as genetic research, digital information flow can double the speed of research and improve the potential for success. Genetic research focuses on DNA, a complex molecule commonly described as the building block of life. The genes in DNA control every living process in the cell, such as the assimilation of nutrients and cellular respiration or the construction of the cell's physical structures. Through a process called *encoding*, genes guide the kind and quantities of proteins created: the proteins actually carry out chemical processes in the cell. If DNA is damaged or mutated, though, it may generate faulty instructions, producing thc wrong amount or altered forms of various proteins and throwing chemical reactions in the cell out of balance. The cell suffers, and the organism as a whole becomes ill or dies.

Genetic research, like science in general, progresses through a series of unexpected connections. The more information that scientists have about the work of other scientists, the more likely they are to fill in gaps of knowledge and connect the dots between seemingly unconnected data. Scientists were among the first group to actively use the Internet to share information more than two decades ago. And geneticists today are making special use of the Internet's unique collaborative properties.

The intensity of this digital collaboration is amazing. Scientists are constantly exchanging ideas with one another and critiquing one another's thinking via e-mail. The Internet allows them to find relevant scientific papers, which are coming out faster. They're able to stay up-to-date on what competitors are doing and where the latest breakthroughs are. When ICOS, a biotech firm on whose board I serve, published new genetic research on the Internet, it quickly drew interest from one researcher studying bone degradation and another studying the ability of women to successfully carry pregnancies to term. Whenever I go to ICOS the scientists are casually talking about their collaboration with one scientist in New York and another in St. Louis and another in the United Kingdom.

Within a biotech company, collaborative tools improve the interchange of information among the DNA researcher, DNA synthesizer, and chemist, who need to work together to find new genes and find compounds that react with the products of genes to create useful drugs. The geneticists who are good at isolating new genes or identifying mutant genes are not usually the same people who are skilled at figuring out the functions of the genes. Both skill sets are needed to develop practical drugs, and digital tools help both. They aid the scientists in the research phase, and they aid the chemists in the analysis phase. Chemists can graphically compare the chemical structure of possible drugs against known chemical compounds in order to surmise the likely chemical behavior of the new find. A compound with a structure similar to one with known toxic effects, for example, would be immediately eliminated from further study.

One of the most exciting connections occurred in ICOS's discovery that overexpression of a gene named Atr may play a major role in many cancers. ICOS was trying to find a way to make tumor cells more susceptible to X-rays so that X-rays might become a more effective cancer treatment. X-rays harm cells by breaking apart DNA. The proteins encoded by Atr are part of the cell's machinery to sense when DNA is damaged so that the cell can begin repair. If ICOS could inhibit Atr in tumors, it could slow down the repair mechanism and make tumors more susceptible to destruction by X-rays.

When ICOS began this project, relatively little was known about the DNA repair mechanism in human cells. But the gene that caused yeast cells to have problems repairing radiation-damaged DNA strands was known. ICOS and its collaborator in the United Kingdom used sophisticated pattern searching and analysis of one of the DNA databases on the Internet to find the equivalent human gene, Atr, on chromosome three of the twenty-three human chromosomes.

Meanwhile the Vollum Institute of the Oregon Health Sciences Center in Portland had found a fragment of human chromosome that contained many genes. This fragment would prevent the body's original, undifferentiated cells, called *stem cells,* from developing into muscle cells. The scientists narrowed the location of the responsible gene to chromosome three and went to the Internet, where they found ICOS's research data. The two organizations then worked together, discovering that Atr was actually the gene that caused cells to continue to proliferate as undifferentiated cells rather than maturing into specialized body cells such as a muscle or nerve cell. The two teams visited an Internet site that has a database on tumors and found that too many copies of Atr are found in breast and prostate cancer and in small-cell lung carcinoma. The conclusion: An overproduction of Atr may cause or promote many cancers.

The Internet mediated this scientific interplay in a way no other medium could. Without the Web, the DNA researchers may not have connected for years, if at all. In the past, connections were the result of luck. The Internet creates a worldwide "chalkboard" on which scientists can jointly work. ICOS was trying to find the "gatekeeper" gene that causes a cell with broken DNA to repair itself before reproducing. By collaborating with the Vollum Institute, researchers got an unexpected "aha!": Inhibiting Atr might do more than simply weaken tumors—it might revert them from tumors to ordinary cells.

It's too early to know whether the work on Atr will lead to an important cancer-fighting agent. ICOS has made the Atr gene and purified it, but now the company has to find an effective inhibitor of Atr. The inhibitor would be the actual cancer-fighting agent. It's like having Cinderella's foot and trying to find the one-in-a-hundred-thousand slipper that will fit it.

MAKING OR BREAKING THE BIOTECH FIRM

Knowing what projects *not* to pursue can make or break a biotech company. Digital information helps eliminate the enormous costs of unnecessary research and improve decision making in the early stages—an important effect, since every successive step in R&D and production tends to be more expensive than the last. Digital systems enable a biotech company to roll the dice more often, and more rolls equate to a better chance of making a medical breakthrough. With still better exchange of information among scientists on such things as the inherent toxicity of compounds, the frequency of hits with each roll of the dice will also rise. Biotech companies need to improve the quality of the candidates being developed. If one doesn't work out, they have to get it pushed aside as soon as possible in order to get another candidate going. Information tools can dramatically reduce the number of false starts and improve the screening efficiency, increasing the number of likely drug candidates in the pipeline.

As more and more scientists are beginning to use e-mail and the Internet, the boundaries between research

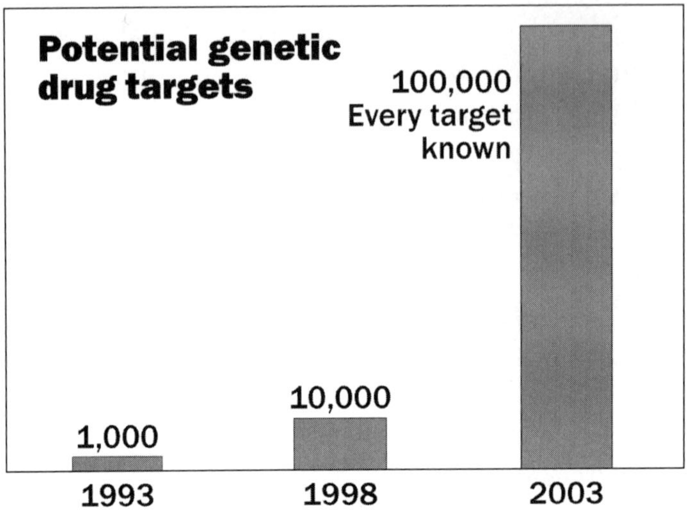

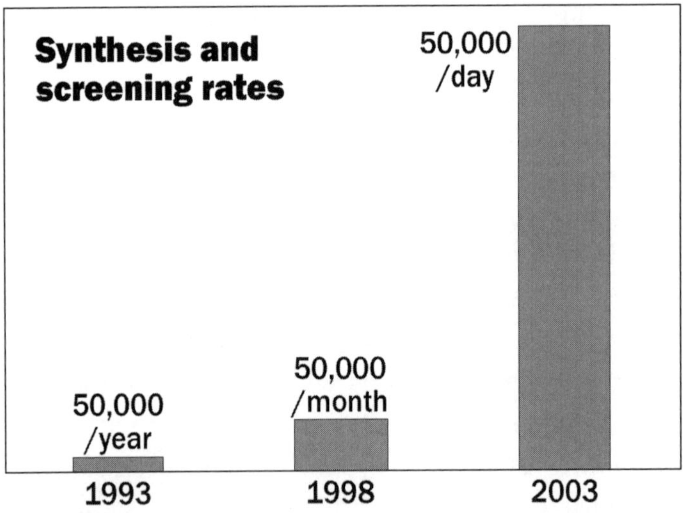

Source: Glaxo Wellcome

Digital tools are providing exponential improvement in the search for cancer cures by identifying and targeting malfunctioning genes that cause most cancers. In just ten years between 1993 and 2003, researchers aided by digital tools will have identified most if not all of the 100,000 to 150,000 separate human genes. Digital tools also help scientists find compounds that chemically react with specific genes and screen those compounds for effectiveness vs. toxicity, rapidly narrowing the search for effective cancer fighters. One large pharmaceutical firm expects to be able to screen 50,000 compounds a day by 2003, up from 50,000 a month in 1998 and 50,000 a year in 1993.

and development and commercial applications are falling away. Electronic tools help manage clinical trials, speed patent searches, and automate much of the documentation process required for FDA review. Companies are beginning to send digital applications to the FDA. In two cases companies actually submitted a physical workstation so that the FDA reviewers could go through the data and review the reports—a bit extreme, perhaps, but better than piles of paper. Digital submissions, which may now be made on floppies, CDs, or digital tape, are still voluntary but are likely to replace paper submissions by 2003. An extranet set up by the drug company for use by its researchers and FDA reviewers, taking advantage of e-mail, videoconferencing, and online discussions, would dramatically improve the interactivity and speed of reviews.

Information available on the Internet, along with inexpensive information tools, enables small biotech start-ups to compete on a more equal footing against companies far larger. A small biotech start-up could not even exist without inexpensive computer technology. At the same time, digital information flow enables larger companies to marshal their intellectual resources worldwide. The small company can play with the big boys; the big company can move as nimbly as a small one.

Information technology in science is about getting the most out of the brains of talented scientists. In the past, scientists—even more than other knowledge workers—have spent the vast majority of their time collecting data and only a small part of their time analyzing it. As better tools enable researchers to apply most of their brainpower to the tough problems rather than to data collection and verification, it's exciting to think how much more progress there will be. As the hunt for Atr demonstrates, the Web workstyle has also made new lines of research feasible.

Comparisons of DNA sequences would be impossible on paper; such data analysis is easy on computers.

Because of the nature of the people they hire and the nature of their work, biotech companies are great examples of the application of the Web workstyle. And since many of them are new, the firms have been able to start from scratch with digital tools. If you ask the employees what's unique about their workstyle, they'll shrug and say they're not doing anything special—just using PCs and LANs and the Internet. Employees take electronic tools for granted.

Digital tools, and the ability of scientists to stand upon the shoulders of others through collaboration on the Internet, will be a major factor in controlling or curing some of the most terrible diseases that still afflict people all over the world.

FINDING COMMON GROUND IN INTELLECTUAL WORK

At first glance, aircraft manufacturers appear to have little in common with biotech companies. At the basic level, though, both industries have complicated physical processes—manufacturing aircraft and physically screening and producing chemicals—that demand the use of digital information to streamline business operations. Both industries face intense review from regulatory agencies focused on short-term and long-term safety. Aircraft manufacturers and large pharmaceutical companies use e-commerce to create closer relationships with suppliers and partners in widely dispersed geographies.

And in the digital age, where information work is at the heart of almost every business, there are many similarities at a deeper level. The core of both businesses is intellectual. For Boeing, the intellectual challenge is such things as designing a wing that has maximum lift and minimum drag and that can be manufactured inexpensively. The company is creating huge, sophisticated machines containing hundreds of thousands of parts that have to fit together and work together flawlessly. For a biotech company, the intellectual challenge is designing a compound that targets a highly specific disorder, usually genetic, with no collateral damage. The company is creating extremely tiny chemical parts that must mesh precisely with the hundreds of thousands of other active chemical parts that make up the body's biological machinery. The intellectual tasks require the collaboration of people all over the company and of partners and others outside the organization. Knowledge management is of prime importance.

Because of the nature of these industries, the companies involved must take big risks. A single successful aircraft can guarantee an aircraft company's future for years and years—the 747 celebrated its thirtieth birthday in 1998. A single successful drug can generate huge profits for a pharmaceutical company and fund many of its other research efforts. The risks are equally huge. Boeing spent $1 billion on the 747 with no guarantee of profitability. A biotech company can easily spend $250 million to $350 million before it has a marketable product.

In a lot of industries, the proper use of digital information may be the only way for a company to differentiate itself from the competition. In high-tech businesses digital information is the only way to drive new breakthroughs. In order to define and solve knowledge problems that have not been tackled before, big wins require big risks—and a digital nervous system to maximize the chance for success. More broadly, how these companies integrate digital tools is an excellent template for how all companies large and small will use the Web workstyle to manage their work in the future. These companies are trading information for time—and risk.

Business Lessons

- ❏ To win big, you sometimes have to take big risks.
- ❏ Risk supported by digital information flow may be the single biggest way to create product and market breakthroughs.
- ❏ With manufacturing, you trade information for inventory. With industries involved in intellectual property, you trade information for risk.

Diagnosing Your Digital Nervous System

- ❏ Are you going digital all the way or only part of the way? Can you digitally link your knowledge management, business operations, and commerce systems to create a seamless digital environment?
- ❏ Does your digital system enable you to take product testing to wherever in the world is most appropriate while retaining proper review and control?

IV

BRING INSIGHT TO BUSINESS OPERATIONS

16

DEVELOP PROCESSES THAT EMPOWER PEOPLE

Man is simply designed wrong for any mechanistic system.

—Thomas Peters and Robert Waterman Jr., *In Search of Excellence*

A business has the equivalent of autonomic processes, the basic human processes such as breathing that keep us alive. One "autonomic" process in a business is the function that defines the company's reason for being—its manufacturing process, for example. This function has to be as efficient and reliable as the beating of a heart. A second kind of autonomic process in business is administrative—the process of receiving payments and paying bills and paychecks, for instance. The administrative processes are as essential to a business as breathing. If the basic operational processes of your business fail, your company fails.

Because the basic operational processes are so important—and so expensive—most big companies began to invest heavily in automating them for efficiency years ago. But too often the operational processes would be automated in isolation, each independent of the other processes in a company. Overall efficiency would be decidedly suboptimal. Until recently, for instance, in the manufacture of some aircraft parts only 10 percent of the original metal actually ended up on an aircraft. The manufacturing process had been optimized at many individual stages along the way rather than as a whole. There was an enormous amount of designed-in waste.

I talk about business operations such as financial and other administrative systems in other chapters. In this chapter I focus on production processes. An automated production process is necessary but not sufficient if a company is to be competitive today. A good digital nervous system can help you develop your line employees into knowledge workers, transforming your company's core production processes into a competitive advantage.

First you need to use information technology to better understand the inner workings of the process itself in order to make it both more efficient and more responsive to changing circumstances. Entergy Corporation of New Orleans, for instance, has increased the uptime and profitability of its fossil fuel and nuclear power plants with a new graphical process-control system that enables plant operators to more finely tune plant efficiency and analyze performance trends in real time. Operators can actually peer inside the generating systems to understand precisely how the machinery is functioning and determine whether a minor repair or an adjustment today might save an expensive repair and extended downtime later. An intelligent PC-based scheduling system ensures that the highest priority items are repaired first. The process-control system actually shows operators the cost of reduced efficiency—if the boiler temperature is ten degrees lower than it should be for optimal production, for instance. By attaching a dollar figure to operational parameters, Entergy is turning its operators into businesspeople, giving them the information they need to run their units efficiently and a lot more responsibility to make decisions. And because production costs for Entergy's plants are available to corporate staff electronically on a minute-by-minute basis, the company can improve its profits by moving power production constantly to those units that are delivering the most cost-efficient energy.

Then you need to be able to extract data from your production process to inform other business systems. The Stepan Company, which produces surfactants, the active agents used in most cleaning products, has developed a state-of-the-art process-control system that has tripled the plant's output and saved the company millions of dollars through more efficient use of its equipment. But the extraordinary efficiency gains are not as valuable to Stepan as the flexibility of its process-control system in meeting changing customer orders and the foundation the system provides for integration with the company's other business systems. Stepan has used its PC infrastructure to build all the necessary "hooks" to allow management to incorporate production data into other processes such as manufacturing resource planning and inventory ordering.

In the future, all Stepan facilities will have common order entry, inventory, and scheduling software; and managers at the Northfield, Illinois, headquarters will be able to get an overall view of the entire manufacturing capability of the company's eleven plants. When a customer requests a change, Stepan will be able to make the change once for all of its plants and make simultaneous deliveries of the product to the customer worldwide. In addition, everything from paper clips to bulk sulfur will be ordered automatically—the sulfur and other key surfactant ingredients according to changing tank levels. Vendors will access the purchasing database to plan deliveries better. Customers will have Web access to view product availability and place orders. Order information in turn will be linked back in real time to Stepan's inventory system, to ensure that enough chemical components are available in the right locations to fill the orders.

Finally, and most important, you need to feed the data from your production process to your line workers so that they can improve the quality of the product itself. If you provide the right technology to help production workers do timely analysis, they'll turn data into actionable information that will help you improve design and reduce defects. Developing a digital nervous system allows you to empower as many of your workers as possible. Information flow is the key.

CREATING HUNDREDS OF SMALL BUSINESSES ON THE FLOOR

General Motors launched the Saturn Corporation back in 1985 to create not only a brand-new car from scratch, but a brand-new way of building cars and empowering workers. The goal was a company in which management and workers would pull together to reach common goals and everybody would care so much about quality that there would be no need for a separate quality assurance department. That dream has produced results. Saturn has won J. D. Power Awards for quality and customer satisfaction for eight consecutive years and is attracting a cultlike following of car owners.

Saturn employees are called team members. Everyone in the workforce of 8,500 people belongs to a team and wears a name badge that identifies the team. The pervasive attitude is "I'm part of a bigger operation here. 'We' is more important than 'me.' " Teams are tight, autonomous units. Some have as few as four members, some as many as sixty, but most have twelve to fifteen people. Each team has a specific function, such as building engines or doors, and each team member is trained to do approximately thirty different jobs in that area so that people don't get stale from doing repetitive tasks. A team hires its own members and has authority to fire a member who consistently shows up late or does shoddy work. With 20 percent of its compensation tied to quality, customer satisfaction, and sales, the team operates a little like an independent small business.

Notice that nothing I've said about Saturn so far involves technology. If you don't believe that all workers have the potential to contribute to your company's success, all the technology in the world won't empower them. Once you assume that every employee should be a knowledge worker, technology will help every employee put his or her full abilities to work on the company's behalf.

NOT USING "THIS OLD STUFF"

Like many manufacturers, Saturn has a supervisory control and data acquisition (SCADA) system to run its $1.9 billion manufacturing and assembly complex—4 million square feet of working space on 2,400 acres of land. The SCADA system, based on GE Fanuc's CIMplicity plant monitoring and control application, monitors more than 120,000 separate data points from an array of sensors, motors, transducers, and electrical switches. Each device is checked at least once a second.

When the Saturn plant was first set up, CIMplicity ran on more than 100 VAX/VMS minicomputers, with the data coming in from programmable logic controllers (PLCs). Workers disliked the system's arcane codes and character-based terminals. If you wanted to log a scuffed door panel, for instance, you'd enter something like "EPSV 1006" and punch in special codes corresponding to that particular quality problem. Workers would fix a problem, but they wouldn't necessarily log the fix, and Saturn was losing important historical data on quality assurance.

In the early 1990s Saturn made the leap to PCs and the still new Windows NT operating system in its manufacturing and assembly plant. This meant working with GE Fanuc to move CIMplicity to Windows NT, as well as giving Microsoft an education in what an operating system needed to do in a complex manufacturing environment. During those early days our development engineers spent many nights on the phone with Saturn engineers.

Today Saturn's manufacturing system includes nineteen PC servers in Production and three in a test bed, plus about seventy older VAX minicomputers. Saturn's manufacturing software includes CIMplicity, a variety of PC server applications and development tools, and standard PC operating systems running on about 3,500 desktop systems and 500 laptops. Even the PLC sensors are being replaced with PCs.

A dispatcher can see all the physical operations of the plant on a single screen or focus down to the level of any one sensor. If a switch fails at Column C, Conveyor 500 of the mezzanine level, for instance, the dispatcher can spot the failure immediately and send over an electrician for repair. All 120,000 points of data are analyzed every six seconds and delivered to dispatchers in a graphical format.

ENABLING PEOPLE TO MAKE A DIFFERENCE

A change as simple as giving all employees easy-to-use graphical computers has produced dramatic effects at Saturn. Anybody in the division can log on to the manufacturing section of the Saturn intranet and see a detailed list of, say, the top ten quality problems that have occurred in end-of-the-line dynamic vehicle tests in the past two hours. Through a Web interface the worker can retrieve data from a database, automatically load the data into a spreadsheet, and pivot through the data to analyze it by part and type of problem—trim, door panels, power train, and so on; fit, paint, weld, assembly, installation, and so on.

By analyzing historical data with off-the-shelf tools—and not having to go to the time and expense of getting a programmer to do a special report—one worker on the power-train team was able to detect a faulty weld in the engine and save Saturn $1.5 million a month in potential repairs.

Three to six internal computer modules control everything on a Saturn from the brakes to air-bag deployment. An engineer reviews diagnostic tests on these modules over the Saturn intranet. Recently Saturn was able to spot, within less than two hours of the first occurrence, a particular kind of failure in the power-train control module. The company got hold of the vendor, who quickly reprogrammed the modules and returned them to Saturn without holding up production.

Saturn also does a pure quality audit of its vehicles by

randomly pulling a dozen or so cars off the line each day. The system downloads into a Windows CE–based handheld PC a three-dimensional schematic specific to the make and model of a car. Using this schematic as a guide, inspectors go through the car and note every irregularity and flaw. If there's a problem with the front left fender, for instance, they'll click on the PC display to get an exploded view of that part. A menu allows them to note the problem.

After each audit, inspectors plug their handheld PCs into the network to automatically synchronize the files with the original database. These engineers and other workers analyze the day's data and compare it with historical daily and weekly results. A part that's routinely scratched during assembly could indicate either a problem with the work of the team or a part that's inherently difficult to install. These pure quality audits have enabled inspectors to work with Manufacturing to fix the fit and finish of a certain model's fuel-filler doors and another model's poor-fitting interior dome lights.

All of the quality assurance data, whether from end-of-the-line inspections or the pure quality audits, is fed back to Product Engineering through Saturn Manufacturing's PC-based information systems. Everyone from manufacturing managers and line workers to design engineers have access to the data, so that teams can work together to improve "buildability"—how well and how easily parts go together. Expertise from the floor is combined with expertise from the engineers to come up with a better design. Saturn workers are qualified to speak because they're information smart.

REDEFINING THE ROLE OF LINE WORKERS

All three of the companies I've talked about in this chapter demonstrate the value of improved information flow even in factories that were already automated. Putting high-quality diagnostic tools in the hands of the people who do the work and building production systems around information flow is essential. Ideally the tools integrate all of the steps that deliver value to a customer, rather than treating the steps as just a series of individual tasks. Michael Hammer likes to say that the "task worker" is the last vestige of the old Industrial Age. In a modern company every worker has to be involved in the entire process—in all the steps. An acquaintance of mine had an uncle who spent twenty-five years at an auto plant in Flint, Michigan, tacking chrome strips and other finish parts onto automobiles. It was a good job in the years immediately after World War II, but it followed the classic Industrial Age approach: Break a process into small, discrete tasks and assign each to one person who does it over and over "the one best way." Compare that approach with the way Saturn workers do their jobs today.

In the new organization the worker is no longer a cog in a machine but is an intelligent part of the overall process. Welders at some steel jobs now have to know algebra and geometry to figure weld angles from computer-generated designs. Water-treatment companies train assembly-line workers in computerized production measurements and math. New digital photocopiers require the service personnel to have an understanding of computers and the Internet, not just skill with a screwdriver.

Human beings remain essential in operational processes that have to constantly improve and that have to constantly adapt to changing circumstances. A flexible production line needs people—well-informed, empowered people. As we consolidate tasks into processes, we give workers more responsibility. Computers will eliminate some jobs, but they will take the drudgery out of many other jobs.

Having people focus on whole processes will allow

them to tackle more interesting, challenging work. A one-dimensional job (a task) will be eliminated, automated, or rolled into a bigger process. One-dimensional, repetitive work is exactly what computers, robots, and other machines are best at—and what human workers are poorly suited to and almost uniformly despise. Managing a process instead of executing tasks makes someone a knowledge worker. And it is good digital information flow that enables knowledge workers to play their unique roles.

From a corporate perspective, another worker-related benefit emerges from good information systems. Only up-to-date and accurate information makes it possible to tie compensation directly to performance, quality, and customer satisfaction. You can't wait until the end of the month to see how everybody did and make adjustments then. You don't want a special "Scoring for Bonus" department to independently measure every team's performance. You have to get performance information directly to every team every day. Without electronic feedback loops, tying compensation to performance—a practice more and more companies want to institute—doesn't work well.

By creating a good flow of information, Saturn is also preparing itself for "mass customization," which combines the efficiencies of high-volume production with the ability to build exactly the model the customer wants. More than most car manufacturers, Saturn already builds a number of custom-made cars. You can imagine the day that a customer in a dealer's showroom or at home uses a PC to order over the Internet exactly the car and the options he or she wants and then gets delivery within a few days. "Build to order," which has become increasingly popular in the PC industry, is bound to become a major part of other manufacturing industries, from cars to clothing to furniture.

Manufacturing lines, though, have to be smart if they're going to handle many custom jobs for complex machines. Because there's no reverse on the assembly line, the special-order chassis and body of a car have to synch up with the right engine and power train. If a problem shows up—for example, if a special-order purple paint doesn't come out perfect on one of the panels—you need the kind of dynamic scheduling system Saturn uses to keep things moving. Saturn's system searches through all the parts on the line, finds the earliest set of panels that will fit the order, and reassigns these panels to the purple car. The car for which the new panels were originally intended is rescheduled farther back in the line, where panels in the color required for it (say, white) are stocked. A problem with a custom job holds up Saturn's assembly line for only fifteen or twenty minutes, not for the hours that would be involved if Saturn didn't have its dynamic scheduling software.

The dynamic scheduling application is a "big bang for the buck" item not just because it solved a major problem, but also because it served as the basis for similar applications in other areas of the plant such as transmission tracking. With a single infrastructure and standard software and tools, Saturn's IT group doesn't have to develop reporting systems from scratch to give autoworkers data. Instead the IT group plugs together standard components that let autoworkers extract the right information for themselves. Every new application can be built in less time and for less money. That's why, over the past five years, Saturn IT projects have grown fourfold while IT budget has increased only half as much.

What Saturn has done will be common sense in the future, but most of the industrial world doesn't work that way yet. Until recently the hardware and systems costs for such capabilities in manufacturing were prohibitive. The interfaces were too arcane. You simply couldn't afford to gather data on defects and analyze it quickly. Small, portable devices will make data gathering even easier. Like Saturn, Boeing has converted its paper-based trouble ticket process into a digital form for handheld PCs, shortening the turnaround time for addressing quality issues during aircraft manufacturing. Other companies are using handhelds to replace paper-based inventory reporting, cutting data collection time in half, improving accuracy, and enabling the reports to be posted on the intranet within hours instead of the week usually required for consolidating paper reports. Wireless networks will make it possible for these devices to go virtually anywhere and report back information even sooner.

Saturn officials were the first from a large industrial company to come to us in the early 1990s and say that they wanted to design all of their business processes around PC tools, from the factory floor on up. Our reaction was, "Wow." They were coming to us because of the vision of where we were going, not because of what we already had in our product catalog at the time. PC hardware grew in power, and so did our high-end system and handheld software. Saturn provided a great deal of information to us on the requirements for industrial-strength software systems. The pieces came together as the result of a strong relationship between the two companies—and between modern technology and manufacturing processes.

Most companies have been willing to give information tools to their high-paid, white-collar professionals who do information work for a living. Entergy, Stepan, and Saturn are proving that building systems around information flow and giving information tools to line workers can also provide enormous value. Entergy is methodically overhauling its key business processes and pushing information and decision making down to the operational level. Stepan is using information to manage its plants as a whole to adapt to changing customer needs. Saturn uses technology to combine the expertise of its line workers with that of its design engineers, to tie compensation directly to performance, and to set the stage for mass customization in an assembly-line setting. All three of these companies are applying knowledge management to business operations to analyze throughput, quality, and failure rates to improve core processes. Digital tools bring more intelligence to their business operations.

Give your workers more sophisticated jobs along with better tools, and you'll discover that your employees will become more responsible and bring more intelligence to their work. In the digital age you need to make knowledge workers out of every employee possible.

Business Lessons

- ❑ The more line workers understand the inner workings of production systems, the more intelligently they can run those systems.
- ❑ Real-time data on production systems enables you to schedule maintenance before something breaks.
- ❑ Tying compensation to improved quality will work only with real-time feedback of quality problems.
- ❑ Task workers will go away. Their jobs will be automated or combined into bigger tasks requiring knowledge work.
- ❑ Look into how portable devices and wireless networks can extend your information systems into the factory, warehouse, and other areas.

Diagnosing Your Digital Nervous System

- ❑ Can line workers get real-time access to data so they can improve the quality of the product?
- ❑ Can you integrate your manufacturing systems with the other systems in your company—for example, to extract data from production processes to drive inventory control or coordinate production with sales?

17

INFORMATION TECHNOLOGY ENABLES REENGINEERING

> I don't see information technology as a stand-alone system. I see it as a great facilitator. And maybe most important, it's a reason to keep asking yourself the question—why, why, why.
>
> —Paul O'Neill, Chairman and CEO of Alcoa

Since Michael Hammer and James Champy introduced the concept of reengineering in 1994, companies the world over have been reexamining their business processes. They're trying to get organizational complexity and internal inefficiencies out of the way of delivering value to customers. When I read Hammer and Champy's book, *Reengineering the Corporation,* three of their ideas about reengineering business processes really stood out for me. The first is that you need to step back periodically to take a hard look at your processes. Do they solve the right problems? Can they be simplified? The second is that if you cut a job into too many pieces and involve too many people, nobody can see the whole process and the work will bog down. The third, closely related to the second, is that too many handoffs create too many likely points of failure.[1]

As often happens with a hot concept, Hammer and Champy's simple but profound ideas about process reengineering have precipitated a deluge of business seminars, training sessions, university classes, magazine articles, and "me too" books from various experts.[2] In the process (pun intended), a variety of businesspeople have used the term *reengineering* to justify almost any organizational change. A couple of years ago a large computer company began a "reengineering" effort by laying off most of the personnel department, leaving no one to rationalize the rest of what was really a downsizing effort. Without personnel experts to guide change, the company made a number of missteps. It bought out the contracts of freelancers and sent them away before they did any more work—even though the company had *already paid* for their services. Highly regarded, newly promoted people were laid off because they were now the least senior people at their new ranks. It's hard to see such behavior as any kind of rational downsizing, and it certainly wasn't reengineering. Michael Hammer said in conversation once that "sometimes reengineering has come to mean almost everything except reengineering." Even though some people go overboard with the idea or use it to mask layoffs, the idea of reexamining your processes from time to time to make them more effective

1. Michael Hammer and James Champy, *Reengineering the Corporation: A Manifesto for Business Revolution,* rev. ed. (New York: HarperBusiness, 1997).

2. An Internet search on the word "reengineering" in October 1998 returned 189,940 documents, ranging from articles on the Year 2000 date-calculation problem to a seminar described as "the serious side of fun." The number of documents was far greater than other important business topics—seven times greater than on knowledge management, for instance.

and to wring out inefficiencies is more important now than ever.

Creating a new process is a major project. You should have a specific definition of success, a specific beginning and end in terms of time and tasks, intermediate milestones, and a budget. The best projects are those in which people have the customer scenario clearly in mind. That's true of process projects, too. The customer may be outside the company or inside, but the idea is the same: How will the person use the product or the process you're developing? How will it be better than the one before?

You also need an understanding of the trade-offs at all levels. Every project has trade-offs. In software projects management always wants the product to be feature rich, small, and done overnight for very little money. Managers want it all, so the trade-offs have to be explicitly understood. If you're clever about making the product rich in features and have to make it bigger, you don't want management coming back to say that you should have sacrificed a few features to keep it small. If you keep a lid on costs, you don't want management to say that you should have spent whatever it took to include more features. The same is true of a project to create a digital process.

You need to be flexible in the face of evolving requirements, without invalidating your original design goals with creeping change. You should have a crisp decision process to evaluate change, including a provision for reevaluating your original project goals.

RENOVATING THE PROCESS FOR PRODUCT DELIVERY

A few years ago a major release of Windows NT came very close to being held up the day it was ready to ship.

Not because of a showstopper bug or some other problem in product development, but because of a missing cardboard box. The artwork for the product container had landed on someone's desk the day that person went on vacation. There the art sat until the finished box failed to reach Manufacturing on schedule. This was just two days before the shipping deadline, and the box normally required ten days for production. Only round-the-clock efforts by the operations people at our manufacturing facility got us enough boxes—ink barely dry—to meet the schedule.

After this incident, the manager of the group responsible for the marketing materials got everybody together to analyze what had gone wrong. The group consisted of almost a dozen people from two internal divisions and two outside vendors. The manager asked one question—a common question at Microsoft I like to ask—"Why are there so many people in this room?" In any meeting I want only the essential decision makers. Everybody else should be off solving other problems. If you find more than three or four decision makers in the room, you can be sure that the sheer number of people involved is a major part of the problem.

This manager challenged the group to simplify the process and to look for similar coordination problems with any of the division's dozen other products. "Look for a pattern, and solve it for everything," he said.

In the short term, the group established the principle of "affirmative acknowledgment," meaning that a handoff wasn't complete until the next person in line said, "I've got it." No more blindly throwing stuff over the transom.

The group also reduced the number of handoffs from five to three. Reducing handoffs may not seem like a major step, but anything that can eliminate "touches" reduces the opportunities for error and helps to assure quality. In a new plant in 1997, Dell Computer redesigned its production lines to cut in half the number of times a hard disk was handled. The company experienced a 40 percent reduction in rejection rates for hard drives in manufacturing and a 20 percent reduction in overall PC failures.

At Microsoft, the people from all divisions who were responsible for getting product components to Manufacturing started having best practices meetings. The senior operations person from Ireland, where we do our European manufacturing, flew in to talk about problems that U.S. practices had created for her organization. Over time we identified a number of process problems in preparing materials for manufacturing. Once, for instance, we'd used special fonts on our product boxes, not realizing that the fonts weren't available worldwide. This caused several of our products to release late for the holiday consumer season in Australia. That hurt.

The process owners in all of the divisions got together to define a global production process that would take advantage of digital tools for improving coordination. We created an application to track all product components, from boxes to box labels to artwork to actual software code. With information about all of these components on the network, product managers and other employees can easily track the status of their build processes. We have a single, well-defined electronic production process that, among other benefits, ensures that when we improve any steps along the way, they are used throughout the organization.

In this same time frame we also began to outsource our manufacturing. This change meant we had to provide complete materials for "turnkey" manufacturing. The process had to be even clearer—process dependent, not people dependent. One goal was: "Operations should not be the hero all the time." The digital tools that improved coordination internally now made it possible to coordinate the final phase of the process, actually building the product, with an external manufacturer. In addition to the application that tracked product components internally, we developed another tool for vendors to determine the release status of product components. Vendors, including the external manufacturer, also use this tool to download digital materials and electronically order nondigital materials. In this case, our digital tools not only enabled us to fix the process problem internally, but also enabled a company that specializes in manufacturing to take on new outsourced work for us—changing the boundaries between our two companies.

One question might be, Why did we ever do manufacturing in the first place? Before we had digital processes, we had no choice. Today our information tools are sophisticated enough to allow us to outsource manufacturing and still be confident that our products are being built to our specifications. We keep a core set of other professionals in house and use the Web as a primary way to coordinate with others outside.

After five or six months these teams not only fixed processes that had already caused problems, but they also found and dismantled a couple of other bad-process time bombs that had not yet gone off. The new tools help identify potential conflicts in the process and let all of the players work together to resolve them before we have collisions or omissions. What is the value to a business of *problems that never occur?*

CREATING A PROCESS THAT STAGES YOUR SOLUTION

The development history of an internal Microsoft application called HeadTrax is a good example of how the symbiosis between business needs and technology works to enable new processes that weren't possible in the predigital world. HeadTrax is a work-flow application that handles the processing of personnel changes. A personnel change can mean an employee hire, a promotion, a transfer, or a change in department.

Our efforts with HeadTrax show that sometimes it takes a series of iterative steps to understand the problem you're trying to solve before getting the process and technology right. Incomplete understanding of the objective is a major concern in every technology project, which is why you're usually better off tackling smaller processes and building on them. No matter how well you plan, you'll often find that you didn't understand everything you should have about the users' needs. If you spend eighteen months delivering a complete solution and realize you haven't got it right, or that business needs have changed in that time, you'll be in pretty sad shape. A better approach is to use software tools that enable you to get something working in less than six months and then improve the solution as you get user feedback.

The first version of our personnel work-flow application looked great until the electronic approval forms started landing in the e-mail in-boxes of our vice presidents. Some executives loved being able to handle most personnel changes online, but others didn't want to review every change, preferring to see just the approval forms for high-level hires or transfers. Executives in big divisions couldn't handle the volume. The old paper system made it easier to delegate, so we needed to add delegation to the digital system. The second version of the application had complete functionality, but the process flow still left something to be desired. At times important approvals were sidetracked at lower levels and minor changes still occasionally landed in the electronic lap of a VP. Working with Andersen Consulting, we realized we had twelve different approval processes in fifteen major groups. Focusing on process, we reduced the twelve to three, which are at the core of HeadTrax Version 3.0.

Today managers originate all employee transactions online. Any reviewer can "push back" a request to have the original requester change the request and resend it digitally. Or the reviewer can approve the transaction with changes so that it continues on its path. All of the people involved with the request will get e-mail with a link to the change request so that they can review it. Historically most Human Resources rejections of personnel change requests have come from minor questions or miscoding problems. HeadTrax virtually does away with those kinds of rejections.

A "work on behalf" feature, which enables a manager to delegate approval responsibilities for any class of personnel requests to other people, has turned out to be the most important HeadTrax function. A vice president might authorize an administrative assistant to approve routine position or personnel changes and authorize senior managers to approve compensation or promotion requests for their teams. "Work on behalf" gives executives a way to create timesaving exceptions and still keep the approval process moving. If a 1,000-person division changes cost centers, or if entire teams are shuffled during a reorganization, an administrative assistant can highlight the groups en masse and make all the changes in the organizational chart with the click of a single button.

A routing feature adds more flexibility. The requesting manager can add someone to the review loop before the request goes to Human Resources—for example, if a senior manager wants to review a particular type of employee transaction such as promotions.

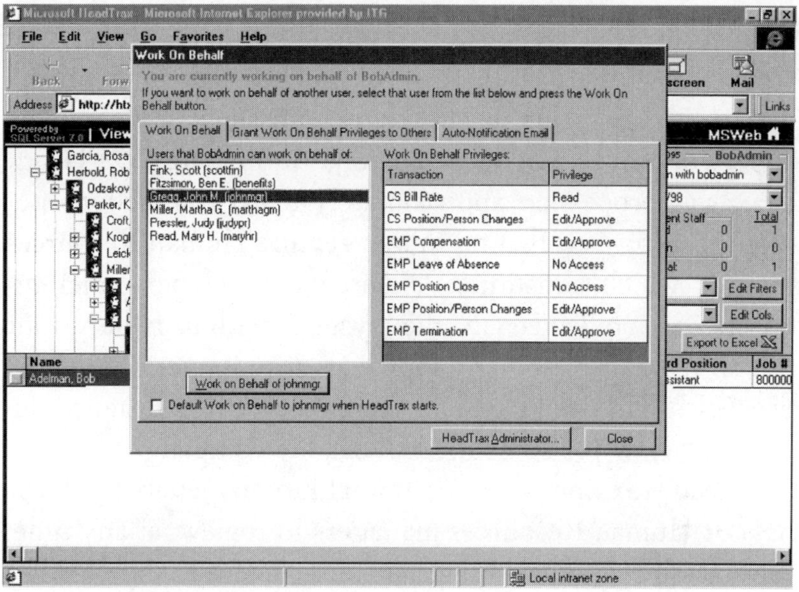

HeadTrax enables managers to handle all personnel changes electronically. A "work on behalf" feature allows managers to delegate approvals to other people, providing flexibility without complicating the process. Implementation of one digital process often uncovers related processes that can be automated. Once HeadTrax was successfully handling personnel changes for regular employees, we realized it could be extended to help manage contingent staff.

HeadTrax is useful for nonadministrative work, too. Starting with whatever employee's name you enter, HeadTrax displays the entire organizational hierarchy, up and down for all staff. HeadTrax also enables you to create organizational charts on the fly and customize views of the charts according to a variety of properties such as full name, phone number, office number, department number, and so on.

Now that it's done, HeadTrax seems like an obvious solution, an application that any medium-size or large company can use. It's more than just a way to eliminate personnel-related paperwork from the desks of executives. It's an engine that drives personnel changes into our accounting and budget systems whenever there's an organizational change. It ensures that all of our business systems stay in synch.

Because the HeadTrax system is new, it's difficult to come up with exact figures for the savings in time and energy it's given us in eliminating missing or incomplete paperwork and hours of data entry. But by late 1998 HeadTrax was processing approximately 8,000 transactions per month. Approvals that no longer require Human Resources review, which constitute 90 percent of all personnel requests, are reflected in the system within twenty-four hours. Human Resources approvals take longer because of processes that aren't tied to technology—for instance, an exit interview for someone leaving the company.

HeadTrax improves accountability by enabling business or Human Resources managers to review, at any time, the status of all outstanding personnel changes. By viewing the head count status in his group, a business manager can track how people are doing in filling job vacancies. If the manager discovers that one of his direct reports has far more open head count than other managers in the department, the senior manager can look into whether the hiring manager needs to spend more time on recruiting or needs more help from our recruiting group.

Human Resources managers recognized that it was not the best use of their time to add their okay to every routine personnel change. Instead they developed an electronic tool for routine actions and for data collection for trend analysis on personnel issues. A senior Human Resources manager might make use of the audit capabilities of HeadTrax, reviewing all rejected changes to see whether a pattern revealed a need for more education of managers on personnel issues or a need for additional functionality in the HeadTrax application. Or Human Resources might analyze whether one operating unit has higher turnover than others and whether there is a pattern in the reasons for people leaving the organization. HeadTrax not only streamlines the process for our businesspeople, it also enables our Human Resources staff to redefine their roles. The ability to immediately see statistics about things such as transfer rates or turnover is worth far more than the lower costs or savings in time.

Identifying the primary, focused objective of any process is the way to begin solving process problems. Whether for production processes or internal business processes, the goal should always be a fundamental kind of simplification: having the least number of people engaged in the least number of handoffs. It's extremely difficult to optimize a paper process. Digital technology makes it possible to develop much better processes, instead of being stuck with variations on the old paper processes that give you only incremental improvements. Real process breakthroughs come through the combination of well-thought-out solutions with digital information flow.

USING DIGITAL PROCESSES TO SOLVE TOUGH PROBLEMS

One of the thorniest business processes at Microsoft is the hiring, management, and payment of contingent staff.

For a company with a lot of projects where work peaks around product releases, the proper management of contingent staff is vital. Temp workers help us handle peak loads in everything from development and testing to marketing to administrative support. Five different groups need to be coordinated in our use of temporary workers: 1) the temps themselves; 2) the 110 agencies for which the temps work; 3) the managers using temp workers in various divisions; 4) our internal contingent staffing group, which manages our relationships with the temp agencies and tracks the hourly rates for temp workers; and 5) Corporate Procurement, which actually pays the bills.

Our business problem was multifaceted. It wasn't just that a lot of paperwork was involved with contracting for services from many different agencies and temps. We also had difficulty ensuring a consistent contracting process, obtaining the correct people at the proper hourly rate, not using them for too many consecutive projects or for too long a time on any one project, and deciding when to convert people to full-time.

A hiring policy developed several years ago established stringent guidelines on the use of temp workers. By policy, all temps had to be hired through agencies, and no contingent staff could work for more than 340 days on any combination of projects without having at least a thirty-one-day break in service. But a paper process makes it hard to ensure that the managers contracting for temps—many of whom were new to the company or new to the role—follow the guidelines. Given the predisposition of our hiring managers to act when things need to be done, the only way we could meet the needs of the departments and prevent mistakes was by throwing a lot of bodies at the problem. People-intensive processes did not make any of us happy.

Further, the paper process did not solve the budgeting problem for senior managers. Because many managers hired temps, and because temps often worked on multiple projects, senior managers in the divisions could not get a handle on the total number of contingent staff being used or on the number of hours they were putting in. We could not with any consistency predict costs for temp staffing. The accounting data on the numbers of workers, hours, and costs that division managers were getting from Finance would be consistently late or would be only estimates instead of actual hours and costs. Payments showed huge spikes and dips month to month.

At first we thought the problem was in the finance department's process, but as we analyzed the data we realized that Finance was getting poor information, too. Our payment process had very few controls. Despite a lot of sign-offs—managers signed time cards for temps, who submitted them to their agencies, who sent us invoices on which Procurement paid—there were actually no financial controls. A manager couldn't verify the hourly rate or the number of hours invoiced. An invoice could be submitted without a signed time card. A manager might agree to a raise for a temp, but contingent staffing might not get the information. Or a temp might get a raise on one project and have the raise applied incorrectly to other projects. We had no way to stop duplicate billings.

Stepping back, the business teams looked at the entire process from beginning to end to determine how digital information could help us manage the complexity.

One management issue was whether the manager had the authority to hire contingent staff to begin with. In our paper system there was no way to ensure management review of the initial decision to get more resources. Once the decision was made to get a temp worker, managers didn't have enough information to know whether they were following the related business rules. For example, did the manager have budget for the work? Was the manager willing to authorize overtime for the project? In addition, the hiring manager had no way of easily knowing the appropriate hourly rate for a particular job or what qualified people might be available. Unless the hiring manager already had a specific person in mind, we had no easy way to identify a potential resource, whether a company, an agency temp, or an independent contractor. We needed a way to automatically calculate the full cost of the assignment up front for proper budgeting.

We decided we needed a new flexible software solution. For each temp, we had to ensure a contract was written and signed up front. Once the contract was approved, the person's card key, phone, and network access had to be available within forty-eight hours. Users had to be able to easily create multiple identical requests for similar positions, a typical situation when you're gearing up for a big project. While the contractor was working, managers needed a simple way to verify the hours worked, the rate being paid, and the amount of money remaining on the purchase order. As the date for termination approached, the hiring manager needed to be alerted automatically. The manager needed to be able to automatically extend the person, but only if there was budget remaining and the temp had worked less than 340 consecutive days for Microsoft. When the termination date arrived, the person's access to the network, e-mail, phone, and buildings had to be turned off.

Our new process had to support changes without holding up the work. If the approval manager was not available when a contract was ready, the hiring manager had to be able to reroute the approval to another person with signing authority. If the manager or cost center changed during the assignment, we had to be able to easily reallocate the cost. The agency should be able to give temps a small pay raise at its discretion but should get the hiring manager's approval for a large raise.

DECIDING WHETHER TO CENTRALIZE

One approach would be to create a huge monolithic application to handle all of these requirements, the "one big app" approach. We did this once with an application intended to enable a dozen of our internal service organizations—the library, security, catering, travel, the company store, the corporate credit card group, and others—to track and respond to employee requests. Ultimately this project became one of the few we've scrapped. The needs of the various groups were different enough that the business rules were too complex for one application to handle. We spent so much time getting the system to work that by the time we finished, the requirements had changed. We learned an important lesson: Very few corporate applications need a "central" point of view. We set each group free to build its own request system. By downsizing the scale of the solution, we squeezed out a lot of complexity and development time. Today all the internal service groups have their own "request" applications, which they improve every few months. They are all great examples of paperless processes that save time and make it easier to track the delivery of great service.

We avoid long development cycles for internal applications. Too much time often nullifies any benefits because business needs change along the way. Smaller, decentralized processes are usually best. Only a few applications, such as our financial reporting system, require centralization. As we have undertaken other business solutions internally, we have kept teams and projects small, keeping in mind the motto of our product development teams: "Shipping is a feature."

In looking at managing contingent staff, we wanted to avoid a monolithic approach but at the same time not end up with half a dozen discrete applications that wouldn't snap together to create an overall business solution. Our strategy, then, was to create a series of modular applications that were designed from the start with the idea of interlinking their digital data.

The primary tools are MS Market, the corporate procurement application on our intranet; MS Invoice, a private Web site on the Internet, or "extranet," which enables our contracting agencies and others to submit invoices electronically; and our SAP system, which handles all of the back-end financial transactions. Since we already had HeadTrax for managing personnel, we used HeadTrax as the user interface regardless of which of the applications actually "owned the code" behind the scenes. The user would simply click on a certain feature in HeadTrax and the correct application would be triggered.

The contracting process begins with digital procurement in MS Market, which I describe fully in chapter 3. The steps in creating, hiring, and managing contingent staff are very similar to the electronic controls that HeadTrax already provides for managing regular staff. MS Invoice provides for electronic submission of invoices and for controls to help both the hiring manager and the vendors stay within budget. With each invoice, the hiring manager has a link to see the amount remaining on the purchase order. Vendors can see which of their billings match up against what invoices. If a vendor attempts to submit an invoice that is more than the amount remaining on the purchase order, the submission is rejected. If the vendor gives the temp employee a raise, the Microsoft manager can approve or deny it with the click of a button.

Astute readers might wonder why we're using invoices at all, electronic or otherwise. After all, leaders in the manufacturing industry have been able to eliminate invoices entirely. The classic example is Ford's elimination of invoices for its inventory ordering. When Receiving accepts a parts delivery, the person enters the receipt of the materials electronically, triggering an automatic payment to the vendor. The manufacturer has the parts; the supplier has payment. Who needs an invoice—even a digital invoice?

We have experimented with a similar approach but uncovered a number of differences where services are involved rather than physical goods. In manufacturing, every item has a part number. It's more difficult to create a one-to-one relationship with time from a temp worker, when what you're "receiving" are hours of time spent on a project. It's difficult for the vendor to relate back an electronic payment to the particular worker and particular week without a separate reference, the invoice number. We have yet to see an invoiceless payment system for services that works for our vendors. The big issue for us was making the temp process fully digital so that all the information was easily available.

A rule of thumb is that a lousy process will consume ten times as many hours as the work itself requires. Many examples in the literature describe how reengineering reduced thirty-day processes to three, or ten days to one. A good process will eliminate the wasted time, and technology will speed up the remaining real work. Our new contingent-staffing application will speed the process, but that improvement won't be the most important benefit. Improving management oversight for the contracting process and ensuring that everyone follows the hiring guidelines and budget are big business benefits. Even more important is that we can relate performance from job to job and maintain a better relationship with these workers.

IMPROVING STEP BY STEP

Be prepared to experiment with new processes and technology solutions. Nobody can predict every possible wrinkle or problem with a new process or application. People have to use it before they and the developers can determine what really works and what doesn't, and users invariably see new ways to extend an application once they get their hands on it. Once we saw how HeadTrax worked for full-time personnel, we realized we could handle contingent personnel. Once we saw how great HeadTrax was for personnel transactions, we realized we could add the ability to track historical information in order to compare head count changes year to year for budgeting purposes. That feature will be part of the next release.

Complexity is the death of all reengineering projects, especially those that involve technology. According to an article in *The Wall Street Journal*, a 1996 survey of 360 companies by the research firm Standish Group International found that 42 percent of corporate information technology projects were abandoned before completion. Complexity was the usual culprit, according to the article, which called the waste "staggering" and added that "the bigger the projects are, the more frequently and expensively they tend to fail."[3]

Projects of only three to four months' duration are going to have much lower failure rates. With short projects you're forced to make important trade-offs that will drive you to simplicity and focus. You'll end up with goals that can be executed. If short projects fail—and a few do, for a variety of reasons—your loss in time and money is much smaller. It's far easier psychologically to pull out and redirect your development team when people haven't spent a year of their lives working on a project that's now going down the tubes.

Even projects that cumulatively take several years can be staged as a series of smaller projects with definable

3. Bernard Wysocki Jr., "Pulling the Plug: Some Firms, Let Down by Costly Computers, Opt to 'De-Engineer,' " *Wall Street Journal*, 30 April 1998.

checkpoints. Such an approach enables the projects to proceed in parallel and gives you the benefit of a faster digital process in many areas even if you get hung up in one or two. Dayton Hudson, the fifth largest retail chain in the United States, wanted to reduce the merchandising cycle time for its 1,100 department stores—the time it takes to order an item and get it on a store shelf. The company broke each business process into discrete steps—design, color and fabric selection, vendor selection, and so on—and then implemented each one quickly and independently. The resulting digital processes were linked together, reducing its cycle time for domestic items from twenty-five days to less than ten for its stores—Dayton's, Hudson's, Target, Mervyn's, and Marshall Fields.

Projects undertaken once your digital environment is established will have more success. If your environment is mostly paper, a new digital application will be outside of the normal business activities, and the normal learning curve for the application could make it seem like a lot of trouble for its worth. If the environment is digital, though, you'll be able to propagate the application quickly. You can leverage training over many applications. Workers who become very adept at using technology also become very demanding when it comes to how well new applications need to work. Once you have a few successful applications working for you, people say, "Hey, why isn't our head count system like our sales system? Why can't we move from summary data to detail here? Do you realize it'd be easy to put in electronic alerts for people there?" They'll point you to other applications or Web pages that you could easily connect to, and you'll end up with a more complete solution.

Taking advantage of your existing technical investments, you can create new digital applications for only marginal costs, creating a huge return. You already need e-mail for ad hoc communications. You need access to the World Wide Web to get information about the world at large. You need external Web sites to promote yourself to customers and partners, and you need internal Web sites for corporate information. Why not use these technologies for every business process? Take advantage of both technology and your existing employee know-how.

OWNING PROCESS CHANGE

At our second CEO summit in 1998, we put together a panel made up of CEOs and CIOs talking about the intersection of business needs and technology. One question to the panelists was, What caused big technology failures? Ralph Larsen, CEO of Johnson & Johnson, said that the most frequent cause of "spectacular failures" is that businesspeople simply turn over big projects to their IT departments or outside consultants "and then run because it's such hard work." Ralph said, "You absolutely cannot do that. All the successes you see come because of strong business-line ownership, not IT ownership. Business-line ownership with strong IT support. The project doesn't belong to the consultants or to IT. It doesn't belong to anyone else but the business owner."

It's impossible to properly reengineer a process using technology without the oversight of someone who can bridge the business and technical teams. This business process owner doesn't have to be the most senior or the most technical person on the business side of your organization, but the person does have to understand the business need and how the technology will be used in actual work. The person must be respected enough in the organization to make decisions stick. That's the person most likely to have insight into developing newer, simpler processes and negotiating trade-offs between business and technical requirements.

Ralph's response got strong support from the CIOs on the panel. Alcoa's CIO, Patricia Higgins, said that the only time she had seen major cost overruns on a reengineering project had been when the business side hadn't been in charge. "Never use new information technology simply to replace old business processes or even legacy IT systems," she said. "Always take the opportunity to review and streamline the process, asking yourself what your business priorities are." The costs come, many companies discover, when you don't redo your processes as part of the new solutions. Invariably you have to bring in someone else later to reengineer the solutions to make them work.

Who should own the reengineering process? Whichever senior business manager is in the greatest pain today or stands to benefit the most tomorrow should own the development of the new process and the technology that supports it.

Business Lessons

❏ Attack process problems from a variety of perspectives and use technology to create streamlined processes that were never possible before. Reevaluate all processes periodically.

❏ Redesign processes to deliver optimal information flow and you'll solve your important business problems.

❏ Process problems boil down to simplification: having the least number of employees engaged in the least number of handoffs.

- ❑ Business leaders, not IT alone, must own decisions about processes involving technology.
- ❑ A lousy process will consume ten times as many hours as the work itself requires. A good process will eliminate the wasted time; technology will speed up the remaining real work.
- ❑ Complexity is the death of all reengineering projects, especially those that involve technology.

Diagnosing Your Digital Nervous System

- ❑ Do your digital systems enable quick deployment of an initial solution and other improvements staged in over time? Do they make it easy for every employee to track status? Do they make it easy to see trends that call for management action?
- ❑ Can you build a large process from several independent smaller processes and link these to create an efficient system?
- ❑ Are you using digital information flow to simplify an entire process from beginning to end?
- ❑ Do you avoid long development cycles by creating smaller, modular solutions that are designed from the start to exchange digital data?

18

TREAT IT AS A STRATEGIC RESOURCE

Information technology so far has been a producer of data rather than a producer of information—let alone a producer of new and different questions and new and different strategies. Top executives have not used the new technology because it has not provided the information they need for *their own tasks.*

—Peter Drucker

Because the handling of information is core to business, CEOs should become as engaged in IT as in any other important business function. Too many CEOs, though, have remained distant from IT. Information systems are often thought of as too complex and unmanageable. Making IT relevant to business strategy seemed like an intractable problem. Discussions always seemed to get bogged down in acronyms. However the CIO tried to say it, the real message was that the old systems were too complex, too expensive, and too inflexible to meet new or changing needs.

With the technology changes of the last couple of years, the CEO now has the opportunity to redirect the company's technology. But this redirection requires three things of a CEO. First, the CEO must be sure to regard information technology as a strategic resource to help the business get more out of its people. IT should not be regarded as just a cost center. Second, the CEO needs to learn enough about technology to be able to ask good, hard questions of the CIO and to be able to tell whether good answers are coming back. IT is no different from sales or finance or manufacturing in this respect. Third, the CEO needs to bring the CIO into management's deliberations and strategizing. It's impossible to align IT strategy with business strategy if the CIO is out of the business loop.

The knowledge of CEOs about technology varies widely, from Paul O'Neill, CEO of Alcoa, who began his career writing computer software for the Veterans Administration, to many others, like Ralph Larsen, the CEO of Johnson & Johnson, who have no background in technology at all. Paul's technical experience meant that he wasn't intimidated by technology. He knew from the start that a company's information systems had to be treated holistically. Ralph's inexperience made him determined to learn. He worked on his own on weekends for two years teaching himself to use a number of PC applications. He knew that without a better understanding of technology he wouldn't have the credibility he'd need to convince Johnson & Johnson's 180 operating companies in 55 different countries to standardize their information systems. At that time, in the late 1980s, Ralph and the other executives at J&J were drowning in paper. Not information, paper. If Ralph needed *information,* he would have to get the finance group to prepare a special report. Ralph and J&J went through a painful process of trying to make sure everybody understood that a common set of systems was absolutely essential to the company's competitive survival.

When the new systems were finally coming on line, Ralph ran into an executive and asked him, "Did you get my note?" The executive said no. Ralph said, "I sent you an e-mail." The executive said, "Well, I don't use a computer." Ralph said, "Then you'll never hear from me again, because that's the only way I'm going to communicate to senior management in written form." Next day the executive had a computer on his desk.

John Warner, chief administrative officer at Boeing, used a leading-from-the-top strategy, too. The first four people to go up on Boeing's new e-mail system were, in order, the CEO, the two operating presidents, and John himself. John knew that if the senior executives were on one e-mail system, everybody else in the company would want to be on that system, too. Boeing thought it would take several years for e-mail to become strategic, but the company learned otherwise only a few months after the system was installed. While a senior executive in Seattle was trying to coordinate with a sales team in Europe to close a big order in 1996, maintenance workers accidentally cut the power to the mail server. Because the machine went down during America's Thanksgiving holiday, it took several days to get it back online. Boeing got the order, but from then on the company put in place the same backup and support capabilities for its e-mail system that it had for other major business systems.

The point of these examples is that the CEO must recognize the strategic importance of technology as he or she does with other important business initiatives and lead the way. You don't have to be a technology expert. In fact, if you know too many technology-related acronyms, you're focusing on the wrong aspect of technology. To know how technology can help your business, you need to start with just a baseline understanding of computers. It doesn't matter how you get it. I know some executives who have had consultants come in every week and teach them the things they need to know about technology. Another way to learn is to have a good relationship with your CIO.

GETTING CIOS TO THINK OF BUSINESS

When Patricia Higgins was asked to become CIO of Alcoa and when JoAnn Heisen was asked to become CIO of Johnson & Johnson, both women had the same initial reaction: to decline. They both saw IT as a "back office" support organization that wasn't integrated into the business. Patricia had been in a variety of business roles at communications companies. Her last job had been president of the communications sector at Unisys. JoAnn had been treasurer and corporate controller of Johnson & Johnson for several years. Her only interaction with the technology group had been challenging the business value of its spending requests. JoAnn asked Ralph, "What have you done to me here? Does CIO stand for 'Career Is Over'?"

But both women became convinced that their CEOs wanted to bring a business eye to the CIO job and to redefine its role. This approach of having businesspeople take the CIO job is a growing trend. Patricia became "an adviser and coach" to the business units on how they could use information as a strategic asset to continue to grow their revenues and profits. JoAnn was the businessperson with good personal skills whom Ralph wanted to bridge "the total disconnect" between the business and IT groups at J&J. "Business managers were frustrated with the level of service, and our technical people felt abused and disrespected," Ralph says. "I needed someone who could talk to both."

At first JoAnn thought it was incumbent on her to learn techno-speak. Then she realized that IT people needed to be able to speak the language of business. That insight was the beginning of sessions in which JoAnn would describe the company's business problems and insist that the technical staff describe in simple nonjargon how technology could help. JoAnn, sometimes described as the walking annual report at J&J, made sure that IT people understood the business issues, the business goals, the changing business issues in health care, and the products moving along J&J's pipeline. Then she challenged the IT teams: How could they support current efforts, and how could they support future revenue growth? This dialogue was the first major step in redefining the role of IT at J&J.

Because CIOs have not always had the best access to CEOs, some CIOs today insist that they report directly to the CEO. That isn't necessarily critical, but however you organize your senior management, the important thing is to have a close working relationship between the most senior technology person and the senior business staff, and the CEO needs to be engaged in their discussions.

At Alcoa and Johnson & Johnson, the CIO sits on the highest-level management committee; and CIOs of the operating companies sit on their companies' management boards. Carlson Companies, an international leader in hospitality, travel, and marketing services, has the CIO on the strategic planning, executive, and capital appropriations committees. Carlson regularly convenes an IT council in which the head of business planning meets with the chief technology officers from the various divisions. The company has two formal meetings a year in which the CEO and other senior executives explain business strategy and what it means for IT to all of the 750 IT employees at its headquarters. Senior technology people gather twice a year to trade best practices supporting business goals.

If your CIO reports to the chief financial officer, though, I'd suggest you take another look at your organization. If IT reports to the CFO, IT is likely to be viewed as an overhead item and the focus is likely to be on cutting costs. IT needs to be viewed in terms of the business opportunities it helps create and should report through the business side. If you've got a business-savvy CFO, the CIO's reporting to the CFO might work. If you don't, you may want to try some other arrangement. At Microsoft the CIO and the CFO both report to Bob Herbold, our chief operating officer, who brings us many years of experience in both business and information services.

Since the founding of Microsoft, I've always applied technology before applying labor to try to solve business problems. Integration of our IT world with our business objectives begins with the business, marketing, and sales plans of the senior executives—Steve Ballmer, Bob Herbold, Jeff Raikes, and others. After reviewing their plans, John Connors, the Microsoft CIO, creates an initial IT plan. John further develops his plan through a series of meetings with Bob, the VPs of all the lines of business, and John's IT heads. This plan, which now contains all the technology initiatives and financial costs, goes to Steve for review, and a consensus plan then comes to me.

For IT as well as all our business units, these annual plans are updated at midyear. In addition, John meets with the executive committee four other times a year on topical issues. Topics in FY '98 were the planned merger of the technical systems for all our Internet properties; the long-term strategy for our physical networking infrastructure; progress on the availability and reliability of our major system products; and the strengths and weaknesses of our core system products in large-scale enterprise environments.

John's recommendations on how we improve our enterprise products come from another complication of his job: He has to use our software before anybody outside Microsoft does. John is charged with using our large IT environment as a real-world lab. We call this approach "eating your own dogfood." It's an inelegant but affectionate name for serious work. If we can't run our own business on our technologies, we're not going to try to make customers do it. Before releasing our Microsoft Exchange e-mail product, for example, one requirement was that it had to be in use as our own internal e-mail system serving our then 14,000 employees.

This requirement to use betas for business—and the makeup of our senior staff, a bunch of whom know more about technology than John does—gives our CIO unique challenges. He probably gets more resources than most CIOs do, but he has more people looking over his shoulder, too. The expectations for his job are very high.

Of course, no CIO has it easy. The IT job is one where you get an "F" if you fail but only a "C" if you succeed—this stuff is *supposed* to work, right? One time, after a particularly difficult IT review, John went home and expressed his frustration to his wife. "She told me my job was like helping design car parts for Henry Ford," John says. "The feedback I give our product people will go to improve life for customers all over the world. She reminded me that I really do have a fun job—and I signed up for it voluntarily."

As we shifted our business strategies to include the Internet in the last several years, John has shifted our IT resources to match. His overall priorities have been to develop the applications needed for us to use the Internet as a communications vehicle for partners and customers and to build out our bandwidth to handle the huge ramp in networking traffic from customers, partners, and our employees worldwide.

We've had few real disconnects between business and IT over the years. The ones that occur usually result from new initiatives within a division by people who do not understand the IT requirements behind their programs. They may announce a public date before they get IT's buy-off. With one online licensing program, the missed signals forced us to use a less-than-perfect ("kludgy") technical solution that IT had to hold together while properly designing the system for the next release. Sometimes customer and market pressure create the same dilemma. A service called Windows Update, which enables users to easily obtain upgrades and software fixes from the Web, had to be available seven days a week, twenty-four hours a day, or "7 × 24 availability," with a very short time to prepare. Fortunately John's team had done enough 7 × 24 projects for our other Internet sites by 1998, when the new service began, that he had the expertise in place to do the back-end work in time.

A good IT staff can handle the occasional unexpected project, but the CEO has to exercise leadership to ensure that IT is not overwhelmed. The CEO has to make sure that all senior executives agree on the top five to eight IT priorities each year and understand the trade-offs on other projects in order to carry out the top ones. The more savvy the CEO is about IT capabilities, the more the CEO can help make the right trade-offs when other urgent projects pop up. Without the CEO enforcing priorities, the CIO and IT staff will try to do too many things. They'll end up doing them all marginally.

PLACING THE RESPONSIBILITY WHERE IT BELONGS

The initial cost of any computer infrastructure is high. IT is and will remain a large part of the corporate cost structure. In thirty years IT will have grown from 5 percent of total business equipment spending to more than 50 percent by the year 2000. In some industries such as insurance and security brokerages, IT constitutes more than 80 percent of the cost of all equipment used. A company has to make the most use of this investment in order to succeed. Often the CIO is expected to justify the cost of the infrastructure, but this responsibility is misplaced. Because the infrastructure benefits all of the company's business functions, the CEO is ultimately the person responsible for decisions on IT spending. The CIO is responsible for advising the CEO, implementing the infrastructure once the decision is made, and building the business applications on top of it. The CIO must also drive the understanding, learning, and thinking about the business down into the ranks of the technical staff and organize them to support business needs. But the business knowledge can be transferred to the IT staff only if the CIO is privy to it.

If IT doesn't "get" business issues, and the CEO does not integrate the CIO into important business decisions, then the fault is the CEO's. If IT doesn't "get" business issues, but the CEO does include the CIO in business strategy, then the fault is the CIO's. Perhaps this situation is why the CIO job is sometimes described as the end of a career and sometimes described as a stepping-stone to the CEO position. Someone who can see how to put technology at the service of business needs is of great value to a company; someone who can't is not helping the company very much.

A requirement is establishing a modern digital infrastructure. Sometimes the CEO has to stand up to division or subsidiary presidents, all of whom are used to making technology decisions independently and all of whom will always say their needs are "different." The major consulting companies can offer advice in this area. One methodology incorporated into an application called IT Advisor helps management assess its IT situation so that it can either avoid or get out of "the IT abyss." A company that's fallen into the IT abyss is seeing rapid IT spending increases, disproportionately high maintenance costs, exploding complexity, and little return on new development.

Based on research by McKinsey & Company, IT Advisor helps companies evaluate current IT assets, IT management processes, and IT business performance based on sixty-nine evaluation criteria. You can see where your company is in regard to IT effectiveness and get a good idea of where to focus your energies, if you have to, to climb out of the abyss. The goal is to reach the IT mountaintop, where you have a robust and flexible infrastructure, IT spending and organization directed at business solutions, and several best-in-class business applications. If you want to get a quick sense of where your company is today, take a look at the interactive IT Advisor on the Web site for this book: www.Speed-of-Thought.com.

Another way to assess your infrastructure is to look at the percentage of IT resources you're spending on buying and managing computers, providing help desk support, and running back-room IT applications. If more than a third of your IT resources go into these routine jobs, your IT operations are inefficient, probably because your infrastructure is overly complex. While trying to figure out how to improve citizen services, the state of South Australia did a study that showed it was spending 55 percent of its IT effort on administration. By comparison, companies with efficient IT organizations spent only 30 percent on the routine stuff. The state figured that a more efficient infrastructure could effectively free up 25 percent more IT resources that could be spent on creating solutions for better citizen

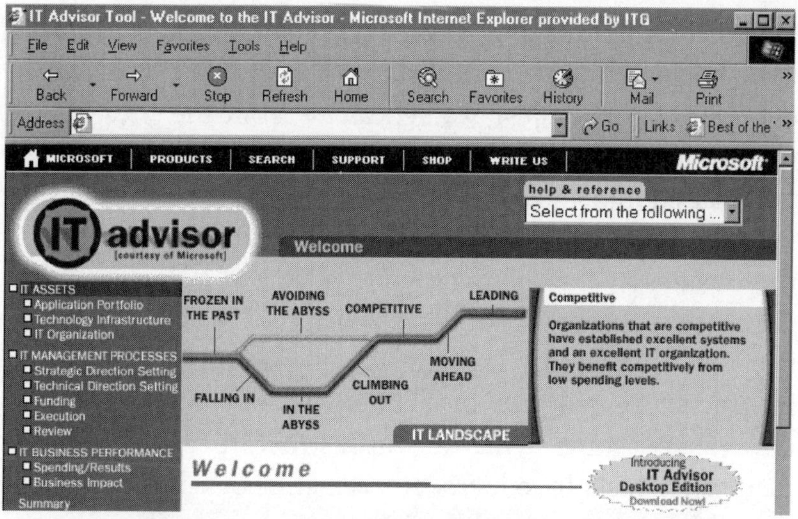

IT Advisor is an online tool that helps companies evaluate their IT capabilities. By answering a series of questions about a company's application portfolio, technical infrastructure, and IT organization and skill set, companies can see whether they are stuck in the past, have fallen into the "abyss" of high IT spending coupled with low IT results, or are using IT to gain competitive advantage. The application, at www.Speed-of-Thought.com, provides guidance to companies on how they can work with their IT departments to become leaders in applying digital solutions to business needs.

services. It moved to a PC infrastructure, standardized its messaging platform, and outsourced maintenance on a fixed-bid basis to ensure that costs were controlled.

Carlson went a similar route in outsourcing the maintenance of its legacy applications. Like South Australia, Carlson wanted to free internal developers to create business solutions. Every situation is a bit different, though. A study by Johnson & Johnson showed that J&J was already more efficient in mainframe maintenance than an outside firm would be. J&J saw no reason to outsource maintenance.

As these examples show, outsourcing works well when the outside vendor brings a set of best practices that are outside of your company's expertise or outside of your primary development focus. I do not, however, recommend outsourcing the development of strategic applications. I talked to one company that was thinking about outsourcing its entire IT effort, and I asked them what would be left of their business! What would that company do if the vendor did a poor job or just walked away from the project one day?

You should measure IT costs carefully, of course, but ultimately you should judge your infrastructure in terms of the business value it gives you. If you're going to spend the money anyway, wouldn't you rather spend it on solutions than on simply keeping the engine running? A good infrastructure will cut baseline costs, but a CEO should always be asking what the infrastructure enables rather than what costs it reduces. It's a matter of emphasis. Each year the company should strive to spend a smaller percentage of resources on routine functions and a greater percentage on new business solutions.

When you review project costs, be particularly careful to avoid the trap of assigning the underlying cost of infrastructure improvement to the first application that will take advantage of it. This approach could make a valuable business solution appear to be financially infeasible. Instead ask how much the second and third business applications will cost. Additional solutions should come in at relatively low incremental costs. A good messaging system, for instance, is expensive; but additional work-flow applications built on that messaging system should be relatively cheap.

Training should be included in infrastructure costs, too. Often companies invest huge amounts of money in hardware and software and neglect to fund the training of the people who use it. What's the point? Every successful application of technology involves generous and ongoing doses of training. Build training into the annual budgets. It'll be the best investment you'll ever make.

It's not a coincidence that most of the companies I've described in this book have taken the approach of driving

IT to undertake specific projects that help increase revenue through improved products, reduced product costs, faster delivery, and improved customer service. These companies have learned a valuable lesson: The purpose of IT is to make money! Rather than focus on keeping IT costs down, evaluate cost in terms of effectiveness for the bottom line. The secret to business success in the digital age is IT success. The secret to IT success is a modern, flexible infrastructure based on PC and Internet standards.

Business Lessons

- ❑ The CEO must understand IT as well as he or she understands any other business function. The responsibility for strategic use of IT can't be delegated to the CIO.
- ❑ The CEO must regard information technology as a strategic resource to help the company generate revenue.
- ❑ The CIO has to be an integral part of the development of business strategy and must be able to articulate in plain language what IT can do to help execute that strategy.
- ❑ Treat training costs as part of your basic infrastructure costs.

Diagnosing Your Digital Nervous System

- ❑ Each year do you spend a smaller percentage of resources on keeping systems running and a greater percentage on new business solutions?
- ❑ Do you have several best-in-class business applications?
- ❑ How expensive is it to add new solutions to your current infrastructure?

V

SPECIAL ENTERPRISES

19

NO HEALTH CARE SYSTEM IS AN ISLAND

Bedside manners are no substitute for the right diagnosis.

—Alfred Sloan, GM Chairman

A few years ago a new Microsoft employee was called back to his home state because his mother had suffered a mild stroke. When she was well enough to leave the hospital, Mrs. Jones (not her real name) stayed with her sister while her son completed arrangements to move her out to the Northwest to be near him. Mrs. Jones largely recovered but was never able to live on her own again, and her periods of good health were punctuated by hospital stays treating more and more acute problems.

The medical events of the last two years of Mrs. Jones's life demonstrate the best and the worst aspects of American health care. She received good care, including a number of state-of-the-art procedures, from three different hospitals and more than a dozen physicians in two different states. As her physical abilities declined, her middle-class family was able to find decent facilities providing greater degrees of care. Medicare and her private insurance paid most of the bills; she and her family picked up the rest. Her many doctors, nurses, and other caregivers were professional and uniformly kind. Mrs. Jones retained her dignity to the end, when she died in her sleep.

Yet the system was far from perfect. When Mrs. Jones left the first hospital for her sister's hometown thirty miles away, a lapse of communication between doctors led to her medication being kept at full strength when Mrs. Jones should have been on a declining dosage. By the time she arrived in the Northwest, side effects of the high dosage required her to be hospitalized immediately. Because her records didn't come with her, a number of expensive tests had to be redone. The same thing happened when she changed hospitals a year later. Her final three-week hospital stay, which did not involve any surgical procedures, nevertheless cost $25,000. At one point her outgoing doctor confused her with another patient and told the next doctor over the phone that her recent hospital stays were an "abuse of the system." This was less than a week before Mrs. Jones died.

These and other problems went on even though Mrs. Jones had family advocates to work through the maze of medical and social services options. Her son and daughter-in-law took turns spending many hours standing in line at one agency or on the phone with another. And it took a year before they could convince one hospital to stop billing them for services that had been paid in full.

Because of the many hospitals, physicians, clinics, pharmacies, care facilities, and public and private agencies involved, the amount of paperwork was unbelievable.

"During periods of Mom's acute care, paper piled up at a rate of exactly one inch per month," her son said.

On business trips he took to carrying an extra binder containing the current paperwork related to his mom's care. When he was caught up with his own work, he would painstakingly reconcile bills, using colored Post-it notes: blue if a bill had been submitted to Medicare; yellow if it had gone through Medicare and been submitted to a private insurance company; red if he'd returned the bill because of errors; and green if the bill had gone all the way through the system and he was ready to write a check for the balance.

Consider the number of people this paperwork represented. For every doctor and nurse who treated his mom, there must have been a dozen billing people in a bunch of different organizations—the hospital or doctor's office, the pharmacy, the social agency, Medicare, the insurance company. It was like an old-fashioned military campaign. For every soldier in the field, you had twenty people behind the lines handling logistics.

Most experts estimate that 20 to 30 percent of the annual trillion-dollar cost of the U.S. health care system is tied up in paperwork. In hospitals that number could be as high as 40 to 50 percent. A single week's stay can generate as many as a hundred pieces of paper. Compounding the cost, about 13 percent of the one to two billion claims filed each year in the United States are returned for errors.[1]

Paperwork and complexity have soared even as the U.S. health care industry has shifted to "managed care" in an effort to reduce costs, prevent fraud, and ensure consistent and appropriate care. Under the managed care model, an organization, whether Medicare or a private insurance

1. Kambiz Foroohar, "Rx: software," *Forbes*, 7 March 1997: 114.

company, will contract with a group of doctors to provide medical services toward managed outcomes and for fixed fees—$1,000 for an appendectomy, $15 for a flu shot, and so on. According to the *1998 Source Book of Health Insurance Data,* more than 160 million people in the United States were enrolled in a managed care plan at the beginning of 1997, the last year for which figures were available.

Doctors appreciate the need to control costs but feel buried in regulations and second-guessed by layers of bureaucrats. They're afraid that their medical options are being limited and that patient care may suffer. They have also complicated matters themselves, treating patient files as business records and often hesitating to share them with competing physicians. And they've been largely computer-averse, although much of that aversion can be attributed to the clunkiness and expense of early medical systems.

Curiously enough, the managed care that many physicians love to hate may turn out to be the primary driver that extends information systems into patient care and returns control of patient care to doctors. When you get enough clinically helpful information in front of physicians they see the benefits and ask for more. Patients, meanwhile, are recognizing how much more information is available to them on the Web and how this information gives them a sense of control and responsibility in the maintenance of their own health.

Clinical benefits have also encouraged health care CEOs to push for better information systems, sometimes against resistance by their boards of directors, which have too often focused on the cost cutting during the mergers of the last several years. Up to now, health care has applied only 2 to 3 percent of its revenues to information technology, compared with, say, the banking industry's 15 percent. Although health care is a high-tech field, the technology

Web Puts You in Charge of Your Own Health

I've personally spent many hours on the Web reading information about health issues facing my friends and family. The degree of detail in medical information on the Web is stunning. But there's lots of quackery out on the Internet, too, so don't believe everything you find. Evaluate the credentials of the people or organization providing the information.

Over time, the availability of so much data will profoundly improve the ability of people to get medical information and become more responsible for their own health decisions. Hamilton Jordan, President Carter's chief of staff, has battled cancer several times. When he was about to give up the first time, a friend told him, "Nobody has more at stake in your health care than you," and convinced Jordan to take charge of his case. For that first cancer, which he believes was caused by exposure to Agent Orange in the Vietnam War, Jordan used libraries for research. A decade later, fighting prostate cancer, he used the Internet to become an expert on his illness and took an active role in treating it.

Intel chairman Andy Grove had a similar experience when he faced prostate cancer several years ago. After going online to see what information was available about the various medical approaches, he quickly realized that there were no valid comparative studies. Ever the scientist, he wrote his own comparative study from the raw data!

Jordan, with a family history of prostate cancer, chose surgery. Grove, with a different history and circumstance, chose a combination of general and "smart bomb" radiation therapy. The important thing is that with good medical advice and their own research, both men made informed decision for themselves.

The Internet is about more than medical information, though. It enables patients who have the same malady to stay in touch, share their experiences, and feel less alone. The community of patients is worldwide, and online forums make it easy for them to connect.

The Fred Hutchinson Cancer Research Center in Seattle is experimenting with a new approach to creating an Internet community. The center is using virtual reality to create a sense of "being there" for patients and their families. The virtual experience appears to be exceptionally valuable before a patient comes to the center, fostering a greater sense of comfort and familiarity. A patient and his family can visit the center over the Internet and do a three-dimensional virtual walk-through of the facility. They can attend presentations on different topics and visit with other patients and their families in common areas. Later, a family member can make an appointment to have an online chat with a specific staff member he's come to know. These virtual experiences don't replace but augment face-to-face personal contact.

has been directed at stand-alone diagnostic systems, not at information flow.

Often the information applications that are used aren't designed to work with other information applications, despite all the health care areas that should share data: the lab, the pharmacy, radiology, the blood bank, medical monitoring devices, charting, and billing systems. Organizations have had to build special interfaces between each and every application. A typical health care organization can have hundreds of these interfaces. One organization currently manages 1,800 different interfaces. This complexity is one reason it typically has taken two years for a health care organization to buy a new system and another two years to install it—too slow by any standard.

Today the situation is more encouraging. The U.S. government has passed legislation requiring the definition of a standard for electronic finance and administrative transactions, including computer-based patient records. Several organizations are working to establish nationwide technical standards for interoperability of medical applications. The Microsoft Healthcare Users Group, which with MS-HUG has one of the friendliest acronyms around, is working to create medical applications that use standard Windows component technology and new Internet technology to "plug and play" with each other.

Better information handling in medical organizations will be a requirement in the future. Some health organizations, recognizing that their patients' needs can't wait, are showing strong leadership. They're proving that a digital nervous system can make invaluable contributions in all areas of patient care: from emergency services through hospital treatment, patient follow-up, and long-term trend analysis.

PROVIDING INSTANT REFLEXES IN EMERGENCIES

More than eighty ambulance services and fire departments in six countries are achieving lifesaving reflex capabilities with PC-based systems. Coupled with global positioning system (GPS) satellites, these systems locate the ambulance nearest a patient's home and map the fastest route to get there. The two largest nationwide emergency services companies in the United States, American Medical Response (AMR) and Rural/Metro Ambulance Service, use PCs to recommend to dispatchers the best redeployment of remaining emergency vehicles once some vehicles have been dispatched.

Rural/Metro in San Diego can calculate how many of its 500 fire apparatus and which vehicle types need to get to a fire. A ladder truck might be required for a high-rise fire, for instance, or hazardous waste equipment might be needed for a factory fire. The Denver Fire Department uses a PC-based system to display the floor plans of major buildings and the locations of hydrants and to alert firefighters to anybody with disabilities living close to a fire who might need to be evacuated.

Perhaps no emergency services firm in the country has made more use of PC technology than Acadian Ambulance and Air Med Services, in Lafayette, Louisiana, which is building a complete flow of information around TriTech Software Systems' VisiCAD for Fire/EMS software. (CAD here means computer-aided *dispatch*, not design.) With 1,200 employees and $90 million in revenues, Acadian is the largest independent ambulance company in the United States. From a single dispatch center in Lafayette, Acadian serves 26 parishes (counties) across 17,000 square miles of cities, towns, sugarcane fields, rice fields, and bayous in the southern part of the state. On a typical day Acadian will handle 500 to 600 calls involving ambulances and medical helicopters.

Users of the PC-based emergency response software system say that it consistently cuts sixty to ninety seconds off immediate response times to 911 emergencies. In a business where life and death can be measured in minutes and seconds, this is a significant advance. But the greatest value is in how the same system enables the emergency medical technicians (EMTs) to give medical help to the injured or the sick, both while EMTs are en route and after they arrive on the scene. While the ambulance is on its way, the software walks the dispatcher through a series of questions to ask the caller about the emergency. The dispatcher downloads the answers to the crew while they're en route and advises the caller on appropriate first-aid techniques pending the crew's arrival. The system even reminds the dispatcher to ask about the presence of a guard dog or other potential hazard to the crew at the scene.

A new ambulance-based pen chart system running on Fujitsu laptops helps ensure that Acadian's EMTs follow standard treatment steps. The PC displays a schematic of the human body divided into seven regions. The EMT taps on the schematic at the part of the body with a suspected problem. Based on whether it's a medical condition such as cardiac arrest or a trauma such as a puncture wound to the heart, the PC offers different treatment guidance.

Replacing the paper reports the crews have used in the past, the pen chart system enables the ambulance crew to quickly create a new patient file. The system prompts for standard information, converts handwritten hospital names to text, and automatically completes the hospital address fields. If the victim is a subscriber to Acadian's monthly subscription program, the pen chart system populates the chart with medical information from records already loaded on the laptop's hard drive.

Intravenous (IV) treatments and a few other procedures require a doctor to sign off when the ambulance reaches the hospital. The signature is obtained with a stylus in a special field on the PC display. If a new treatment is entered later, another signature by a doctor is required, ensuring medical review of all procedures.

Once a report is completed, it is uploaded via remote access into Acadian's network. Encryption technology protects confidential patient information. The pen chart system reminds the crew every day about any files that are incomplete. If a file is not completed and uploaded within five days, a "late report" is automatically e-mailed to the crew's supervisor, who follows up.

The pen chart system has improved the level of accuracy in reports from the 60 percent to the 90 percent range.

Eventually Acadian plans to integrate its information systems so that the initial entry of data by the EMTs will roll directly into accounting and EMT hours entered into the pen chart will roll seamlessly into payroll. The same infrastructure will automatically coordinate training, EMT licensing, OSHA requirements, and the like; automatically requisition supplies for vehicles according to usage; and enable smarter maintenance of the vehicles themselves, which are the most expensive equipment that Acadian has.

But these operational improvements are only part of the story. The data Acadian collects is helping the company to become even smarter with patient treatment. EMTs face the quandary of whether to establish an IV at the scene and delay departure to the hospital or start for the hospital first, even though vehicle motion might make it harder to get an

IV going. By analyzing data collected on the new pen-based PCs, Acadian learned that the success rate was identical either way. The company made en route IVs the standard procedure, cutting minutes off arrival time.

Analysis of pen data also enabled Acadian to provide specific training to EMTs who had a low success rate with IVs or intubations (the insertion of a tube in a patient's throat to help breathing). Analysis also indicated that Acadian could stop carrying two types of medicine that invariably expired and were disposed of before they could be used.

With the old paper reports, analysis of these issues and others was difficult at best. Even with shift commanders reviewing the tickets, it was impossible to spot any but the most obvious issues for follow-up, such as substantial delays or a rare major mistake by a crew. The 500 to 600 tickets a day simply piled up, useful only as historical records of individual cases, not for anlayzing trends. Going forward, Acadian will have enough local data to understand and respond to almost any medical trend. The company won't have to wait for long-term national studies.

Acadian and other ambulance services are also pursuing the next step, transferring digital data along with the patient, to the receiving hospital. In Birmingham, Alabama, ten local hospitals have begun to use TraumaNet, a software program that enables a paramedic to transmit basic patient data electronically from the ambulance. The data goes to a Trauma Communications Center, which directs the ambulance to whichever hospital has the appropriate emergency treatment available and sends the patient data to the hospital so that the hospital can prepare for the patient's arrival. Ultimately the goal is to use digital systems to provide a holistic picture of the patient's status by the time the ambulance pulls up to the emergency room doors.

CAPTURING THE COMPLETE DIGITAL RECORD FOR PATIENTS

Once in the hospital, a patient benefits from information systems that provide the medical staff with more information about the patient's history, capture the details of care to date, and relieve doctors and nurses of excessive paperwork so they can spend more time focusing on the patient. A good illustration of how a hospital can integrate all this patient information is found at Children's Hospital and Regional Medical Center in Seattle. Children's Hospital is a 208-bed nonprofit pediatric hospital affiliated with the University of Washington School of Medicine. The hospital has 180 hospital-based physicians and 100 residents at the hospital, plus another 240 residents who rotate in from other programs. Affiliated with more than fifty outpatient specialty clinics in Alaska, Idaho, Montana, Washington, and Wyoming, Children's also takes pediatric referrals from those five states.

When a patient is admitted, all identifying information is entered once into a PC and stored in a central database. More than 1,500 PCs are stationed throughout the hospital, on every floor, in every department, and in close proximity to every bedside. Whenever anyone in the hospital interacts with the patient, the encounter is entered into the same database. Any staff member, even a clinician at one of the Children's off-site specialty and outpatient clinics, can tap into this information. If a nurse needs to notify a doctor about a patient's status, she can page the doctor, and he can log on to a PC at the hospital or remotely through a dial-up connection and review the patient's condition.

Every treatment, test, medication, and procedure administered at Children's is entered into CareVISION, a patient information management system from Health-

VISION Corporation. A CareVISION file gives the hospital a complete digital record of the patient and what the hospital has done for him. Developed in coordination with Children's clinicians who worked along with the IT staff as part of the project team, the CareVISION system can capture data as minute as how often a nurse visits a patient, turns her in her bed, or gives her a bath. A physician can click on a patient name to review the record, drilling down to as much detail as needed. All lab reports and other information that were once part of the 100-pages-per-week-per-patient paper flow are now stored digitally in a database. Everything is captured electronically so that the hospital has a complete, instantly available picture of every time and every way the hospital touches the patient.

Soon the hospital will add a decision-support module to alert medical staff in real time to treatment conflicts and duplications. For example, upon entering a drug order for a child, a physician might be alerted by the system that the medication interacts adversely with another drug the child is receiving or that the child is allergic to the drug. Or the doctor might order an X-ray, and the system will say, "We just ordered an X-ray yesterday. Do you really want another one?"

As Acadian Ambulance analyzes its data to identify trends and develop appropriate emergency treatments, Children's uses its system to develop "best practices" in caring for patients. The industry term for this is *clinical pathways*, and it means defining optimum courses of care for specific maladies. Most hospitals have always had clinical pathways for treating certain illnesses, but they were paper based and often ended up on a shelf, where few people could access and use them. Even when they were used, paper-based pathways made it difficult to collect and evaluate data for improvement.

At Children's, care data is captured automatically, giving pathway teams ways to track trends and build even better pathways. The teams then program new standard paths into the CareVISION system and "push" them to doctors at the bedside, where they're administering treatment. When a physician prescribes a certain drug or treatment, the system double-checks whether the prescription is compatible with the hospital's pathway for that problem. The system alerts doctors to new procedures they might otherwise overlook.

This ability to sift through data to develop better medical practices is especially important to Children's Hospital in its capacity as a teaching organization. To assist residents and students, CareVISION will contain preselected orders that follow the hospital's current best-practice guidelines. If the resident is not familiar with the order set, the system can e-mail background information to the resident for later reading. The online references will contain the latest data explaining the pros and cons, in terms of cost and effectiveness, of different treatments. If a resident places an inappropriate order, CareVISION will prevent the order from going through, send additional information to the resident as to why the order was stopped, and possibly alert the attending physician to areas where the resident may need more training.

Integration of the new system with the legacy billing system at Children's protects the hospital's investment in existing technology, and the new system meets stringent patient confidentiality and security criteria. The system makes it easier to get reimbursed, since extensive documentation is available to insurance providers. Because the system captures all patient care data digitally, the hospital has the ability to run audit trails and produce extensive management reports.

Because the system is standards based, Children's will be able to modify or augment it in just about any direction it wants. Children's plans to incorporate digital imaging into its system so that doctors will be able to review images of patient problems from wherever they are.

Children's knew that implementing a world-class information system focused on patient care would take time, cost money, and involve a few surprises. But Children's also realized that the cost and the risk of not making the change to a digital system was far greater. "Yes, it's expensive. No, it's not as easy as it should be. And yes, it's taking us a while to roll this thing out," John Dwight, Children's chief information officer, says. "But we really do not have an option. Hospitals simply will not be able to survive in today's health care world unless they invest in digital information systems that let them track and analyze care data. It's do a better job of tracking our care, or go out of business."

PROVIDING ONGOING CARE

PC and Web technology benefit patient care not only in hospitals, but also in daily clinical practice. Sentara Health System of Norfolk, Virginia, a health care provider in southern Virginia and northern North Carolina, is using the Internet to put doctors in touch with patients whether the patients are in the hospital or at home receiving ongoing treatment.

Sentara has created an intranet-based application called SpinWeb that provides its network of 2,000 physicians and 5,000 office staff with instant access to patient records and other hospital information systems over the Web. Doctors dial into Sentara's PC servers from their offices or homes to check patients' current medical status and to read lab reports, patient discharge summaries, other patient news, medical reference materials, and insurance information. A surgeon might dial in the night before surgery to check on a patient's condition. SpinWeb also enables a doctor to review, edit, and electronically sign patient documents via a PC from a remote location. E-mail enables communication among physicians and between Sentara and physicians.

These capabilities save a doctor from having to drive to the hospital, often from a rural area, every time a routine step in a patient's treatment is completed. It also saves the administrative burden in disseminating all the paperwork.

For a large category of high-risk patients, such as individuals with diabetes, Sentara provides disease management education and daily monitoring. Today caseworkers do preventive checkups with these patients on a daily basis, sometimes multiple times a day, checking blood sugar levels and other critical indicators. Using SpinWeb, the patient will soon be able to log on to the Internet and enter her own daily reports that will go to both the caseworker and her physician. The SpinWeb application will be able to make preliminary patient recommendations on its own. If the patient's blood sugar is below a certain level, SpinWeb might instruct her to drink a glass of orange juice. Otherwise the caseworker and the physician can provide proactive and preventive care for the patient from any location. SpinWeb will also enable Sentara to gather trend information. In a diabetes case it could become clear that the patient's blood sugar level is high every day around four P.M., prompting the physician to recommend a change in diet.

Internet-based applicants such as SpinWeb are broadening information access to the many rural physicians and patients Sentara serves. When a patient is referred to a specialist in a nearby city, the hometown doctor can follow the patient's condition via posted reports on the SpinWeb site. Before too long, if a patient needs medical treatment away from the area, SpinWeb will provide the patient's medical records online for any other medical team with proper authorization. A Sentara emergency health card will have a toll-free telephone number that another medical facility can call to get access to the Sentara Web site. Within minutes the remote medical team will know as much about the patient's medical history as the local doctor.

TRACKING UNSEEN MEDICAL DANGERS

In addition to improving both immediate care and ongoing doctor-patient dialogue, information technology can yield answers for improving care through the longer-term capture and analysis of symptoms, illnesses, and treatment. The U.S. Air Force is a leader in using data gathering and analysis to monitor and protect its forces overseas from medical dangers.

A number of American service personnel returning from both the Vietnam War and the Persian Gulf War complained of maladies that doctors couldn't figure out. Vietnam veterans believed their ailments were caused by exposure to Agent Orange, an herbicide used by the United States to defoliate vegetation. Speculation on the cause of "Gulf War syndrome" has ranged from oil-fume inhalation to delayed reactions to vaccines to possible exposure to Iraqi chemical weapons. Adding to the confusion, at least one study claims that the number of unusual illnesses reported by Gulf veterans is no higher than the number reported by soldiers who did not serve in the combat zone. Without the consistent tracking of symptoms in the field and later, and of events that might have caused the symptoms, no one can say with certainty whether such illnesses were war related or what the causes were.

After concerns about a possible Gulf War illness became serious in the mid-1990s, Brigadier General Klaus Schafer, chief medical officer for the U.S. Air Force's Air Combat Command, made a decision: "I'm not about to let Agent Orange or Gulf War syndrome happen to my people. I want to know what environment I'm putting them into and what is happening to them." General Schafer went to the official Department of Defense medical establishment, the Military Health Service (MHS), and asked for help in developing a digital, field-deployable clinical records system that would enable him to gather health-related data on the environments his people were going into. Although the MHS thought such a system was a great idea, MHS said it would be two to three years before that organization had the capability to help develop one.

That wasn't soon enough. General Schafer and his top information systems officer, Lieutenant Colonel Edward Kline, along with a group of technical experts, turned to off-the-shelf PC software, mobile computers, and low-cost servers. The goal was to track and analyze what the military calls "disease non-battle injuries," a broad category that covers health problems other than injuries incurred in battle. The result was an application called Desert Care, which enables the air force to precisely diagnose illnesses and see illness trends areawide. In tracking the welfare of troops, Desert Care can also uncover possible unseen health-endangering activities of the enemy.

From start to finish, development took about four months and cost a mere $200,000. Today Desert Care is deployed in Southwest Asia—the Persian Gulf and the Middle East—supporting the air force's 28,000 people who rotate through there annually. Within a year Desert Care could be "institutionalized" throughout the air force, in all of its hostile theaters, providing medical intelligence on thousands more individuals and dozens more environments. The U.S. Army and Navy are interested in adopting Desert Care in their own theaters, so its impact may widen.

PROTECTING INDIVIDUALS AND THE ENTIRE FORCE

Before Desert Care, one service person's ailment would be just an isolated symptom in the middle of nowhere. The ailment would be dosed with medicine, recorded on a paper-based system, and forgotten. Now when an air force doctor treats service personnel, she also enters the data into a mobile computer. This information is e-mailed back to the United States daily, where it's merged with reports arriving from elsewhere in the theater. Several teams of university and military statisticians in the United States analyze the data to establish norms, build a bigger picture of what's going on medically, and watch for any patterns of sickness to emerge. If other people on the same base or within, say, a 300-mile radius report similar symptoms, the air force knows about those cases right away and can respond. The goal is to provide "force protection"—to enable the military to respond quickly to a chemical or biological attack.

Desert Care proved itself quickly, although in mundane fashion, by picking up on a pattern of sick calls that indicated a slide in food sanitation standards at a particular base kitchen. Without digital assistance it might have taken the air force weeks to realize that there was a problem and institute tighter hygiene.

Desert Care also establishes a great deal of baseline data that will be useful in treating service people after they return home. Suppose a serviceman walks into Andrews Air Force Base Medical Center in Maryland a year or two after returning from Kuwait and reports intermittent bouts of dizziness and depression. Doctors will be able to consult the data and find out what was going on in the area during his service there. Did anyone suffer those symptoms while in Kuwait? Are other veterans suffering similar symptoms now? Did the serviceman receive an anthrax vaccination before he was sent to Kuwait? If any event can be correlated with these symptoms or similar problems at a certain time or place, Desert Care gives doctors the best opportunity to find out.

General Schafer plans to make the system even more powerful for spotting areawide medical problems. When they become commercially available, he plans to introduce handheld DNA probes that will enable medical personnel to make on-the-spot diagnoses of bacteria or viruses through blood and urine samples. Desert Care will then become a field treatment tool as well as a diagnostic tool. Field physicians and medics will also be equipped with digital cameras to take photos of skin lesions or other symptoms, and they'll incorporate the photos into the overall electronic health record for either stateside diagnostic assistance or retrospective case review.

This tracking of long-term medical trends for widely scattered military personnel provides a good template for civilian applications. With digital records we'll be able to study illnesses in a variety of population groups to help discover long-term correlations in environment, genetic predisposition, age, and gender, without having to institute specialized studies. At least one hospital in the American Midwest is experimenting with long-term tracking of patient populations to determine what treatments are most effective in preventing more serious complaints.

EVOLVING A COMPLETE HEALTH CARE SYSTEM

Imagine you had a health care system in your local community built on the components I've described. An intelligent, adaptive emergency system gets you to the hospital quickly, and all critical information on your medical history and the current medical situation feeds immediately into the hospital's computers. A doctor uses a touch screen, keyboard, pen, or (fairly soon) voice recognition system to order your treatment. Digital instructions are fired off to the labs and the pharmacy. PC-based instruments post lab results electronically. These and other reports are online for easy review by any physician on site or off. Alerts automatically pop up for any potential treatment conflicts or deviations from the approved clinical pathway. Inventory and billing are handled automatically. Transaction-processing systems detect fraud or unusual use and, over time, learn appropriate countermeasures. Instead of spending half their time on paperwork, doctors and nurses spend virtually all their time treating you and their other patients. Test results and bills reach you in simple, understandable language. All your treatment and medication information is evaluated automatically over the longer term to help prevent adverse reactions.

Your follow-up care is also scheduled automatically. You research medical information on the Internet and have more informed and engaged interactions with caregivers, whether you communicate with them over the Internet via e-mail or you go in for an appointment. You use e-mail to ask routine questions of your health giver and to receive reminders about ongoing health programs, or medication that's about to expire. When you change health plans all your medical history goes with you instead of being lost or trailing after you several months later. It stays with you throughout your life. Doctors use your history to identify trends in blood pressure, cholesterol levels, and other factors to look for patterns that might reveal a serious developing problem. Systematic medical analysis of the whole community alerts authorities to any alarming public health trends much sooner and more accurately than has been possible before.

If health care communities take an approach based on PC and Web technologies, such capabilities do not have to be outrageously expensive. Estimates for creating an integrated patient-data system involving doctors, hospitals, and managed care providers vary widely. *Medicine & Health* magazine estimates the cost for a large hospital, health maintenance organization, or other health system at between $5 million and $50 million annually during the start-up phase. The high-side estimates presuppose the continued use of incompatible systems, the use of highly specialized diagnostic equipment, and the continuing development of medical systems as huge, monolithic projects.

PCs enable a step-by-step approach using more off-the-shelf software. The examples of patient-data systems in this chapter, all developed independently, together cover most aspects of short-term and long-term medical treatment. Because they were all built on the PC platform, they would be simple to link without expensive systems integration. PCs are also now being used as the front end of specialized devices such as ultrasound, body scanners, and blood and tissue analyzers, reducing their costs and enabling integration of their data. PCs are powerful enough to handle hundreds of thousands of claims per hour or heavy query loads into patient records. PCs can tie into existing back-end systems if health organizations need them to. All told, the applications described in this chapter, if implemented as a single solution, would cost less than the $5 million figure cited by *Medicine & Health*.

Distance Medicine to Improve Treatment, Training

PC-based video technologies are also changing the face of medicine. Acadian Ambulance plans to link onshore doctors by PC-based TV to more than a hundred emergency medical technicians already on oil platforms in the Gulf of Mexico. Telemedicine should improve both diagnosis and on-site treatment, eliminating many of the emergency helicopter flights that cost oil companies between $4,000 and $12,000 for each trip.

Australian state governments use telemedicine to provide care to remote areas of Australia and even to other areas of Southeast Asia. Malaysia plans to use the PC-based TV technology as the basis of a "telehealth" program throughout the country. The goal is to provide not simply acute care, but lifelong prevention programs to help its citizens avoid the heart disease and other lifestyle-related illnesses that have become common in the West.

Columbia/HCA in the United States is using Internet-based video to provide medical training to physicians, becoming the first hospital to do a heart operation live over the Internet. The doctors demonstrated surgical techniques over the video, and an accompanying slide presentation provided technical details. The video can be replayed at any time so that surgeons at all of Columbia's clinics and hospitals can gain exposure to advanced techniques that would otherwise not be available to them.

The Internet is also being used to broadcast important medical conferences for people who can't attend in person. The first broadcasts, in the spring of 1998, were of a pair of Johns Hopkins conferences on clinical care and issues for patients with HIV. Thousands of online participants sent positive feedback, encouraging Johns Hopkins to schedule video coverage of several upcoming AIDS conferences—one of which will be broadcast in three languages—as well as other conferences.

This is not a trivial amount of money, but it is minor compared with the amount most health organizations spend for paper-based transactions and stand-alone computer applications today. With paperwork making up 20 to 30 percent of the $1 trillion–plus per year revenues of the U.S. health care industry, the current overhead runs $200 billion to $300 billion annually—more than the gross national product of many countries.

Today the lack of information systems in doctors' offices represents the biggest obstacle to improving patient care. Only about 5 percent of physician practices in the United States use computer systems in their clinical work. Computerizing a doctor's office will cost from $10,000 to $50,000 for each one, but doctors can quickly recover the costs. A five-physician clinic in Hammond, Louisiana, invested about $50,000 in PC patient systems that made data entry easy for doctors; the clinic saved $60,000 the first year in transcription costs alone.[2]

Because of inertia, it will take a big commitment by health care providers to reshape health care through digital information. The technology is available today. An investment in a common infrastructure and tools will enable not just a huge reduction in costs, but better health treatment for everyone. Change will be driven by two groups: knowledgeable patients who insist on more information and more involvement in their own health; and Internet-savvy health professionals who use these new tools to provide better care. Together they'll use a digital nervous system to turn the islands of health care into a single continent of integrated care.

2. Fred Bazzoli, "Automating Patient Records," *Windows in Healthcare*, Summer 1998: 20–28.

Business Lessons

- ❑ The Web lifestyle enables patients to find out more about their health and take more responsibility for it. The Web lifestyle provides a new way for patients and doctors to communicate.
- ❑ Managed care has provided the economic impetus to extend information systems into clinical practice, but the real benefit of digital systems is improved patient care.
- ❑ Digital systems provide a way to create a holistic picture of a patient's health status and needs throughout the entire cycle of care: emergency services, hospital care, maintenance, and trend analysis.

Diagnosing Your Digital Nervous System

- ❑ Are you designing your medical systems with the idea of patient data flowing seamlessly from emergency services to hospital to doctor?
- ❑ Do digital systems enable your professionals to spend less time on paperwork and more time with patients? Do your digital systems support doctors in their medical decision making?
- ❑ Can you easily provide patient data to another medical facility if your patient needs medical care away from home?
- ❑ Are you preparing for the day in the near future when patients insist on communicating over the Web?

20

TAKE GOVERNMENT TO THE PEOPLE

We must empower citizens to act for themselves without having to go through a bureaucracy. This is sometimes hard for the bureaucracy to understand. Government agencies have to think of themselves as a resource to citizens and not as an office regulating citizens. But guess what? It's fun to help citizens solve their problems.

—Bill Lindner, Secretary, Department of Management Services, State of Florida

Government, perhaps more than any other organization, can benefit from the efficiencies and improved service that stem from digital processes. Developed nations will lead the way creating paperless processes to reduce bureaucracy. Developing nations will be able to provide new services without ever having to deal with cumbersome paper methods. Yet most governments are far behind business in using the tools of the digital age. Businesses going digital are stuck with many paper forms because governments are not yet online.

The reason for this lag is not a lack of money so much as a lack of organizational focus. Because government processes are paper- and people-intensive, "streamlining" in the past meant a reduction in service. It's not uncommon for legislatures to forbid agencies to close any offices, which simply forces them to struggle to do more with less. At the same time, there are few metrics to create economic or motivational incentives to provide better service. Citizens can't take their business to another tax agency or licensing bureau. Government agencies end up focused on their own internal organizational needs and narrow charter rather than the broad needs of citizens and businesses. As an example, consider the paperwork involved in hiring a child-care provider in the United States. The employer has to know that five agencies are involved, each with its own set of forms. This complexity, more than a desire to avoid paying the taxes, explains why compliance with all the rules is low. In this and many other cases, government, to the average citizen or business, remains an intimidating knot of uncoordinated agencies and regulations.

Yet digital processes and the Web lifestyle give government the opportunity to reinvent itself around constituents rather than the bureaucracy. Governments can take five major steps to help make the digital age a reality in their countries. The first two involve improving government services; the last three involve creating an infrastructure so that a country's businesses can compete in the digital age.

1. Put government employees on e-mail and eliminate paper filing. Make sure that all information being shared inside government is digital.
2. Put government services online with an interface designed for the user. Publish everything on the Internet.
3. Attract investment by technology companies and encourage electronic commerce, sometimes with financial incentives but more often with cooperative

projects. Create a framework for electronic authentication of businesses and citizens.

4. Deregulate telecommunications and encourage major investments in the telecommunications infrastructure.
5. Lift the skills of citizens by using technology as part of education and training systems at all levels (discussed in chapter 22).

REPLACING PAPER FLOW WITH DIGITAL PUBLISHING

Just as businesses can make better use of productivity tools and e-mail to get far more benefits from technology investments, so too can government. In developed nations many government employees and public officials already have PCs on their desks. And developing nations can put in a PC infrastructure for a modest cost. The use of e-mail alone promotes interagency cooperation and enables public officials to be more responsive. Some U.S. legislators are beginning to use e-mail to stay in touch with constituents, for instance, and Australia's national parliament is using digital work flow to ensure follow-up on inquiries from constituents.

Governments need to establish policies to use digital information flow in place of paper. Internet publishing should become the default. Printed documents should be the exception, not the rule. The savings would be immense. The U.S. government alone spends $1 billion annually printing documents that are already available on the Web. Most copies of these documents—30 million copies of the Federal Register, 1 million copies of hearings reports, and 65,000 copies of the president's budget—are for public officials whose offices are already online. Most of the printed copies end up in trash bins in the nation's capital.

Another example: By publishing state-employee phone numbers, mailing addresses, and building locations online, Florida saves $295,000 in printing and distribution costs annually and eliminates a 30 percent error rate caused by personnel changes that can't be reflected in an annual paper phone book. Multiply this simple action by the fifty U.S. states and the federal government, and you have additional huge savings.

The U.S. federal rules for hiring and firing employees weigh 1,080 pounds in printed form, and military sugar cookies demand a fifteen-page description. Web publishing of all government manuals can reduce costs and make information far more accessible. Digital systems are also better for complex specifications. The government bid requirements for a cargo plane weigh 3.5 tons in printed form, but the data would easily fit on a couple of CDs.

PROVIDING AN ACCESSIBLE FACE TO GOVERNMENT

An online approach does more than simply reduce paper expenses. Web technology makes it possible for governments to provide a single point of contact for the public, a single online "face" to structure information according to what is important to the citizen.

In several Swedish municipalities, for instance, Web pages organize a variety of related services from various levels of government. Citizens can quickly locate tax authorities, national insurance offices, and passport bureaus. They can access minutes from public meetings and other public documents. They can even get real-time commuting schedules based on sensors in transit vehicles, either via the

Internet or kiosks. A kiosk is just a PC designed for public use. In the United States, the state of Ohio provides one place on the Web for people to see all open jobs in both the public and the private sectors.

Australia's state of Victoria is taking such a "one-stop shopping" approach with its MAXI online system. MAXI is organized around "life events" that change a person's legal status or impose a reporting requirement: marriage, becoming of legal age, moving. If you change residence, for instance, you fill out the change information once from a PC or a public kiosk. The Web application automatically updates the records of the four state agencies that need to know. Citizens have to know only what they want to do, not the locations and procedures of different agencies. MAXI is handling 20,000 transactions a month and rising.

To foster economic development by businesses considering a new location, the Hampshire County Council in the United Kingdom has organized all of the relevant resources in the county, such as office parks, educational institutions, and recreational activities, onto a single Web site. If you set up such a site to entice people to inquire about your area, be sure to make it easy for them to ask follow-up questions over e-mail.

PROVIDING ACCESS TO EVERY CITIZEN

As the Internet provides the best way to interact with government, all citizens need access, even if they don't have PCs themselves. Electronic kiosks that function like bank ATMs will ensure that every citizen can participate equally in the new way of working with government. Placed in post offices, libraries, schools, and other public buildings, kiosks can help governments improve services while trimming the cost of delivery. The national government of Australia, for instance, has replaced its system of index cards on bulletin boards with digital kiosks that display job postings. In addition to providing more complete and updated information, kiosks enable the government to provide unemployment services quickly in an area with a sudden loss of jobs—say, if a plant closes—without the time required to set up a full office.

Online systems, accessible by kiosk or PC, are most useful for citizens and cost-effective for government when they're multipurpose. Governments should review all the transactions that require citizens to stand in line or fill out forms (name, address, ID number). Government should bring together the agencies involved to develop a single system for handling all the transactions. The Irish government, using An Post, the Irish postal service, has done this best. An Post kiosks process utility payments, issue passports, issue licenses for vehicles, disburse entitlement payments, offer savings and investment plans, sell lottery tickets from a kiosk system—even sell stamps. Each kiosk is a mini city hall, covering the work of half a dozen bureaus. With many of the 1,000 An Post sites in remote towns having fewer than 2,000 residents, the kiosks serve 1.26 million people each week—half the Irish population—and handle more than $9 billion (U.S.) in transactions each year. Updating or adding new applications is very easy.

For government transactions such as these, as well as for all commercial transactions, security is a prerequisite. Security has two dimensions: protection of personal data while it's in transit over the network and authentication of the person carrying out the transaction. Encryption technology exists that is strong enough to protect the confidentiality of any electronic transaction on a network, but U.S. export controls on encryption technology restrict U.S.

firms from integrating it into their products. Since this restriction hinders honest users without keeping encryption technology out of the hands of criminals, the software industry is working to change the U.S. government position. In practice, the encryption that can be integrated is strong enough that in most cases the security of data in transit is not the weak link. Electronic data is as safe as data in other forms.

Authentication of the user is equally important. You don't want an impostor getting into your government records any more than you'd want an unauthorized person to see your bank account. The need for authentication is why today governments that do online transactions usually limit them to transactions where impersonation would not be a problem, such as renewals of licenses or an automobile registration or the payment of taxes and fines. I don't think people would object if someone pretended to be them to pay their traffic tickets.

If someone could impersonate you and see your tax return or vote, though, the public would be in an uproar. Smart cards, which users can "swipe" on a PC or at a kiosk, are a solution to identity problems, as with an ATM card for a cash machine. Smart cards, combined with a personal identification number (PIN) or similar password—and in some cases thumbprints or voiceprints—will securely identify users trying to access personal information about benefits, taxes, or payment histories or to initiate a transaction. In Spain a new kiosk system will let anyone find out general information about social benefits by going through a touch-screen menu, but the person needs a smart card to access any personal information such as pension amount and status.

Though such cards are the equivalent of bank cards used around the world, some people are concerned that the government might collect too much information about citizens. Some nations have privacy laws that prevent a single card or database from containing all information about a citizen, and it is likely that in some nations two types of smart cards will emerge: one for financial transactions with business or government and another for health care.

Widespread information access and the ability to put a lot of information onto smart cards will cause societies to revisit the question of how information can be used. Should any prospective employer be able to see an applicant's arrest record? Or just organizations such as schools, which hire people who work closely with children? How will legitimate requests be distinguished from the nosy neighbor who simply wants the information? Ultimately these are political questions rather than technological issues.

Each country will have to decide on the kinds of personal information that will be allowed on smart cards. Even if their use is restricted to identification only, the streamlining of process and elimination of fraud is well worth the investment. Combined with back-end business systems that immediately post welfare or other payments directly to a central accounts database, smart cards make it very difficult to make fraudulent or duplicate claims. In London, 200 trial kiosks of a system like An Post's are credited with reducing welfare payment fraud by £750,000 in the first year. When deployed at all 1,500 post offices, the kiosks are expected to save £150 million per year.

STREAMLINING GOVERNMENT THE DIGITAL WAY

As governments embrace digital systems, software will streamline processes by having special work-flow logic for key functions. Software solutions for the legislative, judicial, and executive branches of any government have recently been created.

Legislatures in several U.S. states are using electronic systems to manage the process for drafting laws. Such systems can eliminate the $3 million to $5 million that most states spend every two years on printing for bill drafting and revision. PC-based systems can manage the process electronically, can more easily track conflicts—within a bill, among multiple bills, or with existing laws or sections of the state or national constitution—and can provide an audit trail of every change to ensure that the final law that is passed is word for word what the legislature intended. These systems make it easy to update Web pages, which several states are using to keep the public informed of the status of legislation and committee meetings.

For the judiciary, PC work-flow systems are enabling courts in the United States and Canada to begin electronic case filings. A typical county court has to place on the docket about half a million documents per year, either manually or with clerks entering basic case information into proprietary case management systems. Leon County, Florida, is developing a system so lawyers can file cases directly via e-mail, have all the information transferred to the case management system electronically, and receive a case number in return e-mail. Next, since court filings and most supporting documents are public records, the county wants to publish the documents on the Web for the court and the public.

Software can also help schedule people for trials. Some U.S. state and federal agencies use digital work flow to manage the scheduling for lawyers and law enforcement officers for court. By reducing the time police spend in court waiting for cases to be called, the application gives police more time on the street.

The executive branch of government can benefit as well from software that solves unique government problems. Florida, for instance, requires state agencies to lease space from the state if any state-owned property is available. Florida agencies can go online to specify the amount of space they need and the location—for example, 5,000 square feet in Miami—and see what is available. The Florida Health Department uses PCs to allocate and reconcile costs such as building leases and staff time among programs funded by different grants or tax allocations. The system electronically matches bills against program accounts and highlights any discrepancies. The department can reconcile its monthly expenses in a few hours instead of three to four weeks of manual reconciliation, and different counties and internal departments get a single bill covering multiple programs.

The state government of South Australia used to publish 5,000 copies a week of its 50-page government listing of job vacancies. Formal publication was delayed until the booklet could be physically printed and distributed to several hundred remote state offices. Closing dates were held up to ensure enough time for remote applicants to reply by paper.

Today a Microsoft Exchange-based work-flow application manages the entire process. Job openings first go via e-mail to legal reviewers and several dozen human resources managers from various agencies, who have first shot at filling any openings. If an HR manager puts a hold on the opening for a state employee who wants to transfer, the hiring manager is automatically notified by e-mail so that no one wastes time applying. Remote sites get the listing electronically. If the posting is not filled internally and moves on to a public announcement, the hiring manager receives e-mail describing the newspapers and dates in which the position will be advertised. Though the state expects to save between 50 and 80 percent of the annual

$350,000 (Australian) production costs with the new system, the main benefit is the speed with which the state can fill jobs while maintaining equal opportunity for people in remote offices.

With new digital systems, governments can open their knowledge systems and business operations systems to the public. The German Federal Ministry for Finance is developing document management and electronic archival systems for public records. The project will include automatic document routing and storage, with documents being published automatically on internal or public Web sites based on classification.

Another example in the United States is Massachusetts's online bidding process. Massachusetts publishes all the state bids, all the documents needed for vendors to respond, and the results of all the bids online. Massachusetts's online procurement system not only handles the entire bidding process less expensively, it also helps other public entities buy goods for less. In most states, the cities, towns, and school districts by law can get the same low prices from vendors that the state gets. In a paper world, though, it's virtually impossible to find the state's price on most goods. Now, a city or school district can quickly find out the state's best price on the Massachusetts Web site.

BUILDING GOVERNMENT SYSTEMS THE DIGITAL WAY

Less developed countries may assume that a digital approach to government is out of reach, but countries without systems can start fresh with new technology, which will be less expensive than manual approaches. Developed countries have older systems that often must be integrated to manage a transition. Leadership examples around the world make it clear that much of the innovation is happening in smaller governments—smaller nations and municipalities, counties and provinces, and the state levels of larger nations. Smaller governments, being less fragmented and less complex, can experiment and deploy solutions on a smaller scale.

For larger governments, the lesson is to pilot smaller projects to develop expertise and evaluate citizen response. Put the initial focus on projects that directly touch citizens and particularly ones that eliminate organizational complexity for the public. King County in my home state of Washington is probably ahead of many governments in the amount of information it publishes online, but the county does not yet package information or transactions simply. To get a building permit in rural King County, an applicant has to cull information from many sources: the phone book, phone calls to the county office, two or three printed pamphlets, and the department's Web site—a site that makes no mention of separate requirements for a land-use permit and a septic permit. A single well-structured Web site, with all the information and links involving all steps in the building permit process, would remove most of the complexity and could automate some of the steps. A meeting with a permit specialist would probably still be needed, but applicants would arrive better able to focus on important issues and not on the steps in the process they overlooked.

Governments should invest in training managers on business process reengineering, as several governments have done, to help stimulate consolidated online approaches. Competitive grants can spur projects to streamline internal processes and improve service delivery. Florida has different agencies compete for a limited number of innovative technology projects, bringing an entrepreneurial spirit to play in budget requests. The state balances such investments with a policy of providing some IT services from its central department only to agencies that fund them out of transaction fees or monthly subscriptions. This "pay as you go" strategy ensures that the state is using its IT dollars for projects that other agencies really want and that have solid cost efficiencies.

Cumulative savings from new digital systems would represent a substantial portion of every government's budget. The Pentagon recently found that it was spending more money to process and approve travel vouchers, $2.3 billion, than it was spending on travel itself, $2 billion. For a reasonable and largely onetime investment, an online expense system would free up billions of dollars in costs every year. "A billion here, a billion there, pretty soon you're talking real money," as Senator Everett Dirkson of Illinois used to say of federal spending. Billions would go a long way against a U.S. budget that annually allocates $27 billion for food stamps, $25 billion for welfare, and $13 billion for public housing. These programs all have enormously expensive paper-based administrative systems that easily consume 30 percent of the funding. Properly deployed digital systems could drive the overhead below 10 percent.

Citizens, becoming more aware of the power of the Web, are no longer willing to accept the idea that government service should be slow or confusing. No consumer would stand in line for two hours to get service from private enterprise. Why should a plumber stand in line for two hours at a government office and lose two hours of pay, when by using the Internet he could get his license or pay his fees in a few minutes and be at work on time?

Government alone, by building key services around the Internet, will provide an enormous incentive for citizens to move to a Web lifestyle. If the government, usually the largest "business" in any country, is a leader in the use of technology, it will automatically lift the country's technical skills and drive the move to an information market. By edict or incentive, it can pull along all the companies that do business with it.

Deregulation of telecommunications is probably the single greatest step that a country can take to create a digital economy. Replacing telecommunications monopolies with open competition around the world will stimulate innovation in Internet service delivery and will reduce rates, which are high and discourage use in many countries.

If a government has policies that are Internet-friendly and invests in a high-tech culture, the benefits can be considerable. Costa Rica followed such a course and won a regional competition for an Intel chip fabrication plant. In the first full year of operation, the plant produced $700 million in export revenues, more than either bananas or coffee, the country's largest agricultural crops.

Building an information economy will make all the companies in the country more competitive. The Information Age benefits from having more participants. As more and more countries join in, the importance increases for all countries. World trade will be done digitally.

No government can put a fully digital approach in place immediately, but every government can begin now with strong first steps that benefit citizens and make them feel that the government is working for them. The practical guiding principle should be that citizens should never again have to fill out multiple forms or go multiple places to get information. As one government official said in conversation about his new Web site, which lets people access a hundred years of county records online, "People can tell when you're trying to help. They know the difference between a government agency trying to help them and one that's just getting in the way."

Business Lessons

- ❑ Governments can use the Web to create a single face to the public, hiding the complexity of internal departmental organization and dramatically improving service.
- ❑ Citizens, becoming more aware of the power of the Web, will no longer accept the idea that government service should be second best. Public kiosks will provide service to people without Internet access at home.
- ❑ Governments should publish information on the Web as the default and publish printed documents only as an exception.

Diagnosing Your Digital Nervous System

- ❑ Do you have a government-wide e-mail system to help streamline communications and improve intra-agency coordination?
- ❑ Do you use the Web to publish government information and provide direct electronic government services to citizens and businesses?
- ❑ Are you starting with technology projects that directly benefit citizens?

21

WHEN REFLEX IS A MATTER OF LIFE AND DEATH

War is such that the supreme consideration is speed.

—Sun-tzu, *The Art of Warfare*

A victory for technology. That's how most people remember the Gulf War of 1991. Cruise missiles hugged the terrain over hundreds of miles to hit heavily fortified targets, and radar-evading Stealth fighters dropped smart bombs on communications centers and bridges. For thirty-eight days during Operation Desert Storm, the U.S. military and its allies controlled the air. Flying 2,500 sorties a day with minimal losses, allied air forces set up the "left hook" ground assault that drove Iraq from Kuwait and ended the war after just 100 hours of ground operations.

The high-tech aircraft of the Gulf War had decidedly low-tech mission support, though. In the Persian Gulf, mission orders were written up on an old-fashioned grease board just as they had been for every air war in the past. Squadron commanders had to manually track which pilots had flown what missions and who was available to fly next. Pilots got face-to-face "threat briefings" on target locations, the best routes in and out, locations of enemy troops, and the possibility of surface-to-air missiles, ground fire, and other contingencies. Then they retreated for a minimum of three hours and usually seven or eight hours of mission planning. They'd look up relevant maps in a file cabinet and photocopy and tape maps together. Then they'd "walk out" distances with a protractor, draw in the route and danger levels with colored pencils, study photos, transcribe intelligence data onto the maps, and calculate the elevations of obstacles.

Only after completing this paperwork did pilots go out to fly their dangerous missions.

Manual flight planning could cause navigation errors of one to two miles, a big margin of error if you're trying to locate an isolated target without many landmarks. And if new intelligence came in, the whole flight plan might have to be scrubbed and the process begun all over again. One computer system per unit (about twenty-four aircraft) was available to help pilots automate some aspects of flight planning, but these computers accommodated only one user at a time, were difficult to use, and frequently broke down, creating bottlenecks in flight support.

After the Gulf War, the U.S. Air Force, like all the services, held a "lessons learned" conference. High on the air force list for running a future high-intensity air war was better flight planning for pilots flying into harm's way. While some active-duty air force personnel wanted to address this need with the military's traditional computer systems, members of the U.S. Air Force Reserve and Air National Guard, who had civilian experience, immediately said, "We gotta do this on a PC."

The reservists turned to a number of commercial software developers as well as to the Georgia Institute of Technology, whose researchers were already experienced with the mathematical models and geographic data sources required for a sophisticated mapping system. The result was FalconView, a PC-based mission planning system developed in eighteen months for about $2.5 million. FalconView cuts the old manual mission planning process for a standard sortie from upward of seven hours to less than twenty minutes. It increases planning accuracy through the use of precise digital data and aeronautical mapping tools. And it's affordable enough and easy enough to use that the air force has deployed it worldwide.

FalconView became so popular with pilots that they began to ask for additional capabilities. Their requests led the air force to embark on a program called Cyber Warrior to bring information technology to all phases of pilot and aircraft deployment, from scheduling to intelligence dissemination to debriefing. The service quickly developed an intelligent scheduling system that tracks pilot assignments, training levels, availability, and special information such as whether a pilot needs to log a night mission to satisfy training requirements. A commander can do a quick search to find candidates for upcoming missions, and pilots can dial in on laptop computers to see when they're scheduled to fly. A PC-based debriefing system helps squadrons reconstruct missions to improve planning for the next mission.

HEADING OFF INTO THE WILD BLUE YONDER

Instead of sitting down with a paper map and a set of colored pencils, a pilot today sits down with a laptop computer containing digital maps of the world, digital images and updates from military intelligence, and an electronic drawing kit customized for military aviators. The pilot can immediately locate landmarks such as bridges or rivers, plot his route, check safety parameters, check weapons systems information and weapons loads, link to a Web-based weather source, and prepare flight plans and maps. Before he flies the mission, the pilot can study mountainous areas or cities to preview what he'll see in the air and get a good idea of the deployment of hostile forces. If the pilot wants to know the elevation of a mountain, he simply clicks on it on his digital map and sees a precise latitude, longitude, and altitude reading—information a pilot used to have to dig up from paper charts.

Fighter pilots load the FalconView pre–mission planning files into the aircraft's computers for use in flight. In addition to providing routine aviation data such as fuel consumption and takeoff and landing information, FalconView has a number of specialized features for military aviation. FalconView data is used in onboard weapons systems for computerized targeting and for checking weapons fusing—whether a bomb is set to explode on the ground or twenty feet in the air. FalconView does drop calculations that take into account the altitude and speed of the plane, the speed and direction of the wind, even the changing weight and balance of an aircraft before and after dropping its payload.

FalconView can mean the difference between a successful mission and an impossible one. During a tour to the Bosnia theater, a pilot took his copy of FalconView along with him to a base in Italy that didn't have access to the software yet. NATO forces had been looking for a particular bridge in Bosnia for three days and couldn't find it on their maps or from the air. The pilot fired up FalconView and located the bridge immediately. They blew it up that afternoon. FalconView displays satellite imagery accurate to within five meters. At the ten-meter resolution of the older system, the bridge wasn't visible.

During the Gulf War, the air force sometimes had to send ten to twelve F-16s to hit a single target. With the higher levels of accuracy provided by FalconView, the air force can now send fewer planes to a target. The goal is for one airplane to hit one target. The greater degree of accuracy from FalconView will enable newer aircraft such as the B-2 bomber to attack as many as sixteen targets on a single mission, a capability that adds up to big savings in lives and money. "The American people are not willing to accept a single casualty," says the lieutenant colonel in charge of the FalconView project, "so every little bit of increased accuracy and certainty we can demonstrate is worth a lot."

Useful as FalconView is, a fighter pilot can't carry a laptop in flight. It might not stay in his lap while he's pulling reverse Gs. As the air force upgrades the avionics computers in its fighter aircraft, though, and as new-generation fighter aircraft join the fleet, FalconView will become fully integrated into cockpit systems and visual displays. Newer planes will have real-time moving map displays tied to GPS systems that show a plane's precise location and its position relative to other friendly air and ground forces. Real-time data links will keep FalconView updated with the latest intelligence feeds coming in via satellite from Command and Control. Updated photographs, maps, and other relevant data will enable a pilot to make last-minute corrections. If enemy ground troops move from one side of a ridge to another while the pilot is en route, late-breaking intelligence will give the pilot a chance to change his flight path either to attack those troops or to avoid ground fire on his way to another target.

Airlift crews already have FalconView's in-flight capability. A crew plugs a laptop into the transport plane's onboard systems, connecting its PC with a live data link to systems on the ground and to other planes. Crews can replan missions, drop zones, and rendezvous points in flight and receive tactical information such as radar readings from other aircraft. Rescue aircraft can get precise range and bearing information on downed aviators. For cargo aircraft carrying food and supplies to civilian populations in such places as Haiti, Somalia, Bosnia, and northern Iraq, FalconView provides drop-zone overlays and calculates wind effects for the loadmaster ready to push cargo pallets out the back of the aircraft.

After Secretary of Commerce Ron Brown and thirty-four other people died in a 1996 Croatian plane crash caused by navigational difficulties, deployment of FalconView became mandatory on all Air Force Distinguished Visitor aircraft, including the president's. By an eerie coincidence, Ron Brown's widow, Alma Brown, was one of several dignitaries who accompanied President Clinton on his trip to Africa in 1998 and was on an air force plane that developed engine trouble. In Africa, runways long enough to handle heavy jets are few and far between. FalconView immediately identified the closest suitable airport and navigated the plane to a safe landing.

GETTING SMARTER WITH EVERY MISSION

Another exciting aspect of a digital military is its ability to dramatically increase rates of learning. Instead of having to fight three wars and lose hundreds of planes and thousands of men to learn which procedures and tactics work, the air force can now examine the records of a few missions and learn the same kinds of lessons a lot sooner. In earlier air wars, including the Gulf War, debriefing was often inconclusive. Combatants in debriefing sessions tended to remember the action through only their narrow views of the situation, and their recollections were usually blurred by the fog of battle. It was hard for commanders to reconstruct the overall scene in order to understand how to improve next time.

In today's debriefing sessions, pilots and commanders pore over the FalconView digital flight plan data and compare it with video footage taken from each aircraft during a mission. A debriefing session might involve the flight plans, four videotapes, and a PC-based debriefing system. The crew can replay an entire mission and see who shot when, whether a bomb was dropped too early or too late, whose plane was in the wrong place at the wrong time, and whose unorthodox but brilliant maneuver saved the day.

FalconView's ability to track, record, and replay mission data is helping the air force develop better flight plans and pilot tactics, for greater pilot safety and military capability. A rule of thumb in military flying is that if you can successfully complete your first 10 combat missions, you can successfully complete your next 100. An awful lot of pilots were shot down in Vietnam during the first 10 missions. With the ability to capture and replay missions, pilots can make their mistakes rehearsing those 10 missions on the ground in front of a PC and then fly those first 10 missions in training rather than in combat, where the consequences of failure are deadly. It's flight simulation taken to a new level.

The next big step will be digitally linking pilots with the U.S. Air Force's Command and Control structures at the higher decision-making echelons. Speed is of the essence in the chain of command. Disseminating orders fast can save a lot of lives. Consider a mission that involves getting a fighter or a bomber to a location eight hours away. With the new capabilities you could get the plane in the air and develop intelligence and target plans while the plane was en route. Up-to-date information would be ready for the pilot on his aircraft display as he approached the target. You would get at least an eight-hour jump on mission execution. As the Gulf War demonstrated, timely mission success in the air can make an enormous difference to troops on the ground. The air force calls this type of air support "the gift of time," allowing ground commanders to pick and choose when and where to best deploy the ground assault.

USING BATTLEFIELD INTRANET TO LINK GROUND AND AIR FORCES

If knowing the whereabouts of friendly and hostile aircraft is important to aircraft in the sky, imagine the value of such a system to ground forces making their way through the jungle or clambering up a hilltop. The U.S. Marine Corps is experimenting with FalconView on laptop computers and handheld PCs in the battlefield.

If you think that a laptop or a handheld PC might encumber a soldier, remember that most marines in the field have traditionally carried four pounds of paper with them. Even sweaty, dirty, bullet-dodging marines couldn't get away from paperwork. A typical battalion has gone to war with twenty to thirty footlockers of paper. Orders, maps, and other intelligence data have been distributed up and down the chain of command via carbon copies of multipart forms.

With the objective of pushing time-sensitive battlefield

information to the soldier in the field, Major James Cummiskey of the U.S. Marine Corps approached Georgia Tech to devise a way to "auto-inject" position information into a field computer. Major Cummiskey happened to talk to the same researchers who had developed the FalconView mapping software for the air force. FalconView turned out to be a perfect fit—not to mention a great leveraging of taxpayers' money.

Major Cummiskey and the Georgia Tech researchers came up with a situational awareness application based on FalconView and the Windows CE operating system for portable computers. The tactical system listens to the marines' wireless data networks, receives position reports, and creates unit symbols plotted on top of FalconView's tactical maps. When any marine unit changes its location in the field, its symbol moves on everybody's maps. Field marines run the application on off-the-shelf handheld PCs encased in a special shock-resistant, waterproof case with extended battery life. These "digital info-stations" let marines know precisely where they are, where their buddies are, and where the bad guys are. I got my first view of the Marine Corps application at Fall COMDEX in 1997, when Major Cummiskey joined me on stage for a demonstration. He promptly threw his handheld machine onto the floor and stomped on it a couple of times. Then he picked it up and put the application through its paces, demonstrating the machine's durability.

Marines testing the system today are operating what is essentially a battlefield intranet. It ties together all the key players—marines in the field, Command and Control, and friendly aircraft overhead—with up-to-the-second information and real-time messaging. Battlefield commanders can see precise images of troop deployment, and individual marine unit leaders can see exactly where they and their buddies are and where they need to go. U.S. aircraft can discriminate between the good guys and the bad guys on the ground. Several security features protect the data from enemy hands, including a "zeroize" button that instantly erases the hard disk—much easier than trying to destroy footlockers full of paper.

PUTTING INFORMATION TO WORK IN THE FIELD

After more than fifteen years of reliance on more expensive computer systems, there's a move across the U.S. military to go to standard PC hardware and software. Fast, low-cost development and the speedy deployment of applications are compelling. The air force's price tag of $2.5 million for FalconView software development was just 1 percent of the $250 million development cost of the air force's earlier mission-planning programs that ran on non-PC workstations. The ongoing cost for enhancements to FalconView is less than $1 million a year, compared with many millions for the non-PC systems. Where the previous system required a special $50,000 workstation for each squadron, FalconView runs on PCs that are part of the existing office infrastructure and therefore cost nothing extra. The air force has deployed FalconView to all active-duty and reserve squadrons, to cover more than 13,000 pilots, navigators, and flight engineers. FalconView is also gaining acceptance by U.S. Army and Navy aviators and is being tested by U.S. Marine pilots.

Marines have been testing the handheld battlefield system in large-scale, battle-scenario training exercises. If approved, the unit could become standard-issue equipment for every marine unit leader in the field. After years of trying unsuccessfully to develop a battlefield solution, the marines have done it in three months, for a total development cost, including incorporating FalconView and communications software, of about $110,000. In the future, marines envision even smaller Windows CE units for the common soldier, wearable in some form.

Inexpensive hardware means that the marines will be able to treat the battlefield handheld as just another standard-issue item. Like a pair of boots, it will do its job and get tossed out when it's done. It's impossible for even the marines to outrun Moore's law, Major Cummiskey says, acknowledging the speed at which PC processing capabilities regularly double and render hardware obsolete. "Knowing that we'll be throwing away all our hardware every few years, it just doesn't make sense to pour millions of dollars into custom computer systems development," he says.

RELATING INTELLIGENCE AND TIME

More than 2,200 years ago, the Chinese military strategist Sun-tzu wrote that "intelligence is of the essence in warfare—it is what the armies depend upon in their every move." According to Sun-tzu, victory belongs to the commander who gets the right information in a timely way: "Complex systems such as battle conditions are rich in information—information that must be acquired immediately. The commander's wisdom must be funded by direct access to persons who serve him as eyes on the site-specific conditions, and who enable him to anticipate the outcome. To be reliable, information must be firsthand. . . . There is thus an important relationship between intelligence and timing."[1]

1. Sun-tzu, *The Art of Warfare,* translated with an introduction and commentary, by Roger Ames (New York: Ballantine Books, 1993): 90.

With declining military budgets, the possibility of continual outbreaks in hot spots around the world, and the unwillingness of the American public to accept high casualty rates, the United States is counting on technology to win wars. Technology doesn't mean simply smart weapons. It means smart soldiers. The rules of war haven't changed. The victory goes to the side that can strike the quickest with the best intelligence. Whether the intelligence is gleaned from spy satellites, unmanned reconnaissance drones, or operatives on the ground, information must get to the warriors in action. And firsthand, site-specific information from the battlefield must reach the strategists as the battle flows back and forth.

The military shares with business a need for organization, supplies, logistics, and tactics. Lee surrendered to Grant at Appomattox not because his troops had lost the will to fight, but because he was out of supplies. Napoleon said that an army marches on its stomach. Churchill's account of Britain's subjugation of the Sudan in 1899 was largely the story of the building of a railroad for logistical support.[2] When Sun-tzu says that the leader must bring the thinking of the people in line with their superiors, rely on strategic advantage and not individual heroic efforts, and attack strategies first, every businessperson understands the application of those precepts to his or her organization and competitive situation. Business, and particularly information technology, has something to offer the military, too. Designing information processes to support organizational objectives and using information flow to empower individuals are good objectives in both military operational and battlefield contexts.

2. Winston S. Churchill, *The River War: An Account of the Re-Conquest of the Soudan* (1899; reprint, London: Medea Books, 1998).

The U.S. Navy's Smart Ship program, for instance, has much the same goal as any labor-intensive industry's: improving operational control while reducing labor requirements. More than half a ship's total lifetime cost is the manpower to run it, and the first "smart ship"—outfitted with a shipboard network and PCs—was able to reduce its engineering watch while under way from eleven people to four.

The new ship came about through a reengineering process that any business might undergo. Navy officials say that the manpower reduction came 40 percent from technology and 60 percent from process restructuring.

And of course the idea of fast organizational reflexes is fundamental to everything the military is about. The navy's new smart ship not only automates navigation and machinery, but sensors can also instantly detect damage to the ship without having to send a crew member into harm's way. The ship can even be captained from the engine room if the bridge is knocked out of commission during battle.

Many projects are also in progress to streamline military business systems. The Defense Department has identified the 240 offices that handle about 80 percent of the department's contracts and has already achieved a paperless contracting environment in more than half of them. As one admiral put it, the United States can use technology to hit a target with a cruise missile from a thousand miles away; it's about time the United States uses technology to pay the supplier across the street.

The new digital systems used by the U.S. Air Force, Marines, and Navy aren't isolated projects, but part of an overall goal by the Pentagon to ensure that U.S. military forces have fast and affordable access to the world's best technology while making better use of taxpayer dollars. For more than thirty years research and development in the commercial sector has outstripped R&D in the military. In the mid-1990s the military began to move away from a reliance on its own specially developed systems to take advantage of the industrial world. The Pentagon embarked on a "dual use" strategy to get military as well as civilian use out of the same technology base. The dual-use strategy has three pillars: investing in civilian technologies critical to military applications; manufacturing commercial and military items on the same low-cost production lines; and inserting commercial components into military systems.

The historic ten-year procurement cycles of military applications collide with Moore's law and the doubling of PC computing power every two years. After seeing the effectiveness of high-tech weapons, who wants to go into battle with technology that's several generations out of date? The best weapons result from the shortest deployment cycles. The same lesson applies equally well to business use of technology.

Location-fixing technology using GPS is fairly specialized today but will become mainstream. Ports and transportation carriers have a need to know where their equipment and personnel are just as the military does. Today most logistics solutions are highly specialized, costing tens of millions of dollars and preventing all but the largest organizations from being able to use digital systems to manage the flow of matériel. PC economics will bring costs down rapidly. It will be inexpensive to put a GPS tracker on a container or any piece of equipment to always know exactly where it is.

Nonindustrial uses of sensing devices are quite innovative. Irrigation wheel lines on farms now come with sensors that beep your pager or send you e-mail if the system breaks down. Farmers around the world are using PC-based GPS systems and satellite sensors to detect differences in soil moisture, fertility, drainage, and other variables. With data downloaded directly to their rigs, farmers can alter the amount of seed or fertilizer in order to maximize yields, or they can analyze this data over several years to find patterns that enable them to make better decisions about how to farm the land. Tiny chips embedded under the skin of cattle will soon be able to not just track the location of livestock, but manage their health. The sensors will trigger personalized feed troughs so that each animal gets exactly the right feed for her age and condition.

To me, it's amazing to realize that the PC has become so flexible and rugged that it's ubiquitous. Whether they're serving the interests of economic competition in a business setting, or military objectives in battle, information applications on the PC enable an organization to empower its workers. In the case of the military, empowerment is a matter of life and death.

Business Lessons

- ❑ In business as well as the military, he who has the shortest procurement and deployment cycle wins.
- ❑ Evaluate whether location-sensing systems would apply to your business needs.

Diagnosing Your Digital Nervous System

- ❑ Are you building on top of the R&D dollars of the packaged software industry or doing one-off projects with lots of unique code?
- ❑ Are you leveraging the low-cost capabilities of the high-volume commercial computing market?

22

CREATE CONNECTED LEARNING COMMUNITIES

Our national commitment to connect every classroom in every school in the country to the Internet will be the greatest advance in quality and equality of education in this century.

—Reed Hundt, Chairman of the U.S. Federal Communications Commission

PCs can empower teachers and students more than any other group of knowledge workers. As I mentioned in describing the Web lifestyle, students are the ultimate "knowledge workers" since learning is all about acquiring knowledge. Teachers will be able to use the Internet to share with each other and to allow students to explore a subject in new ways. PCs can be a catalyst for reaching the educational goals that parents, educators, and government have set forth, such as collaborative learning, critical thinking, and lifelong learning skills. With a solid infrastructure in place, some schools are already benefiting from incorporating PCs in the classroom. Even as most schools struggle to find the resources for these new tools, innovative programs have shown that there is a payoff for the effort.

The success of PCs as educational tools requires teacher involvement. Without teacher training and integration into the curriculum, PCs will not have a big impact. Many PCs have gone into computer "labs" where they sit, seldom used. Schools need to shift from treating the PC as a subject unto itself—teaching about technology—to integrating the PC throughout the curriculum, teaching with technology. More and more school districts are now demonstrating that with the involvement of teachers, PCs used as learning tools can have a profound effect.

In the Western Heights Independent School District, just west of Oklahoma City, Oklahoma, teachers surprised administrators with their enthusiasm when the district provided training the summer before it rolled out PCs. More than 200 of its 230 teachers signed up, causing the district to scramble to schedule enough sessions to handle the demand. Most teachers have a great love of learning, and they'll get excited about anything that will help kids learn. What teachers don't want is to be thrown into something they have not had the opportunity to learn about and become comfortable with.

Western Heights is a small, seven-school district with a moderate industrial tax base. The student population is a multicultural mix of white, black, Native American, Hispanic, and Asian descent. About 65 percent of the kids qualify for free or reduced-cost lunches in the school lunch program. This is not the school district that you might expect to lead the charge into the Information Age. Yet in the last three years the district has overwhelmingly voted three times to spend a total of more than $6.8 million in local funds to create perhaps the leading technology-driven curriculum in the country. The community sees the investment as the only way to break the cycle of poverty that could repeat with its children if they go unprepared into the digital world.

A PC can be a powerful new teaching tool for teachers coming from the world of blackboards and chalk. Using PowerPoint, for instance, teachers find they can spark kids' interest in the subject by including photos, film clips, and links to Internet pages. One civics teacher at Western Heights starts his class each day with fresh news from the Internet. First is a science photo of the day from a NASA Web page; then news clips from abcnews.com; then a story that leads into his curriculum topic, which could be campaign-finance reform or government checks and balances.

PCs are part of each teacher's life in class at Western Heights, not something outside. Teachers use e-mail to communicate with one another about common issues. They don't have to wait for the district meetings that occur a couple of times a year. They can reach out to a colleague with a question and get an answer back quickly. This collaboration occurs among teachers in each grade level or among teachers coordinating curricula across grade levels, in disciplines such as science, math, and language. Computers are allowing teachers to more easily reach out beyond the confines of their classrooms and interact with their peers.

"People may not realize how alone teachers are in the classroom," Western Heights superintendent Joe Kitchens says. "Most teachers remain behind closed doors all day. They have little time for sharing experiences or interacting with other teachers. There are only a few times a year when they can gather with their peers. E-mail eliminates that isolation." Kitchens laughingly complains that teachers are able to "bug him" more than before, too. Traditionally the superintendent would have limited dialogue with teachers. Now they expect him to answer their questions immediately over e-mail.

Western Heights' PC-based network runs on seventeen miles of fiber-optic cable among the schools and administration building. Each of the 230 classrooms has at least two PCs on the network—one for the teacher, the other for kids to use. Each room is wired for another three PCs to be on the network, and each school has a computer lab. A huge monitor in each classroom enables teachers to display material off the Internet, or films from a central video server, or presentations from another classroom.

University of Oklahoma instructors have taught classes remotely. The meteorologist from the local TV station has taught classes about tornadoes and other weather topics, and students have broadcast weather reports back for public broadcast. Dayton Tire, the area's major employer, has participated in videoconference sessions on topics such as job-interviewing skills and chemical engineering. The TV station and the local tire plant were included in the district's fiber-optic system for just this kind of community involvement in teaching. The university connects through Oklahoma's high-speed education network.

Students have used the videoconferencing system to take virtual field trips to the East Coast, to England, and to other places in Europe, visiting museums and studying with sister schools. Students throughout the district watched the space shuttle launch with John Glenn in late 1998 live over their PCs. Several classrooms are set up specifically for distance learning via PC-based TV. These setups have enabled Western Heights to add advanced math classes in its middle school by TV instruction from the high school. It's not a perfect solution, but it's better than no advanced math class. Teachers have benefited from a videoconference course through the University of Kansas to help them enhance class content and curriculum with new technologies.

Distance learning has also enabled students at home with injury or illness to keep up with their classes. One teenager was home for months with injuries he sustained protecting his mother from a gunman. Previously the school would have sent out a "home teacher" three times a week for an hour a day. The home teacher would pick up homework, hand off more assignments, and answer a few questions. This time around, Western Heights put a PC, camera, and monitor in the student's bedroom and set up a high-speed link to his home.

Not knowing how well the interactive link was going to work, the school began by connecting him with only one class, but his classmates complained loudly when he "wasn't there" at their next class. The school immediately extended the televised sessions to include all his courses. Biology class was probably the most interesting for him, since the other kids were always sure to hold the really gross dissections up close to the camera, play similar pranks, and otherwise make him feel like part of the group. This home-PC link was cheaper than a home teacher, and the student learned far more. He kept up with his work and grades, but more important, he was never lost as a member of the class. In another instance, a teacher helped direct the work of substitute teachers and stay in touch with her students while she was home because of medical treatments.

CONNECTING WITH PARENTS AND THE COMMUNITY

Another school making similar investments in the future is Reading's Highdown School, a publicly funded state school in a town of 140,000 people west of London. Highdown is in the heart of the U.K.'s Silicon Valley. A large number of the country's high-tech firms are located within twenty miles. Highdown's proposal to create a connected learning community became one of twenty-three trials accepted as part of the country's digital Superhighways Initiative.

Highdown decided to make technology a central part of the educational experience: to connect the entire community with the school, including museums, libraries, and government offices. Educators wanted a sustainable model so that the approach would not fall by the wayside after the initial enthusiasm waned. They wanted to raise educational performance standards and motivate lifelong learning.

Highdown's network connects more than a hundred PCs in the school with interactive CDs and filtered content from the Internet. As Highdown moves from trial to a long-term program, the local council has joined in to help expand the network to all forty-six schools in the borough. Students have individual computer accounts so they can access productivity applications, e-mail, and the Internet from home.

Parental involvement has been instrumental in the success of the program. Thirty parents participated in the initial development and were able to routinely log in from home to check the school's intranet and find out about their children's activities. Another thirty teachers are connected at home. The school is about to extend the opportunity to link from home to all its parents and is adapting learning materials to allow student learning to be supported at home. Highdown's intranet home page has information on the school and on the subject being taught. The Web site shows parents what students are supposed to learn each week and the approach teachers are using. Parents can link to the materials used by the students. The Internet solves the age-old problem of parents asking their children whether they have any homework and being unable to verify the answer when the children invariably say, "No." Parents also have immediate access to teachers via e-mail, in addition to personal meetings several times a year.

Like Western Heights, Highdown is integrating technology into the classroom. Its Web page provides special curriculum features that would otherwise not be possible, such as a virtual art tour that links to important museums around the world. Technology makes it easy for teachers to scale classes to age and ability and individualize learning. An eleven-year-old art student, for instance, can go online to access age-appropriate materials prepared by the teacher to support the concepts presented in class on the theory of color. An online test measures understanding of complementary colors, and the student can link to artwork by Seurat to show how he used the eye's perception of colors to create pleasing visual effects.

An independent review of the Highdown experiment by government researchers listed six major benefits of technology-based instruction. These were improved subject learning; improved "network" literacy, meaning skills in using PCs and the Internet to learn; improved vocational training; better motivation and attitudes toward learning; improved skills in independent learning and research; and better social development.

LIFTING THE SKILLS OF ALL CITIZENS

Using the school infrastructure to support education for the entire community is an important way to take advantage of—and to justify—technology investments. One type of education is basic literacy skills in computers that can be applied at any job. Another type, with great potential for people seeking employment, is training in information technology itself. In most countries, one out of every ten IT jobs is going unfilled, with the United States and Europe each needing more than half a million new trained IT professionals in the next several years. Rapidly developing areas such as India and Latin America may have proportionately greater shortages.

Because the prosperity of the Reading area is based on technology and because traditional funding sources for schools are unlikely to be sufficient for its plans, Highdown School envisions a public-private partnership to pay for needed infrastructure, an "investment loop" whereby the business community invests in schools today and receives, down the road, more highly trained workers.

Also, because the community will use the network for long-term education, Highdown educators expect the community to contribute. Adults can get online technical training either at the Reading schools, which open on evenings and weekends for that purpose, or at home. Fees for this service go toward maintaining and expanding the IT system.

Many schools around the world are moving rapidly to prepare for the digital age. Israel has a national education network that lets students gather knowledge and use e-mail either at school or from home. The network improves parent-teacher interaction. Costa Rica is providing every public high school student with access to the Internet and e-mail. High school students in Issaquah, Washington, in the United States planned, built, and manage a district network of 2,000 PCs used to teach advanced academic skills. Students in Kentucky are also being trained to support their network, which spans the entire state—176 districts—and includes connections with the state government and, eventually, local businesses and higher education.

ARMING EVERY STUDENT FOR SUCCESS

Most knowledge workers in the United States have their own PC, yet even at the best of schools the ratio is often no better than seven students to every PC. It's expensive for schools to buy PCs for every student, especially when PCs become out-of-date every three years or so. For this reason there's a fear that the gap between the "haves"—those families that can afford PCs at home—and the "have-nots"—those that cannot afford PCs at home—will create a major gap in opportunities. Creative approaches in providing PCs to every student show great promise in helping resolve this dilemma.

One-to-one access—one PC per student—started in the early 1990s in Melbourne, Australia, where Bruce Dixon, a teacher interested in technology, saw significant differences in teaching results when he could scrounge a half dozen computers for his classes instead of just one. For PCs to achieve their full potential, he realized, students had to use them as a tool for all their work—in all their classes and at home as well as at school. Out of many discussions, conferences, and brainstorming with teaching colleagues emerged the radical idea of having all the students finance their own machines. Dixon, by then a technology consultant to schools, worked out a financial model. For a monthly fee, students lease a machine and software; the vendor provides maintenance and upgrades; and when the student graduates the family keeps the machine.

Affordability is still a big challenge with this approach. Families that are well-off can afford the typical $40 monthly fee over a three-year period. Many families can afford to pay some modest amount, if not the full fee. Business, community organizations, and grants can make up the difference for the rest of the kids. Regardless of the amount, the family contribution is fundamental to this program, as it gives the student and their parents a sense of ownership of and responsibility for the laptop and its role in the student's learning. In the first several years of laptop programs, damage, loss, or theft of the PCs has been minimal. Educators say the reason is that students have a vested interest in taking good care of their machines. Interestingly, students from underprivileged neighborhoods generally have less loss or damage than do students from rich schools. The only consistent problem with damage has stemmed from students closing laptops with pens or pencils inside. This habit, a carryover from books, cracks the screen. Students are now warned up front about the danger posed by writing instruments.

Laptop programs have spread to schools worldwide. More than 60,000 students and teachers at 500 public and private schools in the United States have participated in the Anytime Anywhere Learning laptop program. The initial sponsor was Toshiba America Information Systems, and many more hardware manufacturers are involved today. This program brings laptops to students, trains teachers in their use, and integrates technology into curriculum. Large-scale programs have succeeded with 500 students in Harlem; 1,500 students in Beaufort County School District, South Carolina; 1,200 students in the Clovis Unified School District, Fresno County, California; and 500 students in the Federal Way School District in Washington State, to name just a few. By working with local businesses and the community, these schools have been able to finance laptops for all students. Both Canada and the United Kingdom have begun piloting laptop programs, and educational delegations from around the world have visited Anytime Anywhere Learning schools to evaluate their use.

The impact of providing laptops for full-time use by

students has been impressive. A recent study titled "Powerful Tools for Schooling: Second Year Study of the Laptop Program" by education researcher Saul Rockman concludes that students who regularly use laptops gain many skills. They write more often and better; have improved research and analysis skills; express themselves more creatively; work more independently and also more collaboratively; more frequently rely on active learning and study strategies; readily engage in problem solving and critical thinking; and adopt higher-order thinking skills. Objective numbers in the study are supported by the subjective reactions by teachers: 66 percent said laptops increased higher-order thinking by their students, and 71 percent said laptops improved student motivation and made students more willing to focus on schoolwork.

Most school systems around the world are just beginning to bring PCs into the classroom. To get started requires leadership at the school board and superintendent level and a technology plan that provides a blueprint for developing and managing the technical infrastructure, for integrating technology with curriculum, and for training teachers. Finally, rallying community support is critical. Voters have proven willing to vote for measures to fund concrete, well-fashioned plans. Communities should think of connecting the schools as the start of a broader effort to create a connected learning community among all civic organizations and to think of technology-enhanced education as a lifelong activity not restricted by age or to schools.

Technology can also reduce administrative overhead in schools and make it easier to compare educational results. The state of Victoria in Australia has deployed an infrastructure that will eventually connect 100,000 PCs, providing a 5-to-1 ratio of students to PCs across the state; Victoria is training every principal and teacher from all

PCs for Every Student Make a Big Difference

Michael's transition from elementary school to middle school at New York City's Mott Hall School was difficult. The challenging classwork and more competitive environment caused him to withdraw. Michael's teacher, Janice Gordon, believed that the school's Anytime Anywhere Learning program, which offered a laptop to every student, would help him overcome the problems with his handwriting and disorganization and give him more confidence.

She was right. Within two months of getting his own laptop PC, Michael was participating in discussions and sharing his work with the entire class. He does extra homework and in-depth research for class projects. His dad calls him "the Michael Jordan of the computer world."

I visited Ms. Gordon's class in the spring of 1998 and saw firsthand how the constant availability of a laptop PC was changing learning for Michael and his classmates. His newfound success is not an isolated result. In more than 500 public and private schools, kids are using laptops to exercise their curiosity and creativity in ways that perhaps only kids can.

A history student used an online encyclopedia and Web sites to create a presentation on the U.S. Civil War covering famous generals and important battles, including statistics and maps. A science student used the Internet to produce a report on how wax improves speed and reduces friction for snowboards and how boots and bindings provide stability. Foreign-language students go to Spanish-language Web sites so they can better understand how the language is used every day.

PCs also provide new ways to approach traditional studies. Fifth- and sixth-grade students created their own database of the planets, gathered data from several sources, used an online encyclopedia to embed pictures, and wrote a paper about what they had learned. High school students took data on the motion of a cart with different forces and masses applied to it and used a spreadsheet to graphically see the changes so they could visualize the mathematical relationship among force, mass, and acceleration.

Laptops also make it possible for teachers to create more comprehensive projects. In an Ohio history class, a "Destination Ohio" project had students use the Internet for research on sites to see in Ohio, a word processor to plan an itinerary of their trip, a spreadsheet to track costs, publishing software to make a brochure for one of their destinations, and presentation software to "sell" this trip to other students.

The depth and breadth of information that comes from access to technology and the ease in analyzing data are improving fundamental skills such as writing ability and analytical ability. By seeing and examining more information from more points of view, students become better aware of viewing sources critically and making independent judgments.

1,750 schools on the integration of technology into schoolwork. Victoria is also employing PCs to handle business processes—for example, using e-mail to disseminate school documents and memos, financial statements, and images to its many remote schools. Administrators will use software to track trends in student absences, which might reveal educational problems, or staff absences, which might reveal morale problems. Administrators plan to use digital tools to easily compare and contrast everything including testing results by region, grade level, or school size. They want to provide more software support for teachers, whether administrative (managing attendance or generating standard letters to parents) or professional (student skill assessment). At Western Heights in the United States, teachers use an application that scans in test papers, grades them, and automatically reaverages the kids' grades. The time saved can now be spent on teaching.

OFFERING A VARIETY OF WAYS TO LEARN

One of the most forward-looking ideas is to use PCs to offer a variety of ways to learn. About fifty different major theories attempt to characterize individual learning styles. Most of the theories identify similar attributes. In the simplest terms, some people learn better by reading, some by listening, some by watching someone else do a task, some by doing the task. Most of us learn from some combination of all these methods. And all people have different levels of aptitude and different personalities and life experiences that may motivate them to learn or demotivate them. A highly motivated student can learn from difficult reading materials, where a poorly motivated student needs accessible materials such as a video to learn.

New software is helping students learn regardless of learning style or pace. Software can present information in multiple forms that can be personalized far more easily than paper methods. In teaching geography to twelve- and thirteen-year-olds, for instance, Highdown School previously relied on videos of Mount St. Helens and a large stack of printed materials. Some kids did well with these resources; others, less motivated, got bogged down in the dense text.

With Web technology the school now structures a series of learning tasks according to complexity. Students are required to complete a certain amount of work to ensure they understand the concept. The first geology task incorporates multimedia animation of moving magma to help every student understand the basics of volcano formation. The most advanced task is an in-depth survey of volcanoes that includes links to the U.S. Geologic Survey Web site. Students who want to explore further—and many do—can drill into great detail on a number of active volcanoes and their effect on nearby towns and the world's environment.

PCs can help change the learning experience from the traditional approach—a teacher talking at the front of the classroom, coupled with reading assignments—to a more hands-on approach that takes advantage of the natural curiosity of students of all ages. PCs enable students to explore information at their own pace, to learn from video and audio as well as from text, to model experiments, and to collaborate with one another.

This self-directed problem-solving approach, usually described as progressive, is not new. John Dewey and other educational reformers were proposing a change from didactic to experiential learning in 1899. But where building a physical facility to give kids a wide range of experience is complex, a virtual world of experiences on computers is available to all connected students.

Web connectivity builds on the PC's capabilities by enabling students to find other people who are exploring the same topics or to find approaches to a subject that might be more helpful or interesting to them than the approach used in class. They may find a nugget of information that they enjoy bringing back to the class, or one that confused them and the teacher can address for the benefit of everybody. A common assignment will be for students to go out and explore a topic on the Internet, then come back together in a group to discuss what they learned.

The great lectures on all important subjects will become widely available on the Internet. Schools will be able to use them as the core presentations, creating study groups and discussion groups around the topics. Schools will vary in how much they take advantage of these lectures. Local teachers will be freed to develop more in-depth material and personalized instruction rather than duplicating the core lectures, as they have to do today.

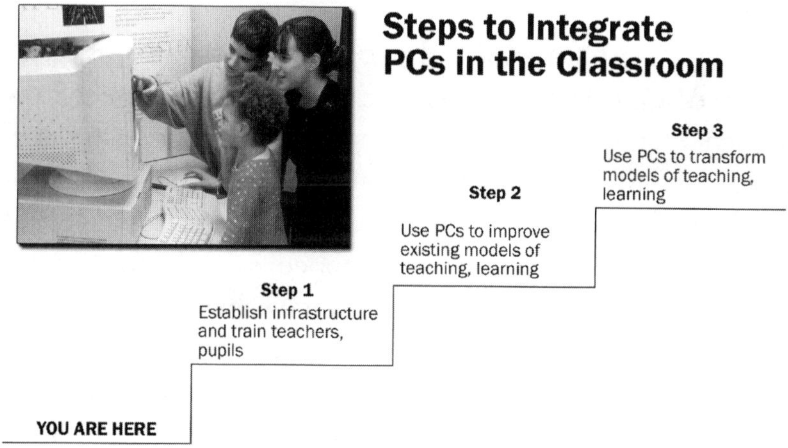

School districts need to have a plan to use PCs to improve education. The first step is to enlist community support, establish a solid technical infrastructure, and train teachers. Next, PCs and the Internet should be integrated into the curriculum, with PCs serving as a learning tool for students. Finally, digital methods can transform learning by making it easier to create and maintain core presentations, freeing teachers to create more in-depth material and personalized instruction.

Ten Hard Lessons on Computers in Schools

More than a decade of use shows that computers can help educate students, but society has learned ten hard lessons along the way. I concur with the conclusions of a November 1997 special report by *The Wall Street Journal:*

1. Computer labs are a lousy place for computers. They need to be in classrooms.
2. Struggling students often get more out of computers than higher performers.
3. Most teachers still haven't been trained on how to use computers in class.
4. School systems must plan computer use carefully.
5. Computers are a tool, not a subject. They need to be integrated into the lessons of other subjects.
6. Kids flourish when everyone has a computer.
7. Hand-me-down machines are not good enough for school use.
8. Computers don't diminish traditional skills.
9. The Internet and e-mail excite kids by giving them an audience.
10. Kids love computers.

Once we have a critical mass of teachers sharing ideas electronically and a higher and higher percentage of the students with access to the PC, the textbook industry will make a fundamental shift to focus on electronic delivery of products. Having textbooks available electronically at lower cost will enable cash-strapped schools to redirect money spent on printed textbooks for other needs. In 1997 elementary schools in the United States spent $3 billion on physical books. College spending was another $2.7 billion. Yet a typical CD can hold all of the reading materials a student needs in a year, with online connections providing the additional breadth and depth. Use of PCs as a primary reading tool will require the breakthrough in screen readability discussed in chapters 3 and 7.

PCs are the primary communications and productivity tools of the digital age. The PC and the Internet fundamentally change one thing: They provide every student in every school and community with access to information and collaboration that before now was not available even to students in the best schools. Educators will take advantage of that access for the betterment of their communities. Educators who embrace PCs as a new teaching and learning tool will be the agents of change.

Business Lessons

- ❑ PCs and connectivity make new educational approaches possible.
- ❑ Use the school infrastructure to support education for the entire community.
- ❑ Successful use of technology in the classroom requires leadership from the community and the school board.
- ❑ Schools need to level the playing field with access to the Internet to help close the gap between "haves" and "have-nots."

Diagnosing Your Digital Nervous System

- ❑ Do you have a technology plan that provides a blueprint for developing the technical infrastructure, for integrating technology with curriculum, and for training teachers?
- ❑ Do PCs in your classroom allow for a more hands-on approach that lets students explore, model experiments, and collaborate with one another? Do PCs in your classroom make learning fun?

- ❑ Do you use PCs to identify the best teaching approach for individual students and tailor the presentation of materials specifically for those students?
- ❑ Do teachers use e-mail to exchange ideas and coordinate curriculum?
- ❑ Do you use technology to streamline routine tasks for school administrators and teachers?
- ❑ Does your school use a Web site and e-mail to get parents more involved in their children's education?

VI

EXPECT THE UNEXPECTED

23

PREPARE FOR THE DIGITAL FUTURE

> Any time there is change, there is opportunity. So it is paramount that an organization get energized rather than paralyzed.
>
> —Jack Welch, CEO, General Electric

Customers are the primary beneficiaries of the increased efficiency of information technology, and the benefits will increase as the economy goes more digital. The other beneficiaries are businesses whose leaders take advantage of digital methods and build advanced solutions faster than the competition. The solutions highlighted in this book are the result of the vision and leadership of businesspeople who brought IT into play with specific customer scenarios in mind. Because technology will change the way you work with customers, and not involve just back-office data processing, the CEO should be more engaged going forward.

Business leaders who succeed will take advantage of a

new way of doing business, a way based on the increasing velocity of information. The new way is not to apply technology for its own sake, but to use it to reshape how companies act. To get the full benefit of technology, business leaders will streamline and modernize their processes and their organization. The goal is to make business reflex nearly instantaneous and to make strategic thought an ongoing, iterative process—not something done every twelve to eighteen months, separate from the daily flow of business.

Investments in technology should provide better information to every worker who might possibly use it. Knowledge workers are the brains of the company. If they're disconnected from the company's important data, how can they function, how can they be empowered? You can give people responsibility and authority, but without information they are helpless. Knowledge is the ultimate power tool.

If information about production systems, product problems, customer crises and opportunities, sales shortfalls, and other important business news gets through the organization in a matter of minutes instead of days, and if the right people can be working on the issues within hours instead of days, a business obtains a huge advantage. This restructuring of processes is more fundamental than any other change since mass production.

Every company can choose whether to lead or follow the emerging digital trends. The companies in this book have decided to be leaders. They're all in tough industries, fighting tough competitors. The Internet is redefining their industries in real time. Winning is no slam-dunk for any of them. They've decided that digital information flow and empowering their employees is part of achieving and sustaining competitive advantage.

KEEPING THE DOOR OPEN DIGITALLY

Though the term may sound cold, *digital processes* is about the empowerment of individuals. Getting people motivated to take on responsibility is not a question of organizational structure so much as organizational attitude. Though we try to keep the number of organizational levels down and the lines of communication short, Microsoft has a fairly traditional organizational chart. I think an open-door policy is more critical than a nonhierarchical structure. Digital tools are the best way to open the door and add flexibility. Depending on the need or urgency, information can move through the chain of command or right to the top, to a single individual or to a team, to anyone in a certain location or to everyone around the world.

A belief in empowerment is key to getting the most out of a digital nervous system. It's knowledge workers and business managers who benefit from more and better information, not just senior management. When employees get a couple of good tools that deliver better results, they demand more. It's another positive cycle.

However you organize your company or motivate your staff, one thing is clear: It is impossible to manage a company totally from the center. It is impossible for a single person or single committee to stay on top of every issue in every business unit or subsidiary. Leaders need to provide strategy and direction and to give employees tools that enable them to gather information and insight from around the world. Leaders shouldn't try to make every decision. Companies that try to "manage down" to direct every action from the center will simply not be able to move fast enough to deal with the tempo of the new economy.

In business the argument between central authority and the individual is the difference between the old-style theory

X mentality, that workers are lazy and need to be driven, and theory Y, that workers are creative and should be given responsibility. Digital processes support the assumption that workers can and will do more if allowed, enabled, and encouraged to think and act.

This center-vs.-individual argument is not an abstraction. The choice affects the design of companies and systems. The mock-up of the first U.S. manned space capsule shocked the original astronauts years ago. There were no manual guidance systems. Not to worry, the NASA scientists explained. The system would fly the spacecraft. The U.S. astronauts, like the monkeys before them, were just along for the ride. The astronauts balked. Veteran combat and test pilots, they knew all too well that "advanced" aviation systems often failed under adverse conditions. The pilots won the showdown, getting the controls and periscope needed to fly these craft manually. On several flights—including orbital missions and the first landing on the moon—it was the local system and the pilot's skill that brought the astronauts home safely when the centrally run, preprogrammed system failed.

The issue is not whether the primitive computer systems of the day could outfly human pilots. Today high-performance aircraft and spacecraft use computer technology extensively to extend the human ability to fly in extreme environments. The issue is whether someone "at the center" and removed from the real circumstances can possibly predict all of the things that can change or go haywire—whether in space or in a business office.

Empowerment of employees on the line requires smart machines at their fingertips. A system built on the concept of "central" vs. "personal" computing is insufficient for a widespread and mobile workforce. Such a system also represents a hostile view of the worker. It says that employees are still Industrial Age cogs, that they should be doing repetitive, single-task jobs. It says that workers should not step outside the box to do their job—the tool, in fact, will prevent them from stepping outside the box.

Having tools to manage a decentralized system is a good thing, but a mind-set to predefine the actions of knowledge workers from the center is counterproductive. Digital tools should stimulate the creativity and productivity of employees. Whatever initial guidance senior management provides, knowledge workers need tools to explore, to collaborate, and to make midcourse corrections as business changes in real time. Digitally empowered employees will enable a few companies in each industry to break away from the pack.

DEALING WITH PUNCTUATED CHAOS

So many parts of business can be improved through digital systems that it will take a number of years to maximize every single part. Every bit of data in a company should be in digital form and easily retrieved. This data will include every file, every record, every piece of e-mail, every Web page. Every internal process should be digital and integrated with every other. A unified view of each customer, for instance, should record every business process related to that customer. Every transaction with partners and customers should be digital. You should give access to customers and partners to every bit of data that is appropriate to them, and vice versa.

Previous economic eras were marked by long periods of stability followed by short periods of industry-wrenching change. Evolutionists would call this phenomenon *punctuated equilibrium*. Today the forces of digital information are creating a business environment of constant change. Evolutionists would call this *punctuated chaos*—constant upheaval marked by brief respites. The pace of change is sometimes unsettling.

The Asian financial crisis of 1998 is an example of how digital information flow is changing the world. A generation ago a boom or collapse in any financial market—stock markets, currency markets—would have taken weeks or months to spread worldwide. Today the participants in these markets are all digitally connected. Any downturn or upturn in a major market creates overnight reverberations in other markets. Businesses have to react quickly to currency changes, new credit risks, and new valuations. Business decisions have to move at the pace of electronic markets. Some companies have been very nimble in responding to these changes, and some have just watched. When it's all said and done, the companies that moved swiftly—for instance, to buy carefully chosen assets while prices were down—will be the ones that come out best. They had to move fast not only to adjust their business, but also to seize the new opportunities.

Similar digital interconnections will soon exist for all markets. The digital world is both forcing companies to react to change and giving them the tools by which to stay ahead of it. Information technology is the only way to have sufficiently quick reflexes connecting business strategy and organizational response.

Today U.S. businesses are ahead of businesses in other countries in the adoption of digital technologies. The many reasons include an openness to risk taking, individual empowerment, and labor mobility. Lower-cost communications and a large uniform market also help. It's always possible to catch up, so American companies don't necessarily have a permanent lead. Each country needs to study the best practices elsewhere in the world. Many of the business leaders I meet outside the United States know they need to adopt a digital approach. In some cases they're held back by the lack of high-speed connections in their country. In some cases they're held back because of a lack of college students' exposure to digital technology in their educational system. They aren't getting a new crop of Web-savvy employees each year. In some cases they're held back because partners and customers aren't ready to join up digitally. Investments in digital infrastructure and education are key to each country's future competitive position.

The areas the United States is behind on include government use of the Internet, government policies on encryption, and adoption of smart cards.

CAPITALIZING ON THE "COGNITIVE NICHE"

Human beings are not the biggest animals. We're not the strongest or fastest. We're not the sharpest in sight or smell. It's amazing how we survived against the many fierce creatures of nature. We survived and prospered because of our brains. We evolved to fill the cognitive niche. We learned how to use tools, to build shelter, to invent agriculture, to domesticate livestock, to develop civilization and culture, to cure and prevent disease. Our tools and technologies have helped us to shape the environment around us.

I'm an optimist. I believe in progress. I'd much rather be alive today than at any time in history—and not just because in an earlier age my skill set wouldn't have been as valuable and I'd have been a prime candidate for some beast's dinner. The tools of the Industrial Age extended the capabilities of our muscles. The tools of the digital age extend the capabilities of our minds. I'm even happier for my children, who will come of age in this new world.

By embracing the digital age, we can accelerate the positive effects and mitigate the challenges such as privacy and have-vs.-have-not. If we sit back and wait for the digital age to come to us on terms defined by others, we won't be able to do either. The Web lifestyle can increase citizen involvement in government. Many of the decisions to be made are political and social, not technical. These include how we ensure access for everyone and how we protect children. Citizens in every culture must engage on the social and political impact of digital technology to ensure that the new digital age reflects the society they want to create.

If we are reactive and let change overwhelm us or pass us by, we will perceive change negatively. If we are proactive, seek to understand the future now, and embrace change, the idea of the unexpected can be positive and uplifting. Astronomer Carl Sagan in his last book, *Billions and Billions,* said: "The prediction I can make with the highest confidence is that the most amazing discoveries will be the ones we are not today wise enough to foresee."

As tough and uncertain as the digital world makes it for business—it's evolve rapidly or die—we will all benefit. We're going to get improved products and services, more responsiveness to complaints, lower costs, and more choices. We're going to get better government and social services at substantially less expense.

This world is coming. A big part of it comes through businesses using a digital nervous system to radically improve their processes.

A digital nervous system can help business redefine itself and its role in the future, but energy or paralysis, success or failure, depends on business leaders. Only you can prepare your organization and make the investments necessary to capitalize on the rapidly dawning digital age.

Digital tools magnify the abilities that make us unique in the world: the ability to think, the ability to articulate our thoughts, the ability to work together to act on those thoughts. I strongly believe that if companies empower their employees to solve problems and give them potent tools to do this with, they will always be amazed at how much creativity and initiative will blossom forth.

APPENDIX

BUILD DIGITAL PROCESSES ON STANDARDS

Business @ the Speed of Thought describes the benefits of a digital nervous system. This appendix describes how to build one—the architecture and implementation choices. You build a digital nervous system with the new digital technologies—PC hardware, low-cost packaged software, and Internet protocols. Because the new systems are built on standards, all of the pieces—hardware, software, and communications—are easier to put together. The appendix outlines a PC- and Windows-based methodology for building a digital nervous system and explicitly covers Microsoft technology for creating a good flow of information. It's a bit more technical than the book overall, but not by much.

A major shift in the computer industry has made end-to-end business solutions much more feasible. The realignment of the computer industry from vertically integrated vendors to horizontally integrated, customer-driven solutions has brought prices down dramatically and offered more choice. In the old vertically integrated computer industry, a customer would buy almost all of the elements of a solution from a single company—the chips, the computer systems built on the chips, the operating system, the network hardware, and service. Every vendor—IBM, Fujitsu, HP, Digital, NCR, and others—had its own vertical solution. Sales volumes were low, and prices were high. Integration among vendors was difficult and expensive. Switching costs for customers were very high since every piece of the solution would have to change.

These vertically integrated vendor solutions are being displaced by the PC approach, in which specialized companies give customers a choice in each of the infrastructure layers: chips, computer systems, system software, business applications, networking, systems integration, and service. Although many companies operate in more than one layer, a customer can choose any vendor in any layer. This new horizontal structure offers customers maximum flexibility.

CREATING THE NEW COMPUTER INDUSTRY

Horizontal integration makes for high volume and low price. The independence of each layer means that competition drives each layer to evolve at maximum speed. Intel and Advanced Micro Devices push each other in chip design. Dozens of companies compete to provide components such as memory, hard drives, and CD-ROMs. Major computer manufacturers vie with one another to use these components to create the fastest and most powerful machines. Apple, HP, IBM, Microsoft, Sun Microsystems, and start-ups such as Be and Red Hat Software compete to improve system software, including middleware. IBM, Microsoft, Oracle, and others compete in databases. Baan, J. D. Edwards, PeopleSoft, Oracle, and SAP compete in financial software packages. Cisco, Lucent Technologies, Nortel, and 3Com compete in network infrastructure. Network integrators include Entex, INS, regional Bell operating com-

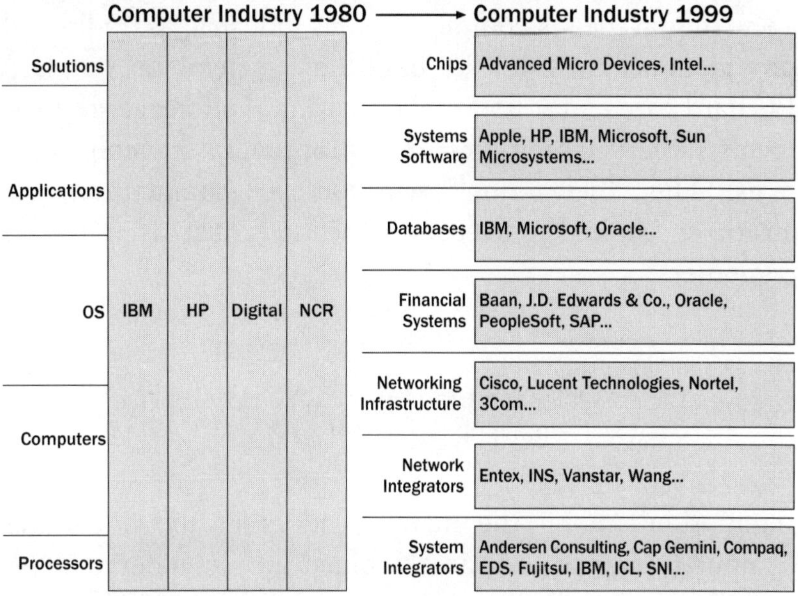

The business model that dominated computing for its first three decades was vertical integration. A single vendor provided most of the hardware and software. Each vendor's solution was stand-alone and difficult to integrate with solutions from other vendors. Costs to switch to another vendor were very high because everything would have to be changed. The new business model built around PC technology is one of horizontal integration, *right.* A set of vendors fiercely competes in every area, driving innovation forward independently of any other area. Every time a company prepares to upgrade its systems, it can reevaluate its vendors—hardware, software, systems integration and so on—based on current capabilities and competitive prices.

panies, Vanstar, and Wang. System integrators include Andersen Consulting, the Big Five accounting firms, Cap Gemini, Compaq, CTP, Fujitsu, HP, ICL, SNI, and Unisys.

Although I've listed the large companies, in some layers a multitude of smaller companies is also very important. In applications software, for example, the diverse needs of each industry are met by smaller companies that provide specialized applications. These thousands of smaller firms depend on the existence of a horizontally aligned market. Their businesses would simply not be feasible without high volume.

A shift from a vertical to a horizontal alignment is also

occurring in the telecommunications industry, as traditional providers are now able to build new systems on standard PC hardware and software systems and the Internet IP protocols rather than on their own proprietary stovepipe systems. This "delayering" will increase competition and customer choice in telecommunications just as it has in computers.

DEVELOPING A DIGITAL NERVOUS SYSTEM: BLUEPRINT REQUIRED

Integration among the many vendors in the horizontal computer industry requires a blueprint. In nature, DNA provides such a blueprint, instructing each cell on how to function to stay in concert with all others. In business, successful organizations have their own blueprints for technology. To date they've all been different. In an age of interconnectivity, businesses need an architecture that extends outward to partners and customers.

Microsoft products are developed according to a blueprint that establishes a single programming model for the future, the Windows Distributed InterNet Architecture. Windows DNA has four parts. The first is a forms approach to the user interface that seamlessly integrates Web pages using HTML with more powerful features found in traditional desktop applications. The Windows family uses HTML—a standard way to display simple graphics—for PCs, simple kiosk-type devices, TV-like devices, and handheld devices, with content rendered appropriately for the capabilities of each machine. Windows also provides more powerful rendering and other operating system services needed to support rich peripherals, quick response, and offline applications. Windows, for example, can display a multidimensional data set without going back to the server every time the user wants to change the view; it can track user actions and calculate what commands the user might want to perform next; and it gives PCs the ability to support speech recognition and natural language processing.

The second is a component object model, or COM, designed primarily to manage business logic across a network. COM is a specification for dividing up a computer program into many different parts, called *objects*, and easily hooking them together so that they interact reliably and securely across a variety of sites. The fundamental concept of components is that a programmer can use them without understanding their inner workings. A programmer just needs to understand how they can be used. When an application needs updating, a programmer can change only the parts needing work and can download components over the network to provide upgrades to users. Components are also valuable because no company is going to rewrite all its applications when new technologies or computer languages come along; components provide access to useful existing code. Windows DNA also specifies how all these objects—especially objects from multiple vendors—communicate and work with one another reliably. Key elements enable any of the objects to run on different networked machines and provide ways to connect Windows-based systems to non-Windows systems.

The third part provides a universal approach to data storage so that any program can access data in any format and in any location, such as on a hard disk, in a computer database or e-mail folder, or practically anywhere else the data is stored. The fourth is a mechanism that enables computer processing to be done wherever it makes the most sense—on the client, on the server, on some combination of both, or replicated from the server to the client for use by mobile employees.

The unique thing about Windows DNA is that it is designed to help existing applications migrate to a distributed world, merging the best of the Web with traditional enterprise applications. Most of the other approaches require a completely new base of applications to be written and restrict developers to a single computer language. Windows DNA allows customers to add value to their existing vertically integrated solutions while gaining the benefits of the horizontally integrated PC platform.

Once a company has a blueprint, another architectural imperative is to design programs with a "three-tier architecture," to separate the logic of a program into three classes: the presentation layer that displays data to the user, the middle layer to encapsulate the business rules of the application—whether a price cut should apply to an outstanding order, for instance—and the back-end layer that stores and retrieves business data. The three-tier architecture makes it possible to logically break up application functionality onto as many machines as needed and to change different tiers without affecting the others.

Using this approach, Merrill Lynch neatly stitched more than fifty separate applications into the Trusted Global Advisor system for financial consultants described in chapter 5. Using Microsoft Office, Outlook, Windows Media Player, and other applications that can take advantage of COM, Merrill Lynch has created one interface that appears to users as a single integrated, handcrafted application on the desktop presentation layer.

Data for many of the fifty applications comes from an existing back-end data tier, which has databases ranging from Microsoft SQL Server and IBM's DB2 on Windows to CICS and DB2 on mainframes. Application servers running Microsoft Transaction Server and Message Queue in the middle tier use COM components to describe the business logic and coordinate the flow of data from the many back ends. Such software systems can remove 40 to 50 percent of the code that developers would otherwise have to write to create distributed applications while handling the complex coordination and security issues. The various components are written in a variety of languages, including Visual Basic, Visual C++, and Java.

Through COM, a mainframe-based 3270 application such as order entry is just another file folder on the desktop, and all Web-based applications, now and in the future, simply work with the shell. Users never have to be aware of the source of the underlying application—Web, local machine, client-server, or mainframe—or when the application is upgraded. New functionality or new applications simply appear on the desktop.

DEVELOPING A DIGITAL NERVOUS SYSTEM: A SOLUTIONS FRAMEWORK

Building a digital nervous system requires a well-defined framework for how to organize and roll out the computer hardware and network, how to make or buy applications, and how to operate the system on a daily basis. The best practices for each of these steps is described in the Microsoft Solutions Framework, a set of guiding principles derived from the experience of Microsoft Consulting Services with a wide range of enterprise customers.

The first hardware decision is the kind of desktop machines ("clients") to give to users. Client hardware has historically required two separate kinds of computers. The first is the dumb terminal, typically used for task-oriented workers. The client machine is passive, primarily displaying whatever work has been done on the host machine or server. This approach allows central control, but network traffic or the server machine can be a bottleneck, and the approach won't work when people are on the move. The second is the PC, an adaptable tool used by knowledge workers. Computing tasks are handled on the PC or server according to business need. This approach is flexible but can introduce management complexity.

Organizations no longer have to make the trade-off between these two approaches. PC technology now combines a high degree of central control with the flexibility required for the new digital infrastructure. A program can run entirely on the server and just the graphical elements appear on the end-user machine, or the same application can run totally on the PC. Since it will be a *very* long time before every device is attached to the network all the time, such stand-alone capabilities are important to knowledge workers. Today's Web-based applications usually don't work if someone is disconnected.

Within a company, employees can use the PC in "terminal mode" to browse for data but retain PC functionality for knowledge work. Factory and supplier planning, for example, can be a more or less automated process that runs on a large server, with a knowledge worker occasionally browsing for any problems with the production schedule. But if negotiating a large order with a customer, that same employee needs to have a tool to run what-if scenarios with the manufacturing schedule to see whether the order can be built in time.

Remember, too, that many single-task jobs will disappear as the Web enables self-service customer support. If a consumer calls a bank's customer-service department, it will be about investment plans and asset diversification and other complex, high-value topics. The communication will likely involve interactive audio and video. The customer and employee will be working collaboratively. The consumer and the employee will both need powerful PCs.

A general-purpose PC is a good choice all around.

PCs do need to become more manageable. The newest versions of Microsoft Office and Windows 2000 let you configure the end-user computers flexibly from a central location. Users can have applications on their local machine, or they can access the application from a server, downloading the minimum amount of code needed to begin. Infrequently used functions can be downloaded automatically when required. If a part of an application is broken, it can be repaired automatically. Also, PCs will reconfigure themselves based on the identity of the person using the machine. People will be able to use any machine in the organization as if it were their own personal computer. When a user changes anything offline or data on the server is changed while the user is offline, the system will reconcile everything when the user reconnects to the network. This management comes through a central directory that stores user, application, and other information across the enterprise.

DEVELOPING A DIGITAL NERVOUS SYSTEM: SERVERS

The next major decision is what servers to deploy at the heart of your network. These servers do everything from running the business processes of your organization to storing the massive amounts of information at the heart of a digital nervous system. The old vertically integrated computing industry created a huge variety of incompatible computers and architectures in the server world. A new

Smarter Software Reduces Cost of Ownership

In 1997 the Gartner Group criticized PCs and Microsoft products for having a high total cost of ownership. Most of this cost was related to maintenance and upgrading. Scott Winkler, who is responsible for the Gartner Group's research on my company, said: "Microsoft has made it worse and more expensive to own these systems over the last ten years, because they were focused on functionality, not cost." Yet by mid-1998 Gartner said that the cost of ownership for PCs running on Windows 2000 networks would be 25 percent less than for previous PC systems. This reduction put PC solutions "neck-and-neck or perhaps a little ahead" of non-PC solutions in lowering TCO. (David F. Carr, "Gartner Group, in a Reversal, Says PC Networks May Cost Less Than NCs," *Internet World,* 6 April 1998.)

Improvements include easier remote installation and management of PCs and software on a network; the ability to centrally enforce standard PC configurations and reestablish user settings if a machine goes down; and tools that automatically upload basic information about a user's machine to a company's telephone help desk or Web support site. This last software eliminates 30 percent of the time a typical support call takes, and the user data can be swept into a database for trend analysis.

We're working on other improvements, too. When a customer adds a new application to her system, the system will one day be smart enough to arbitrate any conflicts between the new software and the software already on her machine. If the system detects a reason to change a setting in a file, it will make the change and not trouble the user unless it's absolutely necessary. If a file becomes corrupted or its settings are changed accidentally, the product will locate and install a correct version of the file, locally or remotely—in effect, healing itself. If the user has to act, her changes will be recorded for a support engineer to review later if problems arise and she does have to call Support. We plan to add similar intelligence to tools for network administrators so they can better centrally manage all of the network resources and users that companies have throughout geographically dispersed offices.

layer of software called *middleware* emerged to try to make them work together.

Middleware, though, brought its own issues of cost and complexity. Boeing had a different computer system to track aircraft parts through each of thirteen stages of manufacturing. Over time Boeing ended up with middleware whose only function was to ensure that the thirteen systems interoperated and still other middleware that kept the data consistent across all these systems. In addition to being expensive to maintain, thirteen different systems generated thirteen different bills of material. Coordinating all of this paperwork slowed manufacturing. Boeing's new production system replaces the thirteen systems with a single source of product data throughout manufacturing.

Geometric leaps in PC performance have eliminated the need for continued deployment of incompatible middle-tier systems. Today PC-based servers support thousands of users yet have 90 percent hardware commonality and 100 percent software compatibility with a desktop computer. This homogeneous platform is one reason PC systems are rapidly growing in popularity for servers. Having the same operating system on the desktop and on the server simplifies development and training and establishes a uniform architecture for distributed computing—applications or parts of applications can move from any machine to any other machine. This commonality also makes it easier to connect knowledge workers to existing back-end data systems. Rather than having to have a middleware software component on every one of 10,000 desktop clients, the interoperability layer can run on a few dozen servers that connect the clients to the data tier.

While the horizontally integrated PC computing model has not yet matched the older vertically integrated model in every aspect of computing capability, it is rapidly closing the gap. Only a handful of business applications in the world today require more scale than PC servers can provide. Within the next few years even these applications will be able to run on the PC architecture. Moving away from the old applications is one of the toughest things for companies to do, but the transition is inevitable. The old mainframe applications weren't designed for rich Web access by tens of thousands of users or to give people access to real-time information.

One reason the ERP vendors are doing so well is that companies are moving quickly to PC technology for major applications. Partly, the move saves money. More impor-

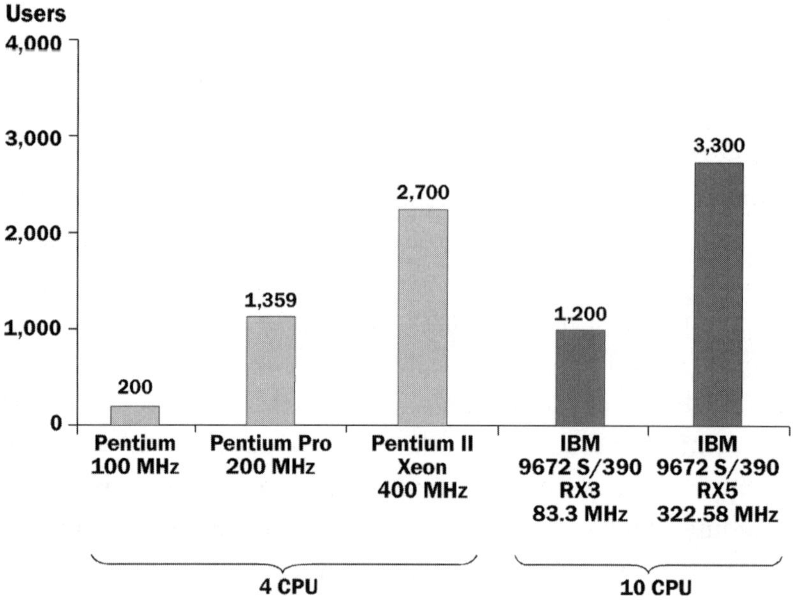

Source: SAP, Intel

The PC market creates economies of scale that enable massive spending on R&D. As a result, PC systems are overtaking older systems in performance. Four-processor systems built on a variety of Intel microprocessors compare favorably with ten-processor mainframe systems that cost substantially more. This benchmark shows the number of users that can be supported on SAP financial software used in many corporations. Though both PC and mainframe technologies continue to improve, high-volume PC systems are outstripping low-volume non-PC systems in the rate at which performance advances.

tant, companies can integrate business data with the PC network and with the PC's ability to analyze information in rich ways.

DEVELOPING A DIGITAL NERVOUS SYSTEM: PHASES OF DEVELOPMENT

Implementation of a digital nervous system has three phases. They usually happen in a certain order but can also occur in parallel. First, knowledge workers receive PCs for productivity use, local area networks are installed to provide document sharing on file servers and Web servers, and a single back-end e-mail system is deployed to improve collaboration. Second comes the investment to link existing business operations into knowledge management systems. Usually this is in the form of data warehousing that converts operational data into a form that it is easy to search and query to glean business intelligence.

The final and most dramatic step is the addition of new back-end applications that connect to existing systems but that use the new common architecture. The goal is to select projects that achieve the greatest reward in the shortest period of time. Electronic commerce is a common one. This approach means you can move to a new architecture without having to throw away your existing investments.

McDonald's, the $35 billion fast-food leader, has evolved its digital nervous system in a way that will be familiar to many companies. Its first systems were mainframes at its Oakbrook, Illinois, headquarters for handling sales and financial reporting. In the mid-1980s many McDonald's outlets installed Unix systems running custom software for bookkeeping, inventory, and payroll. Sales data was faxed back to headquarters twice weekly to be keyed manually into the mainframe. In the first phase of creating a digital nervous system, McDonald's added PCs and departmental networks at its headquarters to handle productivity tasks and file sharing. However, every major business operations system at McDonald's was custom-built. The systems required significant integration to work together.

In 1997 McDonald's resolved to get more out of the company's technology investment. After eighteen months of research and pilot projects with help from the Gartner Group and Computer Sciences Corporation, McDonald's came to the conclusion that its old systems were too complex and would always be a cash drain. McDonald's decided to make a dramatic leap from proprietary mainframes and minicomputers to a single architecture involving a single desktop standard, standard networking services, and Web-based information sharing. This new system uses the same architecture for the business operations systems in each outlet as for the knowledge management systems at headquarters. The new infrastructure, being implemented in late 1998, will give McDonald's the kind of real-time sales feedback Marks & Spencer gets and the granular, up-to-date information on trends that Jiffy Lube managers get.

McDonald's used the best technology available to solve its business problems at every point in time. The problem is that the original technologies were proprietary. Computing paradigms shifted every decade or so, from mainframe to minicomputer to client-server to Web-based. Complexity grew, too. The rare company that achieved most of the capabilities of an integrated system had to pay a fortune to create the system and even more to maintain it. It's a testimony to the skills of all IT shops historically that they could get these systems to work together at all.

DEVELOPING A DIGITAL NERVOUS SYSTEM: DECIDING WHAT TO BUY

Using commercial, off-the-shelf software packages that are built on the same architecture is another way that companies can reduce the cost and complexity of building a digital nervous system. The successful companies select a few standards and enforce them strictly. The elements of a company's infrastructure that benefit most from standardization are desktop systems, desktop productivity applications, e-mail systems, database systems, and network services.

Most companies have standardized on a Windows desktop, and many have standardized on desktop productivity applications. Coke, Jiffy Lube, Glaxo Wellcome, and many others have standardized on Microsoft Office. Having a standard corporate desktop and standard productivity software on top of that—spreadsheets, presentations, text documents, databases—provides the basic set of tools that knowledge workers need. The value of standard productivity applications applies not only within a company, but also across companies. I can't imagine how we could work with our development and business partners, our accountants, our public relations consultants, or our law firm without being able to easily exchange, edit, and annotate documents. Desktop applications are more than productivity tools. They are the access point into your company's most important data as well as the components for your customized line-of-business applications.

Document exchange requires a powerful e-mail infrastructure. Through independent departmental decisions, acquisitions, and other factors, companies can end up with multiple messaging systems, some used for e-mail and some used for groupware. Trying to hook these systems together keeps administrative costs high and makes it difficult to obtain the advantages of e-mail: the ability to quickly and easily exchange documents and the ability to integrate work-flow applications throughout the entire company. Some host-based and Internet e-mail systems do not integrate well with desktop applications or the Internet, so you need to be sure your e-mail system embraces the PC platform and Internet messaging protocols and standards. Do e-mail right. Install a single e-mail system for your company geared to support the activities of knowledge workers.

Database decisions are highly influenced by the choice of underlying operating system, so you could start by picking a small number of operating systems to support. Components also make business and application logic much more independent of any one back-end database system, providing flexibility in integrating different database systems and preserving application investments.

A single network operating system goes a long way toward simplicity in otherwise complex back-end systems. People are just beginning to understand the value of such features as a comprehensive security model for the network and all of the applications that run on it. A user can log on to the system once and access every application for which he or she has privileges—whether database, e-mail, or Web page. An administrator can use a single set of tools to manage users, applications, and networked resources such as printers. The ability to search for data across the network and across multiple formats—database, e-mail, and documents of any kind—is dramatically simplified.

Standardizing important elements of the infrastructure doesn't mean that every department or user should be forced to use only the applications decreed by "central planning." In general, companies should standardize software packages corporate-wide when they affect corporate-wide communication and integration. Otherwise departments and business units should be free to choose best-of-breed applications particular to their business needs—project management, brochure design, marketing analysis, product development, and so on. As long as the business applications run on the mainstream platform, the central IT department won't have to be greatly involved in the decision process for individual business units.

DEVELOPING A DIGITAL NERVOUS SYSTEM: DECIDING WHAT TO BUILD

If packaged software does not solve your business needs out of the box, look for software products that are easy to customize. It's better to start with commercial software and customize the package than to build a custom application from scratch. A three-tier architectural blueprint combined with commerical software that uses a component approach makes customization much more possible.

Interaction with partners of all sizes requires component technology that works for companies of all sizes. You won't find mainframe technology in small and medium-size companies. It's just too expensive. But companies of all sizes have one thing in common: PC technology. The fact that Windows DNA is pervasive in all Windows systems makes it very attractive to software developers.

Windows DNA enables the integration of all data types, including voice and video, with computer applications. One decision, then, is when a company should merge its physical voice and data networks. The telephone network is today a different set of wires running different standards from those of the data network. Major telecom suppliers such as Lucent and Nortel are embracing computer networks, and major data networking suppliers such as Cisco are embracing voice communications. The standards for integrating data and voice will be Internet based, and the competition will be intense. For organizations, putting in a single voice-data network is a big infrastructure investment. Every CEO should consider such a transition during major remodeling or new construction but otherwise take a long hard look at the costs vs. benefits of replacing the entire physical structure.

SAVING ON INFRASTRUCTURE

The financial savings from standardizing on a single infrastructure can be very high. McDonald's predicts an 18 percent annual savings with its new infrastructure. Dayton Hudson, the retail chain, spent $100 million in creating its new infrastructure and saved that much in the first year. The all-time record for infrastructure realignment and cost cutting, though, may go to Lockheed Martin, the largest defense contractor in the United States.

When Lockheed and Martin Marietta merged in March 1995 in the largest deal in aerospace history, the new company had a combined $1 billion IT budget. Martin Marietta was sixteen months into IT consolidation stemming from its merger with GE Aerospace, Lockheed still had twelve separate IT organizations, and several attempts had failed to consolidate IT in many of the business units in both companies.

Joe Cleveland, then internal information systems vice president for Martin Marietta, promised to cut IT spending in the merged company by a total of $700 million over five years, reduce IT head count by 25 percent, and improve service to the business units. He got the top IT job in the new company and in just two years bettered the target of $700 million cumulative budget reduction—three years ahead of schedule. He succeeded by standardizing infrastructure and using a virtual organization to extend the resources and services of IT.

Cleveland, now president of enterprise information systems (EIS) for Lockheed Martin, replaced the 24 existing e-mail systems residing on 900 servers with a single corporate messaging system on 117 servers, for an 87 percent reduction in servers and related cost. Message delivery was reduced from one day to less than three minutes for internal messages and less than ten minutes for Internet messages. He consolidated volume and leveraged economies of scale to reduce costs on voice, video, and data networks, collapsed a number of data centers into two major centers, consolidated numerous server centers into server farms, consolidated maintenance contracts, and developed strategic partners to reduce procurement costs.

To optimize IT resources, Cleveland implemented the concept of a virtual organization in place of the traditional geographic organization, which had limited the capabilities of the organization to assets and skills in a particular location. Lockheed Martin created four consolidated IT functions and aligned a CIO for each of Lockheed Martin's business sectors to translate business requirements to IT solutions. When a business unit identifies an IT requirement, a virtual team is formed from a program manager and representatives from each of the IT functional areas. This team completes its roster from a pool of more than 4,000 skilled IT professionals according to needs rather than to work location. The team utilizes collaborative tools such as e-mail, Web site forums, teleconferencing, videoconferencing, and NetMeeting to work virtually. When face-to-face meetings are required, people travel; but collaborative tools keep travel to a minimum.

This virtual organization helped Lockheed Martin to convert 100,000 users to Microsoft Exchange e-mail in a little over a year because all of the IT people who had anything to do with networks and messaging were on the same team. IT staff working on projects across different business sectors are also spotting common business processes early, helping business units leverage existing solutions to save time and money. Because they engage with their business counterparts directly, IT employees are encouraged to actively contribute new ideas.

Having met its initial goal of consolidating technology spending, Lockheed Martin is now willing to spend technology dollars to help business. Technology people are now thinking much more like businesspeople, which is how it should be.

DESIGNING FOR INFORMATION FLOW

As McDonald's, Dayton Hudson, Lockheed Martin, and others have learned, even the first steps in implementing the right architecture can eliminate enough complexity to pay for the transition. The digital revolution means that big companies can buy most of a rich software infrastructure rather than build it from scratch. Small or medium-size businesses can afford a rich software infrastructure for the first time. They're no longer priced out of the game.

The new horizontally integrated computer industry provides the best business and technical model for the future. The inexorable competition in each layer of the industry—chips, systems, software, solutions, and service—drives each area ahead independently of any other. This high-volume model attracts more and more software developers who create packaged software that reduces the cost of business. More developers mean more and more of the innovative work is occurring first or exclusively on the new platform. This positive feedback loop has drawn in virtually all traditional enterprise vendors as important supporters of the platform and has created the largest service capability in the computer industry. A major success in the horizontally integrated approach is Windows computing, which by standardizing the operating system creates incredible variety in the hardware systems on which it runs and in the software solutions that can be built upon it.

Scale economics for research and development in the PC industry dwarf what any one company can do in an old vertical approach. The PC industry as a whole spends more than $15 billion a year on R&D, while Sun, about the only "pure" vertical player anymore, spends less than $2 billion on R&D. (Apple, which also sells an entire hardware-software system, has primarily been a desktop company rather than a provider of enterprise business solutions.)

By staying in the mainstream, businesses can ride the massive R&D investments and the innovation that is concentrated in the horizontal model. Quite simply, the high-volume world is beating the low-volume world in the speed of technological advance. Over the years, more and more of the traditional vendors have taken an increasing PC focus, including Fujitsu, HP, ICL, NEC, Unisys, and others. IBM is not purely in either camp, continuing its vertical strategy with mainframes and minicomputers while also developing a business around the horizontal PC model.

When you pick PCs to build business systems on, you're retaining your choice of hardware without hurting your software investment. You can go to whichever hardware vendor has the best service or the fastest or cheapest machine today. Every few years, when you renew your hardware systems, you can reweigh those criteria and rebid the purchase without worrying about having to change your software applications or any of your training. Current software investments will carry forward as the PC evolves into new form factors such as tablet devices and devices that recognize speech.

Your organization's computing architecture should be a unifying design that maintains overall integration while enabling incremental change, especially at the departmental level. Flexibility is important because it's impossible to de-

Y2K Issue Shows Short-Term Software Thinking

Unless updated, many software programs can't tell the difference between the year 1900 and 2000, causing them to miscalculate such things as pension amounts. This "year 2000" problem stems from a failure of people thirty years ago to think of software as a long-term asset. They believed that the primary asset was the hardware and that the software was transitory. History has taught us the opposite. It's the hardware that goes obsolete first, while software applications stay around seemingly forever.

Every major computer vendor offers some form of compliance for being "Y2K ready," with a series of processes to test and upgrade customer systems. As of early 1999 any organization that is not well on its way to implementing Y2K solutions can only practice triage. A company should identify its most crucial business applications—or the most crucial modules in those applications—and move them to a modern solution. It should deal with other applications later, according to priority.

A component approach will eliminate the next Y2K problem, whatever it happens to be. Developers will be able to alter individual modules such as those that calculate dates instead of going through millions of lines of code to make changes. But shifting the role of technology from a sunk cost to a capital investment will happen only if companies recognize the long-term nature of software investments and choose software platforms and strategies accordingly.

fine in advance a single computing approach across the entire enterprise. In large companies such plans inevitably become too rigid and can fail to keep up with the pace of business change. Faced with inflexibility, business managers have felt justified in going around IT to create their own solutions. This is how PCs and PC networks came into many companies in the first place.

The standards of the digital revolution—the PC, the microprocessor that will make other new digital devices possible, and the Internet—provide companies a way to implement a unified architecture without busting the bank. Companies can move to the new architecture step by step. Many are already implementing the first phase of migrating knowledge workers to a standard platform, network operating system, and e-mail. The next steps, which can happen project by project, are to connect these knowledge systems with existing business operations systems, to build new business systems on the new architecture, and, over time, to replace older business systems.

Diagnosing Your Digital Nervous System

- ❑ Do you reduce cost and complexity by using commercial, off-the-shelf software packages whenever possible?
- ❑ Do you use a single e-mail system company-wide?
- ❑ Does your architecture provide a good top-level framework for corporate-wide applications while enabling bottoms-up development of departmental applications?
- ❑ Do you practice three-tier application development so you can logically break up applications on as many machines as you need and change different parts of the code without affecting the others?
- ❑ Do you use component technology to integrate software?
- ❑ Are you using standard Internet technologies?
- ❑ Do your digital systems unify corporate-wide applications while facilitating bottoms-up development of departmental applications?

GLOSSARY

Automated Waste. The idea that a company may spend money on expensive systems to support inefficient processes instead of using digital systems to create new and more efficient processes.

Auto PC. A PC device for vehicles that provides access to e-mail, voice messages, phone calls, navigation instructions, and similar functions. The interface is primarily through voice commands so that drivers can keep their hands on the steering wheel and attention focused on traffic.

Bandwidth. The amount of data that a communications system can carry. Sometimes refers to how many projects a person can think about or work on at once, as in "She's got a lot of bandwidth."

Batch, Batch Files, Batch System. The practice of storing transactions for a period of time before they are posted for processing, typically overnight. Many batch-processing systems are giving way to online transaction systems so that business users see results quickly and can respond to fast-changing business situations.

Beta Test. The testing of software by volunteer customers shortly before the formal release of a product. Designed to uncover problems that may appear in actual business use but cannot be found through internal tests. If beta testers find serious problems, the developer fixes those and conducts more beta tests before releasing the software commercially.

Boundarylessness. The idea that solutions to business problems should encompass everyone involved, whether inside or outside the formal borders of a corporation.

Cable Modem. A modem that sends and receives data at high speed through a coaxial television cable instead of telephone lines, as with a slower conventional modem.

CAD, Computer-**A**ided **D**esign. The digital design of models ranging from simple tools to buildings, aircraft, integrated circuits, and molecules. In the field of emergency services, CAD stands for computer-aided dispatch.

Client. A computer on a network that accesses resources provided by another computer called a server. A dumb client, or dumb terminal, is limited in capability. A smart client, or PC, also provides computing power for work that logically should be done on the client instead of the server.

COM, Component **O**bject **M**odel. A specification for building software components that can be assembled into new programs or add functionality to existing programs. COM components can be written in a variety of computer languages and can be updated and reinstalled without requiring changes to other parts of the program.

Database Marketing. The creation of special offers for a set of customers based on information in a database. Simple database marketing might involve nothing more than a general offer to residents in a certain location. Sophisticated database marketing is based on demographic data such as the recipient's income or buying patterns.

Data Marts. A scaled-down version of a data warehouse that is tailored to contain information likely to be used only by the target group. See also *Data Warehouse*.

Data Mining. The process of identifying commercially useful patterns or relationships in databases or other computer repositories through the use of advanced statistical tools.

Data Warehouse. A database that can access all of a company's information. While the warehouse can be distributed over several computers and may contain several databases and information from numerous sources in a variety of formats, it should be accessible to users through simple commands.

Digital Nervous System. The digital processes that enable a company to perceive and react to its environment, to sense competitive challenges and customer needs, and to organize timely responses. A digital nervous system is distinguished from a mere network of computers by the accuracy, immediacy, and richness of the information it brings to knowledge workers and the insight and collaboration made possible by the information. No company has a perfect digital nervous system today; rather, it's an ideal use of technology in support of business.

Disintermediation. The removal of the middleman from a transaction involving a producer and a consumer, usually through digital transactions on the Internet.

Distance Learning. An educational system in which the teacher and students are separated in time or space and use technology such as television broadcasts or the Internet to communicate.

Dogfood, Eating Your Own. The practice of a company using its own products internally as a final test of capability before selling the products to customers. An example is Microsoft's policy of deploying its software for its own business use before releasing the software commercially.

DSL, Digital **S**ubscriber **L**ine. A regular twisted-pair telephone line that carries digital rather than analog signals, increasing the bandwidth of the line.

Dumb Terminal. A terminal that does not run programs locally and is typically capable of displaying only characters and numbers and responding to simple control codes.

E-commerce, Electronic Commerce. Commercial activity that takes place by digital processes over a network. Most new business-to-business and business-to-consumer transactions are being delivered on the Internet.

EDI, Electronic **D**ata **I**nterchange. A set of standards controlling the transfer of business documents such as purchase orders and invoices between computers. EDI has eliminated paperwork for many large businesses but is generally too complex for small and medium-size businesses. New Internet-based transactions are likely to be built on XML instead of EDI. See also *XML*.

EIS, Executive Information System. A set of tools designed to organize information into categories and reports for senior executives. Many EIS systems were difficult to integrate with other corporate information systems. Today EIS usually stands for "enterprise information system" and is designed to provide information to a wider range of people in an organization.

ERP, Enterprise Resource Planning. Software used in a number of industries to coordinate sales and order information with the manufacturing system in order to accurately schedule production, fully utilize capacity, and reduce inventory.

Extranet. An extension of a corporate intranet using World Wide Web technology to facilitate communication with the corporation's suppliers and customers in order to enhance the speed and efficiency of the business relationship. See also *Intranet*.

FAQs, Frequently Asked Questions. Pronounced "facts." A common feature of Web sites that includes answers to common questions related to that site.

Feedback Loop. A system to gather reactions from customers about a product or service in order to create a continuous cycle of improvements, more feedback, and more improvements.

Fiber-Optic Cable. A cable containing dozens or hundreds of strands of glass or other transparent material known as optical fibers. Each strand carries light beams that are modulated to transmit information. Fiber-optic cable can carry far more data than most other means of transmission.

Friction-Free Capitalism. A concept first expressed in *The Road Ahead* that digital processes can remove most of the friction in business transactions by removing middlemen. The Internet makes it easier for buyers and sellers to find one another, provides buyers more information about products and services, and provides sellers more information about customer preferences and shopping patterns.

Gantt Chart. A bar chart that shows individual parts of a project as bars against a horizontal time scale. Gantt charts are used as project-planning tools for developing schedules.

GPS, Global **P**ositioning **S**ystem. A satellite-based navigational system that enables users to determine their location with very high precision.

Groupware. Software that enables a group of users on a network to collaborate on a particular project. Groupware incorporates e-mail, collaborative document development, scheduling, and tracking.

Handheld. A lightweight palmtop computer that provides specific functions such as a calendar, note taking, and e-mail. Handhelds are the first generation of devices becoming known as personal digital companions, which will come in a greater variety of shapes, small sizes, and functionality.

HDTV, High-**D**efinition **T**ele**v**ision. A method of transmitting and receiving television signals that produces a picture with much greater resolution and clarity than does standard television technology.

Horizontal Integration. A business model for the computer industry in which each layer of technology—chips, systems, software, solutions, and service—is provided by a different set of companies. Fierce competition in each area drives technology ahead rapidly and creates a high-volume, low-price model. Compare *Vertical Integration.*

Host. The main computer in a system of computers or terminals, usually a mainframe.

HTML, Hyper**T**ext **M**arkup **L**anguage. The language used to format documents for viewing with a browser on the user's machine or on a network, including the World Wide Web. HTML tells browsers how to display type and images to the user and describes responses to user actions such as activation of a link by a mouse click.

Hyperlink, Hypertext, Hypermedia. A connection between an element in a document such as a word, phrase, symbol, or image and a different element in the same document or in another document. The user activates the link by clicking on the element, which is usually underlined or in a special color. Also called *hot link, hypertext link*. The term *hypertext* describes documents. *Hypermedia* emphasizes animation, sound, and video. See also *HTML*.

Inflection Point. In mathematics, the term that describes the point at which the shape of a curve shifts from concave to convex; in business, the term that describes a sudden and massive change in a business market or technology use. Popularized by Intel chairman Andrew Grove.

Information Work. A phrase coined by MIT's Michael Dertouzos to describe the transformation of passive data into active information by human brains or software.

Institutional Intelligence, Institutional IQ, Corporate IQ. A measure of how easily a company can share information broadly and how well people within an organization can build on one another's ideas and learn from past experiences.

Intranet. A network designed to organize and share information and carry out digital business transactions within a company. An intranet employs applications associated with the Internet such as Web pages, browsers, e-mail, newsgroups, and mailing lists but is accessible only to those within the organization.

IP, Internet **P**rotocol. The technical specification that governs the sending of data across the Internet. Standardization of most networks on IP in the last several years has made possible for the first time an efficient worldwide network for exchanging data. As phone systems become digital, IP connections will be used for both voice and data.

IT, Information System, Information Services, Information Technology. The formal name for a company's data-processing department. This book uses the acronym *IT* to refer to all aspects of the company's central computing department and systems.

Just-in-Time. A system of inventory control based on the Japanese *kanban* system in which materials are delivered just in time for manufacturing. The better the information system between a company and suppliers, the less inventory the company has to stock and the lower its costs.

Kiosk. A freestanding PC that provides information to the public, usually through a multimedia display. Kiosks will become a common way for government agencies to provide services to citizens who do not have PCs or Internet access.

Knowledge Worker. Employees whose fundamental task is analyzing and manipulating information. PC systems can turn more employees into knowledge workers by giving them better information about the processes they are carrying out.

LAN, Local **A**rea **N**etwork. A group of PCs, servers, printers, and similar devices connected over a network in a relatively limited geography.

Legacy Application or **System**. A computer system that remains in use after an organization installs more modern technology. Compatibility with legacy systems is important when new software is installed. Legacy systems based on mainframe computers are being replaced in many organizations by PC-based architectures.

Memex. A device described by scientist Vannevar Bush in 1945 that would enable people to store and display all books, records, and communications and connect to data through hyperlinks, which he called *associative indexing*. Though based on mechanical terms of the era, the memex anticipated the concept of a PC connected to the Internet.

Meta Data, Metadata. Data about data. For example, the title, subject, author, and size of a document constitute metadata about the document.

Middleware. Software that sits between two or more types of software and translates information between them.

Moore's Law. Intel cofounder Gordon Moore's rule of thumb, which has turned out to be true, that microprocessors would double in processing power every eighteen to twenty-four months.

Natural Language Processing. A field combining computer science and linguistics in order to create computer systems that can recognize and react to human language, either spoken or written.

OLAP, OnLine Analytical Processing. A database capable of handling queries more complex than those handled by standard relational databases, through the ability to view data by different criteria, intensive calculation capability, and specialized indexing techniques.

Paperless Office. The idealized office in which information is entirely stored, manipulated, and transferred digitally rather than on paper.

Perfect Price. Adam Smith's concept that a free and open market will enable a buyer and seller to find one another and agree on the theoretically correct price for any goods or services. The wealth of information and ease of connection enabled by the Internet make it possible for buyers and sellers to approach the perfect price.

Plug and Play. The ability of hardware devices such as an extra disk drive to plug into PCs and work without the user having to reconfigure the system manually; the ability of software components to work together without requiring other software layers to exchange data or synchronize processes.

Point-of-Sale. The place in a store at which goods are paid for. Computerized scanners for reading tags and bar codes, electronic cash registers, and other special devices record purchases. POS systems connected with digital analysis tools enable real-time analysis of sales and faster response to changing customer demand.

Portal. A Web site that becomes a user's primary starting point for access to the Internet. AOL, MSN, and Yahoo! are examples of portal sites.

Reengineering. The design of new business processes, usually in conjunction with digital systems, to improve corporate responsiveness to changing business conditions.

Server. A computer system that controls access to a network and network resources such as printing and file sharing. Some servers provide access to information in databases or on Web sites, while others coordinate the flow of data and computer processes among other servers and back-end systems. See also *Three-Tier Computing*.

Skunkworks. Any small team that goes off by itself to develop a new product outside of a company's normal development processes. Named for the secret group at Lockheed that developed a number of high-technology aircraft.

Smart Card. A credit card containing an integrated circuit that gives it a limited amount of "intelligence" and memory. Smart cards are being used for identification and to encode information such as a person's medical history.

Soft-Boiled Egg Rule. The principle that software should be simple enough that a user can do most transactions in less than three minutes, or about the time it takes to soft-boil an egg.

Supply Chain. A phrase describing all the companies involved in delivering a product to consumers. Paper-based systems or old digital systems make communication difficult and create slow, complicated intercompany processes. Compare *Value Network*.

Task Worker. Employees assigned to a single, repetitive task with little autonomy. Modern business principles encourage the use of technology to automate many tasks and redesign others to take advantage of a worker's skills.

TCO, Total **C**ost of **O**wnership. The cost of owning, operating, and maintaining a computer system. TCO includes the up-front costs of hardware and software, plus the costs of installation, training, support, upgrades, and repairs. Industry initiatives designed to lower TCO include centralized network management of PCs, automated upgrades, and "self-healing" PCs.

TGA, Trusted **G**lobal **A**dvisor. Merrill Lynch's intelligent interface to software systems that enable financial consultants to spend more time on analysis and less time on data collection.

Three-Tier Computing. A computing architecture in which software systems are structured into three networked tiers or layers: the client or presentation layer, the business logic layer, and the data layer. PCs usually provide the presentation layer. PC servers in the middle tier, or business logic layer, coordinate interactions between the user (client) and the back-end data tier. The data tier often includes a variety of PC and non-PC systems.

Throughput. A measure of the data transfer rate through a communications system, of the data-processing rate in a computer system, or of the production rate of other systems.

Time to Market. The amount of time it takes a company to go from concept to initial shipment of a product.

USB, USB 1394, Universal Serial Bus. A technical standard that enables a number of digital devices to be easily connected together and work properly: for example, a new hard drive or modem connected to a PC.

Value Network, Value Chain Initiative. A web of partnerships enabled by digital information flow so that a company and all its suppliers can easily communicate and act together. In a value network, everyone who touches the product—from retail to distribution to transportation to manufacturing—must add value, and communications go both forward as well as back among all companies involved. Compare *Supply Chain.*

Vertical Integration. An older business model for the computer industry in which most layers of technology—chips, systems, software, solutions, and service—were provided by a single vendor. Sales volumes were low and switching costs for customers were high since every piece of the solution would have to change.

Videoconferencing. Teleconferencing in which video images are transmitted along with sound.

Video-on-Demand. The ability to play movies or other recorded events whenever the user wants, rather than at the times set by broadcasters.

Web Lifestyle, Web Workstyle. The new way of living and working that will become common as consumers and workers take advantage of digital devices and digital connections to transform the way they work and their approach to living. Once the infrastructure is in place, new unforeseen applications will emerge, just as the telephone, radio, television, and computer emerged only after electrical use became commonplace.

Windows 32. The application programming interface used by developers to create software that operates on the Microsoft Windows family of operating systems.

Windows CE. A scaled-down version of Microsoft Windows designed for use with handheld PCs, other digital companions, and embedded devices.

Windows NT, Windows 2000. Microsoft's operating system designed primarily for business use. Originally named Windows NT, the product has been renamed Windows 2000 to indicate it is moving into more general use.

Wizard. An outstanding and creative programmer or a power user, or a software help system that guides users through each step of a particular task, such as opening a word-processing document in the correct format for a business letter.

XML, e**X**tended **M**arkup **L**anguage. An updated version of HTML that not only describes the way to lay out content on a Web page for display or printing, which HTML does, but also describes the nature of the content. XML provides a way of indexing data for retrieval and for other kinds of manipulation. XML provides a simple way to handle data exchange over the Internet.

Year 2000, Y2K Problem. The inability of some computer programs to distinguish between the years 1900 and 2000. After January 1, 2000, computers could miscalculate such things as pension amounts. Major computer vendors have published a great deal of information on how they are complying with issues related to the year 2000. Microsoft's program is described at a link from www.Speed-of-Thought.com.

CUSTOMER ACKNOWLEDGMENTS

I'm deeply indebted to the many people from other companies who took time out of their busy days to talk with me or my researchers. So many people helped that I'm bound to have overlooked someone. If that's you, it is strictly an oversight for which I sincerely apologize.

Customers are listed alphabetically by organization:

Clay Henry, Bob Richardson, John R. Zuschlag, Acadian Ambulance & Air Med Services; Tracy Maxwell, Advanced Research Systems; Cary Auderer, American Medical Response; Stephen M. Shapiro, Andersen Consulting; Martin McAdam, An Post; Juan Andres Hall, Argentine Security and Exchange Commission; Jim Payne, the Associates; Australian officials from several organizations: Bronte Adams, Mike Allen, Tracy Anders, Hon. Dr. Michael Armitage MP, Evan Arthur, Peter Bailey, Robert Ceramidas, Paul A. Doherty, Ray Dundon, Graham Foreman, Peter Fowler, Anthony Hudson, John Maunder, Anthony O'Shea, Rosie Simpson, Randall Straw, Roseanne Toohey, Phil Turner, Peter Wilson.

Also, David Greenberg, Avio Corporation; Jay Evans, Azron; Alcino Rodrigues de Assunção, Aluizio Borges, Douglas Tevis Francisco, Odecio Gregio, Banco Bradesco; Michael Ippoliti, Bethlehem Steel Corporation; Phil Condit, Scott Griffin, Pearl Martin, Kathy Martinson, Richard Metz, Larry Olson, Patricia Paolucci, John Warner, Ronald Woodard, the Boeing Company; Myrtle Hudson, Pauline Pillow, Autumn Wagner, California State Automobile Association; Merilyn Dunn, Adina Levin, CAP Ventures; Jack Bergstrand, Bill Hensel, Bill Herald, Tom Long, Ira Tolmich, the Coca-Cola Company; Rick Engum, Coca-Cola Enterprises; John White, Compaq Computer Corporation; Bruce Dixon, Computelec; Reiner Schaaf, Computer2000; Doug Hockstad, Comshare; Tripp Johnson, Crestar Bank.

Also, Dennis Breck, Rochelle Chase, Sandy Draves, Susan Eich, Shelley Hyytinen, Michael Peterson, Mark Sauceman, Paul Singer, Vivian Stephenson, Robert Ulrich, Dayton Hudson Corporation; Michael Dell, Debra Dudgeon, Scott Eckert, Bill Morris, Lora Canney Zarbock, Dell Computer Corporation; Thomas McDermott, Gary S. Schmidt, Delta Control Systems; John Heim, Jeff Viehmeyer, Distribution Architects International; Janet Johnson, eFusion; Lynn Ochman, Ronald E. Phillips, Jeff Richardson, James Rider, Entergy Corporation; Kevin Huntley, Environmental Systems Research Institute; Pam Hoodes, Bruce Jones, Michael Murphy, Escher Group; Florida officials from several organizations: Randall C. Baker, George C. Banks, Pete Butler, Henry Cummings Jr., C. Derick Daniel, John A. DelVecchio, Mary Dozier, Doug Duncan, Jerome Gary, Marsha Koppe, Lynn Larson, Bill Lindner, William C. Manley, Linda Nelson, Paul Rowell, Jacqui Rudd, Rick Swaine, Linda Willis; Tony Albers, Dennis Schneider, Ford Motor Company; Glenn Phillips, Forté; Brian Fink, Randal A. Simonetti, Frontier Corporation.

Also, Gary Hare, Paul Johnson, Randy Rowe, General Electric Company; A. J. Romanelli, GIS Solutions; Malcolm Mitchell, Glaxo Wellcome; Michael Hammer, Hammer and Company; Stuart Mowat, HarperCollins; Lisa Paul, Healthcare Informatics; Chris Poole, Highdown School; Michael Cicirelli, Jodi Couch, Kerry W. Fowler, Michael Gallatin, Jeff Gardine, Jeff Hesselberg, Merl F. Hoekstra, Joy Jarvis, Dina Leviten, Kate Loughney, Howard Mendelsohn, ICOS Corporation; Howard High, Dean Isherwood, Shannon Johnson, Jason Rawlins, Tom Waldrop, Albert Yu, Intel Corporation.

Also, Michael Scholl, Jiffy Lube International; Ann Heller, Jackson Tung, Michael Wang, John Deere Healthcare; Stephen Piron, Johnson & Johnson; Sharon McAvinue, Johns Hopkins University; Hamilton Jordan; Don Deshler, University of Kansas; Jim Knight, University of Kansas Learning Resource Center; David Couch, State of Kentucky; Bernadette Cafferty, Kurt Salmon Associates; James H. Mann, Lawson Products; Pat Anderson, Bill Buonanni, Joe Cleveland, Charlie Hargraves, Ralph Sandridge, Lockheed Martin Corporation; Richard H. Ferrans, Louisiana State University; Malaysian officials from several organizations: Muhammad bin Ibrahim, Dato' Dr. Muhammad Rais Bin Abdul Karim, Janet Kong Meow-San, Dato' Dr. A. Jai Mohan, Rosma Osman, Ramli Saad, Lim Poh Sim; Robert Harris, Philip Osprey, Cathy Ryan, Marks & Spencer; Jill Jenkins, Thomas Marder; Michael Pusateri, Carl Wilson, Marriott International; Kathy Bezek, Arthur Kingfield, Joseph F. Norton, McDonald's Corporation; Lang Davison, Bill Meehan, McKinsey & Company; Erik Iversen, MediaServ.

Also, Deb Brennan, Bobbie Collins, Steve Eubanks, Philip Gilligan, Paul Kanevsky, Debbie Kone, Sandy Kurinsky, Blaise Masone, Anthony Pizi, Peter Sargent, Howard P. Sorgen, Andrew Williams, Merrill Lynch & Company; Sen. Terry C. Burton, Don Flowers, Amy Tuck, state of Mississippi; Michael Schrage, MIT Media Lab; Peter Krey, Steve Lieblich, Alan Scheuer, Morgan Stanley Dean Witter & Company; Joseph Farrelly, Larry Fisher, David Klein, Eileen Murphy, Jeanette Oliveira, Pamela Summers, Frank Wiggins, Nabisco; Donald P. Jacobs, dean, Anthony J. Paoni, professor, J. L. Kellogg Graduate School of Management, Northwestern University.

Also, Vivian Adler, Diane Skelly Bernhardt, Jann Davenport, Dale George, Terri Griffith, Danita Hundley, Jo Ann Hunt, Joe Kitchens, Laurie McCracken, Michael K. Roberts, Linda Yarbrough, Western Heights Public Schools, Oklahoma; Thomas Ficho, Orchard Medical Group; Kelly Wong, Orient Overseas Container Line; Sharon Bishop, Parents Reaching Out to Oklahoma; R. Britton Mayo, Pennzoil Company; James Champy, Perot Systems Corporation; Tom Shaver, J. D. Power and Associates; Charles C. Fry, the

Prometheus Group; Julie Baughman, James T. Harvey, Mary Stone, Promus Hotel Corporation; Chris Dayton, Vasilis Koulolias, Matthew Wilson, Pythia Corporation; Don Awalt, RDA Consultants; Daniel Bosch, Robert Mondavi Winery; Wayne Robertson, Robertson Associates; Becky Argenti, Bruce Bemisderfer, C. Randy Fowler, Alan Hale, Roger Kash, Scott Pendleton, Stuart Smith, Anthony Wall, Saturn Corporation; Mark A. Del Beccaro, John B. Dwight, Seattle Children's Hospital and Regional Medical Center; Carla J. Bryant, Sentara Health System; Sergio Otero de Oliveira, Serpro; Jeff Mason, Sequoia Software.

Also, Ioannis Charalambous, Wes Smith, Shell Services International; Michael Kaye, Kurt Keiser, Chris Muench, Ed Rebello, Arnold Testa, Siemens AG; Singapore officials from several organizations: Tay Yong Chin, Chin Li Fen, Cheong Wai Harn, Tan Chiam Huat, Jimmy Seah Cheng Hwee, Khoo Mui Kheng, Ang Puay Koon, Chng Eng Leok, Lim Poh Sim, Robert Chin Him Soon, Yong Chin Tay, Eric Lui Chew Wah, Ng Kin Yee, Leong Chin Yew.

Also, Karyn Beckley, Roy Hayes, SpaceLabs Medical; Robert Fine, Joseph Harms, Rick Lindquist, Gregory Warner, Stepan Company; Snorri Ogata, Taco Bell Corporation; Rick Diaz, Chris Lowde, Lyle Meier, Ed McDonald, Ken Morris, Clara Woo, James Wright, Texaco; Chris Maloney, Tritech Software Systems; Lieutenant Colonel Robert D. Coffman, Lieutenant Colonel Edward H. Kline, Brigadier General Klaus O. Schafer, U.S. Air Force; Lieutenant Colonel Joe Webster, U.S. Air Force Reserve; Major James Cummiskey, U.S. Marine Corps; Tom Warring, U.S. Naval Surface Warfare Center; Anthony M. Cieri, Captain Grey Glover, Commander Craig Madsen, Captain Michael O'Leary, U.S. Navy; Robin Berman, Joseph Grant, Maurice Holmes, Janice Malaszenko, Patricia Wallington, Xerox Corporation; and Norio Sasaki, Yamanouchi Pharmaceuticals Company.

INDEX

Acadian Ambulance and Air Med Services, 339–42, 354
Advertising, 230–32, 243
"Affirmative acknowledgment," 298
Aircraft manufacturers, 107–108, 180, 263–69, 276–77, 282, 292
Air Force, U.S., 348–51, 373–79, 384
Alcatel, 126
Alcoa, 315, 318, 320
Allard, J., 163–64, 167–68, 170–71
Amazon.com, 70, 79
American Airlines, 228
American Express, 44
American Internet User Survey, 101
American Medical Response (AMR), 339
Amsterdam, the Netherlands, 127–28
Andersen Consulting, 301–302
Anderson, Jon, 9
Annual reports, 47
Anytime Anywhere Learning laptop program, 396–97, 398
Army, U.S., 350, 381
Associative indexing, 165
Assunçao, Alcino Rodrigues de, 148
ATMs, 229–30, 363
Auctions, online, 76, 78–79, 92
Australia, 125, 359, 362, 395
  state governments, 326–27, 354, 361, 366–67, 397–99
Automobile industry, 6–11, 141–43, 180, 219, 239, 284–93, 310
Auto PCs, xv
Autoweb.com, 92
AXI, 44

Bad news, 159–83
  acting on, 181–82
  converting to good news, 184–200
    by collecting and analyzing customer feedback data, 192–95, 197–98
    with customer guarantees, 187–92
    helping users step through problems, 195–97
    prompt response to customer queries, 198–99
  digital nervous system's role in responding to, 160–61
  disbelief and, 162
  ignoring, dangers of, 177–81
  Microsoft's response to the arrival of Internet, 161–77
  rewarding bearer of, 179
  speed of responding to, 160
Ballmer, Steve, 9, 34, 56–57, 215, 322
Banco Bradesco, Brazil, 146–49
Bandwidth, 124–26, 323
Banks and banking, 228–29, 234
  bill payment, electronic, 118–19
  differentiation of a company from its competitors, 11–13
  Internet and, 147–48
  time to market and, 146–49
  Web lifestyle and, 118–19
  see also Financial services companies

Barnes & Noble, 79
Benefits programs, 45, 50, 51, 53
Bertelsmann, 79
Best practices, 145, 299, 327, 344–45, 413
Billions and Billions (Sagan), 414
Bill payment, electronic, 118–19
Biotech companies, 270–76, 277
Boeing, 107–108, 180, 263–69, 276–77, 292, 319, 427
Bogg, Keith, 223
Book publishing, 145, 225, 402
Boundaries, redefining business, xxi, 70, 133–40
  as employee opportunity, 136–39
  flexible staffing, 134–35
  outsourcing and, 133–35
  with web of partners, 217–19
Brand planning, 241–45
Britain, 125, 130
Brokers, 79–90
Brown, Mike, 9
Brown, Ron and Alma, 377
Building a digital nervous system, 37, 417–40
  blueprint required for, 420–22
  deciding what to build, 433–34
  deciding what to buy, 431–32
  designing for information flow, 436–39
  guiding principles for, 423–25
  horizontally integrated vendors and, 417–20
  phases of development, 429–30
  saving on infrastructure, 434–36
  servers, 425–29
  "three-tier architecture" for, 422–23
"Build to order," 290
Bush, Dr. Vannevar, 165
Business operations, xix, xx–xxi, 281–329
  basic operational processes, 281–82
  business-line ownership of process change, 314–15
  production processes, *see* Production processes
  reengineering, *see* Reengineering
  treating IT as strategic resource, 317–29

Cable modems, 125, 127
CareVISION, 343–46
Carlson Companies, 321, 327
Censorship, 128
CEOs, *see* Senior management
Champy, James, 295–96
Charitable donations, 46, 50
Chief Executive, 68
Children's Hospital and Regional Medical Center, Seattle, 343–46
Chrysler Corporation, 92
CIO (chief information officer), 318–25
  relationship with CEO, 318, 320, 321, 322, 325
Cisco Systems, 92, 207
Cleveland, Joe, 434–35
Clinical pathways, 344–45
Coca-Cola Company, 207–208, 216, 241–45, 256, 258–60
  Inform (Information For Marketing), 242–45
Coldwater, Michigan, 130
Collaboration, 255, 258–60
  corporate IQ and, 239
  electronic, xvi, xx, 34, 138, 177, 265–66, 269, 270–75, 276, 277, 389
College campuses, Web lifestyle on, 117, 167–68
Collins, Jim, 262
Columbia/HCA, 354
Commerce and the Internet, xvi, xix, xxi, 63–156, 224
  boundaries, redefining business, 70, 133–40
  comparison shopping, 73, 75
  cross-selling, 73, 93, 148–49
  customer service, individualized, 91–113
  customer support, 109–11
  early start, benefit of, 111–12

financial service companies, 79–90, 92
flexible pricing, 76–77
friction-free capitalism, 73
interactive Web sites, 102, 104, 112
judging the quality of your site, 107
linked Web pages, 102–103
matching buyers and sellers, 73, 75–76
middleman, 67, 78–90
personalizing site experiences, 103, 112, 227–28, 231
projections for, 92
registration information, 77
resistance to technology and, 197
savings for companies, 73–74, 96
service cost savings, 96
time to market, *see* Time to market
transaction cost savings, 73, 74
voice connection, 110–11
Web lifestyle, *see* Web lifestyle
Commerce Department, U.S., 118
Community building, Web lifestyle and, 116, 128–30, 393–94
Compaq Computer, 149–54, 179–80
enterprise resource planning (ERP) system, 150–52
publish-and-subscribe technology, 153–54
Compensation and performance, linking, 290, 293
Computer-aided design (CAD), 142, 237, 268
Computer notebooks, 66
Comshare, 17
Condit, Phil, 265, 269
Connors, John, 322–23
Contingent staff, management of, 305–11
Contributions, charitable, 46, 50
Core competencies, 34, 133, 135, 139
Cornell University, 167–68
Corporate culture, 155, 167, 182, 217, 255
bad news and, 178–79
Corporate IQ, 236–61
Costa Rica, 370, 394
CRAFT (customer requirements and fulfillment tools), 209–10
Crestar Bank, 12
Criddle, Linda, 56–57
Cross-selling, 73, 93, 148–49, 214
Cummiskey, Major James, 380, 382
Customer communication, 24
e-mail and, *see* Electronic mail (e-mail), customers and
feedback, *see* Customer feedback
Internet commerce and, *see* Commerce and the Internet
promptness in responding to, 198–99
Customer feedback, 112, 185–95
to drive product development, 197–98
prompt response to, 198–99
Customer relationship management (CRM), 230–32
Customers:
analyzing areas of weakness, 36
communication with, *see* Customer communication
customer service, *see* Customer service
data mining information about, *see* Data mining
feedback from, *see* Customer feedback
guarantees, 187–92
targeted advertising to, 230–32
technical support for, *see* Technical support
Customer service, 4, 67
customer complaints and improvements in, xxi, 185–92
digital information analysis to enhance, xx, 203–205, 206
freeing employees up for, xxi, 59–60, 223–24
Internet commerce and, 91–113
Jiffy Lube and, 201–205, 206, 207
see also Customer feedback
Cyber Warrior, 374

Data entry, digital, 206–208, 219
Data marts, 225

Data mining, 225–33
cost of, 232, 233
marketing and, 228–32, 233–34
product development and, 233–34
targeting advertising and, 230–32
Data warehouses, 27, 225, 226
Dayton Hudson, 313
Dayton Tire, 390
Dell, Michael, 94, 95, 100, 108, 112
Dell Computer, 92, 93–100, 108–109, 111–12, 199, 299
back-end systems, use of, 98–99
cost savings from Internet commerce, 96
developer resources, prioritizing, 98
inventory, 99–100
Premier pages for corporate customers, 97, 100
Denver Fire Department, 339
Department of Defense, U.S., 349, 369, 384–85
Dertouzos, Michael, 13–14, 15, 20, 239
Desert Care, 349–51
Digital Equipment Corporation, 151, 179, 180
Digital information, xiii–xviii, 65, 68
advantages of, xiv, 206–208
all-digital workplace, *see* Paperless office
digital nervous system, *see* Digital nervous system
flow of, xiii–xiv, xv, xviii, 412
key steps to achieving, xx–xxi
to knowledge workers, *see* Knowledge management
Digital nervous system, xviii–xxii, 15–20, 22–38
advantages of, 4–5
assessing your infrastructure, 325–28
availability of data with, 24–25
building a, *see* Building a digital nervous system
business operations and, *see* Business operations
chart of components of, 15
commerce and, *see* Commerce and the Internet
conversion to, 85, 220
defined, xvii–xviii
differentiating your company with, 3, 11–13, 220
government and, *see* Governments and government agencies
for health care industry, 339–55
knowledge management and, *see* Knowledge management
obstacles to, 219–20
purposes of, xix, 24, 36–37
signs of excellence in, 37
strategic planning with digital tools, 25–33
see also names of individual companies
Direct-mail marketers, 76, 77
Disabled, software features for, 147, 194
District sales managers, 35
Dixon, Bruce, 395
Douglas Aircraft, 180
Downsizing, 136
DSL (digital subscriber line), 125, 127
Dwight, John, 346

Eastman Software, 55
"Eating your own dogfood," 323
Eckert, Scott, 99
e-commerce, *see* Commerce and the Internet
Eddie Bauer, 92–93
Education, *see* Schools
eFusion, 110–11
Egghead.com, 78
Egypt, 128
Electronic books, 230, 232
Electronic Data Interchange (EDI) systems, 151, 219–20
Electronic mail (e-mail), xiv, xx, 19, 58, 68, 138, 174–77, 195, 319, 323, 347, 350, 352, 359, 366–67, 394, 399
benefits of, 176–77, 182

at Coca-Cola, 241, 258–59
customers and, 228
reminders to customers, 205
responding to e-mail from, 198–99
technical support, 110
in the future, xvi, 65
hiring process and, 41, 42
knowledge sharing with, 239–40
for meeting preparation, 20, 174
responding to unplanned events and, 167, 169, 170, 174
scientific research and, 270, 273–75
teachers and, 389–90, 393
for technical support, 110
Emergency medical service, 339–42, 352
Employee benefits, *see* Benefits programs
Employee handbook, 43
Employee stock purchase plans, 45–46, 51
Encoding, genetic, 270
Encryption, 124, 341, 362–63, 413
Encyclopedias, electronic, 54
ENIAC, 13
Entergy Corporation, 282–83, 292–93
Enterprise resource planning (ERP) system, 150–52
Error messages, software, 196
Error rate:
digital information and reduction of, 142, 206–207, 210, 215, 341
electronic forms, 53, 55
reducing handoffs and, 298–99
E * Trade Securities, 79
Executive information systems (EIS), 17
Expense reports, 58
Extranets, 10, 153–54, 218, 237, 275, 310
see also Intranets

Failures, *see* Bad news
FalconView, 374–80
Feedback, xx–xxi
from customers, *see* Customer feedback
employee, 55, 56–57
Fidelity Investments, 45–46
Fields, Debbi, 187
Finances, personal, Web lifestyle and, 118–19
Financial reporting:
reserved for senior management, 16, 17, 18
standardization of, 8, 9
Financial services companies, 223, 234
banks, *see* Banks and banking
Internet and, 79–90, 92
FIND/SVP, 101
fine.com, 107–108
Flat organization, 166, 176
Flexible pricing, 76–77
Flexible staffing, 134–35
Florida, 360, 368–69
Food and Drug Administration (FDA), 275
Forbes, 218
Ford Motor Company, 142, 180, 219, 239, 310
Forms, electronic, 41–54
employee feedback on, 55, 56–57
frequently asked questions (FAQs), 55
Forrester Group, 79, 101
401(k) plans, 45–46, 51
Fraud prevention, 352, 364
Fred Hutchinson Cancer Research Center, 337
Freelancing, 136–39
Frequently asked questions (FAQs), 55, 247
Friction-free capitalism, 73

Gap, The, 76
Geffen Records, 93
General Electric, 218
General Motors, 6–11, 180
Saturn Corporation, 284–93
Genetic research, 269–73
Geographic constraints on workforce, easing of, 138, 139
Georgia Institute of Technology, 374, 380

German Federal Ministry for Finance, 367
Global positioning systems (GPS), 339, 376, 385–86
Glossary, 441–51
Goldman Sachs & Company, 163
Good news, 182
  converting bad news to, *see* Bad news, converting to good news
Gordon, Janice, 398
Governments and government agencies, 357–71
  building digital systems, 367–70
  citizen access to online systems, 360–64, 369–70, 414
  digital information, exchange of, 49, 275, 357, 358
  executive branch, 366
  judiciary, 365
  legislatures, 365
  paper-based systems, 49, 275, 357–58, 359–60, 369
  publishing online, 358, 359–60
  streamlining, 364–67
  U.S. government, *see* U.S. government
Grocery stores, 219
Grove, Andrew, 64, 177–78, 337
Guarantees, customer, 187–92
Gulf War, 348, 349, 372–73, 375, 378, 379

Hammer, Michael, 289, 295–96
Hampshire County Council, 361
Handheld PCs, xv, 120, 207, 292, 379–82
Hands, Rich, 101
HarperCollins, 225
Harvey, Tim, 190
Hayes, Pat, 26–33, 34
Health care system, 333–56, 364
  daily clinical practice, 346–48
  emergency services, 339–42, 352
  of the future, 352–55
  incompatible information systems, 336–38
  integrated patient-data system, 353–55
  Internet and, 336, 337, 347–48, 352, 354
  managed care, 335–36
  paperwork and, 334–35, 342, 344, 352, 354–55
  patient records, 336, 343–46
  tracking unseen medical dangers, 348–51
Health VISION Corporation, 343–44
Heisen, JoAnn, 320–21
Herald, Bill, 241
Herbold, Bob, 322
Hewlett Packard, 5
Higgins, Patricia, 315, 320
Highdown School, Reading, 391–93, 394, 400
Horizontal integration, 417–440
Hotels, 224
  bookings and pricing of rooms, 190
  customer guarantees, 187–92
  Internet access in, 108
  Marriott International, 93, 103–109, 111–12
  personalizing stays at, 190–91
  Promus Hotels, 187–92
HTML (HyperText Markup Language), 171, 259
Human Resources, *see specific functions, e.g.* Benefit programs

IBM, 179–80, 184
ICOS, 270–73
IMAGINE project, 129–30
India, 138, 394
Inflection points, xvi, 64–67, 177
InfoDesk Web site, 246–48
Information flow, xiii–xv, 3–60
  digital, *see* Digital information
  knowledge management, *see* Knowledge management
  paperless office, *see* Paperless office
Information technology (IT), 10, 394
  assessing your infrastructure, 325–28
  budget for, 52, 234, 324–25, 328
  building on your existing, 313–14

corporate investment in, xiv–v, 33–34, 324–25, 328–29, 336
as enabler, 241
incompatible systems, 23, 336–38
intertwining of business and, 6, 153, 301, 320–24, 325
outsourcing, 327–28
reengineering and, *see* Reengineering
as strategic resource, 317–29
treated as expense to control, 241, 318, 322
"Information work," 13–15, 20, 239
In Search of Excellence (Peters and Waterman), 179
InSite Web site, 256
Institute for the Future, 163
Insurance companies, 92, 233–34
Intel, 143–45, 177–78, 370
Interest-based communities, Internet and, 128–29, 131
Internet, 12–13, 40, 65, 408
boundaries of organizations changed by, 133–34
commerce and, *see* Commerce and the Internet
content ratings, 128
familiarity with, 68–69, 70, 106–107
filtering technologies, 128
in the future, 69, 119–20, 126–27
Web lifestyle, *see* Web lifestyle
Web workstyle, *see* Web workstyle
governments' uses of, 358–70, 413, 414
hotels, access in, 108
medical information on, 336, 337, 347–48, 352, 354
memex machine, 165
Microsoft's response to arrival of, 161–77, 181
portals, 70, 148
sales data via, xx, 19, 34
scientific collaboration on the, 270–75, 276
searches, results of, 259
significant capabilities of, xvi
as teaching tool, 387, 389, 392–93, 400–403
Web lifestyle, *see* Web lifestyle
Web workstyle, *see* Web workstyle
word of mouth and, 91–92
"Internet Tidal Wave, The" (Gates e-mail memo), 171–74
Intranets, 346–48, 392
battlefield, 379–81
at Microsoft, 42–60, 194, 237–38
see also Extranets
Inventory:
Internet commerce and, 99–100
just-in-time, 213
management of, 218, 219, 283–84
Investment online, 79–90
Invoicing, electronic, 310–11
IQ, corporate, 236–61
Ireland, 362
Iridium, 126
Israel, 394
Issaquah, Washington, 394
IT (information technology), *see* Information technology (IT)
IT Advisor, 326, 327

Jiffy Lube, 201–205, 206, 207
Johnson & Johnson, 16, 318–19, 320–21, 327
Jordan, Hamilton, 337
Just-in-time delivery, xxi, 217
Just-in-time inventory, 213

Kent State, 54
Kentucky, 394
King County, Washington, 368
Kiosks, electronic, 361–63
Kitchens, Joe, 389–90
Kline, Lieutenant Colonel Edward, 349
Knowing your numbers, 201–21
as basis for understanding your business, 214–16
collecting the data, 206–208
to create a web of partnerships, 216–19

Knowing your numbers *(cont.)*
customer service and, 201–205, 206
to extend your business, 216
factors holding companies back, 219–20
Jiffy Lube example, 201–205, 206, 207
paper vs. digital form, 215–16
reshaping a company's behavior by, 210–14
sales process, enhancing the, 208–10
Knowledge management, xix, xx, xxi, 159–278
bad news, *see* Bad news
for brand planning, 241–44
building blocks of, 257–58
data mining, *see* Data mining
defined, 238–39, 260
knowing your numbers, *see* Knowing your numbers
knowledge sharing, xx, 239–60
product development and, 250–57
product support and, 245–48
risk taking and, *see* Risk taking
shifting people into thinking work, 222–35
technical support and, 245–48
training and, 248–50
Knowledge sharing, xx, 239–60
rewarding employees for, 240, 255–57
Knowledge workers, empowering, *see* Digital nervous system; Knowledge management; *specific business operations*

Laptops, 340–41, 374–75, 377, 379, 396–97, 398
Larsen, Ralph, 16, 318–19, 320
Learning communities, *see* Schools
Line employees, 166
empowering, in production processes, 282–93, 410–11
information flow and, 18, 19
numerical analysis and action by, 215
Lockheed Martin, 269, 434–36
Long, Tom, 244–45
Lusk, Wyoming, 130

McDonald's, 5–6, 19, 429–30
McKinsey & Company, 326
Malaysia, 354
Manufacturing, xiii, 11, 14
product delivery process, 297–300
production processes, *see* Production processes
risk taking and, 263–69, 276–77
time to market and, 141–45, 149–54
see also individual companies
Marine Corps, U.S., 379–82, 384
Maritz, Paul, 164
Marketing, 241–45
data mining and, 228–29, 233–34
targeted advertising, 230–32
digital information flow and, 203–205, 213–14
strategic planning with digital tools, 25–33
Marks & Spencer, 210–14, 218, 222–23
Marriott International, 93, 101–109, 111–12
Massachusetts, 367
"Mass customization," 290, 293
Mature industries, 263
Medical care, *see* Health care system
Medicine & Health, 353
Meeting planners, 105
Meetings, face-to-face, 170–71
efficient use of, 20, 34, 174
Mellon Bank USA, 228–29
Memex machine, 165
Merrill Lynch & Company, 80–89, 422–23
Microsoft, xxi–xxii, 262–63, 409
bad news:
converting to good news, 184–85
responding to, 161–77, 181
construction information, 235–37
contingent staff, management of, 305–11

digital ordering by customers of, 207
HeadTrax, 47, 300–305, 310, 312
integration of IT with business objectives, 322–23
intranet at, 42–60, 194, 195, 237–38
MS Invoice, 310
MS Market, 43, 51, 52–53, 56–57, 310
MS Reports, 47–48
MS Sales, 27, 31, 32, 35, 47
customer analysis, 36
DISCO (district comparisons) report, 32
investment in, 33–34
new employee, tracking experience of, 42–49, 50
OnTarget, 48
outsourcing by, 134, 135, 136, 299–300
paperless office at, xvii, 40–60, 309
Product Improvement (PI) team, 192–95
product support, 246–48
research on future technology, 54
standardization of financial reporting, 9
strategic planning, digital tools used in, 25–33
Web site, *see* Microsoft Web site
Windows 95, 161, 163
Windows CE, 185, 288, 380, 382
Windows Media Player, 240
Windows NT (Windows 2000), 164, 185, 286, 297–98, 426
Microsoft Access, 185
Microsoft Excel, 47, 185
Microsoft Exchange, 323, 366
Microsoft Expedia, 103, 185
Microsoft Healthcare Users Group, 338
Microsoft Internet Explorer, 194
Microsoft Investor, 185
Microsoft NetMeeting, 111
Microsoft Sidewalk, 185
Microsoft Site Server Commerce 3.0, 227–28
Microsoft Web site, 41, 42, 92, 108, 164, 171, 172–73, 175, 194–95, 199
Middleman, 105
elimination of, xxi, 67
value of, xxi, 67, 78–90
Middle managers, 35
bad news and, 177, 178
information access for, 18–19, 35
Middleware, 427
Military, 372–86
Mistakes, *see* Bad news
MIT Media Lab, 54
MOET (Microsoft Order Entry Tool) Web site, 207
Moore's law, 143, 382, 385
Morgan Stanley Dean Witter, 223
Mrs. Fields, 187
MSN, 164
Mundie, Craig, 162
Murphy, Eileen, 253–54
My Years with General Motors (Sloan), 6–7

Nabisco, 250–57, 258
Nasser, Jacques (Jac), 239
Navy, U.S., 350, 381, 384
Smart Ship program, 384
NCR, 229
Negroponte, Nicholas, 154
NetMeeting, 138
Networks, xiv, 40, 269, 393, 394
Internet, *see* Internet
wireless, 292
1998 Source Book of Health Insurance Data, 336
Nippon Telephone and Telegraph, 162
Numbers, knowing your, *see* Knowing your numbers
Nyberg, Lars, 229–30

Ohio, 361
OLAP (online analytical processing), 225–27
O'Neill, Paul, 58, 318
Only the Paranoid Survive (Grove), 177

Operations, business, *see* Business operations
Ordering, digital, 100, 207, 208–209, 267, 283, 284
Oregon Health Sciences Center, 272
Organizational structure, 166, 176, 322, 409–11
OS/2, 184, 185
Outsourcing, 133–35, 136, 299–300, 327–28

Paper, information on, xiv, xx, 40, 53–54, 220
  bills, 118
  governments and, 49, 275, 357–58, 359–60, 369
  health care system and, 334–35, 342, 344, 352, 354–55
  paperless office, *see* Paperless office
  "paper numbers," 215–16
  replacing paper forms with electronic forms, 41–53
Paperless office, xvii, xx, 39–60, 309
  appropriate uses of paper, 53–54
  Dell Computer's ordering process and, 100
  early visions of, 39–40
  at Microsoft, 40–60
  nonfinancial benefits of, 52–53
  savings from, 49–52
  scanning paper documents from outside sources, 55
Parthenay, France, 129–30
Partners (partnerships), 135, 139, 147, 216–19
  digital data from, 34, 49
  between GM and its dealers, 7–11
  sales data shared by, 34, 217–18
  value network, 217–19
Part-time work, 139
PCs, *see* Personal computers (PCs)
Pen chart systems, 340–42
Pentagon, *see* Department of Defense, U.S.
Performance reviews, 48–49, 256
Personal computers (PCs), xiv, xv, xx
  adoption of, 117, 118
  in the future, xvi, 65, 68, 119, 138
  health care information systems based on, 339–55
  IBM PC, 179–80
  Internet, original, 165
  kiosks, electronic, 361–63
  laptops, 340–41, 374–75, 377, 379, 396–97, 398
  military systems based on, 373–86
  networked, *see* Networks
  online sales of, 92, 93–100, 108–109
  in Saturn's manufacturing process, 286–87, 288, 292
  in schools, 387–404
  see also Personal digital devices
Personal digital devices, xv, 65–66
  in the future, xvi, 68, 120
  handheld, xv, 120, 207, 292, 379–82
  smart cards, xv, 363–64, 413
Peters, Tom, 179
Pivot tables, 223, 226
Platform for Internet Content Selection (PICS), 128
Platinum Software, 55
Portal sites, Internet, 70, 148
"Powerful Tools for Schooling: Second Year Study of the Laptop Program," 397
Prange, Gordon, 181
Priceline.com, 75
Privacy laws, 364
Problems, *see* Bad news
Processes, business, *see* Business operations
Procter & Gamble, 217
Product companies:
  changing nature of, xiii, 154–55
  time to market, 154–55
  see also individual companies
Production processes, 282–94
  efficiency and responsiveness of, 282–83

empowering line workers in, 282–93
extracting data from, 283–84
Product planning, 47–48, 233–34, 250–57
Product support, 245–48
see also Technical support
Promus Hotels, 187–92
Proxies, 47
Publish-and-subscribe technology, 153–54
Publishing industry, 145, 225, 402
Punctuated chaos, 412
Punctuated equilibrium, 411
Pusateri, Mike, 101, 102, 104, 106–107
Pythia, 138

Quality, 3, 4, 144, 218–19, 299
automobile industry and, 141–43

Radio, 120
Raikes, Jeff, 25–26, 28, 29–30, 33, 322
Real-time data, xx, 19, 150–54, 225
Recruitment, 41–42
Reengineering, 295–316
business-line ownership of process change, 314–15
contingent staff, management of, 305–11
creating a new process, 297, 300–305
step by step improvements, 311–14
focusing on core competencies, 133–34
key principles of, 295–97
product delivery process, 297–300
reducing handoffs, 296, 298–99, 305
trade-offs, understanding, 297
Reengineering the Corporation (Hammer and Champy), 295–96
Restrac, 41–42
Résumés, 41–42
Retailers:
changing nature of, xiii, 154–55
Internet commerce, *see* Commerce and the Internet
see also individual companies
Return on investment (ROI), 30, 31
Risk taking, 262–78, 412
by aircraft manufacturers, 263–69, 276–77
by biotech companies, 270–76, 277
Rockman, Saul, 397
Routine tasks, freeing employees from, xx, 59–60, 222–24
with data mining, *see* Data mining
Rural/Metro Ambulance Service, 339

Saffo, Paul, 163
Sagan, Carl, 414
Sales data, 58, 202–204
digital tools to analyze, 225–27, 242
Microsoft's MS Sales, *see* Microsoft, MS Sales
partners sharing, 34, 217–18
real-time, xx, 19, 150–54, 225
Sales process, tools to enhance, 208–10
Salomon Smith Barney, 46–47
Satellite communication systems, 125–27
Saturn Corporation, 284–93
dynamic scheduling software, 291
SCADA system, 285–86
Schafer, Brigadier General Klaus, 349
Schools, 387–404
college campuses, 117, 167–68
computer labs, 388, 390, 402
distance learning, 391
individual learning styles, catering to, 399–402
the Internet, uses of the, 387, 389, 392–93, 400–403
parental and community involvement with, 391–94
student access to PCs, 395–99
teachers' uses of PCs, 387, 388–91, 399–403
Screen technology, 54, 119–20, 402
Security, 345, 362–63, 381
Self-employment, 136–39
Senior management, xiv, 407–408
bad news and, 177, 179

Senior management *(cont)*
CIO, *see* CIO (chief information officer)
knowledge sharing by, 239–40
preparing for new digital world, 68, 106–107, 318–20
reorientation of company behavior by, xviii
treating IT as strategic resource, 317–29
reserving "the numbers" for, 16, 17, 18
transition to digital nervous system, 220
Sentara Health System, 346–48
Service, customer, *see* Customer service
Service Breakthroughs: Changing the Rules of the Game (Heskett, Sasser, and Hart), 187–88
Sherlund, Rick, 163
Shopping online, *see* Commerce and the Internet
Siemens AG, 144, 208–10
Singapore, 125, 129
Sinofsky, Steven, 167–68, 170
Sloan, Alfred P., Jr., 6–10, 20
Smart cards, xv, 363–64, 413
Smart vending machines, 208, 216
Sony Corporation, 5
Sorgen, Howard, 80–81, 83
Southwestern Bell, 162
Spain, 363
Speech, *see* Voice
Speed-of-Thought.com Web site, xix–xx, 326
SpinWeb, 346–48
Spreadsheets, electronic, 9, 223, 226
Staff, *see* Workforce
Standardization, 8, 9, 52, 124, 150, 241, 318, 338, 417
Standish Group International, 312
Stepan Company, 283–84, 292, 293
Stock options, 45, 46–47, 49, 50, 51
Strategic planning, 24
digital tools used in, 25–33
treating IT as resource in, 317–29
Students, *see* Schools
Sun-tzu, 382, 383
Suppliers, 213, 217–19
benefits of electronic links with, 142, 265–66
paperless office and, 53
publish-and-subscribe technology and, 153–54
see also Partners (partnerships)
Sweden, 360–61

Teachers, *see* Schools
Technical support, xxi, 109–11, 195–97, 245–48
error messages and, 196
trends in, 199
Telecommunications, deregulation of, 359, 370
Tele-Communications Inc. (TCI), 162
Telecommuting, 138
Teledisic, 126
Telemedicine, 354
Telephone, 138
digital, 120
Internet telephony, 138
technical support by, 109–10
Television (TV), 120, 122–24
digital, 120, 122–24, 230, 232
interactive, 122–24, 162
targeted advertising, 230–32
telemedicine, 354
Temporary staffing, management of, 305–11
Texas Instruments, 256
Third Age Web site, 129
Time magazine, 161
Time to market, xxi, 144–56
conquering cycle time, 149–52
increasing complexity and, 143–45
increasing power and decreasing time, 152–54
of physical products, 154–55
quality and, 141–43, 144

Tong, Rich, 246, 247
Toyota Motor Sales, 11, 142–43
Training, 191, 248–50, 313, 328, 359, 368, 393–94
 medical, 342, 354
 military, 377–78
 see also Schools
TraumaNet, 342
Travel, 369
 hotels, *see* Hotels
 Internet sites, 75, 92, 101–102
  Marriott, *see* Marriott International
 online system for corporate, 44, 51–52
Travel agents, 105
TravelWeb, 103
TriTech Software Systems' VisiCAD for Fire/EMS, 339

U.S. government, 363, 413
 agencies and departments, *see under specific names, e.g.* Commerce Department, U.S.
 setting of standards, 338
United Way of America, 46
Universal serial bus (USB), 124
University of Kansas, 390
University of Oklahoma, 390
Unplanned events, 23
 flexible staffing and, 134–35
 keeping focused, 170
 Microsoft's response to arrival of the Internet, 161–77
 real-time systems to respond to, 150–54
USWeb, 249

Value network, 217–19
Vending machines, smart, 208, 216
Vendors, 73, 219, 237, 284, 367
 see also Suppliers
Vertical integration, 417–18, 419, 427
Videoconferencing, 138, 168, 390–91
Voice, 126
 Internet voice connection, 110
 voice recognition systems, 123
Vollum Institute, 272–73

Wall Street Journal, The, 312, 402
Wal-Mart, 217–18, 232
Wang, 179, 180
Warner, John, 319
Waterman, Robert, 179
Web lifestyle, xvi, xix, 111, 114–32, 414
 activities comprising the, 115–16
 adoption of technology for, 117–18
 bringing about the, 119–20
 on college campuses, 117, 167–68
 community building and, 116, 128–30, 393–94
 generational differences in adapting to, 117
 governments and, 369–70
 the home and TV experience, 121–27
 social implications of, 127–30
 statistics on Web use, 116
 throwing off old limits, 131–32
Web workstyle, xvi, xviii, xix, 133–40, 266, 275–76
 as employee opportunity, 136–39
 flexible staffing, 134–35
 outsourcing, 133–35
Welch, Jack, 218
Western Heights Independent School District, Oklahoma, 388–91, 399
White, John, 151
Wilson, Carl, 101, 107
Windows 95, 161, 163
Windows CE, 185, 288, 380, 382
Windows magazine, 161
Windows Media Player, 240
Windows NT (Windows 2000), 164, 185, 286, 297–98, 426
Windows Update, 324
Winkler, Scott, 426
Workforce:
 contingent staff, management of, 305–11

Workforce *(cont.)*
empowering your, *see* Digital nervous system; Knowledge management; *specific business operations*
flexible staffing, 134–35
geographic constraints, easing of, 138, 139
outsourcing and, 133–35, 136
part-time work, 139

Xerox Corporation, 40, 54
XML (eXtended Markup Language), 259

Yahoo!, 70
Yamanouchi Pharmaceuticals, 245–46
Yankelovich Partners, 101–102
Year 2000, Y2K issue, 438
Yu, Albert, 145